Fundamental Aspects of Educational Technology

Fundamental Aspects of Educational Technology

YOGENDRA K. SHARMA

KANISHKA PUBLISHERS, DISTRIBUTORS
NEW DELHI-110 002

KANISHKA PUBLISHERS, DISTRIBUTORS
4697/5-21A, Ansari Road, Daryaganj
New Delhi -110 002
Phones : 2327 0497, 2328 8285
Fax : 011-2328 8285
E-mail : kanishka_publishing@yahoo.co.in

Fundamental Aspects of Educational Technology
First Published-2002
Edition-2018

ISBN: 978-81-7391-525-3

PRINTED IN INDIA

Published by Madan Sachdeva for Kanishka Publishers, Distributors, 4697/5-21A, Ansari Road, Daryaganj, New Delhi-110 002, Typeset by Sunshine Graphics, Delhi, and Printed at Rajdhani Printers, Delhi.

Preface

The present work in your hand is the result of your appreciation of my following works in the subject for which I express my gratitude, indebtedness and heartfelt thanks to you.

1. *History and Problems of Education,* Vols. I & II;
2. *Foundation in Sociology of Education;*
3. *Doctrines of Great Indian Educators;* and
4. *Doctrines of Great Western Educators.*

Educational Technology is a fast growing science committed to converting raw-hand teachers into really effective and efficient ones by equipping them with practical teaching skills and qualities of creative teaching. Teaching technology has, in recent years, undergone revolution in respect of new methods employed in teaching at different levels. New methods has greatly enhanced the value of Teacher Education and has made teaching interesting, effective and purposeful.

There is a practical need for bridging the gap between traditional and modern approaches of teaching and learning, because these days teaching strategies are touching new heights on account of modernisation as a result of interdisciplinary contributions, which need to be understood by future teachers and teachers alike. The work in hand is a sincere effort in this direction.

The work at hand covers the development of methods

application and evaluation of systems, techniques and aids needed to improve the process of teaching and learning. It deals with the efforts being made in educational institutions for the application of scientific methods with a view to organise new sets of equipment and material needed for effective teaching and learning.

The work at hand is comprehensive enough to meet the requirements of syllabi for B.Ed. and M.Ed. courses of almost all the universities in India and hence, useful for pupil teachers undergoing training in any university. In addition to it, this book will inspire all working teachers, educational administrators and general readers because it contains up-to date knowledge on various aspects of educational technology.

I have tried my best to make this book as a textbook for students and reference book for the teachers and educationists, the readers are the best judge of its merits. Suggestions for improvement are, therefore, cordially invited.

YOGENDRA K. SHARMA

Contents

1

Basic Ingredients of Educational Technology

The present age belongs to science and technology, hence we find that intellectuals belonging to each and every walk of life opt to adopt scientific and technological phrases in place of traditional phrases concerning their vocations with a view to project that their way of working and their vocational know-how is most modern and in a position to keep pace with modern technological developments concerning their vocation. B.C. Mathis defines educational technology in the following words:

"Educational Technology refers to the development of a set of system methods and practical knowledge of designing, operating and testing schools as educational system."

Everyday we hear about the names of various technologies in the present scientific and technological age, such as—sugar technology, paper technology, cloth technology and glass technology. In educational field too, the term 'Educational Technology' is being used with great interest.

Scholars believe that with the proper use of science and technology in the field of education, desirable results can be achieved in teaching, learning and testing spheres as tremendous progress is taking place in the various fields of agriculture, health and industry. Keeping in mind the same objective educational technology was developed and education was placed in science faculty.

To understand the meaning of Educational Technology, understanding of terms 'Education' and 'Technology' is essential. Therefore, we are throwing light on the meaning of the terms education, science and technology in this chapter.

Meaning and Nature of Education

Etymological Meaning of Education

The Latin word 'Educatum' means to train. 'E' means from inside and 'Duco' means to draw out, to lead out or to bring up. By combining the two education comes to mean to draw from within. Education is a process which draws from within. Each child is born with some innate tendencies, capacities and inherent powers.

Education draws these powers out and develop them to the full. Latin words 'Educare' and 'Educere' mean to bring up, to lead out and to develop etc. In this way the word education means to develop the inborn qualities of a child to the full.

Narrower Meaning of Education

In its narrow sense, school instruction is called education. In this process, the elders of society strive to attain pre-determined aims during a specified time by providing pre-structured titbits of knowledge to children through set methods of teaching.

The purpose is to achieve mental development of children entering school. In the process, the teacher is the most important factor and the child is assigned a subsidiary role. The teacher is expected to instil ready made dozes of knowledge in the child's mind.

Such knowledge strangles the natural development of the child and hence is of no use to him for his actual future life. In spite of this, school education has merits of its own. In the words of John Stuart Mill, "The culture which each generation purposefully gives to those who are to be its successors, in order to qualify them for at least keeping up, and if possible for raising the level of improvement which has been attained."

Following opinions of some educationists represent the narrow meaning of education.

1. "In narrow sense, education may be taken to mean any consciously directed effort to develop and cultivate our powers."

—*S.S. Mackenzi*

2. "Education is a process in which and by which knowledge, character and behaviour of the young are shaped and moulded."

—*Prof. Drever*

3. "The influence of the environment on the individual with a view to producing a permanent change in his habits of behaviour of thought and attitude." —*G.H. Thompson*

Wider Meaning of Education

In its wider sense, education is not the communication of information by the teacher or the acquisition of knowledge by the child but the total development of child's personality. Education consists of all those experiences in the process by which an individual freely develops his self according to his nature in a free and uncontrolled environment. It is a life long process of growth and development. It is not confined to the limits of time, place and individual.

Any person who gives the child a new experience is a teacher and any place where this giving and receiving takes place may be termed as a school. Thus, education is essentially a process of growth and development which goes on throughout the whole life. Rousseau developed his philosophy of naturalism keeping this wider concept of education in his mind. Following eminent scholars interpret education in the wider context.

1. "In the wider sense, it is a process that goes on throughout life, and is promoted by almost every experience in life."

—*S.S. Mackenzi*

2. "By education, I mean the alround drawing out of the best in child and man—body, mind and soul". —*M.K. Gandhi*

Analytical Meaning of Education

(1) *Not Limited to Knowledge Imparted in Schools.* Education cannot be confined to the processes of giving knowledge to children in schools. Its programme goes on from birth till death. Everyone learns something or the other throughout life by various experiences and activities. All this is education.

(2) *Education as the Development of Child's innate Power.*

Education is developing the native endowments of a child rather than something forced into the mind from outside. Addision has rightly remarked, "Education, when it works upon noble mind, draws out to view every latent virtue and perfection which without such help are never able to make their appearance."

(3) *Education as a Dynamic Process.* Education is not a static but a dynamic process which develops the child according to changing situation and times. It is a purposive activity always pursuing some aim of life to which an individual devotes himself fully.

(4) *Education as a Bipolar Process.* In his book *Evolution of Educational Theory* Adams has interpreted education as a bipolar process. He analysed education as under—

(i) "It (Education) is a bipolar process in which one personality acts upon another in order to modify the development of the other."

(ii) "The process is not only a conscious one but a deliberate one. The educator has the clearly realized intention of modifying the development of the educand."

(iii) "The means by which the development of the educand is to be modified are two folds:

(a) The direct application of the educator's personality to the personality of the educand, and

(b) The use of knowledge in its various forms."

According to Adams, the bipolar education has two poles. At one end is the teacher and at the other is the child. Both are equally important in education. If the teacher instruct, the child follows. If the teacher gives, the child receives. Thus, in the process of education there is interaction between the teacher and the child.

The teacher tries to mould and modify the behaviour of the child so that the latter develops his personality to the full. With the active cooperation of the teacher and the child, the process of education goes on smoothly and efficiently.

(5) *Education as a Tripolar Process.* Like Adams, John Dewey also regards education as a process of development. But while accepting the psychological view, Adams emphasizes the importance of teacher and the child, John Dewey emphasizes the sociological view point. Hence, according to John Dewey,

education has two aspects—(1) Psychological, and (2) Sociological. He accepts the contention that education of the child should be according to his native endowment.

He further asserts that the development of a child does not take place in a vacuum. It takes place in and through the society in which the teacher and the child both live. It is the society which will determine the aims, contents and methods of teaching. In this way, the process of education contains three poles, namely—(1) the teacher, (2) the child, (3) the society. These three factors actively co-operate in the efficient and successful working of the educational process.

Broader True Meaning of Education

In its true meaning, there is dynamic coordination between narrow and wider meaning of education. It is because the education in narrow meaning is limited to its conservative nature. This meaning considers education as keeping the pupil in controlled environment and forcibly imposed education to lead a particular life style. This suppresses his interest, attitude, capacities, abilities and needs.

In broader meaning, education is liberal. According to this broader meaning, natural development of the pupil is emphasized by keeping him in uncontrolled environment. If the broader meaning of education is accepted, the social and spiritual development of the pupil is necessarily difficult, if not impossible.

In such condition, both narrow and broader meanings of education are not correct. Both need coordination. After coordination in both the meanings, education is presented as that dynamic process which brings the changes in the behaviour of the pupil and develops him intellectually, socially, culturally and spiritually in such a way by allowing reasonable independence and keeping in view, consciously or unconsciously the personal interests, attitudes, capabilities, abilities, social ideals and needs of the pupil so that both the individual and the society may touch the peaks of the progress.

T. Raymont, a well known educationist, has similar idea that, "Education is the process of development which consists the passage of human being from infancy to maturity, the process whereby he adapts himself gradually in various ways to his physical, social and spiritual environment."

Thus, education is a process of development. To understand its nature and rate of progress, one must know the data of education.

Data of Education

The data of education consists of the following four factors—

(1) *The Child.* The foremost data of education is the child. Each child has certain innate powers. His natural development is possible only according to these native endowments. As such, the child's nature should be known to those who provide education for his development.

(2) *Heredity.* Hereditarians believe that education of a child is predetermined by heredity. According to them, hereditary impressions influence a child from his infancy before any formal education begins. As the impressions are often indelible, therefore education has to follow the lines laid down by these impressions generated and formed by parents and other related elders of society.

These innate tendencies and qualities are the firm foundations for his education. These also delimit and define the highest achievements to be achieved by him. Without hereditary traits and impressions of a musician, a child can never be developed into a noted musician of repute by education or any other process. Thus, to be hereditarians, education is development according to lines pre-determined and prelaid by the heredity of a child.

(3) *Environment.* Another factor of education is environment. Every child is born in a family at a particular place and time. His upbringing also takes place in a specific environment. This environment is either controlled or uncontrolled. Both types of environments exert their influence upon the growing child in different ways. Controlled environment leads to controlled growth and uncontrolled environment promotes uncontrolled growth.

According to environmentalists, heredity factor is only a myth. They assert that if the environment is not desirable, no amount of heredity will be able to develop the child according to desirable lines and standards of growth. According to them, environment is a powerful factor which influences the development of child consciously or both. One cannot escape its influence at any cost.

The environmentalists hold that as the child gradually comes into contact with the physical and social environments, his innate tendencies flower out and his behaviour begins to change. In this sense, it is the environment and not the heredity which makes a child a musician or an artist.

Thus, according to environmentalists, education is a process based on and conditioned by the environment in which the child is brought up.

(4) *Time.* During the process of development, specific activities are indulged by the child at specific times. To understand this process of development, one must have a clear understanding of the various stages of development. As different and specific tendencies sprout out of these various stages, education must correspond its plans and programmes to these budding capacities. Then only, the development of the child will be normal and natural. Hence, education should correspond and suit the mental level of the child, otherwise it will create complexes and mar the development.

Both the hereditarians and the environmentalists assert one side of the truth. The two factors are not contradictory. They are mutually complementary and supplementary. Both work together to develop the child smoothly and in a balanced way. Both are essential for the proper development of a child.

Western Concept of Education

Educational thinking, like every other branch of knowledge, started in the philosophical deliberation of the ancient Greek philosophers. Thus, the meaning of education in west is initially available in the works of Plato. It is interesting to note that thousands of years ago, Plato gave a meaning to education which is even now followed in the West with slight changes here and there.

Plato defined education as a life-long process starting, "from the first years of childhood and lasting to the very end of the life". He used the term education in a very wide sense, "which makes a man eagerly pursue the ideal perfection of citizenship and teaches him how rightly to rule and how to obey."

Education not only provides knowledge and skills but also inculcates values, training of instincts, fostering right attitude and habits. In *Republic,* Plato points out that "true education, whatever that may be, will have the greatest tendency to civilise and humanise them in their relation to one another and to those who are under their protection."

This humanist definition of education propounded by Plato is still the most widely accepted meaning of education in the West. Education everywhere has been taken as a process of inculcating values. As Plato said, "Now I mean by education that training which is given by suitable habits to the first insticts of virtue in children."

These views of Plato have been universally accepted in West as well as in the East. Education has been defined differently by the idealists, the pragmatists, the naturalists and the realist philosophers. However, its meaning has been generally idealistic. Without some sort of idealism there can be no education worth the name.

In the words of Robert R. Rusk, "We may accept the aim of education is the enhancement or enrichment of personality, the differentiating feature of which is the embodiment of universal values". The Western educational philosophers have generally agreed that the growth of the human child is the essence of education.

In the words of A.G. Hughes, "The essence of discipline is, thus, not forced subordination to the will of the hated tyrants, but submission to the example of admired superiors." In the middle ages Comenius declared education to be a process whereby an individual developed qualities relating to religion, knowledge and morality, and thereby established his claim to be called a human being.

According to Froebel, "instruction and teaching should be passive and protective not directive and interfering."

The principle of liberty has found most eloquent expression in the definition of education given by Rousseau when he said, "Let us obey the call of Nature. We shall see that Her yoke is easy and that when we give heed to Her voice we find the joy in the answer of a good conscience."

Others have laid emphasis upon the social meaning of education whereby it aims at making an individual fit in the society. It was in this sense that Aldous Huxley said, "A perfect education is one which trains up every human being to fit into the place he or she is to occupy in the social hierarchy, but without, in the process, destroying his or her individuality."

All the foregoing definitions have stated that education is the process of development. It, therefore, becomes necessary to discover what is implied in this development. Although the ability to learn depends upon development, but development is not synonymous with education. Development means the gradual and continuous progress of mind and body. Through this development the child acquires the following elements:

1. Knowledge of the environment by which he is surrounded.
2. The necessary motor control to fulfil his individual needs.
3. Linguistic abilities to enable him to converse.
4. Some knowledge of individual and collective relationship.

The development of all these elements begins at home itself. The educator's task is to continue this process and to encourage it while the child is at school.

In fact, this process of development continues right through an individual's life-time. Consequently, it is accepted that education in its general sense continues throughout a man's natural span of life.

Even the successful teacher or educator himself remains a student throughout his life. On the one hand, he teaches certain things to some people but at the same time he learns something from them. All successful educators experience that the development undergone by their thoughts, personalities and abilities would have been impossible otherwise. In much the same way, people other than the educator, teach and learn simultaneously.

Indian Concept of Education

Turning to the Indian approach, it becomes necessary to include the spiritual aspect also because it is accepted as a part of the development by education. In fact, Indian thinkers have placed special emphasis upon this. Yajnavalkya opined that only that is education which gives a sterling character to an individual and renders him useful for the world. Shankaracharya said that education is that which leads to salvation.

Even the more recent educationists have stressed the importance of the spiritual aspect. In the words of A.S. Altekar, "Education has always been regarded in India as a source of illumination and power which transforms and ennobles our nature by the progressive and harmonious development of our physical, mental, intellectual and spiritual powers and faculties."

This spiritual tradition has been carried on by contemporary Indian philosophers of education in their integral approach, synthesis of idealism and pragmatism, rationalism and humanism, diversity in unity and harmony of the individual and society.

It was due to this emphasis on the spiritual meaning of education that Vivekanand said, "Religion is the innermost core of education."

In the words of Sri Aurobindo, "The child's education ought to be an outpouring of all that is best, most powerful, most intimate and living in his nature, the mould into which the man's action and development ought to run is that of his innate quality and power. He must acquire new things but he will acquire them best, most wholly on the basis of his own developed type and inborn force."

M.K. Gandhi expressed the same idea when he defined education by saying, "By education, I mean an all round drawing out of the best in child and man, body, mind and spirit. Literacy is not the end of education not even the beginning. It is one of the means whereby man and woman can be educated. Literacy in itself is no education."

Synthetic Definition

It is clear from the above discussion of the meaning of education in West and India, ancient and modern that it may be synthesised since all these accept some common characteristics of education. The following points, concerning the meaning of education, emerge from a review of the meaning of education in the West and in India:

1. *A Life-long Process.* Education, according to most of the philosophers, continues from birth to death. As Madam Paul

Richard pointed out, the education of man, "should begin at his very birth and it is to continue the whole length of his life."

2. *Unfolding.* Education is a gradual unfolding. In his allegory of the cave Plato observed that "the power and capacity of learning exists in the soul already, and just as the eye was unable to turn from darkness to light, without the whole body, so too, the instrument of knowledge can only, by the movement of the whole soul, be turned from the world of the becoming into that of being and learn by degrees to endure the sight of being and of the brightest and best of being or in other words of the good."

It is in the same sense that Sri Aurobindo said, "The chief aim of education should be to help the growing soul to draw out that in itself which is best and make it perfect for a noble use."

3. *Based on Child Psychology.* Western thinkers unanimously agree that true education should be based on child psychology. This again has been accepted by Indian philosophers of education. According to Sri Aurobindo, "Nothing can be taught to the mind which is not already concealed as potential knowledge in the unfolding soul of the creature."

Educational theory must be based on sound psychology. As Sri Aurobindo points out, "The true basis of education is the study of the human mind, infant, adolescent and adult."

4. *Individual as well as Social.* True education is individual as well as social. Plato brought out a scheme of education according to each individual's capacities to serve the society. Philosophers, in the West, have everywhere laid emphasis upon individual as well as social aims of education.

Contemporary Indian philosophers also exhibit this tendency. M.K. Gandhi said, "I value individual freedom, but you must not forget that man is essentially a social being. He has risen to his present status by learning to adjust his individuality to the requirements of social progress."

5. *Total Development.* Thus, education by general agreement is a total development, physical, mental and spiritual, individual as well as social. This total development is the meaning of self-realisation. This synthesis of the different aspect of man's development is characteristic of not only idealism but also

naturalism, pragmatism and realism. It is again the meaning of perfection, acclaimed as the aim of education by so many thinkers. It is also what is known as complete education. It is again the humanist meaning of education since man is a complex being having several aspects of his personality all of which require full development.

According to Sri Aurobindo, education should help the individual to grow "into a fullness of physical and vital energy and utmost breadth, depth and height of his emotional, his intellectual and his spiritual being". The total development lays equal emphasis upon physical as well as spiritual growth. Without physical culture mental training has been considered as one-sided.

In the words of Aldous Huxley, "Where the body is maladjusted and under strain, the mind's relations, sensory, emotional, intellectual, conative, with external realty are likely to be unsatisfactory."

Education aims at an all round and total perfection of the individual and society. Hence, physical culture should form an important part of the educational process. As Sri Aurobindo puts it, "If seeking is for a total perfection of the being, the physical part of it cannot be left aside, for the body is the material basis, the body is the instrument which we have to use."

Similar quotations may be hunted from other philosophers of education in West and East. The total development involves character development, development of social virtues and individual skills. It includes all the various aims of education. It involves all the functions of education in human life such as development of natural abilities, character building, personality integration, preparation for adult life, control and sublimation of basic instincts, creation of useful citizens, development of a sense of community, progress of culture and civilization, social welfare, use of leisure and synthesis of national as well as international consciousness.

Modern Concept of Education

To understand the modern concept of education, one has to make a comparative study of the old and modern concepts. Following are the differences between the old and the new concepts:

(1) *Meaning of Education*. Education is derived from the Latin word 'Educatum' which means to draw out, to foster growth and to develop. Hence, the modern concept of education seeks to develop the inherent capacities of a child in the social environment. In the old concept, education was taken to mean as a process to thrust ready made titbits of knowledge into the mind of a child as if it was an empty vessel. The old concept has exploded under the weight of psychological researches and democratic values. The mind is a dynamic self-adjusting and self-learning force needing proper guidance for wholesome growth and development. Modern education seeks to develop the mind according to its own inherent capacities in a social environment.

(2) *Aims of Education*. Ancient education emphasized scholarship and mental development. It kept an indifferent attitude towards other aspects of personality. Acquiring more and more knowledge was regarded as the prime aim. On the contrary, modern educationists lay equal stress upon other aspects of development viz. physical, mental, emotional and social. Thus, the aim of modern education is to develop individuality to the full and attain social efficiency and dynamism.

(3) *Curriculum*. In the old curriculum, only subjects promoting mental development were included and emphasized. Thus, old curriculum got rigid and stratified. It was confined mostly to classroom activities and experiences. Modern curriculum is flexible, varied and progressive in the sense that it tries to meet the needs of the developing child as well as the demands of ever-changing modern society.

(4) *Methods of Teaching*. As the methods emphasized cramming and stimulated rote memorization education was a lifeless, dull and drab process. Modern methods condemn rote memorization and promote the adoption of lively and effective methods life Play way, Learning by doing, Learning by experience etc. These methods stimulate motivation, interest and attention.

(5) *Discipline*. Old concept of discipline emphasized the use of rode and punishment to enforce obedience and discipline in children. This concept of enforced discipline through repression has now been given up. The modern concept is self-discipline leading to natural obedience.

(6) *Examination*. The old method of essay type examination

encouraged cramming and rote memorization. Modern techniques evaluate as well as examine. These include objective tests, progress reports, cumulative records, interviews and practical performances.

(7) *Agencies of Education.* According to old beliefs, school was the only agency for the education of children. According to modern views, all formal and informal agencies are harnessed to the task of education.

(8) *Teacher.* Old education put the teacher at the top of the educational process. In modern times, a teacher is considered as a friend, philosopher and guide.

(9) *Child.* According to old concept, the child was a mere passive recipient of whatever the teacher instructed. Modern education is child-centred. The entire educational process is to cater to his needs and develop him according to his nature. He is to interact actively with the teacher and his class-mates to achieve effective learning promoting his own development and the development of the society of which he is an integral part.

(10) *School.* According to old concept, school served as a shop for selling knowledge. Everything was pre-planned in advance. Teachers were concerned with the input and bothered little about output. Modern concept of education regards school as miniature of society laying emphasis more on output in comparison with input.

(11) *Education as a Discipline.* In ancient times, education meant only training of something for some aim. Modern education is a separate discipline of deep study, investigation and research. It is a very important process of human development in all fields of human activities. It has its own distinct special feature and factors to promote it as a vital formative process.

The following chart clarifies the modern concept of education:

S. No.	*Aspects of Education*	*Old Concept of Education*	*Modern Concept of Education*
1.	Meaning	Instruction	Development
2.	Aims	Knowledge	1. Development of Total personality 2. Social Efficiency.

Contd.

S. No.	*Aspects of Education*	*Old Concept of Education*	*Modern Concept of Education*
3.	Curriculum	Subject centered	Activity centered, social efficiency.
4.	Methods	Rote memorization	Learning by doing, Project etc.
5.	Discipline	Rigid, Repressionistic	Self discipline.
6.	Examination	Essay type tests	Objective type tests, Evaluation.
7.	Agencies	Formal (School)	Formal and Informal both.
8.	Teacher	Instructor	Friend, Philosopher and guide.
9.	Child	Passive recipient	Active, dynamic.
10.	School	Teaching shops	Miniature of Society.

Difference Between Education and Instruction

(1) *Field.* Education is the full development of all innate powers of a child. Nothing is thrust into his mind by force from outside. It develops the child physically, mentally, emotionally and socially. Thus, its field is wider than that of instruction. Instruction means forcing into the mind of a child *predetermined* dozes of knowledge in a pre-planned way to achieve mental development. It is one-sided development and that too of memory only. Thus, its field is narrow in comparison with education.

(2) *Place of Child.* In education, the place of child is central, pivotal and of prime importance. Teacher's role is subsidiary. In instruction, the place of teacher is central. The role of child is secondary. Thus, the role is reversed.

(3) *Interests, inclinations and abilities.* Education pays full attention to the interest inclinations and abilities of the child. Nothing is forced into his mind without his will. Instruction neglects interests, inclinations and capacities of the child. Ready-made dozes of knowledge are forced into his minds.

(4) *Preparation.* Education prepares the child for real life. Instruction prepares the child to pass an examination.

(5) *Nature of Learning.* In education, all learning is self-learning. It remains stable and permanent and can be applied to solve the problems of future life. In instruction, cramming is encouraged. It is soon forgotten and, thus, cannot be applied to meet the challenges of life successfully.

Parts of Education

According to John Dewey, education is a tripolar process. It has following three important ingredients:

(1) *The Teacher.* In ancient times, the teacher had the main role to play while the learner's role was subsidiary. In modern time, the role has been reversed. Though the place of teacher has now become secondary, yet his responsibility has increased because a teacher is not only an important factor in the educational environment of the learner, he is also a builder of the whole educational environment which is very comprehensive and all inclusive.

In the process of education, a teacher's role is of two fold. First, being the important factor of the educational environment, he influences the personality of the learner through his own magnetic personality. Second, as a builder of the educational environment, he provides suitable experiences to the learner to develop and use fully his skills and capacities to achieve the good of his ownself and the welfave of his society, of which he is an integral part. Besides, by his own attitudes and behaviour, the teacher builds the character of learners and infuses in them respect for moral and spiritual values.

This is only possible when the teacher is himself a man of strong moral character. He must be well aware of the modern strategies, tactics and techniques of teaching. He should be capable of using them to the best of his knowledge to make teaching-learning most effective. Thus, to develop the learner as well as the society, a teacher is a very. important factor in the educational process of today.

(2) *The Learner.* According to psychological findings and democratic feelings, education starts from the child. Thus, education has become child-centred today. Adams was the first educationist to point out this truth by his remark, "The teacher teaches Latin to John". John is more important than Latin.

Modern educationists are unanimous about the importance of child in the educational process. Education should develop the personality of the learner according to his interests, inclinations, abilities and capacities. Everything concerning education is now child-centered. Aims, curriculum and methods keep the child at the centre of their formulation and planning of educational programmes.

No teacher can be successful in his activities if he fails to understand the learner with which he is to deal. To make teaching-learning normal, natural and effective, the teacher should not only be the master of content but also know fully well the stages of child development and their characteristics.

(3) *Curriculum.* The essential link between the teacher and the child is the curriculum. It serves as a vehicle for the realization of educational aims. The teacher uses the items of curriculum according to modern methods of teaching to educate children to realize the predetermined aims of education. In the wider sense, curriculum means all the experiences and activities from which a child learns something or the other.

The teacher and the child both co-operate in building and formulating experiences conducive to learning. Curriculum is structured according to the ever-growing needs of children and changing demands of dynamic society.

This is the difference between the curriculum of despotic as well as democratic countries. In the former type, all activities are rigid, predetermined and fully controlled by the state, while in the latter pattern, there is flexibility, freedom and adjustment.

Meaning of Science

The science is that systematised knowledge which a person acquires through his tests and experiences. Remember that the science establishes relationship between cause and effect by presenting the knowledge in a systematic, well-planned and organised way before us. It develops scientific attitude aiming us. As a result of this, our wrong conceptions come to an end. As the scientific attitude develops. We say good or bad because these have some goodness or drawback. In this way, as the scientific attitude develops in the human being, his decisions and conclusions start having objectivity. Hence, we should follow the scientific laws in search of truth.

Meaning of Technology

It is most important to understand the meaning of Technology first and then the meaning of Educational Technology. It is because the entire creation and construction which the science has encouraged is all due to the medium of Technology. The progress of developed countries like America and Russia took place on the basis of science and technology only.

Now, science and technology are being used in our country too so that our country may progress like America and Russia. In the opinion of Ofiesh that the technology is the use of science in art. Hence, the basis of technology is science and its function is to develop experimental art.

It should be remembered that the technology, on the one hand, constructs new organisations, models and designs, while on the other hand, it organises the human being and the process of machine system. It is to be cared that the technology is neither a mere machine or hardware nor a human-system or a software, but it is the combination of all these.

Hence, it would be a mistake if it is delimited to the hardware only. In short, the technology is the application of science in art and it is concerned directly with the production or construction. The technology means the use of scientific knowledge to meet the needs of daily life or the practical form of scientific knowledge is called technology. In this way, when the knowledge of science is used in the practical tasks, it is called technology.

Relationship Between Science and Technology

Both the science and technology are closely associated. The science makes us aware about the fact that why an object or principle should be known while the technology makes it clear how that object or principle should be known? Hence, the science is mere a principle and the technology is the experimental and practical aspects based on the skill 'How to know the principle?'.

In this way, the straight concern of the technology is with efficiency. The national life of those nations which have followed the relationship of science and technology, is growing prosperous and happy by using both science and technology properly and by enjoying various advantages.

In our country, the cramming of the principles of science takes place among pupils, but they are kept away from the practical and skill aspects of those principles. Thus, the science education cannot by converted into technology in our country. That is why, a student who passes M.Sc. in Physics, possesses the entire theoretical knowledge about 'Electricity', 'Sound', and 'Light', but he cannot even repair the devices of daily use such as radio, taperecorder, television and scooter etc. because of lack of technical know-how.

Contrary to this, an illiterate mechanic repairs quickly all those devices with the help of his technical know-how in the case of any break-down. Hence, we should provide technical knowledge too along with the knowledge of science to the students. Only then the problem of unemployment can be solved in our country and the progress will be effective in the areas of agriculture, industry, commerce, trade, health and security etc.

Origin of Educational Technology

The birth story of educational technology is not too old. We see that even in nineteenth century, the educational technology existed in the form of educational toys and other learning tactics. But its frequent use came to light in 1926. In Ohio state university, it was used in the form of a teaching machine by Sidney Presscy. Then around 1930-40, Lumsdain and Glaser tried to make education as mechanical by presenting some special types of scrambled books, cards and boards.

It should be remembered that the most important work was carried out during 1950 when B.F. Skinner developed Programmed Learning while carrying on experiments with animals.

In 1950, Brynmor, in England, used educational technological steps for the first time. It is to be cared that in 1960, as a result of industrial revolution in America and Russia, other countries also started progressing in the field of educational technology. In this way, the beginning of educational technology took place in 1950 from America and Russia and now it has reached England, Europe and India.

Now we see in teaching, due to various technological inventions like radio, tape-recorder, television, computer, CCTV i.e. closed circuit T.V., electronic video tapes and other audio-visual aids, many other numerous technologies have developed which are being used in the areas like industry, commerce, health, security and education.

We observe that the development of these devices has helped in the indoctrination of behavioural technology and in the field of teaching technology, models and designs. In other words, now the process of teaching has been mechanised.

As a result, now in the three aspects of human knowledge, various types of machines are being used through which an effective teacher can provide benefits to the large groups of the students with the help of his knowledge. In this way, the concept of educational technology has developed in the field of education as a result of the mechanisation of teaching.

Meaning of Educational Technology

J.K. Galbraith, in his book *The New Industrial State*, has given two main characteristics of every technology. These are: (1) systematic application of scientific knowledge to the practical tasks, and (2) the division of the practical tasks into sections and sub-sections.

In the field of education, any subject which meets these two norms of the characteristics, is called educational technology.

Always keep in mind that educational technology does not determine the educational objectives. It is the function of political thinkers and philosophers. This function is carried out keeping in view the wider aspects of society and values.

Educational technology defines teaching-objectives in behavioural terms. It is that science on the basis of which various methods and techniques are developed and constructed in order to achieve pre-determined teaching objectives.

Thus, when the teaching objectives got determined, then educational technology comes into existence to achieve them. First of all, it creates conditions by interpreting the input during the teaching process. It selects and applies the appropriate strategy for achieving the teaching objectives.

In the end, looking at the output or abilities of the pupils, it is evaluated whether the teaching objectives have been achieved or not. If not, then what changes should be brought about in the teaching strategy or strategies so that the teaching objectives may be achieved. Hence, educational technology includes three processes. These are:

1. Functional analysis of teaching-learning process in which the teacher observes all those components which are applied as input and these come to light through output.
2. Separate or combined search and analysis of those components which are used in the teaching-learning process during input and output.
3. Presenting the acquired learning experiences in the form of research-outcomes.

It is clear from the above account that the educational technology is that behavioural technology which presents the art of teaching in a new fashion and it controls educational influences with the help of those factors which are used for achieving teaching objectives.

It is to be remembered that certain steps are to be followed in order to achieve these objectives. These steps are—(1) Teaching Objectives; (2) Contents; (3) Teaching Material; (4) Educational Environment; (5) Behaviour of the pupils; (6) Behaviour of the teacher; and (7) Interaction between teacher and pupil.

Hence, educational technology is that dynamic, progressive and important mechanism in the field of education which modifies and analyses the various steps of teaching and learning with the help of indoctrinated principles and laws of modern psychology, sociology, engineering, administrative theory, mathematics and other social and physical sciences.

It develops educational efficiency by formulating and remodelling according to the needs. Also, it plays its important role not only in the classrooms but also in the entire school environment, educational administration and educational references.

Definitions of Educational Technologies

The following definitions suggested by the different scholars are being given in order to make the meaning of educational technology more clear—

"Educational Technology is the form of detailed application of psychology of learning to practical teaching problems."

—*John. P. Dececco*

"Educational Technology is the application of scientific knowledge and learning and the conditions of learning to improve the effectiveness and efficiency of teaching and training."

—G.O. Leith

"Educational Technology may be defined as the application of the laws as well as recent discoveries of Science and Technology to the process of education." *—S.S. Kulkarni*

"Educational Technology is the application of scientific process to men's learning conditions." *—Robert A. Cox*

"Educational Technology is that branch of educational theory and practice concerned primarily with the design and use of massages which control the learning process." *—E.E. Hadden*

"Educational Technology is concerned to provide appropriately designed learning situations which, holding in view of objectives of the Teaching or Training, being to bear the best means of instruction." *—Richmond*

"Educational Technology is an applied or practical study which aims at maximising educational effect by 'Controlling' such relevant facts as educational purposes, educational environment, conduct of student, behaviour of instructors and interrelations between students and instructors."

—Takashi Sakamato

After conducting an analysis of above mentioned definitions, the following conclusions may be derived—

1. Educational Technology studies the effect of science and technology upon education. In other words, science and technology are used under educational technology. Hence, it is the practical aspect of science.
2. Educational Technology is a continuous dynamic, progressive and effect-producing method.
3. The basis of educational technology is science.
4. New conceptions are possible only due to educational technology such as programmed learning, micro-teaching, simulated teaching, interaction analysis, video-tape, tape-recorder, projector and computer etc.
5. Engineering Technology is not the educational technology because the engineering technology has manufactured radio, tape-recorder, video-tape and T.V. etc., which are used in teaching as audio-visual aids, but still engineering technology is different from educational technology. In education, it is accepted as a hardware approach only.

6. Educational Technology accepts schools as a system. In this system, the school-building, furniture and teacher act as input while various methods, techniques, strategies and the teaching and examination with the help of audio-visual aids function in the form of a process. Lastly, the output is in the form of ability of the pupils.
7. Audio-visual aids cannot be termed as educational technology. It is because its concern is only with the process-aspect of educational technology and not with the input and output aspects. But if these audio-visual aids are used to achieve educational objectives, then it can be put in the category of Educational Technology.
8. Educational Technology cannot solve each and every problem of education. It can be used successfully in teaching and instructional system only.
9. Programmed Instruction is also different from Educational Technology. Its main cause is that the student learns himself during the programmed instructions. It does not allow interaction between pupil and teacher. Hence, it can be used only for limited objectives and limited subject-matter. Therefore, programmed instruction is merely a part of educational technology.
10. Some people assume that educational technology will replace the teacher which will make the teacher unemployed one day. It is their mistake. Educational Technology can never replace the teacher. It is because of three aspects of educational technology. These are—(1) Input, (2) Process, and (3) Output. Input is the teacher's job and therefore, educational technology cannot snatch the place of a teacher.

In spite of this, educational technology develops cognitive domain only and not the affective domain. Affective domain can only be developed when an interaction between teachers and pupils takes place. Hence, educational technology cannot replace the teacher. However, a teacher can provide benefits to the large groups of students with the help of radio, tape-recorder and television etc.

Objectives of Educational Technology

The main objectives of Educational Technology are as follows:

(i) The first objective of educational technology is to modernise the learning methods and techniques after systematising them so that these may be turned effective according to the needs of the changing era for the unknown future.

(ii) The second objective of educational technology is the desirable modifications in the behaviours of the teachers and pupils by improving the teaching, learning and evaluation conditions.

(iii) The third objective of educational technology is to make the classrooms teaching easy, clear, interesting, effective, understandable, objective and scientific.

(iv) The fourth objective of educational technology is to help in increasing various facilities by solving the most complicated problems of human life so that the human life may carry on its progress continuously.

Types of Educational Technology

As Lumsdane suggests, educational technology has the following three forms—

1. Hardware Approach.
2. Software Approach.
3. System Approach.

1. *Hardware Approach.* The use of engineering machines in teaching is called Educational Technology-1. It is to be remembered that physical science and engineering technology have given birth to Educational Technology-1. Davis has said clearly that Educational Technology-1 or Hardware Approach is the application of physical science in education and teaching with which the teaching process is being mechanised gradually so that maximum pupils may be educated in minimum time and at low cost.

Educational Technology includes cinema, gramophone, radio tape-recorder, projector, computer, closed circuit television (CCTV) and electronic video-tape etc., all the teaching machines the use of which makes the teaching more and more effective in order to achieve the teaching objectives. It has already been mentioned that the human knowledge has three aspects. These are—(1) Preservation (2) Transmission, and (3) Development.

It should be remembered that the history of preservation of the knowledge is believed to exist since the printing machines started. The knowledege is preserved with these machines in the form of books which are shelved in the Libraries. Not only this, now we see that the knowledge is also preserved through tape-recorder and films in addition to books.

The second aspect of human knowledge is its expansion or transmission. A teacher can impart knowledge himself to his pupils but such direct benefitters happen to be small in number. Now a days, transmission or expansion of the knowledge is supported by machine like mike, radio and television etc.

With these, thousands of pupils enjoy this home-delivery of such benefits. In this way, due to educational technology-1, surprising changes have occurred in the process of education. The correspondence courses and open-university are the gifts of educational technology.

The third aspect of the human knowledge is its development. For this aspect, provisions are made for research work. In the research programmes, the main function is the collection and analysis of data. For this purpose, presently the researcher uses the electric machines and computers. Hence, all the three aspects of knowledge allow the use of machines. In short, now the teaching process has been mechanised. This mechanisation of teaching process is termed as Educational Technology-1 or Hardware Approach.

2. *Software Approach.* Educational Technology-2 or Software Approach is also named as Instructional Technology or Teaching Technology or Behavioural Technology. It must be remembered that Educational Technology-2 does not allow the use of engineering machines. However, psychological principles of teaching and learning are utilized so that desirable changes in the behaviour of the pupils may be brought about. If the machines are even used, this is done only to make the subject-matter effective. Hence, the Educational Technology-2 is concerned with the teaching objectives in behavioural terms, principles of teaching, methods of teaching and techniques, reinforcement of instructional-system, feed-back devices and evaluation.

In nut-shell, in Educational Technology-2 or Software

Approach, it is tried to develop all the three aspects i.e. Input, Process and Output.

The above description makes it clear that the Educational Technology-1 or Hardware Approach means the use of machines in teaching, while Educational Technology-2 or Software Approach means the use of teaching and learning principles. In this way, there is close relationship between Educational Technology 1 and 2.

3. *Systems Approach.* Educational Technology-3 or System Analysis is also known as Management Technology. It was developed after World War-II. It has provided a scientific basis to the decision-making regarding the problems associated with administration, management, commerce, industry and army. Remember that Educational Technology-3 helps to study the problems of educational administration and management in a scientific and conclusive way. By using it, we can make the educational system, educational administration and management effective. In short, Educational Technology-3 helps in the development of educational administration and formulation of instructional out-line. By using it educational system, educational administration and management can be made more effective and less costly. Hence, these days the educational technology-3 occupies an important place in the field of teaching.

Functions of Educational Technology

The main functions of educational technology are as follows:

(*i*) To convert behavioural objectives into the learning conditions in the context of educational objectives.

(*ii*) To analyse the characteristics of the learners.

(*iii*) To organize the contents.

(*iv*) To formulate or construct the media of presenting the contents.

(*v*) To evaluate the performance of the pupils with reference to the achievement of educational objectives.

(*vi*) To provide reinforcement and feedback in order to modify the behaviour of the pupils.

Importance and Need of Educational Technology

Educational Technology enjoys special importance in all the countries of the world. Hence, every country is applying educational technology in accordance to its educational system. We are throwing light on the importance of educational technology as follows—

Increasing the Effectiveness on Teaching-Learning Process—Educational technology brings desired improvement in teaching-learning process by making it effective. It develops to the maximum the cognitive, affective and psychomotor aspect of the pupil.

Maximising the Output—Educational technology has maximised the learning facilities. It is because it uses the principles indoctrinated by Psychology, Sociology, Mathematics, Engineering and other social and scientific subjects. Their input maximises their output in the form of their competency by this technology.

Optimum Use of Resources—The developing countries possess very limited resources. They lack experts, machinery or tools, school building, stationary and time. Educational technology emphasizes the maximum use of available resources in the learning situations, which may benefit all the pupil of the nation from those limited resources which are available for teaching work. We make it clear to the readers that the teaching technology has developed the techniques like radio and television with which appreciable assistance has been sought for the expansion of mass education.

Instructional Design

Instructional Design occupies an important place in teaching. Till recent, teaching remained based upon learning objectives only. It did not encourage desired achievement. Hence, in order to bring desired changes in the pupils' behaviour, the teaching situations, working tools and new approaches are also considered important in addition to the learning principles.

The composite form of all these is called instructional design. Remember that among the new approaches, the following three approaches are main as schools of thoughts—

Training Psychology. Training psychology is an important method of teaching and learning. Its development results out of the research work carried out on the complicated training problems and situations.

Training psychology emphasizes that the whole training talk should be divided into 3 parts. These parts are—*(i)* Preparing outline of the task, *(ii)* Task analysis, and *(iii)* Putting the task elements in such a sequence that the desired objectives are achieved. It is clear that the instructional designs depend upon training psychology.

The main role of training psychology is in Teacher Education. It is because the modern training programme is in a vogue condition. Still in most of the training departments, the pupil-teacher educators don't know what they are to teach to the pupil-teachers? How skills are to be inculcated in them? They must study the training psychology so that they may also learn to formulate teaching objectives and to analyse the elements of the training programme. In America, various models have been developed for the teacher on the basis of training psychology.

Cybernetic Psychology. Cybernetic Psychology is also a part of training psychology. Its reason is that this training is more close to the research. Remember that Cybernetic Psychology accepts human being as a machine. It also emphasizes that every human being uses the process of cybernetic through his senses to control and modify his behaviour. In other words, for human development, the theory of cybernetic is an important theory.

Hence, cybernetic psychology emphasizes the fact that all the methods of feedback bring about the desired changes by controlling the behaviours of the pupils considering the dynamic feedback and self-regulation as its goal. In short, this method is considered more important for self-learning.

Remember that the cybernetic psychology which controls the learning behaviour on one side, has more importance in individual teaching than collective teaching on the other side. Programmed instruction is its most appropriate example. In this, the answers given by the pupils are compared with the correct answers. The correct answers put the pupil on right track during feedback or cybernetic.

In short, the result of the individual behaviour works as feedback or cybernetic for him and controls his future behaviours. Therefore, the feedback or cybernetic occupies an important place in the progress, growth and development of the human being.

System Analysis. A system is concerned with such an organisation of entire sequence in which inter-relationship between various elements and with the entire sequence occurs.

In the words of Unwin, "A system is the sum total of parts working independently and working together to achieve the required results or outcomes based on needs."

A system has three components—*(i)* Purpose, *(ii)* Process, and *(iii)* Content. The 'purpose' describes what is to be done, the 'process' includes various activities, and the content is concerned with the sub-parts or sub-components of the system.

As a matter of fact, the system is a problem-solving process in which the needs of the management are diagnosed and lastly by using an appropriate method for solving the problem, evaluation is carried out. In this way, in organising teaching-learning, the solution of the arising problems, in organising teaching-learning a system is a scientific and valid tool by which learning behaviours are controlled.

The assumption emphasizes the fact that each behaviour of the human being function as a part of an organized system. Therefore, each problem of the human being can be solved by analysing it and as a result of this, the system can be made effective. Remember that the educational administration is benefited to the maximum by system analysis. It helps the administration by result-oriented analysis.

We can present the instructional design with reference to its three approaches on the basis of following three aspects—

Instructional Design

Approach Point	Training Psychology	Cybernetic Psychology	Systems Analysis
Focus	Task Analysis	Feedback control and self-regulation	Systems Development
Function	Input	Process	Output
Implications	*(a)* Classroom Teaching	*(a)* Teaching	*(a)* Instruction
	(b) Programmed Instruction	*(b)* Instruction	*(b)* Management

Scope of Educational Technology

Educational technology got developed as a new subject in the field of education for the last few years. The term 'Education' includes teaching, learning, instruction and training, similarly the scope of educational technology is also much wider. The below mentioned technologies are included in it—

1. Behavioural Technology
2. Instructional Technology
3. Teaching Technology
4. Instructional Design
5. Training Psychology
6. Cybernetic Psychology
7. System Analysis.

In view of the definitions and characteristics of educational technology, some general working-areas of educational technology can be pointed out—

(i) Area of Curriculum Construction. In the present technological and psychological age, the application of scientific and technological knowledge is much essential for the curriculum construction. The curriculum construction has become a very tedious job in the field of education. The task of the curriculum construction can be simplified with the help of educational technology.

(ii) Selection of Teaching-Learning Strategies. The selection of teaching-learning strategies turns easy with the help of educational technology.

(iii) Selection of Audio-Visual Material. Another important working-area of educational technology is that the teacher can select easily the audio-visual aids with its assistance.

(iv) Determination of Educational Objectives: The software aspect of educational technology contributes in the formulation of teaching objectives.

(v) Areas of Teachers' Training: The new innovations in educational technology can be used successfully in teachers' training and it is actually being done, such as micro-teaching, simulated teaching, system approach, class-room interaction and teaching models etc.

(vi) Area of Feedback. In the field of education, educational technology has emphasized on feedback for evaluation. Many experiments have been carried out in this area.

(vii) Area of the Hardware. One form of educational technology also occurs as Hardware Devices such as teaching machines, tape-recorder, television, computer and satellite etc. The learning in the classroom can be made effective with their use.

Characteristics of Educational Technology

1. Educational technology is based on the application of the scientific knowledge.
2. Educational Technology has contributed in developing various methods, for example, micro-teaching method, simulated teaching, interaction analysis, audio-visual aids and programmed learning method.
3. In the field of educational technology, psychology, science, technology, system, art, audio-visual aids and machines are used.
4. Educational technology is helpful in making the teaching process objective, easy, clear, interesting and scientific.
5. In educational technology, the provision of measuring tools is emphasized for the evaluation of learning outcomes.
6. A desired changes is possible in the behaviour of teachers and pupils.
7. Educational technology is a continuous dynamic technology.
8. Educational technology encourages learning by controlling the environment.

Schools of Teaching Technology or Educational Technology

Rationalism, realism, idealism, humanism, neo-humanism, eclecticism, instrumentalism are the ideas that reflect various efforts to link teaching and the curriculum with a coherent and consistent set of values. But these labels have remained unknown to teachers engrossed in developing introductory departmental course and major programmes. Hence, the labels and associated views would apparently seem irrelevant to many teachers. Yet, implicit in school and college programme developments and teaching orientations, there are five acceptable distinctive philosophical views:

(i) theocentric—makes divine sovereignty and glory the central truth with all other truth dependent upon or emergent from that ultimate source.

(ii) ideocentric—emphasizes the worth of the accumulated knowledge in the discipline.

(iii) Sociocentric—places individual services to society (or to the nation) at the centre of education.
(iv) ideocentric—assumes that a democratic society requires maximal individual development.
(v) eccentric—highlights the individual instructor as a model for emulation.

Traditional and other institutions operating in the context of fundamentalist religious commitments tend to be theocentric. The professor who asserts that his sole objective as a teacher is, "to do God's will to the best of my ability" well exemplifies this position. Liberal arts colleges committed to distribution requirements are predominantly ideocentric. Programmes dominated by the social sciences and by interdisciplinary problems courses often operate from a sociocentric viewpoint. Programmes committed to individual (idiocentric) development tend to result from faculty commitments to humanistic psychology. The eccentric conception emphasizes professorial rather than student ideocentricity. The number of really excellent teachers on most campuses is small, and thus they are indeed.

QUESTIONS FOR ANSWER

1. What are the types of Educational Technology? Clarify the differences between Instrumental Technology and Teaching Technology.
2. Define Educational Technology and write a note on its scope and significance in Indian context.
3. Explain 'Hardware' and 'Software' approaches to education and differentiate between the two. Also write their relative importance.
4. Write short notes on the following:
   (a) Functions and Need of Educational Technology
   (b) Instrumental Design
   (c) Characteristics of Educational Technology
   (d) Objectives of Educational Technology
   (e) Relationship between Science and Technology
5. "Knowledge of Educational Technology is useful for a teacher". Justify.

2

Kinds and Components of Educational Technology

The opted prime objective of education determines the kind of educational technology. The society or the state opts this educational objective. On the basis of these educational objectives Hardy and Dressels have identified and defined four kinds of educational technologies. This classification is mainly based on central objective of education and accordingly stresses on the technology of teaching to achieve the opted objective of education, therefore, Hardy and Dressel have named them as teaching technologies, which are being discussed as follows:

1. In discipline-centred teaching, the content and structure of the discipline are rigidly determined and in no way modified to meet the requirements, needs, or special concerns of either the teacher or learner.
2. In instructor-centred teaching, the teacher is the expert and the main source of knowledge. He is an authority on the subject matter and the discipline. The instructor, around whom all class activity revolves, is the focal point in the teaching-learning process. The student is a passive recipient rather than an active participant.
3. In student-centred cognitive teaching, intellectual development is held to be the most important outcome of the teaching-learning process. Both content and teaching practices are selected and adjusted to

accommodate the cognitive growth of the student toward teacher-specified objectives.

4. In student-centred affective teaching, the personal and social development of the student is the focus of the teaching-learning process. Both the content and the teaching practices are adjusted to foster the total development of each individual. The individual is expected to develop idiosyncratically rather than to adapt to content or to the demands of the teacher.

Discipline-Centred Teaching

In discipline-centred teaching, the course content and the structure of the discipline are rigidly defined and are not modified or rearranged to meet the requirements, needs, or special concerns of either the teacher or learner. The professorial obligation is to assure that each segment of the discipline covered by the cause is presented in a sound scholarly manner. Learning is the obligation of the student.

The course content includes those concepts, methods, theories, and materials that seem to present best that segment of the discipline as defined by scholars in the discipline. The preferred method of instruction is a series of lectures planned to cover the specified content systematically and according to a fixed schedule.

The classroom setting tends to be formal, with emphasis on scholarly authority and objectivity. Interactions between students and of students with the professor deal almost exclusively with issues arising out of the classification of course content. Students are given the same or very similar assignments to be pursued through use of the text and standard reference materials.

Students are evaluated and graded on specific skills and items of knowledge and on traditional or standard ways of presenting them. The professor's self-image is that of an authority in the discipline. The professor is responsible for presenting a defined segment of that discipline to students, each of whom is assumed to be motivated to acquire an understanding of it.

Students are regarded as prospective majors in the discipline or in a field to which the discipline has direct relevance. Course coverage and teaching methodology are the same for all classes, regardless of heterogeneity or size. Neither individuality nor creativity is sought because objectivity is prized.

Teaching in the disciplinary mode may be very effective with students who are vitally interested in the course and the discipline, and especially so with graduate students. Teachers so oriented may be vital, warm human beings interested in those students who share an interest in the discipline and demonstrate potential for success in it.

Instructor-Centred Teaching

In instructor-centred teaching, the teacher selects and develops the ideas presented to students. Students are expected to adjust to the professors and to learn more from them than from reading, discussion, or critical thought. Students are regarded as a admiring audience.

Course content is based upon personal preferences and may include practical applications or interrelations with other disciplines that the professor finds interesting and complementary (also complimentary) to his or her personal insights and scholarship.

The instructional procedures are chosen to highlight the teacher's personality and eccentricities. Classroom discussions, which may exhibit the instructor's humour, critical facilities, and versatility, focus upon and clarify the instructor's views.

Assignments likewise reflect the instructor's interests and points of view. The instructor evaluates and grades students on their ability to imitate, reflect, and elaborate on professional perspectives, conceptions, and formulations.

The professor's self-image is that of scholar and teacher of stature—a recognized authority. The professor may make conscious or unconscious adaptations to an audience, but the adeptness are based on affective rather than cognitive concerns. The instructor-centred teacher may not give much thought to adoption to individual students or student groups and may even, without fully realizing it, ignore, or resent student originality or creativity as competition.

The standards of instructor-centred teachers tend to be highly personal and idiosyncratic. Subjectivity and objectivity are not always distinguishable. Within this instructor-centred category there are identifiable subtypes. Some simply and uninhibitedly express their natural personality. And some have had such a range of experiences and are so talented in communication with them that, without conscious intent, they become the course.

These talented types are those whose names recur in the advice (sometimes good) given to students by other students, graduates, and professors: "Be sure to take a course from Professor X". This instructor-centred orientation is found in some of the best and most inspiring teachers and also in some of the worst. An over-weening ego may make the reputation of a professor, but it may not result in good teaching.

Student-Centred Cognitive Teaching

In student-centred cognitive teaching, the intellectual maturation of the student is regarded as the goal of the teaching-learning process. Both content and teaching techniques are chosen to foster the cognitive development of the student. Emotions (affect) are not ignored but are expected to be controlled and directed by intellect.

The cognitively oriented teacher regards students as individuals who are becoming self-reliant and capable of self-direction. The knowledge that they will acquire and the ways they will use it are not predictable by the teacher. This cognitive emphasis is conjoined with an awareness that affect cognition. It may also be acknowledged that, in the nature of the human being, there are moments in which affect reigns supreme. There is joy in scholarship and intellectual performance.

Course content is chosen to be interesting, stimulating, and productive of student intellectual growth. Teaching methods or learning experiences, chosen primarily to encourage or even force students to think, may include student discussions or any experience that stimulates curiosity, thought, and understanding.

The classroom atmosphere may be exciting and yet relaxed, encouraging participation of students and stimulating them to become creative, analytical, and logical in their thinking. Student discussions and interactions are used as processes to encourage understanding and application of concepts and principles.

However, the teacher, always focusing on cognitive development, may intervene and redirect discussion whenever it strays from the point. Assignments are designed to develop cognitive abilities and to motivate the student toward self-reliance and intellectual maturity. Students are evaluated and graded on their ability to define and solve problems that require new resources and strategies.

The teacher's self-image is that of one who both models effective thinking and encourages student emulation. Accordingly the teacher's role is to develop the students' capability in inquiry rather than to present an organized body of knowledge. The cognitively oriented teacher undertakes to foster in students the ability to generalize the mode of inquiry and to extend it well beyond the course content to problems more typical of those that occur in life.

In so doing, the teacher finds individualization and adaptation desirable, both as motivation and as providing real problems for which neither the means of solution nor the answers are readily available in the text. The teacher encourages objectivity while recognizing that complete separation of cognition and affect is neither possible nor desirable.

Standards are high but harder to define than in a discipline based course because the objectives and the tasks are broader and more inclusive. Furthermore, as students are encouraged to move toward defining their own standards, uniform appraisal procedures may become impossible. The cognitively oriented teacher is less concerned with covering a specified body of content than with fostering students' interest in learning as well as their understanding and ability to use what they have learned.

Student-Centred Affective Teaching

In student-centred affective teaching, the personal, social, and intellectual development of the individual is the primary goal of the teaching-learning process. Moreover, affective and social development, as a composite, is taken to be a prerequisite to significant intellectual development.

Both course content and educative activities are selected and adjusted to accommodate this goal. Education is seen as therapeutic, and intensive interaction of individuals in groups is, therefore, regarded as an essential part of it.

In this orientation, content is secondary and is selected to help students mature and to confirm to them their emerging status as adults. The preferred instructional methods encourage student involvement, with emphasis on discussion sessions led by students or instructors (or perhaps simply convened with no leadership).

Informality, frankness, and student interaction characterize the sessions. Since students are encouraged to work toward self-expression and self-determination, formal assignments are seldom evident. Students are evaluated or evaluate themselves on the basis of participation, self-expression, affective development, and personal satisfaction.

Grades in the traditional sense are not used. The students' remarks tend to be highly objective and personal, although subject to group discussion and appraisal. In this mode, it is uncertain whether students become objectively subjective or entirely subjective by decrying objectivity.

The affective orientation is found most commonly in the social sciences, occasionally in the humanities, and rarely in mathematics and the natural sciences. This distribution reflects distinctions among the disciplines and differences among the individuals attracted to them.

Cognitive Versus Affective Orientation

Student-centred teaching may be focused on cognitive development, on affective development, or on the complex but natural co-mingling of affect and intellect that characterizes all human beings. Some people would regard this conception of teaching as based upon a humanistic point of view. Since we believe that cultivation of the intellect is the primary concern of higher education, we doubt the validity of teaching that is completely affective in orientation.

Though self-insight, self-acceptance, and a start toward self-realization can be deeply educational experiences, such experiences, even when successful, are not necessarily accompanied by acquisition of skills and the ability to use them. The individual experiencing such affective development may be happier and better able to cope with life, but there seems to be no more reason for granting credits or degrees for this than for giving credits or a degree in medicine to someone who has recovered from infectious hepatitis.

At the other extreme, pure cognitively oriented teaching is impossible. For example, most teachers attempt to communicate to students both values and preconceptions of the discipline and the satisfaction that accompanies knowing and using ideas, concepts, and methods that characterize it.

Some teachers appear not to have recognized any other view, whereas others have recognized affective potentials but have consciously striven to avoid them in their teaching. This conscious avoidance of affect is in itself an affective commitment, although not always so recognized. With some people, that avoidance results from profound convictions and deep-seated biases.

The distinction between cognitive orientation and affective orientation may be theoretically possible, but the complete separation of cognition and affect in actual teaching and learning is artificial, if not impossible. The difference between the two orientations is more one of intent and emphasis than it is a complete dichotomy.

Similar arguments could be made for the interdependence of all four orientations. For example, an otherwise discipline-oriented teacher may be sensitive to individual differences and adapt assignments to them in reference to either ability or interest.

In fact, our observations and experiences to-date with these four orientations suggest that most teachers fall athwart all four rather than into any one, and they may shift in emphasis from one to another as they deal with different content, course levels, and students. This is facilitated by that fact that the four orientations are related in pairs.

The disciplinary orientation and the student-cognitive orientation can be regarded as extremes on an objective disciplinary continuum. At one extreme, the emphasis is on presenting the discipline as an organized body of knowledge, with some attention to modes of inquiry. At the other extreme, the emphasis is on developing student cognition by assimilation of the modes of inquiry.

The instructor orientation and the student-affective orientation present a continuum along which the human element takes precedence over the discipline. Some teachers who find themselves preferring one continuum may have an eclectic disciplinary or human (personal or student) orientation rather then any extreme position. Other teachers may combine an instructor-centred orientation with either an orientation to a discipline or a student-cognitive and student-affective orientation. The one combination that seems unlikely (from observations of teachers and their responses to this structure) is that of discipline orientation and student-affective orientation. But even this composite may characterize some teachers in psychology or sociology.

Practical Analysis of Orientation

These possible combinations have been pointed out to emphasize that the four orientations are not necessarily discrete types or that each teacher could perfectly fit in one or other category.

The four orientations are the result of observation and the logical analysis of tendencies rather than of statistical analysis seeking independent types. The whole intent has been to develop a pattern of orientations that might be useful to teachers in self-analysis.

Many would favour the student-cognitive orientation and question the extreme positions on the student-affective instructor centered, and discipline-centred orientations. But effective and stimulating teaching—based upon any of these orientations or composites is surely possible for some teachers selected courses and disciplines serving specified students.

These teacher orientations have value as way to improve teaching and learning by making teachers more conscious of their stances and the relevance of these stances to their objectives, courses, and students. Teaching practices and their underlying values are thereby brought to the teachers' attention and the tendency to imitate others or to fall rote patterns may be overcome.

Emphasis on Learning

If learning is embraced as the criterion of effective teaching may be misplaced. The verb teach may be either transitive or intransitive, but the intransitive usage implies nothing about the nature of teaching. The sentence "Jones teaches" states that only that Jones engages in activities designated as teaching, whether by self-characterization or the judgment of others. The statement conveys no information about what Jones does or about the attendant circumstances.

A learner may be self-taught. The statement that Jones teaches history uses teach as a transitive verb, but it is no improvement over saying that Jones teaches. A disciplinary attachment is indicated, but the learner, the object of the teaching, is not. The sentence suggests that Jones does something to history, although history surely does not change significantly because of Jone's teaching. In fact, we should say that Jones teaches students about history rather than that he teaches history to students.

The success of teaching must be determined by whether and what the students learn, not by what the teacher does or asks students to do, and most certainly not solely by the scholarly precision and verve with which the teacher may present the historical materials.

This is not to say that the materials, content, and forms of presentation are unimportant or irrelevant; rather it emphasizes that these are subject to choice by the teacher guided by a concern for their effectiveness in promoting learning by students. Teaching and learning must always take place in some context and involve some content.

The term content evokes such words as discipline, knowledge, subject matter, values, abilities, and skills. But close examination reveals that these are by no means equivalent terms. A discipline is both an organized body of knowledge and an organized mode of accumulating and ordering knowledge. As such, it includes disciplinary methods, skills, strategies, concepts, principles, structural elements, value commitments, and analytic and synthesizing modes of thought.

Knowledge, understanding, and mastery of the methods, skills, and strategies are not taught so much as they are exemplified by the teacher and the materials used. Students emulate, assimilate, and learn in individual ways and often in ways not well understood by either the teachers or the students.

Components of Teaching Technology

Components	*Discipline-Centred Teaching*	*Instructor-Centred Teaching*	*Student-Centred Teaching (Cognitive Approach)*	*Student-Centred Teaching (Affective Approach)*
Course content	Based on disciplinary concepts, principles, theories, and methods.	Based on teacher's preferences and perceptions.	Composed of materials interesting to students and productive of cognitive outcomes.	Secondary-used to help students in maturation.
Method of instruction	Lectures and standard text, with systematic coverage of the body of knowledge.	Lecture of teacher dominated discussion highlighting teacher's personality.	Discussion, with special lectures to focus on important issues.	Emphasis on student involvement and interaction as a means personal and social development.
Classroom setting	Emotion free, with emphasis on scholarly objectivity.	Teacher dominated and controlled.	Somewhat relaxed but intellectually stimulating.	Highly informal, encouraging free student expression of feelings and concerns.
Student faculty interaction	Familiarity and intimacy with students discouraged.	Discussions with students focused on clarifying lecture points.	Interactions planned to be intellectually stimulating to students.	Interactions in groups, with instructors acting as moderators.
Assignments	All students in course given the same assignment.	Reflect the teacher's interests and views of the discipline.	Geared to cultivate the desire to move towards intellectual maturity.	No formal assignments students encouraged to work towards self-expression.

Objectives and evaluation	Students judged and graded by comparison with mastery standards.	Students judged and graded on ability to imitate professional approaches, perspectives, and formulations.	Students judged and graded on tasks that require new resources and strategies.	Students evaluated (perhaps by themselves and their peers) on participation and self-expression.
Professional self-image	Identifies with the discipline rather than with teaching role.	Has strong ego and radiates self-confidence.	Developer of student's ability to analyze, reason, use language effectively, and solve problems.	Counselor and "resource person".
Students	Viewed as would be majors and graduate school candidates.	Viewed as an audience or a source of acolytes.	Regarded as individuals who must become self-reliant in using their knowledge.	Viewed as individuals who must achieve self-insight and accept full responsibility for their own behaviour and goals.
Adaptation to or in student groups	Course coverage standard for all sections.	Some adjustments made for different audiences.	Emphasis on the how and why of knowledge.	Group interaction used to motivate students to learn.
Originality or creativity	Students encouraged to use the standard way of solving pre-structured problems.	Originality in student responses acceptable if it does not clash with teacher's views.	Originality in thinking encouraged.	Each student expected to achieve self-realization.

Contd.

Components of Teaching Technology *(Contd.)*

Components	*Discipline-Centred Teaching*	*Instructor-Centred Teaching*	*Student-Centred Teaching (Cognitive Approach)*	*Student-Centred Teaching (Affective Approach)*
Individualization	Assignments designed to help students master materials presented.	Students expected to adapt to teacher's interests rather than develop their own.	Students encouraged to develop their own analytic abilities.	Allows individuals to develop and acquire new resources and new ways of organizing ideas.
Source of standards	Standards of mastery set for each unit of learning by experts in the field.	Teacher standards based upon acceptance of his or her views.	Students expected to develop and use high standards in their own work.	Standards individually derived and self-imposed.
Objectivity	Expression of opinion in the classroom minimized.	Teacher's seeming objectivity actually highly subjective.	Analytical, objective, and logical instructional methods.	Understanding and acceptance more prized than objectivity.

Components of Educational Technology

Components of educational technology mainly concerns with methodology of teaching and related aspects to achieve the objectives of education. Educational Technology may be divided into the following three components:

1. Behavioural Technology
2. Instructional Technology
3. Teaching Technology

1. Behavioural Technology

Behavioural technology is the important component of educational technology. It puts emphasis on the use of psychological principles in learning and teaching so that the behaviour of the teachers and pupils may be modified in accordance with the teaching objectives. It must be remembered that the present education is child-centred.

Therefore, every teacher should possess the precise knowledge of child-psychology, i.e., the age, standard, mental capacity or capability and individual variations etc. Only in that case, the teacher can acquire the desired behavioural changes by creating learning experiences in the pupils in order to achieve teaching objectives.

B.F. Skinner designates teaching an interaction which exchanges the contents between teacher and pupils. Hence, we can divided teaching into two elements according to the following diagram. These elements are—

1. Content
2. Communication

The contents can be presented before the students either by the teacher or through the programmed instructions. It should be remembered that the contents can be presented at the three levels. These levels are—

1. Memory
2. Understanding
3. Reflective

Hence, it should be clarified to the readers that the different objectives, different methods and techniques of presentation and different evaluation methods are required to present the contents at the three levels.

At the time of presenting the contents before the pupils, where the teacher is required to be active on the one side, it is also required that he should provide complete freedom to the pupils for the expression of their ideas in order to bring about the changes in the behaviour of the pupils on the other side. In other words, for successful teaching, a frequent interaction between the teacher and the pupils is must.

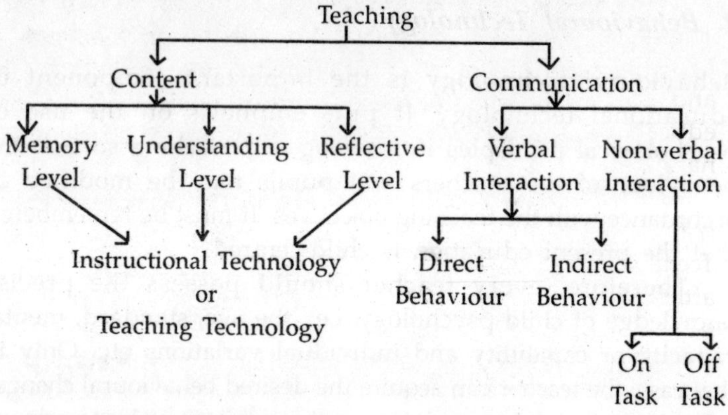

The above description suggests that the communication of the contents or the behaviour of the pupil and the teacher may be of two types—

1. Verbal
2. Non-verbal

Asking the questions by the teacher and responding to them by the pupil is said to be the verbal behaviour. But, contrary to it, the non-verbal behaviour is symbolic in which the teacher and the pupils contribute in the development of the lesson through their facial expressions, gestures displaying, the body-parts and any sort of signals.

A skilled teacher succeeds in making the education clear and alive through his non-verbal behaviours. In America, some tools have been constructed as a result of many research works in order to measure objectively that verbal and non-verbal behaviours of the teacher and pupils with the numerical and qualitative methods. With the help of these tools, by gaining knowledge about pupils' and teachers' behaviour and after slight adjustments in their study methods, techniques and strategies, some desired modifications in their behaviours can be brought about.

At one hand, educational technology tells us how the desired changes in the pupil's behaviour may be sought, while at the other hand, it also describes the observation of teacher's class-room behaviour, its analysis, interpretation and techniques of its development.

It is a true fact that everybody is not an inborn teacher. There are such few persons who are inborn teachers—like Mahatma Gandhi, Rabindra Nath Tagore, Shri Aurobindo Ghosh and Vivekanand etc. But these handful inborn teachers cannot educate compulsorily all the pupils of any such democratic nation.

Hence, those persons who are not inborn teachers, are trained as teachers in training institutions. Behavioural Technology suggests us how such desired changes can be sought after going through the behaviours of such teachers in order to develop teaching skills. The contents of behavioural technology for bringing about the changes in the behaviour of the teacher is:

(i) Meaning and definition of the teacher-behaviour.
(ii) Principles of the teacher-behaviour.
(iii) Observation methods of teacher-behaviour.
(iv) Analysis and Nature of teacher-behaviour.
(v) Evaluation and Norms of teacher-behaviour.
(vi) Models of teacher-behaviour.
(vii) Various techniques of developing teacher-behaviour. For Example—*(a)* Programmed Instruction, *(b)* T-Group training, *(c)* Interaction Analysis Techniques, *(d)* Simulated Social Skill Teaching, and *(e)* Micro-teaching.

All these techniques are being used with much interest in the universities and schools of America with the purpose of bringing about changes in the teacher-behaviour. In our country too, initiative is being taken.

Assumptions of Behaviour Technology. Behaviour technology is based upon the following assumption—

(i) Teacher's behaviour is social and psychological.

(ii) Teacher's behaviour is observable.
(iii) Teacher's behaviour is measurable.
(iv) Teacher's behaviour is modifiable.
(v) Teacher's are not inborn only, they can be produced even.

Characteristics of Behavioural Technology

(i) The basic foundation of behavioural technology is psychology.
(ii) Reinforcement and feed-back are emphasized in behaviour technology.
(iii) In this technology, the teaching acts are evaluated from the objective point of view.
(iv) Behavioural technology is more focused on psychomotor objectives.
(v) This technology is based upon software approach.
(vi) This technology is used more in the teacher's training institutions.
(vii) The attention of behavioural technology can be focused upon individual differences of pupil-teachers.

2. Instructional Technology

In instructional technology, the presentation of the contents is described in or out of the class. In both, instruction and teaching, the pupils are motivated for learning, but still there is much diiference between these two. Instruction means—communication of information.

This can be done by other persons and methods than a teacher. For example, various types of audio-visual aids can guide the students. The correspondence course upon university may accomplish the task of instructions successfully through press and television.

Actually instructional technology is based upon Hardware Approach. The teaching material prepared on the basis of machines like tape-recorder, record player, television and projector etc. comes under this. With the help of this, large groups of the students may be provided with the knowledge in minimum time and expenses.

It needs attention that the instruction is no doubt helpful

in making teaching easy, precise, interesting and effective, but instructional technology cannot replace a teacher. The only reason is that the teaching job can be performed by the teacher only. Remember that in teaching, interaction between teacher and pupils is must while in instructions, especially in programmed instructions, the pupil can learn himself.

Instruction is used in teaching and hence, teaching can be named as instruction but instruction cannot be termed as teaching because in instructions, interaction between a teacher and pupils is not essential.

It is clear that the basis of instructional technology is the machine system. It provides assistance in teaching work through machines prepared with the help of science and technology.

In the words of S.M. McMurrin, "Instructional technology is a systematic way of designing, carrying out and evaluating the total process of learning and teaching in terms of specific objectives, based on research, on human learning and communication and employing a combination of human and non-human resources to bring about more effective instruction."

The above description clarifies that the instructional technology motivates learning process. In this, the instructional material is selected keeping in view the objectives. Simultaneously, for presenting the lesson, various methods, techniques, strategies and audio-visual aids are used so that the objectives may be achieved. In the end, the achievement of the objective is evaluated. If, owing to any reason, the objective is not achieved, then again the decision regarding any proposed change is taken so that the desired change in the pupils' behaviour may be brought about.

Assumptions of Instructional Technology. The development of instructional technology is based on the following assumptions:

(i) A pupil can learn according to his needs and capacities.

(ii) A pupil can learn even in the absence of the teacher.

(iii) Reinforcement can be provided by using instruction continuously.

(iv) Learning objectives can be achieved through instructional objectives.

(v) The subject-matter can be divided into its various elements or sections and each sections can be taught independently through this technology.

Characteristics of Instructional Technology

(i) Instructional technology is helpful in achieving cognitive objectives.
(ii) This technology can meet the shortage of effective teachers.
(iii) With the help of this technology, the pupils can learn according to their needs and speed.
(iv) This technology can control the individual differences.
(v) In this technology, conditioned Response Theory of Learning is also used.
(vi) Analysis of contents in depth is carried out in this technology which encourages optimism regarding the impressive presentation of the contents.

3. Teaching Technology

Teaching is an art. Teaching technology makes this art more easy, precise, practical and objective by using scientific principles. We have mentioned earlier that the teaching has two elements—

(i) Contents, and
(ii) Class-room behaviour or communication.

Teaching technology includes both contents and communication. Hence, teaching technology includes both instructional technology and behavioural technology. But neither is adds in itself only the major aspect, i.e., programmed instruction nor its studies only some contents like various principles of teaching behaviour, techniques of behaviour development and class-room behaviour models in behaviour technology even the observation of class-room behaviour, analysis, interpretation and evaluation are also considered the contents of teaching technology.

Here we want to clarify our readers that these days, the teaching is considered as 'Student Centred' and not 'Teacher Centred'. In other words, the learning by the students, instead of teaching by the teacher, is emphasized. Not only this, now the teaching work is compared with an industry in which the teacher manages for the pupils learning like a manager or administrator. In such a set-up of teaching and learning, the content is studied by dividing it into four phases.

(i) *Planning*—Planning is an important phase of teaching-learning. In this phase, the teacher analyses the contents, determines and defines the learning-objectives and at the end, he writes those objectives in clear terms. Hence, in this phase, the teacher performs three activities—*(a)* Task-analysis, *(b)* Identification of objectives, and *(c)* Writing learning objectives.

(ii) Organisation—Organisation is the second phase of teaching and learning. In this phase, teacher creates such an effective environment by selecting teaching methods, techniques, strategies and essential aids by which the pupils may achieve learning objectives through the acquisition of appropriate learning experiences.

(iii) Leading—Leading is the third phase of teaching-learning. In this phase, teacher motivates the pupils to such an extent that they may start taking interest in teaching and the learning objectives are achieved.

(iv) Controlling—Controlling is the fourth phase of teaching-learning. In this phase, the teacher observes the extent to which the 'organisation and leading' phase have achieved the learning objectives. He uses various techniques of measurement and evaluation for the purpose. If he concludes that the objectives have not been achieved, then in that case, he brings essential changes and modifications in his activities related to "Organization' and 'Leading' phases.

Assumptions of Teaching Technology—Teaching technology is based on the following assumptions—

(i) The nature of teaching process is scientific.
(ii) Teaching activities are modifiable.
(iii) Teaching and learning can mutually be related.
(iv) Appropriate conditions can be created by teaching for effective learning.
(v) Pre-determined learning objectives can be achieved by teaching activities.

Characteristics of Teaching Technology

(i) Teaching technology can make the teaching more effective.
(ii) Pupil-teachers and in-service teachers can have the advantage of teaching technology.
(iii) In this technology, assistance can be sought from philosophy, sociology and psychology.

(iv) In teaching technology, input, process and output are involved.

(v) Objectives of all the three domains namely Cognitive, Affective and Psychomotor Domains, can be achieved by using this technology.

(vi) With the help of teaching technology, teaching from memory level to reflective level can be organized.

A Comparative Study of Behavioural, Instructional and Teaching Technology

Sl. No.	*Aspects*	*Behavioural Technology*	*Instructional Technology*	*Teaching Technology*
1.	Exponents	B.F. Skinner, Flander, Ober, Amidon	Lumsdam, Bruner, Asubel, Glaser	I.K. Davis, Hunt, Morrison, Herbart.
2.	Objectives	Development of *(i)* Cognitive, *(ii)* Affective, and *(iii)* Psychomotor aspects	Development of Cognitive Domain	Development of *(i)* Cognitive *(ii)* Affective and *(iii)* Psychomotor aspect
3.	Base	Psychological basis	Psychological and Scientific basis	Philosophical, classical and psychological base.
4.	Level	Memory and Understanding Level	Understanding Level	Memory, Understanding and Reflective Levels.
5.	Place of teacher	Secondary	Helper	Manager
6.	Application	For producing effective teachers	Self-study, correspondence Remedial study	For making class-room teaching purposeful and effective.
7.	Examples	Micro-teaching Simulated Teaching, T-group teaching, Interaction Analysis	Correspondence course, Self-study, Programmed Learning	Planning Organisation, Leading and Controlling

QUESTIONS FOR ANSWER

1. Make a comparative study of Behavioural, Instrumental and Teaching Technology.
2. Make a difference between Discipline-Centred and Instructor-Centred Teaching.
3. Make a difference between Student-Centred Cognitive and Affective Approaches Teaching.
4. Write a note on Components of Educational Technology.
5. Write short notes on:
   (*a*) Practical Analysis of Orientations.
   (*b*) Characteristics of Behavioural Technology.
   (*c*) Assumptions of Instrumental Technology.

3

Teaching Technology—Some Basic Aspects

Teaching Technology is the prime area of educational technology. Teaching technology consists of three parts—basic aspects (concepts), teaching methods and teaching aids. Therefore, this chapter is devoted to define the fundamental concepts concerning teaching technology and particularly basic aspects of teaching technology—Teaching. "Teaching is the system of actions intended to induce learning", says B.O. Smith.

Teaching is a social process on which the political system, social philosophy, values and culture of every nation leave their impression. As the political system and philosophical ideology a nation will have, so would be the effect of political system and philosophical background on teaching process of that country. In the following lines, we are explaining the meaning of teaching on the basis of political set-up.

Meaning of Teaching

Meaning of Teaching in Autocracy. In autocracy, the public will is suppressed by preferring the will of the autocracy. Hence, in autocracy too, the place of the teacher is primary and that of pupils is secondary. As a result of this, the teacher considers himself as an ideal and imposes forcefully the knowledge externally into the pupils' mind by crushing their interests, attitudes, capacities, competencies and needs. In this way, in autocracy, only the teacher remains active at the time of teaching and the pupils sit like fearful and passive listeners in the class-room and follow his instructions.

H.C. Morrison (1964) has defined teaching from this point of view as—"Teaching is an intimate contact between a more mature personality and a less mature one which is designed to further the education of the later."

Meaning of Technology in Democracy: In democracy, the will of the public is appreciated by preferring public will. Hence, in democracy, the place of the pupil is primary and that of teacher is secondary. As a result of this, at the time of teaching, an independent interaction occurs between the teacher and the pupil. In this way, in democracy, both teachers and pupils influence each other.

"Interpersonal influence aimed at changing the behaviour potential of another person", says N.L. Gage.

Meaning of Teaching in Laissez-Faire. In Laissez-faire set-up, the teacher is like a friend. At the time of teaching, the pupil is more active than the teacher. In such a political system, the function of the teacher is to create such conditions which have gaps or which have some obstructions.

The pupils try to overcome those obstructions by filling up these gaps. In this way, the teacher provides opportunity to the pupils for solving their problems by avoiding his interference in the activities of the pupils in laissez-faire political system. This develops their creative powers.

"Teaching is an arrangement and manipulation of situation in which there are gaps and obstructions which an individual will seek to overcome and from which he will learn in the course of doing so."—Brubacher.

The above account makes it clear that the teaching has multi-meanings from political-system's view point. According to the eminent educationist Adams, "teaching is a bi-polar process, its one pole is teacher and another is the pupil."

The teacher brings desired changes in the behaviour of the pupils by the influence of this own personality and the pupil is influenced by following him. In this way, this process between teacher and the pupil goes on. In this process, the efforts of the teacher are called teaching and the task performed by the pupil is termed as learning.

Like education, there are narrow and broader meanings of teaching too. In its narrow meaning, the teaching means to impart knowledge and counselling to the pupils in the class-room. In other words, to impart knowledge to the pupils is the narrow meaning of teaching. But in broader sense, every person or an object goes on teaching one or the other thing to the pupil right from birth till death.

In other words, teaching is a relationship with which the pupil develops his all the powers. According to the eminent American educationist John Dewey, the process of education has three components. These are—

(i) teacher,
(ii) pupil, and
(iii) society or curriculum.

Definitions of Teaching

We are giving the definitions as suggested by the following scholars in order to make more clear the meaning of teaching—

H.C. Morrison (1943): "Teaching is an intimate contact between a more mature personality and a less mature one which is designed to further the education of later."

Edmund Amidon (1967): "Teaching is an interactive process primarily involving class-room talk which takes place between teacher and pupil and occurs during certain definable activities."

Yoakum and Simson: "Teaching is the means whereby the experienced members of the group guide the immature and infant members in their adjustment of life."

Ryburn: "Teaching is a relationship which helps the child to develop his powers."

B.O. Smith: "Teaching is a system of actions to induce learning."

John Brubacher: "Teaching is arrangement and manipulation of a situation in which there are gaps or obstructions which an individual will seek to overcome and from which he will learn in the course of doing so."

Difference between Teaching, Instruction and Learning

In order to understand the real meaning of teaching, it is essential to understand the difference between *(i)* teaching, *(ii)* instruction, and *(iii)* learning. Hence, we are clarifying the differences in these three terms in the following lines—

(i) Teaching. In teaching, an interaction occurs between the teacher and the pupils. As a result of which, the pupils are diverted towards the objectives. In other words, the main elements of teaching, i.e. the mutual relationship or the interaction between the teacher and the pupils advances the pupils towards objectives.

(ii) Instruction. The instruction does not involve an interaction between the teacher and the pupil. Still the instruction can divert the pupils towards objectives. The main difference between teaching and instruction is that the teaching includes instruction but the instruction does not include teaching. Hence, the teaching is instruction but the instruction is not teaching. In spite of this, all the three cognitive, affective and psychomotor aspects of the pupils can be developed by teaching, while by instruction, only cognitive aspect can be developed. Hence, no instruction can replace the teaching. In short, instruction is that process which diverts the pupils towards the objectives of cognitive aspects.

(iii) Learning. Learning means—*(a)* activities, and *(b)* experience. Both teaching and instruction influence learning through various activities and experiences. Hence, the learning and teaching mean the modification of pupils' behaviour through activities and experiences.

Difference between Education and Teaching

The meanings of 'Education' and 'Teaching' have been explained earlier in this book. Now, we are making the difference between these two in the table on page 58.

Difference between Teaching and Indoctrination

The process of indoctrination is the highest order of the teaching process. The maximum use of intelligence is expected to reach this highest level. In this process, the beliefs, ideas and assumptions etc. are impressed upon others. In teaching, the indoctrination can be included but it is not sufficient. The teaching can be possible even without indoctrination but indoctrination is not possible without teaching.

Sl. No.	Education	Teaching
1.	Education is a social process according to John Dewey.	Teaching is a method by which the process of education is made impressive.
2.	Teaching is a life-long process and every experience of life enriches it according to S.S. Mackenzi.	Teaching arouses the learning Curiousity in the pupils by mutual communication or establishing contacts among *(i)* the teacher *(ii)* the pupil and *(iii)* society or curriculum.
3.	The process of education carries on knowingly or unknowingly.	Teaching is done knowingly only in a formal way. The teaching has some purpose. The achievement of the objective means the teaching is successful otherwise it is unsuccessful.
4.	In formal education all aspects such as the objectives, curriculum and teaching methods etc. are considered	The teaching familiarizes the pupils only with the curriculum.
5.	The results of formal education are definite but in informal education—these are indefinite.	The teaching is done in the formal way. Hence, its results are definite.

Difference between Teaching and Training

The term 'Training' is used to shape the habits, while the term 'teaching' is used to form habits. Both the terms are closely related, but these terms are not the same. The training is only an element of teaching. Actually the term 'training' is more nearer to the conditioning. The training includes the process of attaining various skills. But it is certain that the training cannot lead the human being to the higher levels of the education.

Impact of Philosophy on Teaching

There are quite different priorities to such matters as disciplinary content, core requirements, physical education, foreign languages, communication and mathematical skills, performing arts, and career development. However, actual programme requirements and the curriculum as a whole emerge from the complex interactions of many additional factors; the influences of students, faculty members, administrators and academic traditions. Educational philosophies are aided or negated various times by pressures from society, professional organizations, employers, donors, politicians, laws, accrediting agencies, and governing boards. Whatever is in the curriculum at any moment is an artifact of diverse circumstances seldom fully recognized, yet so ensconced that threat of major alternation generates unified resistance. The needs of students and the implications of these needs for revising educational objectives and experiences are easily ignored in the resulting turmoil.

The five philosophical views also imply differing conceptions of learning and teaching. In theocentric commitment, man is but one manifestation of Divine Will.

In the remaining four philosophic commitments (ideocentric, sociocentric, idiocentric and ecentric), there is obviously much in common with the four teaching orientations. The disciplinary orientation is ideocentric. Intrinsic worth is assigned to ideas of great significance.

Specific knowledge or intellectual ability, whether of immediate practical significance or rendered important by social whim, is of lesser or extrinsic worth. The idiocentric and sociocentric commitments, both the student-centered (cognitive), on the one hand, and student centered (affective), on the other, are more complexly related. The disciplinary organization of knowledge is regarded as one of those constraints. The individual becomes the measure of the worth of everything.

Dynamic Nature of Teaching Technology

Countless classroom filled with hundreds of thousands of students are being staffed by thousands of men and women called teachers. There are many voices—teachers explaining and questioning, children answering and whispering to their neighbours. Every day, five days a week, from 9.00 A.M. to 3.00 P.M., teachers and children come together and face one another for six hours. This is the reality of teaching.

Teaching is this dynamic, evolving activity. It is characterized by mess and noise, by people—lots of people—by caring and heartache, and most of all, by uncertainty and vagueness. Why are teachers' lives fraught with endemic uncertainties?

Uncertainty in teaching appears to be inherent in the kind of work teachers do and in the population with which they do it. In every new session, teachers are faced with 25 to 30 new students, unique individuals, all of whom display separate personalities and demonstrate different needs. Methods of interaction and instruction that were successful with last years' students may or may not be successful with this years' class.

Teachers are never able to achieve a status quo when dealing with constantly changing materials—each new year's students bring new challenges and new questions that have to be overcome.

What about the kinds of things teachers do with students? Teachers set educational objectives, develop curricula and instructional units, work with individual students as well as groups, and try a whole range of teaching approaches without ever really knowing whether students have "gotten it".

Because "no uncertainty is greater than the one that surrounds the connection between teaching and leaning". Teachers can only do the best they can and hope that their efforts are positively affecting the development of their students.

But what should the aims of education be, what knowledge is of most worth? Again, there is no single answer to either of those questions, despite the scores of books that have attempted to provide just that—a single answer. Should schools socialize students or educate them? Should they "teach minimal levels of competence or develop a wide range of talents and possibilities?"

The goals of education appear to fluctuate according to the whims and needs of society, so that during one era the curriculum is child-centered, while in another it focuses on social needs. "The result is that individual teachers make their own translations of policy and that, in general, the profession is riddled by vagueness and conflict."

In their work, teachers get very little support. Till date induction system is not highly developed or organized, leaving teachers to fend for themselves when they enter the complex culture of the school. The way the school day is divided provides teachers with little extra time to intact with other teachers or supervisors. When supervision is provided, it is generally more evaluative than nurturing, and teachers are measured against ambiguous and multiple criteria.

Teaching is a lonely profession in which teachers spend their days primarily with children and are rarely given the time or opportunity to work with other adults, share frustrations or just talk. As a result, observation becomes equated with evaluation and teachers learn to be private and to guard their classroom domains jealousy. The price of this isolation is that teachers are unable to share their successes. However, this isolation also allows teachers to keep their failures private.

Teaching as Science

In the modern ages, the teaching is recognized as a science. The teaching is considered as science on the basis that all the activities of teaching can be supervised and analysed. In spite of this fact, the teaching activities can be studied in an objective way. In short, we can say that the teachers can be prepared by a special type of training. In this teaching-learning process, the use of reinforcement and feedback can prove effective. Hence, the teaching is being recognized as a science.

Relationship between Teaching and Learning

It is essential to establish the relationship between teaching and learning. The understanding of the relationship between the teaching and the learning requires the understanding of meaning of these two. The meaning and definitions have already been mentioned.

The meaning of learning can be explained by various definitions. According to Woodworth, "The process of acquiring new knowledge and new responses is the process of learning."

Crow & Crow have considered that the "learning is the acquisition of habits, knowledge and attitude."

J.P. Guilford has accepted learning as any change in behaviour as a result of behaviour.

Pavlov's view is that the learning is habit formation resulting from conditioning.

The main function of the teahing remains focused on

learning. Whenever there is teaching, it will be followed by learning too. But B.O. Smith contradicts this view. According to him, it is not essential that the learning is induced by teaching. He considers both as different from each other. According to Smith, "Teaching is a system of actions intended to produce learning".

Thomas Green has explained that the learning cannot be possible without teaching, but without learning, the teaching is possible. Gates has also explained about learning that "It is modification of behaviour, through experiences and activity."

It is very much clearer from various definitions of learning that the modification of behaviour and formation of habits is called learning. Hence, a relationship of teaching and learning is clear from the meaning of learning.

Objectives of Teaching

Teaching is a continuous process and it is a purposeful process. It lacks entity in the absence of objective. Hence, objectives are essential for a successful teaching process. Some main objective of teaching are as follows—

(i) The main objective of teaching is helping the pupils so that they can understand the realities properly and may adjust in a better way.

(ii) Enabling the pupils to establish the contact with truth and to take the decisions by teaching.

(iii) Another objective of the teaching is that the teaching process should make a pupil the best worker and the best thinker.

(iv) There is another objective of the teaching. It is to help one or the other everyday so that the new experiences are gained and that pupil may perform some constructive task.

Teaching Variables

A good teaching has been explained as having a provision of learning experiences so that the teaching objectives may be achieved as a result of desired modifications in the behaviour of pupils. For this, the knowledge of various aspects and activities of teaching is necessary for a teacher. Hence, in this unit, by explaining the various aspects of teaching and variables therein, we are throwing light on various teaching activities in detail. John Brubacher rightly says: "Teaching is an arrangement and manipulation of a situation in which there are gaps and obstructions which an individual will seek to overcome and from which he will learn in the course of doing so."

Meaning of Variables

Meaning. A variable has been defined as 'Any response or behaviour which can take different degrees'—For example, effects of various amounts of study on school performance.

A teaching process has three variables—

(i) The Teacher. The first variable of teaching is 'the teacher' The teacher is said to be an 'independent variable'. The teaching organization, planning and its organisation is carried on by the teacher.

(ii) The Pupil. The second variable of teaching-process is 'The pupil'. The pupil is considered as the 'dependent variable' because the teaching has to be active in accordance with the planning, organization and presentation.

(iii) The Content and Teaching Methods. It is the third variable of the teaching: It has been termed as 'Intervening variable.' Interaction between pupil and the teacher, teaching method and the nature of teaching material the intervene in the responses of the pupils.

Types of Variables

The variables are mainly of three types which are as follows:

(a) Independent Variable. An independent variable is that variable in which the experimenter can bring changes and that variable brings a change in the dependent variable. We can manage the independent variable according to our will.

(b) Dependent Variable. The dependent variable is that variable which acquires changes as a result of changes occurred in some other dependent variable.

(c) Intervening Variable. A variable located or active in between an independent and a dependent variable is an intervening variable. Example—In the teaching process, the teacher is an independent variable, the pupil is a dependent variable and the methods to be used in teaching, motivation techniques, contents etc. are all examples of intervening variables.

Functions of Variables

In the teaching process, the following are the functions of variables—

1. Diagnostic Function

The diagnostic function is the first aspect of the process. In this, the teacher decides about the pupils entering-behaviour and the teaching objective can be achieved on its basis. Hence, the teacher considers only two things under the diagnostic function. These things are—*(i)* the pupil, and *(ii)* the content.

He, first of all, determines the previous knowledge or entering behaviour of the pupil. Then, he arranges the elements of the contents to be taught in a sequence by analysing them logically so that the teaching activity may be performed in a psychological sequence. In this way, the diagnostic function is the foundation of the remedial aspect of the teaching.

This function is performed in accordance with the pre-active phase. In this function, considering, the following variables, the teacher takes decisions—

(i) Analysis of Teaching Problem. The first variable of diagnostic aspect is the analysis of the teaching problem. Hence, the teacher should decide about the entering behaviour of the pupils while giving a thought to the problem related to that content with far-sightedness and depth which is to be studied by the pupils.

It is also to be decided whether that content is according to their capacity or not. In other words, the teacher should take the decision concerning the pupils and the content so that the desired objectives may be attained.

Remember that the decision taken by the teacher as stated proves fruitful for the remedial aspect or the inter-active phase of the teaching.

(ii) Determining the Entering Behaviour of Student. The second variable of the diagnostic aspect is to determine clearly the entering behaviours of the pupils. After this, he should present the new knowledge to the pupils.

Its advantages is that after presenting the new knowledge, the information of changes in the behaviour of the pupils will be easy to acquire. Hence, for determining the entering behaviours of the pupils, the teacher should prepare and use such evaluative questions keeping in view the contents, which should be reliable and valid.

(iii) Individual Differences. The third variable of the diagnostic aspect is the consideration of individual differences of the pupils. The principle of individual differences means that every pupil has different interests, attitudes, capacities, abilities and needs.

Keeping in view the individual differences of the pupils as the teacher should perform the teaching task at the average level on one hand, he should guide sympathetically the talented and backward pupils on the other hand, which leads the teaching to the attainment of the objectives with a success.

(iv) Task Analysis. The fourth variable of diagnostic aspect is the task analysis. The teacher should analyse carefully the learning activities related to the contents. Its reason is that the success or the failure of the lesson depends upon the task-analysis. The readers are requested to study the task analysis chapter in this book.

(v) Analysis of Content in view of Types of Learning. The last variable of the diagnostic aspect is the analysis of the content with regard to the type of learning. The teacher should know the nature of learning. Also, he should know the tactics and principles to be used in the various situations so that the teaching may become easy, clear, effective, understandable and scientific.

2. Remedial Function

In the remedial aspects, an effort is made to bring the desired changes in the behaviours of the pupils. Hence, the teacher should make decision regarding the use of teaching methods, strategies and tactics and mutual relationships between various variables keeping in view the individual differences of the pupils in this aspect.

In this aspect, assistance must be sought from action research in order to solve the various problems which arise during the teaching. In this way, in remedial aspect, the teacher should manage the teaching variables in such a way that the maximum teaching-objectives are attained by deciding the teaching-techniques and tactics. This aspect has the following variables—

(i) Selection of Teaching Strategies and Tactics. The first variable of teaching strategies and tactics is their selection. It should be remembered that the success of teaching and learning depends upon the appropriate selection and use of teaching strategies and tactics.

The teacher should perform this important function in accordance with his ability and experience at the time of planning the teaching, so that the teaching objectives may be achieved while presenting the content using the selected strategies and tactics and by making the lesson easy and clear.

(ii) Arrangement of Feedback Devices. The second important variable of diagnostic aspect is the arrangement of feedback devices. Here, it is essential to state that the feedback is the soul of successful teaching. Its reason is that the feedback provides reinforcement to the pupils which, in turn, provides motivation and encouragement for learning.

Hence, while teaching, the teacher should provide necessary feedback by using praise and blame techniques for motivating and encouraging the pupils so that the teaching objectives may be achieved by producing maximum learning experiences and desired behavioural changes in the pupils.

3. Evaluative Function

The evaluation is the third important variable of teaching. In this aspect, the diagnostic aspect is evaluated. It should be remembered that the criterion of evaluation is the achievement of the objectives. If the objectives are achieved, the remedy by the teacher is correct, otherwise it is defective.

In other words, if the teaching objectives are not achieved, the teacher should not blame pupils for his failure. He should change the variables of diagnostic aspect so that the objectives may be achieved. It should be remembered that this aspect is in accordance with the post active phase. This aspect has the following important variables—

(i) Construction of Criterion Test.
(ii) Evaluation of Behavioural Changes.
(iii) Diagnostic Phase.

(i) Construction of Criterion Test. The first variable of evaluation aspect is the construction of criterion test which provides clear information regarding the changes brought in

the behaviour of the pupil by remedial teaching.

The main characteristic of the criterion test is its objectivity. In other words, this test is reliable and valid. Its aim is to evaluate the determined objectives. Hence, the teacher should construct the criterion test with great care.

(ii) Evaluation of Behavioural Changes. The second variable of the evaluation aspect is the evaluation of pupils' behavioural changes. The teacher should perform this function on the basis of criterion test.

(iii) Diagnostic Phase. The last variable of evaluation aspect is the diagnostic phase. This diagnostic phase means to know, by evaluation, the extent of the success of teaching. If it is not successful, then what modification should be brought about.

The diagnostic phase means to know the evaluation, the extent to which the teaching objectives have been achieved as a result of using the methods or strategies or tactics at the time of teaching.

If the teaching objectives have not been achieved as a result of their use, then the planning organization, leading and controlling of the teaching process should be repeated (see chart below).

Variable of Teaching

Diagnostic Function	Remedial Function	Evaluative Function
(i) Analysis of Teaching problem.	Selection of teaching Strategies and Tactics.	Construction of Criterion test.
(ii) Determining Entering behaviour of pupils.	Arranging feedback devices.	Evaluation of Behavioural changes.
(iii) Individual differences.		Diagnostic phase.
(iv) Analysis of Task-elements.		
(v) Analysis of Content.		

Phases of Teaching

The activities in teaching carry special importance. Its main cause is that through these activities, the pupils get much assistance in learning. In other words, the learning experiences are acquired in a natural way through these activities. It should be remembered that these activities are different in the different phases of teaching. The teaching phases are as follows—

1. Pre-active Phase of Teaching

In the pre-active phase of teaching, the planning of teaching is carried over. This phase includes all those activities which a teacher performs before class-room teaching or before entering the class-room. Hence, the following activities are included in the pre-active phase of teaching—

(i) Fixation of Goals.
(ii) Decision making about the subject matter.
(iii) Arranging/Sequencing the elements of content for presentation.
(iv) Decision about the Strategies of Teaching.
(v) Distribution of Teaching Strategies.

The above activities can be explained in short as follows—

(i) Fixation of Goals. First of all, the teacher determines the teaching objectives which are then defined in the form of behavioural changes. Thus, he ascertains the teaching objectives and what changes he requires in the pupils by achieving those objectives. These objectives are of two types—

1. In the form of entering behaviours of the pupils.
2. In the form of terminal behaviours of the pupils.

It is remarkable that these objectives are determined according to the psychology of the pupils and needs of the school and the society.

(ii) Decision Making about the Subject Content. After fixing the teaching objectives, the teacher makes decisions about that content which is to be presented before the pupils and as a result he wants to bring the changes in their behaviours. This decision is taken by the teacher while focusing on the following points—

(a) What is the need of the curriculum proposed by the teacher for the pupils?
(b) What is the terminal behaviour of the pupils?
(c) Why the pupils need it to learn?
(d) What level of motivation can be effective for the pupils?
(e) By which methods the teacher should evaluate the knowledge related to the subject-matter?

(iii) Arranging/Sequencing the Elements of Content for Presentation. After making decisions regarding the contents to be presented to the pupils, the teacher arranges the elements of content in a logical and psychological sequence so that the arrangement of content-elements may assist in transfer of learning.

(iv) Decision Making about Strategies of Teaching. After sequencing the contents, the teacher makes decisions regarding the proper methods and strategies keeping in view the contents and the level of the pupils with the help of which the contents can be marked on the brain of the pupils very easily.

Hence, during the teachers' training, the emphasis should be on the development of this skill, so that, after training, the teaching objectives can be achieved after making decisions about appropriate methods and strategies.

(v) Distribution of Teaching Strategies. It should be remembered that the decision-making regarding the teaching methods and strategies for presenting the sequenced contents to the students is not sufficient. But the teacher is also to decide how and when he will make use of which method and strategy during the class-room teaching.

In other words, what type of questions he will ask the pupils? When and where will he use the chart or map? When will he deliver lecture? When and how will he use the black board? And, when will he ask the evaluative questions? etc.

All the above activities should be determined by the teacher at the pre-active stage.

2. Inter-active Phase of Teaching

In the inter-active phase of teaching, all those activities are included which a teacher carries over right from entering the class-room till the presentation of the contents.

"The teacher provides pupils verbal stimulation of various kinds, makes explanations, asks questions, listens to students' responses and provides guidance."—*P.W. Jackson.*

The following activities are included in the inter-active phase of teaching—

(i) Sizing up of the class.

(ii) Diagnosis of the learners.

(iii) Action and Reaction of Achievement.

The action and reaction activities include the following—

(*a*) Selection of the stimuli.

(*b*) Presentation of the stimuli.

(*c*) Feedback and Reinforcement.

(*d*) Deployment of strategies.

We are throwing light on the above mentioned activities in the following lines—

(*i*) *Sizing up of the Class.* As the teacher enters the classroom, first of all he perceives the size of the class. He throws his eyes on all the pupils of the class in a few moments. He comes to know the pupils who can help him in his teaching and the pupils who can create a problem for him as a result of this perception.

He can recognize those pupils who are to discourage him and those who are to encourage him by their face-reading. In this way, the teacher can feel the class-size in a few moments.

In the very same way, the pupils can feel the personality of the teacher in a few seconds. Hence, at this stage, the teacher should look like a teacher. He should possess all those characteristics which are supposed to be present in a good teacher. Here, it can be summed up that a teacher should be efficient and effective.

(*ii*) *Diagnosis of Learners.* After having a feeling of class-size, the teacher makes efforts to know how much the new-comers or pupils have previous knowledge. He tries to know this thing in the following three areas—

(*a*) Abilities of Learners

(*b*) Interests and attitudes of learners.

(*c*) Academic background of learners.

The teacher starts teaching activities after diagnosing by questioning in the following sequence—

Teacher

Perception → Diagnosis → Response

(*iii*) *Action and Reaction or Achievement*. Two types of activities are involved in the teaching—

(*a*) Initiation, and (*b*) Response. Both these activities occur between the teacher and the pupils. Both these activities are known as verbal interaction. In other words, when a teacher performs some activities, the pupils react him or when pupils perform some activities, the teacher reacts those activities and thus the inter-action in the teaching goes on. We can present the inter-action of the teaching by the following diagram.

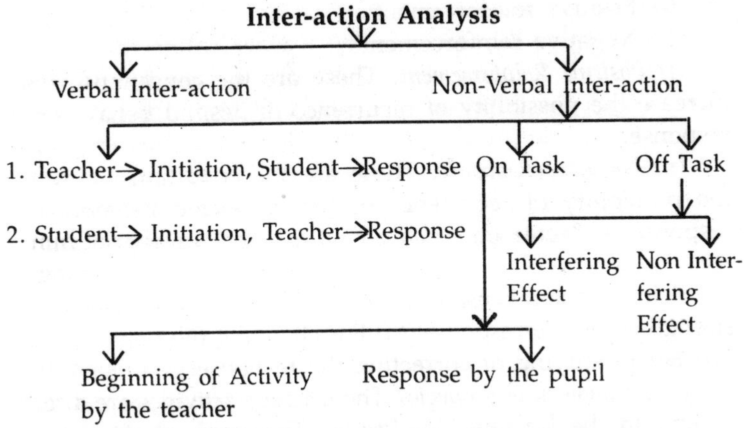

The teachers performs the following activities in order to analyse the nature of verbal and non-verbal inter-action of teaching activities—

(a) Selection and Presentation of stimuli
(b) Feedback and Reinforcement
(c) Deployment of Strategies

(a) Selection and Presentation of Stimuli. The motive or new knowledge is a process of teaching. It can be verbal or non-verbal. The teacher should be aware of the motive which would prove effective and which would not be so for a particular teaching situation.

The teacher should select the appropriate stimulus as soon as the situation arises and an effort should be made to control the undesired activities to create the situation and for desired activities.

After selecting the stimuli, the teacher should present them before the pupils. The teacher should present that form of the stimulus which can motivate the pupils for learning. During such presentation of stimuli, the teacher should keep in mind the form context and order of the stimuli.

(b) Feedback and Reinforcement. Feedback or reinforcement is that condition which increases the possibility for accepting a particular response in future. In other words, those conditions which increase the possibility of occurrence of a particular response are termed as feedback or reinforcement. These conditions may be of two types which are as follows—

(i) Positive reinforcement

(ii) Negative reinforcement

(i) Positive Reinforcement. These are the conditions which increase the possibility of recurrence of desired behaviour or response.

(ii) Negative Response. These are the conditions in which the possibility of recurrence of the undesired behaviour or response is decreased, such as punishment or reprimanding etc.

Reinforcement is used for three purposes. These are—*(i)* For strengthening the response, *(ii)* For changing the response, and *(iii)* For modifying or correcting the response.

(c) Deployment of Strategies. The teaching activities are directly related to the learning conditions. Therefore, at the time of interaction the teacher produces such activities and conditions by the reinforcement strategies which effect the activities of the pupils.

The deployment of the teaching strategies turns the pupil-teacher interaction impressive. From the very moment, the teacher starts the teaching task and till the moment that task goes on, the verbal and non-verbal behaviours of the pupils are controlled by the reinforcement strategies and cooperates in presenting the contents in an impressive way.

In the deployment of the teaching strategies, three areas should be considered. These are—*(i)* Presentation of subject-matter, *(ii)* Levels of learning, and *(iii)* Level or context of learners, their background, needs, motivation, attitudes, cooperation and opposition.

We should keep in mind the fact that in the interactive stage, these activities are carried on not only by the teacher, but also carried on by the pupils. The pupils also feel about the teacher and diagnose his personality as a teacher. In order to be impressed themselves and to impress the teaching, they deploy the various strategies by selecting the different stimuli.

Operations at the Interactive Phase

We can present the activities of the interaction through the following chart—

Teacher			Student		
P	D	A	P	D	A
(Perceptual)	(Diagnostic)	(Achievement)	(Perceptual)	(Diagnostic)	(Achievement)

3. Post-active Phase of Teaching

In this phase, as the teaching task sums up, the teacher asks the questions from the pupils, verbally or in written form, to measure the behaviours of the pupils so that their achievements may be evaluated correctly.

Therefore, evaluation aspect includes all those activities which can evaluate the achievements of the pupils and attainment of the objectives. The following activities are considered in the post-active phase of teaching—

(i) Defining the exact dimensions of the changes caused by teaching.

(ii) Selecting appropriate testing devices and techniques.

(iii) Changing the strategies in terms of evidences gathered.

(i) Defining the Exact Dimensions of the Changes Caused by Teaching. At the end of the teaching, the teacher defines the exact dimensions of the changes in the behaviours as a result of teaching which is termed as criterion behaviour. For this, the teacher compares the actual behavioural changes in the pupils with their expected behavioural changes.

If he deserves the desired behavioural changes in the maximum number of pupils, he concludes that his teaching strategies and tactics worked effectively with the help of which teaching objectives have been achieved.

(ii) Selecting Appropriate Testing Devices and Techniques. The teacher selects those testing devices and techniques to compare the actual behavioural changes with the desired behavioural changes which are reliable and valid and which can evaluate the cognitive and non-cognitive aspects of the pupils. Therefore, criterion tests are more preferred than the performance tests.

(iii) Changing the Strategies in Terms of Evidences Gathered. While, by using the reliable and valid testing devices, the teacher

gets the knowledge regarding the performances of pupils and attainment of objectives on one hand, he also gets clarity regarding his instruction, teaching strategies and tactics on the other hand.

He also comes to know about the required modifications in the teaching strategies and situations along with the drawbacks of his teaching in order to achieve the teaching objectives. In this way, through evaluation, the teaching activities are diagnosed and these can be made effective by necessary modifications and changes in them.

It is evident from the above description that to achieve the teaching objectives, 'the three aspects of teaching activities should be arranged in such a way that when the changes occur in the thinking and working systems of the pupils, creative thinking should also be developed in them so that, by recognising reality, they may become efficient in coordinating their external experiences with their inner organisation.

Characteristics of Good Teaching

The following are the main characteristics of good teaching—

1. *Good teaching must have desirable informations.* The human knowledge is going on increasing since the rise of civilization. He has learnt all this by trial and error, insight and imitation. We should provide desired informations to the students in a well organised form regarding this store of knowledge. It saves time. Also, the pupils will not face any difficulty in achieving knowledge.

2. *Good teaching must motivate for self-learning.* A good teaching is not merely to impart informations to the students, but it is also to arouse the will of self-learning in them. The teacher should explore the interests, attitudes, capacities, competencies and needs of the pupils and guide them accordingly. From this point of view, the teaching should be so much natural and interesting that the pupils get motivated for self-learning. It means to say that the good teaching is to provide assistance in developing the pupils by motivating them for self-learning and enabling them for establishing the contact with the different subjects of the curriculum and environment themselves.

3. *Good Teaching must have efficient Planning.* The pupil cannot

be taught everything all the time. Various stages are meant for achieving the different aspects of knowledge. Also, the pupils have different interests, attitudes, competencies and needs on the basis of individual differences. So there must be some useful planning of teaching in view of the above things.

4. *Good Teaching must be selective and useful.* The human being is struggling continuously since he came on this earth. As a result of this struggle, his knowledge-store is going on enriching day-by-day. Such an explosion in knowledge cannot be learnt in such a short time-span. Therefore, through teaching, the pupils should be told some selected and useful things. In other words, disseminating the selected knowledge is called good teaching.

5. *Good Teaching must provide opportunities for activity.* The pupil remains active by nature. This activeness is based upon his basic instincts. Hence, each pupil performs desirable and undesirable activities under the influence of his instincts. The teacher should study the pupil's basic instincts and direct these activities for purposeful and useful directions. In this way, it is the duty of the teacher to construct such an environment before the pupils so that the pupil himself goes on acquiring, by doing desirable activities, the best and useful experiences. In short, the good teaching is that in which the maximum opportunities are provided to the pupils for doing desirable activities.

6. *Good Teaching must be Sympathetic.* Psychology has proved that when the pupil gets involved in the emotional disturbance while struggling mentally, his all mental powers cease to function smoothly. From this point of view, the successful teaching essentially requires emotional stability and security. Hence good teaching is sympathetic.

7. *Good Teaching must be Cooperative.* Teaching does not mean forceful imposition of knowledge in the pupils brain. Remember that the teaching and learning process is an alive and active process. Hence, the desirable results can only be achieved when the teaching is based on the cooperation of the teacher and the pupil. From this view-point, the teacher should not be instructive while the pupil acquires new knowledge. However, he should offer good suggestions. In short, good teaching is based on the cooperation of both the teacher and the pupil.

8. *Good Teaching is Organisation of Learning.* Marshall, in his book *Successful Teaching*, has written that the organisation of learning means the unification of all the components of teaching. Hence, the activities of the teacher and the pupil should be unified. It is essential to include all tasks, teaching methods and conditions in these activities. In short, good teaching is the organisation of learning.

9. *Good Teaching must be Democratic.* Modern age is the age of democracy. These days, the real education is considered to be that education which prepares the pupil for life by the life. In the light of this, we should prepare the pupils for democracy democratically.

But to achieve this objective, the teaching should be based on democratic ideals, objectives, curriculum and teaching methods. In short, good teaching should be democratic.

10. *Good Teaching must be Progressive.* The real education of the pupils is based upon his personal experiences. Good teaching presents new knowledge keeping in view the previous experiences of the pupil. This changes and modifies the pupil behaviour. Also attributes like initiative, self-confidence and self-reliance etc. get developed in him gradually. Hence, we can say that the good teaching is progressive.

11. *Good Teaching must lead to emotional stability.* Every pupil has inborn instincts. These powerful instincts make efforts for their expression. If these instincts are left uncared, then the pupil will not behave properly in the society. Also, the suppression of these instincts is harmful for the pupil. Hence, the training of all the instincts and emotions of the pupils is most important. Good teaching produces emotional stability in the pupil.

12. *Good Teaching must help the child to adjust himself to his environment.* As the pupil develops, he has to face the complicated and complex natural and social environments.

In other words, the whole life of the pupil is a story of struggle. In this struggle, he either adapts to the environment or tries to change the environment according to his own needs. Good teaching helps the pupil in adjusting in both types of environment.

13. *Good Teaching is a means of preparation.* To prepare the pupil for future life is an important function of education. The

teaching is such a process by which the physical, mental, emotional and social development of the pupil occurs.

The pupil learns to lead his life properly in the present and for the future as a result of this all-round development. In short, good teaching is an important means of present and future preparations.

14. *Good Teaching is both diagnostic and remedial.* Today, we are in a position to know conveniently about the intelligence of the pupil, his attitudes and his weaknesses on the basis of psychological researches. Not only this, we can also identify very easily the competencies, capacities and emotional traits of the pupils by objective tests.

We can make the teaching as diagnostic by these means. Also, we can make the teaching remedial by knowing about the individual differences. Hence, good teaching is diagnostic and remedial. It is very clear, from the above description, the teaching means establishing an appreciable relationship between the teacher, pupil and curriculum.

By establishing this relationship, an all-round development of the pupil takes place. In other words, good teaching imparts desired informations to the pupil, also he gets opportunities for self-learning by keeping himself active. As the good teaching is planned, therefore, only the selected knowledge is given to the pupils by this good teaching. Remember that the good teaching is sympathetic and in this, the cooperation between the teacher and the pupil is emphasised.

Hence, a good teaching is that learning method which becomes so much dynamic in the democratic shade that the emotional stability in the pupils develops in a natural way. With this, the pupils get ready for adjustment in the future life in complicated natural and social environment. In short, the good teaching, being diagnostic and remedial, is such a relationship between the teacher, pupil and the curriculum by which an all-round development of the pupil occurs.

This enriches the pupil with the feeling of using his energy in the all-round progress of the society after becoming the responsible component and nation's high-character citizen. It means to say that by good teaching, both the society and the individual go on reaching at the peak of the progress.

Utility of Teaching Activities

Every society establishes educational institutions in order to transfer its culture and values through the teaching and brings desired changes in the behaviours. Therefore, teaching always enjoyed a place of importance in every nation, period and society and it will remain as such in future too. We are throwing light on the importance of these teaching in the following lines—

(i) The teaching activities are especially important for pupil-teachers. When the pupil-teachers are being trained about the teaching activities in the training colleges, he possesses an idea which is very clear to him that what activities should he be performed before entering the class-room, after entering the class-room and in the class-room, so that these pupils and these activities may produce learning experiences and objectives may be attained by achieving the teaching objectives.

(ii) The teaching activities assist in understanding the nature of teaching variables and their mutual relationship.

(iii) An effective interaction between the teacher and the pupils occur by presenting the teaching activities systematically and the teaching objectives are achieved successfully.

(iv) The teaching activities influence the various types of learning by creating learning situations. This results in the close relationship between teaching and learning.

(v) All the three levels of teaching, i.e., memory, understanding and reflective levels can be explained successfully by considering the teaching activities.

(vi) The teaching activities present the scientific basis for preparing the instructional design.

(vii) The teaching activities encourage micro-approach.

(viii) In-service teachers can also make the teaching more effective while developing their teaching skills after acquiring the knowledge of teaching activities.

It can be concluded that the teacher always remains in the contact of young children. But mind it, teaching is not a child's play. It is the most complex activity or process. Its reason is that it is the only teaching which can determine clearly the limit upto which the pupils have learnt.

Hence, any person who wants to become a good teacher or he wants to use the principles of educational technology in his teaching, he should analyse the teaching behaviour with regard to all the three aspects of teaching and the activities of the above mentioned three aspects of teaching should be followed in a dynamic and creative way.

QUESTIONS FOR ANSWER

1. What is teaching? Explain the nature of teaching. Throw light on the relationship of teaching and learning.
2. Define 'teaching' and explain the relationship of teaching and learning.
3. Explain the nature of teaching by differentiating the terms 'teaching' 'education', 'training' and 'indoctrination'.
4. What is the concept of teaching? Give its definition and write the characteristics of teaching task.
5. Give a suitable definition of teaching by explaining its meaning.
6. Explain the difference between Education and Teaching while describing Good Teaching.
7. Explain the various activities occurring in each phase of teaching while throwing light on the different phases of teaching.
8. What do you mean by teaching activities? Why these have importance for a teacher?
9. Explain the different variables of teaching along with their functions.
10. Explain in detail the operations of interactive stage of teaching. How are these operations differ from those used during the pre-active and post-active stages of teaching?
11. Write short notes on the following:
    (a) Impact of philosophical thoughts on Teaching
    (b) Teaching is a Dynamic Technology
    (c) Importance of Teaching Activities

4

Principles and Maxims of Teaching

Great educator and intellectual Mr. Huges and Huges rightly says—

"It has been well said that 'teaching' means 'causing to learn'. Nothing has been given until it has been taken; nothing has been taught until it has been learnt. Teaching is more than the efficient delivery of thoroughly prepared lectures."

This observation clearly states that for successful teaching, it is essential to know how the pupil learns and by which methods he learns. Since the teaching methods or strategies are based on certain principles, therefore, it is essential for a teacher to follow these general or basic principles while teaching.

The principles are necessary to control the behaviour of the teacher, the following two types of teaching principles are emphasized—

1. General Principles of Teaching
2. Psychological Principles of Teaching

1. General Principles of Teaching

Principles of Motivation. The motivation is that method which creates pupils' interest in the content. The meaning of motivation from this view-point is to create interest in the pupils for acquiring knowledge. It is a psychological fact that when a teacher motivates the pupils to acquire knowledge, the process of teaching and learning goes on smoothly. In the absence of proper motivation, the pupil takes no interest in memorizing the contents.

Hence, every teacher should follow the principles of motivation. Now the question arises how the pupils are prepared to gain knowledge. For this, the teacher should use the pupils' innate tendencies carefully. It is an experience that the pupil is very much curious to know about the new things regarding environment.

Therefore, the teacher should create such situations in which a curiosity is aroused in the pupils regarding the acquisition of the latest knowledge concerning the novel things and contents about the environment. For example, while teaching history, a curiosity can be aroused in the pupils regarding the knowledge of historical events, concerning the Taj Mahal by showing its model or picture.

Similarly, the pupils can be motivated for learning the poems by heart with the technique called *Antakshri* while arousing curiosity and feelings of self-esteem.

Principle of Interest. The principle of interest means to create interest of the pupils in the subject-matter in order to make the teaching useful and effective. When the interest of the pupil is created in the subject-matter, he acquires knowledge very conveniently. In other words, he faces no difficulty while studying.

There are various methods for this, for example—

1. Curiosity of the pupil should be aroused and the objective of the lesson should be made clear. The clarity of the objective to both the pupil and the teacher definitely creates the interest of the pupil for the lesson.
2. Establish a relationship of contents with the pupils' activities and objectives.
3. The principle of learning by doing should be followed.
4. The teaching should be linked with the active life of the pupil.

For example, if a pupil has no interest in learning a poem, he should be provided with an opportunity of participating in *Antakshri*. When the same pupil observes his team defeating, he will develop his interest automatically regarding the learning of a poem.

Principle of Learning by Doing. The principle of learning by doing means the teacher should produce activity in each type of lesson. This activity is of two types—

1. Physical and
2. Mental.

The physical activity means to produce activity in the body organs of the pupils, and the mental activity means to activate the sense organs of the pupils.

Psychologically, each pupil is temperamentally active. Therefore, activity is in accordance with his nature.

According to McDougall, every child has inborn instinct of construction. As a result of this instinct, the child remains busy all the time of this instinct, the child remains busy all the time in doing some or the other activity. The more the activity of the pupil, more would be the teaching-learning process.

Therefore, for a successful teaching the teacher should make use of the pupils instinct of construction. In other words, at the time of teaching, the maximum use of the pupils' basic instinct will make the teaching effective to the maximum.

Both, the physical activity and mental activity depend upon each other. Its evidence is that the pupil becomes active just after taking the birth and as he grows, his area of mental activities becomes more broader. As the pupil's mind and body work together, he shows more interest in learning something new.

Froebel has indoctrinated this principle of learning-by-doing considering this very fact and he also indoctrinated his kindergarten system based on this principle. Most of the people often derive wrong meaning of the principle of learning by doing. It is to be disclosed here that the principle of "learning by doing" does not mean that the pupil himself should only be active for learning by doing, but it also means that the teacher should also make the pupil active for learning the new things.

For example, while teaching history, the pupils can learn the historical facts and incidents very conveniently if these are shown in the form of Plays as compared to the learning from books. Similarly, an interest can be created in the pupils regarding geography if geography is taught by using the models, charts, and diagrams or by getting these things prepared by the pupils themselves.

Good feelings arise in the pupils by keeping themselves active. Their efficiency increase. For this, there are some modern methods, such as—Montessory Method, Kindergarten Method, Heuristic Method, Dalton Method, Project Method and Basic Method etc. These are based on this principle.

It becomes very clear from the above description that the principle of activity is very useful. Therefore, it should be used in each class and in all the school activities, such as—school council, declamations contest, various societies, meetings, conferences, clubs and games etc. This will develop the appreciable habits in the pupils and they will get proper and sufficient training of social service.

Principle of Linking with Life. From Psychological point of view, the pupil of each level has his own world. In other words, as the pupil grows, he begins to imagine his world in his own way. In this way, the pupil shows his interest in those subjects or activities which are linked to his personal world. Keeping in view this thing, the activity and the subject have been linked with the learner's life in this modern age.

The principle of linking with life means relating the subject-matter with the life of the pupils.

In other words, the pupils learn rapidly and conveniently those things which get related to their life. According to Ryburn, "Life is a continuous experience. Everything we do is linked up with what has gone before and with what comes afterwards."

Therefore, it is necessary to relate the new experiences with hour previous experiences. After a relationship between new and old experiences, the new experiences or knowledge become a part of the pupil's life.

Principle of Selection of Contents. The principles of selection of content is an important principle. It is necessary to explain that there is a close relationship between the contents and the objectives of education. In other words, the contents are selected according to the objectives. Now, it is urgent of know that since the human being appeared on this land, he has collected huge and complex knowledge.

Its reason is that some things are essential and some are

non-essential. The non-essential things confuse the pupils. Hence, according to this principle, the teacher should select only those facts which the pupils can understand in order to achieve some definite objective.

In other words, the teacher is to select what and how much is to be taught to the class. In short, the teacher should select the content according to the definite, clear and predefined objective. This benefits both the teacher and the pupils. The teacher develops the lesson successfully and all the pupils acquire knowledge very conveniently.

Principle of Recognizing Individual Differences. This principle means the individual differences of the pupils should be taken into consideration. The psychological researches have proved that the pupils are not alike in intelligence, nature, ability, interest, potentialities and needs. That's why each pupil is not at the same level.

In other to develop all the pupils and for equal opportunities, the teacher should impart proper guidance to the talented pupils, sympathy should be shared with the abnormal pupils, and in order to bring the mentally retarded and backward pupils to the normal level, affectionate behaviour should be exhibited.

Principle of Definite Aim. The meaning of this principle is that every lesson must have some definite aim or objective. In the absence of an objective, the teacher is like that boatman who has no knowledge of his aim and the pupil is like that oarless boat which is sailing in the seawaves blindly. From this point of view, there must be some definite, clear and completely defined objectives in order to make the lesson interesting and impressive.

The objectives and the teaching methods are closely related. In other words, every teaching method is based on some objective. The teaching method is used according to the objective. For example, if our objective is the appreciation of the poem, then its method would be entirely different from that method which has an objective of teaching a poem to the pupils.

Not only this, the pupils and the teachers must have full knowledge about that. This provides success to the teacher in his teaching task and the interest of the pupils is created in the lesson.

Principle of Revision. The meaning of this principle is that whatever the subject-matter is taught to the pupils, it should be revised by the pupils. The psychological experiments and researches have shown the revision is very much essential in learning.

In other words, without experiments and revision, everything is forgotten. Therefore, the acquired knowledge should be revised by the pupils not only immediately, but also repeatedly. The frequency of the revisions depends upon the nature of the lesson. Hence, more the lesson is difficult, more its revisions should occur.

Principle of Creation and Recreation. This Principle means those activities carried over by the pupils which are recreational and which can develop the creative power of the pupils. This will create interest in the pupils regarding the teaching activity without any fear of the teacher and the school.

They will try for new innovations and will have an opportunity of expressing creative activity. From this point of view, the principle of recreation is very essential for successful teaching. In twentieth century, so many teaching methods have been developed which are based on the principle of learning by play-way.

Principle of Division. The meaning of this principle is that the subject-matter should be divided into some units for presenting it in certain order. The division of the content should be followed by the presentation in such a manner that each unit should seem to be complete in itself. One unit should create curiosity for other unit.

In this way, by presenting the contents after dividing it into units, the lesson becomes very easy for the pupils. They acquire knowledge easily without any difficulty. Hence, for a successful teaching the division of the lesson into an order of units or steps is necessary.

Principle of Democratic Dealing. According to democratic principle, the teacher should adopt democratic attitude with the pupils and it should not be dictatorial. In the dictatorship, the pupil's personality gets repressed. This instigates them for revolt sometimes. Contrary to this, in a democratic set-up, every pupil is considered as a holy and valuable property of the society. Hence, he gets maximum opportunities for developing his self-thinking and independent expression in order to develop his personality.

The modern age is dominated by democracy, the teacher should adopt democratic attitudes for the pupils. It should be remembered that the democratic attitude means the development of the lesson occurred with the help and the cooperation of the pupils. He should ask maximum questions and the pupils should be allowed to remove their doubts.

This creates the habit of thinking independently in the pupils. Also, their personality will rise to the heights by developing the merits like self-confidence, self-esteem and self-respect etc.

Principle of Planning. To make teaching successful, this principle of planning is essential to be followed. The meaning of this principle is that the teacher should ascertain the teaching sequence and after proper planning, the lesson-plan should be prepared. This enables him to solve every problem concerning teaching very conveniently.

It means to say that a teacher should decide how much he can seek the cooperation of the pupils in order to solve a problem with the help of which method and at what stage before preparing a lesson plan.

It can also occur that a problem arises at the time of teaching which had never been imagined. In such a situation, a teacher should solve the problem immediately in accordance to his ability. He can deviate from the lesson-plan for this. Its reason is that the lesson-plan is a helper of the teacher and not his master.

2. Psychological Principles of Teaching

The psychological principles of teaching affect the teaching-process directly or indirectly. These principles are used for turning the learning-process effective. These psychological principles are as follows :

1. *Principle of Motivation and Interest.* The motivation and the interest have been considered most important in the teaching-learning process. According to this principles, both the teacher and the learner are to work with interest and motivation.

2. *Principle of Imparting Training to Senses.* To encourage effective learning, the proper development of the senses is very

essential. All types of potentialities or capacities are required for all the aspects of learning such as observation, identification, generalization and experiments etc. These capacities or potentialities can be attained only through the sense organs.

3. *Principle of Encouraging Creativity and Self-Expression.* To encourage the creativity and self-expression becomes the duty of the teacher or he should develop the habit of innovations in the pupils. The pupils should be capable of presenting their views and attitudes.

4. *Principle of Reinforcement.* The term 'reinforcement' is used in teaching-learning process. It is concerned with making the learning process effective. In teaching process, the reinforcement means—the utilization or presentation or removal of such stimuli so that the possibilities of recurrence of any response increases. For example, if a teacher gives some reward to the pupils for correct answers, the possibilities of the similar behaviour from the pupils increase.

5. *Principle of Remedial Teaching.* Sometimes there are errors in the pupils and the teaching activities. The teacher should identify these errors and he should provide remedy to his erroneous teaching activities. It is known as remedial teaching. This task is not so easy. In this, the teacher has to overcome many obstructions.

6. *Principle of Sympathy and Cooperation.* If a teacher exhibits sufficient sympathy for pupils and contributes in overcoming their difficulties, he can be good guide of the pupils. Such teachers act as motivator for the pupils.

7. *Principle of Repetition and Exercise.* Everybody has come to know that the process of forgetting starts in the pupil due to the disuse of the acquired knowledge. Thorndike has experimented in this regard. Hence, repetition and exercise should occur in the class daily. The utility of this principle increases among the small children.

8. *Principle of Recreation.* At some occasions, the pupil feels fatigue in the class. It is due to lengthy teaching task. This fatigue creates boredom in the pupil and he shows disinterest in the task. The use of this principle is much needed in the lower classes. Hence, the principle of recreation should be followed in the class.

Maxims of Teaching

Maxims of teaching deserves more careful consideration of the teacher to enable him to make the teaching and learning go forward. Practical application of these maxims is a must for effective and efficient teaching and are indicative of teacher's ability. Utility of the maxims of teaching may be understood as follows:

"Maxims of teaching have been discovered, not invented. They are simply statements of the way in which teaching and learning go forward. They ensure effective and efficient teaching."

Meaning. Distribution of the knowledge and the teacher's ability, both are separate. A teacher is said to be a failure if he is unable to distribute the knowledge to the pupils even though he has abilities, merits and mastery of the subject. The reality is that the teaching is an art and to acquire efficiency in this art, the teacher needs two things—

1. The complete knowledge of the subject-matter.
2. The scientific knowledge of the teaching style for disseminating the knowledge to the pupils.

Psychology tells us that the various laws of learning derived from many experiments from time to time along with the essential elements of the learning. The educationists have presented their experiences and decisions in the form of maxims considering these laws and elements as basis of teaching.

These experiences and decisions presented in the form of maxims have been named as maxims of teaching. By following these teaching maxims, teachers get amazing results in their teaching task, i.e., the pupils acquire success very conveniently.

The educationists who have contributed in developing these teaching maxims are Herbart, Spencer and Comenius. In short, for a successful teaching, the use of teaching maxims is essential.

The principles of teaching cannot be used without following these maxims. Hence, for making teaching effective, every teacher must use maxims of teaching.

Usually, a new teacher or student-teacher faces many difficulties while performing teaching functions. Therefore, they must acquire the knowledge of these maxims of teaching during their training period. This will make clear to them when the teaching should be started and in what sequence it should be done and how it should be done?

Since these maxims of teaching convey us the starting point of the contents the direction in which we should move in order to achieve objectives. Some main teaching maxims are as follows:

Some Essential Maxims of Teaching

1. *From Known to Unknown.* The meaning of 'from known to unknown' is that the basis of the pupil's new knowledge should be his previous knowledge. It is a psychological fact that it becomes very difficult to acquire the new knowledge if it is presented before the pupil at once. But he takes interest in learning new knowledge if it is linked with the pupil's previous knowledge.

Hence, it is the duty of every teacher that before teaching anybody, he should activate his previous knowledge and present new knowledge on the basis of that activated previous knowledge of the pupil. It means to say that those small and simple informations with which the pupil is already familiar, should be made basis for imparting unfamiliar informations.

Every teacher, especially pupil-teacher, should move forward after establishing relationship between that known and the unknown. In other words, whatever the pupils know, the new knowledge of the unknown should be given on that basis.

For example, if a pupil is already familiar with the soil of the surrounding plains, facilities of water and the production of that area then it would be easy to provide him knowledge about the cultivation of that state on the basis of that previous knowledge while teaching geography.

2. *From Seen to Unseen.* The meaning of this maxims is that the pupils should be made aware of those things which are at perceptional before them first and then those things should be presented which don't exist before them. Its only reasons is that psychologically, the pupils ranging from 6 to 14 years functions at perceptional level only.

From this point of view, first of all the knowledge of present should be imparted to the pupil and then regarding past and future. In short, the teacher should use the seen or perceptual things in order to impart the knowledge regarding unseen or non-perceptuals along with concerned example. This facilitates the necessary knowledge concerning non-perceptual things (unseen).

3. *From Simple to Complex.* A key to successful teaching is creating interest in the pupils for new knowledge and developing self-confidence in them. From this point of view, if the teaching is to be made successful, it is essential to use a maxim called 'From Simple of Complex'.

This maxim means the teaching of simple to the pupil first and then the complex contents should be taught afterwards. If this is not followed, the pupils will lose their confidence. This will reduce their interest in the subject, they will lose their heart and they will not concentrate their mind in the studies.

Therefore, we should divide the subject-matter in such a way that the simple aspects should come first and these should be followed by the complex one in an order. Now the question arises that which aspect is simple and which one is complex. It should be remembered that the things simpler in teacher's view may be complicated for pupils.

For example, drawing a straight line may be simple for a teacher but it may be difficult for a pupil. It is also possible that the things which a teacher considers difficult for the pupils may be easier for those pupils. For example, drawing an animal's picture may be viewed by the teacher as a difficult task for a pupil but it is actually very easy for that pupil.

In this light, the teacher should decide what is easy and what is difficult keeping in view the interest, attitude, ability, potentiality and needs of the pupils. In short, as the pupil's mental development occurs, the lessons should be made complicated gradually. This will keep the interest of the pupil and the teacher will achieve success in the Teaching work.

4. *From Particular to General.* This maxim means that the specific examples should be presented before the pupils first and then the general laws or principles should be derived from those specific examples.

According to this maxim, the teacher should present some specific examples before the pupil. Then the same example should be evaluated and after understanding the fact, pupils should be motivated to derive general principles.

For example, if a teacher wants to explain his pupils that when the solids are immersed in a liquid, they lose their weight. He should perform two experiments before his pupils. First, the solids should be weighed in air. After this, the same solids should be weighed in a liquid. When the pupils conclude this, from their own observation and testing, that the solids lose their weights while immersed in a liquid, they will derive this general principle themselves without any difficulty.

In this way, in any subject, especially while teaching science, mathematics and grammar, various laws can be derived with the help of pupils.

According to this maxim, pupils get sufficient opportunities to derive themselves general principles through observation and testing. This encourages them and they start taking interest in doing tasks.

When the pupils learn themselves by doing, they need not to cram the knowledge, however, it becomes a permanent and clear part of their thinking. The above description of the maxim tells its utility. Therefore, in the inductive method of teaching, this maxim is used.

5. *From Indefinite to Definite.* It is a psychological fact that the pupil's intellectual development proceeds from indefinite to definite. As the pupil grows, his senses develop. Through these sense organs, the goes on graining the knowledge regarding different objects while living in the contact of his parents, brother-sister, other family members and the surrounding social environment.

On the basis of this gained knowledge he gradually makes his personal concepts regarding each object. These concepts or ideas are generally vague, unclear and uncertain. It is the duty of the teacher that he should provide certainty to the uncertain knowledge of the pupils by using concrete objects, pictures and examples.

6. *From Concrete to Abstract.* It is a psychological fact that the mental development of the pupils begins with the concrete objects and afterwards he gains micro-words for them. Therefore, to begin the education of pupils, the concrete object and fact should be made known first.

In other words, when knowledge about small things (micro)

is to be imparted to the pupils of lower classes in order to provide a definite shape to their ideas, the same objects should be shown or their models, pictures and lines can be used.

For example, while teaching geography, the knowledge of mountains, lakes, rivers and oceans can be either imparted through seen or perceptual things or through their models, pictures and lines very successfully.

7. *From Whole to Part.* In the twentieth century, Gestalt psychologists proved that we first perceive the object as a whole and then its parts. In other words, we gain knowledge about the 'whole' first and then about the 'parts'. For example, when we see our fan working in our room, first of all, the whole picture of the fan comes before us and then of its parts.

Similarly, when we see some tree, our attention goes on the entire tree, then on its stem, branches and leaves etc. This is called Gestalt theory. Remember that it is essential to study the background and environment of the object about which the knowledge is to be gained according to this Gestalt theory.

Hence, the teacher should present before the pupils the new teaching matter as a whole and in an organized way first and then its parts should be explained on the basis of this 'whole' and organized teaching-matter.

According to this maxim, by starting with the 'whole' object, the teacher imparts knowledge about each and every part of the object to the pupils. While teaching a language, first the sentences should be taught and then the words. In this concern, it should be pre-decided what the 'whole' is?

While teaching Geography teacher should not consider the earth as a 'whole'. He should not give, first, the knowledge about the entire earth and then about all the countries and then its various party.

Remember that the quantity of the 'whole' increases with an increase in the knowledge of the child. For example, for 6 year old pupil, his lane is 'whole' and for 12 years old pupil, his state is 'whole'. Hence, first of all the 'whole' for the pupil should be decided beforehand. Then its parts should be studied.

8. *From Psychological to Logical:* This maxim means to follow a sequence from psychological to logical while providing knowledge to the pupils. According to psychological order, the knowledge about some object or subject should be presented according to the age of pupils, curiosity, interest, needs and acquiring power.

Contrary to this, logical order means the present action of the knowledge before the pupils after dividing it logically into various units. While presenting the knowledge logically, the pupil's interest, age and acquiring-power are over-looked and only logical presentation of the subject-matter is emphasized whether the pupils understand it or not.

Therefore, the presentation of the knowledge in psychological order or sequence is definitely better and useful instead of teaching in a logical manner. Remember that the presentation of knowledge in a logical manner was considered good in old days, but in this modern age, the psychological order is being considered better as psychology has gained more importance.

Therefore, the education of language is started with the sentences now-a-days instead of alphabets and sounds.

In short, we should teach in lower classes according to his maxim by using psychological order instead of logical order. But, the logical order must be adopted as the pupil enters higher classes along with mental development. In other words, we should proceed from psychological order to the logical order.

9. *From Analysis to Synthesis.* Initially, the knowledge of pupils is vague, uncertain and unorganized. In order to make his knowledge clear, define and well-organized, a maxim named "From Analysis to Synthesis" is used essentially.

Analysis means to divide a problem into such living components which on assembling them may solve the problem. In other words, in analysis, the problem is separated into its various elements and then they are studied. For example, while teaching geography, if the pupils are to be taught about earth, we shall study by dividing it into different parts on the basis of climate.

This system can be used in geography, geometry science and grammar in which the problems can be made distinct and which can be divided into different parts.

Attention is to be paid to the fact that not only by analysing the problem, the pupils will gain a clear and definite knowledge about the problems, we need synthesis too for this. Synthesis means to understand by connecting the knowledge acquired from the analysed and living components of a problem.

For example, while teaching geography, we shall study the geographical fact of some place. Then a comparative study will be done and in the end, by assembling each component, we shall gain the knowledge of entire earth. Remember that the analysis and synthesis are supplementary to each other.

Hence, for an idealistic teaching, the mixture of both methods is essential. In short, if we want to provide clear, definite and well-organized knowledge of various subject to the pupils, then each teacher should use "Analytic—Synthetic" method.

10. *From Empirical to Rational.* This maxim means to make the pupil's empirical knowledge more rational so that it becomes valid and definite. Remember that the empirical knowledge is that which a pupil gains through his own observations. The pupil observes usually the freezing of water in winter and converting water into steam in summer.

Similarly, he looks every day rising up and setting down the sun. If the same pupils are questioned about the freezing of water and its steaming, these pupils, perhaps, will not be able to answer scientifically and logically.

In such a situation, according to this maxim, it is necessary for a teacher to make the pupil's empirical knowledge more rational. This will make the pupil's knowledge more true and definite.

11. *Follow Nature.* The meaning of this maxim is to regulate the eduction of a pupil according to his nature. Hence, all the sources of education should be based upon the principles of physical and mental development of the pupil.

In other words, whatever knowledge is to be given to the pupil that should be according to his physical and mental development. Hence, the teacher should follow the pupil's nature instead of his discretion.

It means to say that the education which obstructs the

development of the pupil in any way, is un-natural and un-psychological. Therefore, the teacher should do nothing which hampers the physical and mental development of the pupil. In short, the teacher should follow the nature of the pupil.

12. *Encouragement to Self-Study.* According to this maxim, self-study has been emphasized. Its only reason is that the actual teacher remains hidden in the pupil. When the pupil is absorbed in self-study and acquires some sort of knowledge then that knowledge becomes an integral part of his mind.

Therefore, great educationists like Rousseau have given important place to the self-study. Dalton's system is based on self-study. Hence, according to this maxim, it is required that the teacher should study the content first and then give it to the pupils for self-study. He should remove the difficulties of the pupils. In short, the pupils should be motivated, assisted and encouraged for self-study.

13. *Training of Senses.* The pupils have mainly five sense organs. These are—(1) an eye, (2) a nose, (3) taste, (4) smell, and (5) touch. All these sense organs are gateways of knowledge. With the help of these sense organs, the pupil forms concepts in his mind about the various sizes in this universe, types, colours, weight, quantity, density, area and temperature etc.

Hence, according to this maxim, the teacher should maximize the training to the above mentioned sense organs of the pupil. If these sense organs are trained properly, the pupil will form concepts of each object correctly in his mind. This will make his knowledge true and definite. Educationists, like Montessorie and Froebel have emphasised the use of this maxim.

By throwing light on above mentioned maxims, it is very much clear that all the maxims help in lesson-planning and guide the pupils keeping in mind the interests, attitudes, abilities, capacities and various levels of development of the pupils.

From this point of view, if the teachers especially pupil-teachers want success in the teaching task, its complete knowledge is essential for them.

QUESTIONS FOR ANSWER

1. Describe the general principles of teaching.
2. What is the importance of activity in the modern teaching? Write a note on the principle of activity.

3. What do you mean by the principles of teaching? Describe general and psychological principles of teaching.
4. How the general principles of teaching are helpful in the task of the teacher? Support your answer with proper examples.
5. What do you mean by the psychological principles of teaching? Explain briefly various principles useful in effective teaching-learning.
6. What is meant by psychological principles of teaching? Explain the implications of a few such principles.
7. What is a "Maxim of Teaching"? Which are the various maxims of teaching? Describe them in detail.
8. Discuss the importance of a maxim of teaching named 'From known to unknown' in class-room teaching.
9. What is the utility of maxims of teaching? Describe any five maxims to explain your views.

5

Educational Technology and the Teacher

Since the earliest days of human civilization in every part of the world and in all developing systems of education in each and every nation teacher had always been the most important factor and had always played the most pivotal role in the development of socio-cultural, socio-economic, socio-political and politico-economic concepts at all times. The present age belongs to science and technology and alike all other works of human life science and technology is playing a very vital role in education too. The influence of science and technology is very wide and most comprehensive, therefore, some people feel that this situation will affect the position of the teacher in the field of education, but I assure you that this will not affect teachers position in education negatively. The fact which I see and feel at present and visualize it to be in future is that it would make teacher's position in education much more pivotal and important which he had ever enjoyed in the past, at any time in the history of human civilization.

The teacher is the pivot in any system of education, whatever be the scheme that is under implementation. It is ultimately the teacher who makes or mars the scheme. Henry Van Dyke said "Famous educators plan new systems of pedagogy, but it is the unknown teacher who directs and guides the young".

As the teacher is an important component in the field of

education, evolving and implementing ideal methods of teacher preparation should be the primary objective of any Government. People even today consider that teaching is an art.

It is their contention that a teacher is born and not made. This is to a large extent true so far as transmitting information to the learner is concerned. But the teacher is no longer an importer of knowledge. The task of the modern teacher has assumed a different significance now. He has to function as a professional diagnostician and a learning facilitator.

Teacher—Some Problems

The teacher faces not only new groups of students coming from homes with weak educational traditional but also has to deal with a vast curriculum. The teacher-learning process has become complicated in view of the fact that the teacher of today has to deal with a large heterogeneous groups in every class. Moreover, the ever expanding horizons of modern knowledge add new dimension to the problem of teaching strategies and maximum use of instructional resources.

Good teaching is basically good communication between people. Teaching requires skilled professional work for which study, training and practice of all the tricks of the profession are necessary. A teacher will derive a sense of complete satisfaction and accomplishment only when he makes use of these techniques with efficiency in the classroom.

For imparting this kind of training, the apprenticeship scheme inherits from earlier days is often devoid of regular and systematic training. The problem is further aggravated by the fact that most of the colleges of education do not even have the model schools attached to them so that trainees can benefit by adopting new techniques of teaching under the close supervision of the college professors.

Consequently, the trainees are being sent to different practising schools in the vicinity for intensive teaching where they do not get any adequate help from the teachers and the college staff. A new analytical approach has, therefore, been developed which has replaced the old slogan 'Master the Model Teacher' with 'Master the Teaching Model'.

Improving teachers and their practice continues to be the most important problem in the field of education. As students are evaluated by their test scores and found to be in need of increased preparation, teachers are singled out as the target for appropriate staff development and new methods of teaching children.

Teachers should be seen as persons in search of meaning who choose to teach mostly for personal reasons. Tension builds when schools offer little support for teaching as a way of life.

Teachers live in a world of continual uncertainty as they struggle to balance personal motives with the realities of classroom life. Successes and failures in the classroom take on a personal meaning, with the failures serving to erode the original motivation to teach. The teacher then needs help from within to restore the motivation.

Frances Bolin points out the need for teachers to reflect on their history as teachers and to face aspects of their work that are discouraging and then take action in areas of need. The teacher's desire to take action may stem from the original commitment to teaching as a vocation. Once the teacher realizes that he or she has been discouraged, encouragement can take place. Reassessment of one's history is followed by efforts to renew oneself by reconsidering personal values and acting to restore them.

Teachers are called to the vocation by something beyond the normal. To have the vocation of a teacher is to permit oneself to be yoked to the interest—educational and vocational—by children and young people. Sometimes their calling is suppressed by those in charge of schools or by others with power over children and young people.

The suppression by and the noises of the powerful cause some of the frustration in the work and life of teachers. Yet it is precisely these frustrations that encourages the person who sees teaching as a vocation to journey outward beyond current meaning and values.

Teaching—A Comprehensive Technology

Teaching is now very much considered a science. The techniques have to be studied with the help of models and practised in the colleges under the supervision and guidance of college teachers. The systems approach, a self-regulating concept, which is adopted in the field of technology, is being increasingly applied in the field of teaching also.

Now educational methods and an array of technologically oriented teaching aids have created new thinking about the ways of using them in the educational system. Against this background, there is need to prepare a kind of teacher who has an experimental attitude. For all this, the colleges of education have to upgrade and renovate their teaching techniques.

When courses are reorganised, an attempt is made to make the entire course theoretical only. *Structured lecturing seminar, slides and tapes, sequence technique, class discussion, library assignment, workbook presentation, team teaching and individualize learning techniques like programmed learning and making use of ingenious devices and materials are referred to theoretically and not practically.*

Colleges of education should organize a resource centre with learning packages. Very little attempt has been made in developing countries like India to explore the potentials of these techniques in actual classroom situations. Neither the Professors of education in the various disciplines attempt to give demonstrations of these new techniques to the student trainees nor the latter are given opportunities to explore the values of these methods in practice.

One limitation in incorporating this kind of experimentation in the teacher education curricula is the absence of a demonstration school in the college campus. Importance must also be given in teacher education programmes training for the development of student study skills. Proper study techniques must be devised in these programmes.

This may include reading skills, essay writing skills and report writing skills, notes taking, evaluation techniques and even job-hunting skills. The purpose of pre-service training is only to initiate and induct a teacher to the teaching profession. This is only the beginning and not an end. Teacher education is now recognized as a continuous process and hence in service programmes should be organized in all the colleges of educaticnal periodically.

Better Techniques and Technology Needed

If teaching is seen merely as a job, then frustration can be accepted as part of the wear and tear of factory labour. If teaching is only a technology and a method, then this frustration requires better methods or techniques, or perhaps finding techniques that are a response to the powerful and which justify not hearing the callings of children and youth.

From the point of view of a profession, these conflicts are grist for new research projects on the part of the *gurus,* and indicators of the need for better knowledge to guide our life, our calling, these and other frustrations are indicators that we are not yet whole, at one with our work.

What we hear today from young people and the powerful is not what we heard when we were first called to be teachers. Previously workable methods no longer fit, and the children and youth are not what they were. These are not isolated changes, but indicators that the world had changed. The meanings and values that we forged in the past be transformed once again, as we are transformed by the new calls and cries in our world.

To be a teacher is to reshape our values as continuously as we are reshaped by the newness of this changing world. What we fight for and against, continues to change as the struggles and conflicts of the world unfold in our place of call and response.

Teacher Education

In view of the advancing Educational Technology which has made teaching a comprehensive technology there is practical need for better teacher eduction to make the present day teacher to perform his duties most effectively for the good of the educants and society. History of teacher education in India is not even 100 year old, yet we are doing our very best to match ourselves with the rest of the world. The history of teacher education in France, Germany, America, and England is as follows:

Teacher Training is generally concerned with preparation in subject matter and professional education, including psychology, methods, and practice of teaching. It is concerned principally, with teacher training for public elementary and secondary schools and continuing education related to that training.

France and Germany began teacher education as early as

17th century and continued to be influential in shaping patterns of training in other countries. With the secularization of schools in Germany, work in teacher education was greatly extended through the influence of Wilhelm Von Humboldt who became minister of education in 1809. He helped establish a planned educational programme, set up regular standards and examinations for teachers, and encouraged the development of pedagogical seminars.

Teacher education in the United States gained acceptance largely between 1820 and 1865. In the northeast the normal school (the original name for teacher-training schools) took root. The common school with equal opportunity for people of all classes led inevitably to support of a normal school to train teachers.

The widening range of ability of students attending school brought an emphasis on teaching methods. Because of widespread establishment of common schools, Samuel R. Hall opened his private normal school at Concord, Vt, in 1823. In 1839, the first of the public normal schools as established by the state of Massachusetts.

Traditionally, however, the training of teachers had been one of purely liberal education, and the effort to professionalise teacher education started a continuing controversy.

Thomas Jefferson at the University of Virginia and George Ticknow at Harvard experimented in elective programmes with subjects of utilitarian value for pre-professional work, and this influence helped the new normal schools to establish themselves.

These early patterns of teacher education had their beginnings at a time when educational responsibility rested primarily with the church. When governments began to assume civil responsibility for establishing and maintaining schools, they also began to determine of the preparation and qualification of teachers. As the percentage of children enrolled in school in the United States increased and higher numbers continued into the secondary schools, standards of certification were raised and collegiate study was increasingly expected of elementary as well as secondary school teachers.

The period from 1920 to 1930 has been described as that in which normal schools became teachers colleges in answer to this expectation.

The training of teachers in England dates from early in the 19th century, when the National Society for Promoting the Education of the Poor and Foreign School Society, first attacked the problem of elementary education on a national scale.

Both societies adopted the "monitorial system", in which older scholars learned their lessons from the adult teachers in charge of the school and then taught to the younger children.

Some training was found to be necessary and training schools were accordingly set up. One of these developed into the Borought Road Training College, which is still in existence. About 1840 James Kay, to whom, more than to any other single man, the English educational system is due, began the movement that replaced the monitors by 'pupil-teachers'; i.e., boys and girls who were regularly apprenticed for a period of five years from the age of 13 and both learned the art of teaching and continued their education under the head teacher of an elementary school.

Kay's scheme also involved training colleges where professional and academic education could be carried to a higher stage after the apprenticeship was completed. He himself founded the college which, as St. John's College. Battersea, London, was taken over by the National Society and furnished a model widely imitated.

In England, the first major development toward increasing educational opportunity came in 1918, but it was not until the Education Act of 1944 creating the modern and technical secondary schools that reform assumed significant proportions.

U.N. and International Efforts for Better Education

In view of advancing educational technologies and need for better teacher education for the good of mass education in all the nations of the world, U.N. and international efforts are on for the good of the educants in every part of the world. India is trying her best to keep pace with the best of educational technologies in the world.

In the 20th century, as the privileges of education were extended throughout the world, the International Bureau of Education and later the United Nations Educational, Scientific, and Cultural Organization (UNESCO) actively promoted international exchange of information and the systematic gathering of educational data.

The predominant institution for the education of elementary teachers was a normal school following completion of the elementary school. These institutions gave courses in both general and professional education. A few countries offered education for elementary teachers at the level of higher education, either through the university or through higher schools of education. Still other countries offered a combination of work beginning at the secondary level and extending into the higher education level.

The preparation of secondary school teachers was both academic and professional. Academic preparation was provided for—

1. through work at the regular universities;
2. through work at special institutions providing both academic and professional training;
3. by bringing in persons with special proficiency (engineers, for example, might teach mathematics; or pharmacists, chemistry);
4. in special schools for music, physical education, or art;
5. in countries with no higher educational institutions, by sending teachers abroad for training. Professional training was provided in a variety of ways.

Courses and Requirements. The professional courses for secondary teacher training fall under three general headings: education, psychology, and practice teaching. Prevalent among education courses are those which deal with teaching methods and general orientation to education.

The psychology courses provide for general psychology orientation and child or adolescent psychology. Practice teaching is uniformly provided but differs in length of time and type of work done by the student. In Austria, a year of probationary service under the guidance of experienced teachers is provided. In the Federal Republic of Germany, pre-academic studies with two four-week periods of practical work in a school during vacations.

The subject taught in primary-teacher-training establishment reflect the following persistent requirements in general education: mother tongue, a second language, history, mathematics, science, and geography. Professional subjects closely approximate the course offerings indicated in the requirements for preparation of secondary teachers.

More specialized provision is made for the study of child development, together with more emphasis on methods. Persistent offerings in special subjects include physical culture, drawing, penmanship, music, handwork domestic economy, agriculture and rural studies, health, and arts and crafts.

These subjects reflected a trend to train teachers in areas that will enable them to contribute to national needs in a agriculture, health, and domestic patterns. Further more, they indicate that primary education universally deals with a wider variety of cultural emphasis than reading and writing alone, and that these subjects are of sufficient significance for recognition in the curricula of a teacher education.

A comprehensive study of teacher training for primary schools in the former USSR and the US revealed many similarities between the four-year course in pedagogical schools for the training of primary schools teachers in the USSR (1955-65) and the four year course of the State Teachers College at Oneonta, NY (now State University of New York College at Oneonta).

The fundamental difference in the two programme was that the Soviet programme gave emphasis to teaching methods in direct relation to subjects, while the Oneonta course gave separate consideration to the child and his curriculum in a two-year integrated methods course.

Just as the beginnings of teacher education took place almost simultaneously in the various countries of Western Europe, so following World War II there was a nearly universal review of the adequacy of education in an effort to extend opportunity to a larger number of people in various countries.

The United Nations Universal Declaration of Human Rights (adopted in 1948), which states that everyone has a right to education made its influence felt in recognizing throughout the world the need to extend compulsory education. The effect of these developments of teacher education was direct Extension of teacher education was needed because of the extension of compulsory education, the increase in population of school age, and the extension of the years of schooling.

In Costa Rica, for example, there were 3,500 students in

secondary schools in 1948 and more than 45,000 in late 1960s. Enrolment in primary schools of Iraq was 90,000 in 1944 and 10,00,000 by the late 1960s. Similar increase in primary and secondary school enrolment were experienced in country-after-country, with consequent attempts to expand teacher Training institutions and programme to keep pace.

The World Survey of Education revealed that in 1930-34, the number of students specialising in education represented 1% of the total enrolment. In 1955-59, they accounted for 2%, an annual increase of 38% over the 1930-34 figure.

The International Bureau of Education has been conducting since 1931, a yearly International Conference on Public Education (after 1945 in cooperation with UNESCO). As early as 1935 pressures were felt on teacher education programmes, and the conference that year was devoted to problems of primary teacher education and problems and issues in preparing secondary schools teachers training.

In 1953 and 1954, the problems of primary teacher education were the subjects of conferences. Reports from various countries and the recommendations of these attending reflected practice and also served as guideposts to ministries of education in formulation programme in teacher education. They revealed discernible trends in the 1960s that were not readily identifiable earlier:

(i) *Longer preparation for elementary teachers and greater specialization for secondary teachers.* No doubt the worldwide stress on newer programme in science and mathematics influenced this development.

(ii) *Elimination of barriers between training of elementary and secondary teachers.* In England and Wales, the McNair Report (1944) and the Robbins Report (1961) made recommendations which, in effect, made teacher-training institutions and organisms part of the universities.

In 1965-66, universities in England, Scotland, and Canada introduced a bachelor of education degree, although it had marked differences as defined by various universities.

(iii) *Technology.* Countries as widely separated geographically as Sweden, Thailand and Hungary reported the use of television with practice teachers to permit viewing of actual classes without disruption of classrooms. Videotape was used in many institutions to permit students to observe their work and improve it. Computer-assisted instruction began to appear in the late 1960s. Techniques for using such devices are included in programmes.

(iv) *Student-teacher relationships.* The expansion of schools to include wider segments of the population increases the importance of the teacher-student relationship. This was reflected in the use of sensitivity training, group dynamics, micro-teaching, interaction analysis, simulation games and emphasis on self-concepts as it affects learning. There was also an influence on the design of courses, such as the section of the required training in Belgium that attempts to focus curriculum spirit, and methods on man and society and their relationship.

(v) *Advanced training centres.* The erstwhile USSR Academy of Pedagogical Sciences is designed to train pedagogical scientists in research, in pedagogical theory, and in development of new discoveries and hypotheses which form the basis of school practices, Turkey's five-year plan of reform provided for the training of 3,000 university teachers and research workers. India developed 97 secondary extension service centres, 45 primary extension service centres, and research centre to serve teachers colleges. The federally funded Research and Development Laboratories and Regional Educational Laboratories also reached beyond existing programmes of teacher education. The US Higher Education Act (1965) and the Education Development Act (1967) were also designed to provide training opportunities for graduate students and colleges and university personnel.

(vi) *Special education.* There is almost universal expansion of training for special education teachers. Examples include the University of Warsaw Chair of Special Pedagogy and Yugoslavia, Education Law of 1958.

(vii) *Nursery School Teachers.* Educational opportunity is being extended to pre-school children in increasing numbers. The Head Start Programme in the United States was one example. Nurseries for children of working mothers were being developed in many newly industrialized countries. This expansion brought about an extension of training for nursery school teachers as well.

Hindrances to Good Teaching

Despite good educational technology and its use by teachers as per its availability in the institutions, there are some hindrances to good teaching, a brief account is as follows:

Teaching is a complex activity, often distorted by various forces and powers. Teachers are impeded by the traditions they serve and which serve them. These traditions have become identified as content that is to be taught.

The very limited question of what to teach and the domination of technical language of behavioural objectives and evaluation clouds understanding: understanding of self, of our work, of young people, and of the traditions themselves. Whereas we tend to see these traditions as having a life of their own, they are carried by and embodied in the people and communities committed to their use, development and criticism. From these derive the traditions of literature in its many forms and critical reflections, and the many changing traditions of print: script, type, and now word processing or laser setting.

To speak of traditions as that which call the teachers is to point to the fact that the teacher is part of a community that itself makes demands. The teacher shows responsibility for the endurance and continuing value of traditions by maintaining their life-forming capabilities of liberation and enslavement.

As teachers are called upon by the new life of children and youth, they are also called by the recollections and hopes of communities that fix structure, meaning, and value of individual and collective life.

Teachers are called to be the trustees of the ways of life that would decay and be forgotten, were it not for their concrete services. The call of traditions also engages us in struggles of values and meaning—this indicates how teaching is a way of life and living.

Struggles over the control of language in listening and speaking, freedom of expression in writing, and access to idea in media occur constantly in the vocation of teaching. We are called to keep language free, a source of freedom. To do so is to struggle against the thralldom of language to those who would shape it for own ends.

Maintaining the liberating quality of the various traditions and keeping them from falling into the hands of people who would use them to ensure others or to shape the public according to their view is a struggle that keeps the teacher awake and alive.

If teaching becomes routinized and we do not participate in the ongoing struggle to maintain these sources of beauty, truth and freedom, then we no longer constructively partake of the unfolding and making of human history.

To have the vocation of teaching is to participate intentionally in the unfolding of this social world. The vocation of teaching does not permit fixed meaning or values. If a teacher becomes fixed and stereotypical, the struggle for meaning and living ends up.

In all probability, some one else is then using the teacher to shape and control the living of others. Thus, it is impossible to have a fixed understanding of a teacher, or of oneself as a teacher.

Exchange of Experience among Teachers

Qualified teachers while making maximum use of educational technology for good teaching may well be advised to exchange their experience with other teachers because it would help them to overcome some of their professional hindrances.

Human life as a journey has narrative structure. Thus, we come to tell our own story and to know the stories of others. A story appears to be a helpful way to speak of a person with a vocation.

How do we give language form to that story? Who or what helps us recollect and shape our experiences into patterns that can be remembered and used to map our future journeys with others?

How do we compose these experiences with young people and traditions, and our struggles in schools, so they continue to make sense rather than becoming repressed burdens? Was it just hard day in school, to be forgotten with a drink, or were we engaged in a new struggle that can result in new meanings and values if we can give voice to them?

A theory of teaching probably cannot help. Being able to tell our story to others and to listen to the stories of other teachers who take their calling seriously might help. The vocation of teaching does not offer security, stability, or comfort; it offers adventure, an invitation to remain open and vulnerable, and occasions to reshape and recompose the story of our life.

Within this television and computer world, how has the struggle to maintain and show the beauty and trustfulness to languages, so necessary for its vitality and our freedom, been incorporated into the story of our teaching?

How does the story of our teaching, our life, undergo dramatic turns, may be even reversals, as we try to hear the calls of children and youth amidst the siren call of drugs, the voyeuristic invitations of television, and the profit call of the industries of war which consume to destroy?

These increasing complexities of teaching are not sings of the decay of teaching, but an invitation to rethink and refeel what is of value and what we are called to do and be. How do we get a picture, a moving picture, of where we have been, where we are, and where we are going?

Journey, narrative, and personal story can also help teachers think about those with whom they work. Again, we have been dependent, on the understanding nets or frameworks of developmental theory. If these are limited and inadequate to help us understand our own story and journey, how can we assume that they are sufficient scaffolds on which to compose the events, activities, and moods of the young people before us?

Can we look at students as we look at ourselves: on a journey, responding to that which calls them into the world? Where did they come from, where are they now, where are they going? How have other persons, events, places influenced their story? How do we help them tell the story of their journey? How do we help them with the scaffolding that will help them make sense of who they are, where they are, and who they might be?

Bringing journey into story form is possible only when a person is invited to be fully present. If a part of oneself remains hidden or suppressed because of threat, shame, or possible ridicule, then that part cannot be incorporated into the story line of the person. Submerged and repressed, it distorts other aspects of the narrative, hence, the value of the story therapy. Given the importance of presence, the teacher is like a host or hostess, helping the student to be comfortable, totally present, and able to be himself or herself and open to others.

If the young person is in an environment that invites any support for presence and openness, the noise of prevailing powers is reduced, and the teacher can hear more clearly and respond more directly to the call. In such situations, the stories of each can be better articulated.

Metaphors of Teaching

Our metaphors of teaching separate teachers from young people and their parents. If teaching is seen through the metaphor of a profession, young people and their parents become clients. If the metaphor is technical, then the young and their parents become part of the data or substance upon which we work.

Therefore, we must know their characteristic so we can use appropriate techniques and materials. In fact, this has happened, for we place emphasis on knowing students and their social and cultural background, not to partake in their story and they in ours, but often to better control or work with them.

The technical metaphor maintains the foreboding distance between teachers and young people, a possible reason for the alienation within schools. It contributes to the suppressed insecurity of the teacher and the desire for more protective armor knowledge and technique. Open communication and the sharing of mutual stories, in fact, the building and inter- winning of shared stories, permit teachers and students to acknowledge their limitations.

Open communication and the recognition that young people also work and live, make meaning and establish values in classroom situations suggests that we have more in common than we acknowledge.

Is the recent interest in teaching moral and spiritual values place education consequence of a collective breakdown in educational communities? This was not a concern thirty years ago.

School as a Community

Under present arrangement, the school is a false or forced community, one of control rather than collegiality. Those who are members of the community by virtue of their control over it often do not share face to face, this is, mouth to ear, contact. They remain hidden, out of sight, embedded in materials, evaluation instruments, and methods. Teachers are drawn into their sets of meaning and values, rather than vice versa. Few people are fortunate enough to be part of a teaching community where vocation is the norm and the guiding metaphor: a listening-speaking community wherein personal story is talked and listened into being, and values and meaning are assessed and reconstituted.

Silence about the working life of teachers inhibits community formation. Is this silence a reason that we tend to think along individualistic ways about education, because we teachers have been isolated, vocationally, from community? Is one of the telltale consequences of our isolation and preoccupation with individual achievement, important to the extent that it does not cover over the social fabric that is the foundation of such individualism?

Perhaps the real partners in this vocation of teaching, besides other teachers, are those who call us to serve them. Young people and their families have the potential to be in coalition with teachers. Too often they are seen as opponents or problems. Young people and their parents cannot minister to us in the same way that we serve them, or that colleagues do and administrators could. They nevertheless could be part of our support matrix in the same way that we could be part of their support matrix if we so choose.

Teachers as Technique Makers

Teachers must act in an imperfect world. To postpone action until the knowledge and technique makers establish the educational millennium is sheer irresponsibility, based on illusions of progress. We have no choice but to risk ourselves. The choice is to consider the risk private or to build a community that accepts vulnerability and shares risks.

To teach because it is a vocation is to recognize, at some level, that need for colleagues, companions, and friends with whom we can communicate and search for new values and meanings. To be in and part of a community with others who accept teaching as a vocation is to be with others who recognize the vulnerability and fallibility of being available, on call, to young people and to the traditions we value. Obviously, this is not what schools are. Nevertheless, this is a consequence of seeing education as a vocation.

We need colleagues and friends who listen and share conversations about what we are doing, about how the young people of this year differ from those of past years, about the developments in our traditions, about the conflicts between young people and the traditions and between young people and school rules.

We need people who listen to us and to whom we listen, who help in the narration of our story, so we can more readily recognize our changing values and meanings.

Our search for new knowledge, new materials new forms of teacher education, and better teacher benefits has gone on, long enough. Of course, it must continue in some fashion, but we must begin to scrutinize and become intentional about the communities within which we teach. We must seek out new coalitions and work intentionally at the social fabric that surrounds those of us who are called to be teachers.

Teacher to Use Traditions Correctly

The other dimension of the teacher's calling is to make available the tradition that is valued. To make this tradition stand out clearly is to provide a background against which the figure and story of the young person stands forth more distinctly. Standing out against a clearly articulated tradition, the young person can more easily imagine a future that integrates present and past and empowers a future.

Such images of possibility, of hope, can become a part of the young person's story, serving as a beacon into a vague land of the future. Unfortunately, this imagining or envisioning of the future in one's story has been neglected or perhaps distorted. In the technical-bureaucratic language that dominates schooling, the future is imagined as objectives or goals, a significant watering down of the language of image or vision.

Dominance of the School Traditions. This conflict between the language of the young person and the language of the school becomes part of the story line of the teacher. The teacher feels caught between the dominant language of the school, his or her own commitment to the tradition, and the story of the young person. The dominance of the school language serves to silence the student, where personal story of living in school is thus repressed. This "caughtness" dominates the teacher's consciousness.

The teacher is a mediator between the young person and the tradition. On the one hand, the teacher represents the tradition to the student in such a way that it can be a factor in the young person's narrative. A tradition need not be made presently or available in any one determinate form or structure, but can be presented and represented in multitude of ways if the teacher is at home in the tradition.

On the other hand, the teacher is called to bring to the surface the present, those dimensions of the young person's past and present that have some bearing on the tradition.

Finally, if the teacher is called by the young person and participates in that young person's emerging or unfolding story, the teacher must be an able listener, who listens the young person into an articulate consciousness and a narrator who has the necessary language to place this episode into the young person's story line.

This narrative function has been left to evaluation instruments, which are a severely limited, restrictive, and perhaps even distorting language. Evaluation instruments answer the question "where are you?" but the answer comes back in terms of impersonal groups or structures removed from history.

These are not answers that compare the young person's past, present, and future. If called by the young person and the tradition, the teacher makes poetry by naming what is for the young person, and perhaps for the tradition, in new ways. It can be poetry that recollects old life, redirects it, and renews it for the future.

Need for Searching New Values

We must ask about way time is used within the teaching community. Obviously, the school day, week, and year are not structured or organized to facilitate the kinds of needed conversation. Teachers are not often available to each other for community building. This is one of the side benefits of team teaching. Part of the reason for this lack of time is the division of labour in our educational enterprise.

Classroom teachers have the problems; college and university personnel have the time. Classroom teachers do not have time to work on and over their problems, so the problems are taken up by college and university personnel, who have the time to mull them over, to research them, and to write and lecture about them.

Teachers become dependent on their time and their presumed solutions to the teachers' problems, whether as theories or methods.

So teachers return to summer schools, or read books to find others' solutions to their problems. Could it be that the social distribution of time in our educational enterprise is part of the problem?

It is also obvious that administrators are not necessarily committed, nor have they been educated, to take their titles seriously. To administer is to minister, to serve. The focus on organization, management, and policy often precludes concern for the teacher as the primary and chief ingredient of any education.

Without the presence of those who are called to be teachers, we would have little need for schools. Yet administrators, often see teachers as the problem.

The primary problem in schools is administrators who have been educated to control rather than to serve and minister to the teacher. What do I mean by an administrator ministering to teacher? The discussion above about the social fabric required for teaching as a vocation provides the context for such meaning.

Hence the work of teaching needs to become part of the story, the life journey of the teacher. Vulnerability needs to be acknowledged, conflicts articulated, values reassessed, and meanings remade. To listen someone else into consciousness, to accept teaching problems as occasions for new growth and development, to explore the social and personal significance of changing characteristics of young people, to search for new structures and opportunities of community that reflect the changing values of community members, to mediate between the principalities and powers and people of the school—these are some of the needed characteristics of administrators.

Teacher's Consideration for Values

Teaching is inherently loaded with value considerations. In fact, it is one of the dominant forms of value maintenance and creation. That we must now attend our framework for thinking about "doing" which education has covered the value considerations inherent in all teaching. Hence, they have been introduced as something special, detached from the everyday of teaching and the ongoing life of teachers and young people. A shift in the metaphor with which we talk about teaching can help us here.

If we shift our metaphor to teaching as a vocation, if we acknowledge that teaching is a way of living, not merely a way of making a living, and if we attend intentionally to the meaning and value-making of the teacher, will we not start to rebuild our educational communities? Then we will not have to teach values; we will be able to work in order to live more truthfully, justly, beautifully, and openly in the classroom. Do we have to teach values if we live them and reflect responsibly on our life together? Life in classrooms deserves attention as an important part of the teacher's life. If we are called to teach, then that becomes the part of the world that is our responsibility, and where we live out that which we value and that which we mean. Is that life part of our own life story, and is that story an integrated story of a person struggling in a very difficult and changing world?

Teacher should have an open Mind

In the life of real people, vulnerability is a prerequisite for and consequence of journey. To be available to the vast otherness of the world, to be able to respond to the call of others, requires that we live without stereotypes and closure. We are required to be comfortable with reasonable doubt, openness, and unsureness, if we are to respond afresh to that which is given to us afresh.

Teaching as a vocation is a part of our open journey, which we understand as a story being composed in response to that which calls us. The lore that has grown around teaching since the early part of this century, buzzard by empirical and scientific methods, denies the vulnerability and insecurity. These are tokens of personal insecurity, which can be overcome by more education, better training, better materials, better organizations, or more talented teachers who will come into the school, if the pay is higher.

The panacean efforts of the past thirty years—teacher-proof materials, new organizations, new curricula, and new methods—indicate that the vulnerability of teachers is much more deeply rooted in the human condition. The insecurity of teaching is what makes teaching a vocation, and is inherent in vocations.

We cannot take on a calling without risk. We cannot respond to the calls of the young, or the communities of tradition, or the conflicts that such a response entails, unless we recognize and accept our vulnerability and fallibility.

We need to find ways to live without being overpowered or overcome by newness and novelty calls. This does not deny the importance of knowledge, methods, materials and organization in the vocation of teaching.

There is no doubt about the significance of inquiry, research and knowledge for the continual improvement of one's own teaching as well as that of teaching in general. But reasonable doubt, openness, and journey are also necessary prerequisites in the sciences. The point is that inquiry, knowledge, and technical developments cannot do away with or cover over the built-in vulnerability of the vocation of teaching.

If vulnerability is done away with, or rather covered over and ignored, we simply turn teaching into a productive technical enterprise that is unresponsive to the people and context within which it happens.

Acceptance of one's vulnerability, insecurity, and fallibility requires a social context of acceptances and support. We can tolerate the pain and discomfort if we are with others who accept them as manifestations of the human conditions and who listen to our flounderings and fuddlings into the uniqueness of our story.

To use knowledge and technique to protect oneself from the insecurity of meetings the otherness of the world, to reduce risk that accompanies vocation, can only result in control and disappointment. Too often, knowledge makers and researchers are interested in problems and insecurities in order to market their wares, to design more research, or to search for grants. They are not, particularly, interested in the school people who are caught responding, however, inadequately, to the newness and otherness of the world.

Fallibility and Insecurity of Teaching Vocation

The fallibility and insecurity that accompany teaching have been covered over by the metaphors of teaching as a profession, as a technology or a method, or as an activity of schooling. The search for a method or technology of teaching carries with it the false promise that better methods of teaching can be given to teachers to reduce their insecurity or vulnerability.

Difficulties and struggles of teaching are assumed to be a result of inadequate method, not an inherent consequence of the vulnerability that accompanies a vocation. To use the metaphor of profession is to see teaching as a knowledge-based activity. This assumes that teachers should be sufficiently well educated to cope with problems, that knowledge is a protection against insecurity and fallibility—it is protective armor. As part of a knowledge-based community, teachers should have access to problem-solving methods or to the problem solutions of others. Conflicts and difficulties with new students or new developments in a tradition are problems to be solved within the profession. They are not, necessarily, personal challenges that ask the teacher to rethink values and the meaning of being a teacher and a human being today. From the perspective of the metaphor of schooling, the teacher's vulnerability is either to see as a sign of weakness or denied. Such signs can be overcome by bureaucratic routines such as finding a replacement teacher, getting new texts, demanding conformity to the syllabus, discipline, or other school-generated techniques.

Career Development for Teachers

Several proposals have been made for career development within the teaching profession, the 'master teacher' merit pay, and the like. All these proposals have value in that they address the need to recognize good teachers. However, those in positions powerful enough to initiate change in schools are often those least cognizant of the realities that teachers face and may have little knowledge of school culture. Similarly, some recent reports have made reasonable suggestions regarding educational improvement in general.

It appears that these proposals are fraught with as much uncertainty as the act of teaching is. For instance, who should be identified as master teachers? What criteria should be used? What kinds of career-ladders should be developed? Who should receive merit pay and how much should they receive? If these questions are superimposed on the teaching uncertainties discussed above, further questions will be generated. What kinds of rewards should master teachers receive?

What should the role and status of master teachers be? Should career ladders be tied to grade levels taught or to particular subject matter? Should master-teacher become supervisors or should they become part of the induction process and assist new teachers? What kind of academic proportion should master teachers or meritorious teachers revive? Should master teachers help establish educational goals?

What about the students—how will these proposals benefit them? All these questions seem to illustrate clearly that one specific change, like the introduction of career-ladders, cannot be made to fit a non-specific system or profession.

What, then, is the solution? Perhaps the profession needs to rethink what it means by vocational choices. The proposals discussed seem to assume that good teachers are leaving the field in frustration and, therefore, need some extrinsic motivation to stay. These assumptions may be faulty.

There is no doubt that good teachers do leave the classroom; they will continue to leave no matter what teaching rewards are introduced, because they are looking for new experiences. On the other hand, good teachers do remain and will continue to do so despite the uncertainty and lack of tangible rewards, because teaching is what they most want to do.

Furthermore, we all know from our own experiences that additional money and titles are not enough to persuade us to remain in positions where we are dissatisfied. Similarly, teacher who choose to remain in the classroom need vocational choices that will offer intrinsic rather than extrinsic rewards.

This raises the question, "How can this be accomplished?" One response to this question is suggested by Richard Wiener, whose article presents curriculum innovation as a vocational choice that is intrinsically rewarding. Another way to provide vocational choices, for the teacher, however, is through staff development.

Staff Development Drives

The idea of staff development is neither unique nor untried. All school systems provide staff development in some form or another for their teachers. However, the quality of this staff development is questionable and appears to be characterized by irrelevance to teachers and teaching; a lack of continuity and coordination among school, district, state, and federal efforts; an absence of feedback to teachers; and less than overwhelming attendance. Current staff development appears to focus on the correction of deficits rather than on the growth of teachers. What staff development offerings should do is to supply teachers with a forum where they can interact with other teachers, talk, exchange ideas, and critically examine their own teaching practices. Staff development must grow from the needs and concerns of teachers and must afford teachers the change to engage in inquiry for the purpose of improvement. This is not to suggest that teachers as a group should work in a vacuum, but rather that good staff development should enable teachers to work on relevant issues in concert with others in the educational field-administrators, researchers, university personnel and the community.

Uncertain Nature of Teaching Vocation

If teachers are unable to share their successes with their principals or subordinates, from where do they derive rewards for their efforts? For most teachers, satisfaction must come from students. But these student-derived rewards are neither constant nor long lasting. One good day may come only after a string of bad days, one bad day is enough to counter a few good ones.

To combat the uncertainty in their professional lives, teachers constantly seek the right answers through the acquisition of more knowledge. After pre-service education, practising teachers take more courses to obtain permanent certification, attend in service workshops, and immerse themselves in staffs development offerings. But the search for definite answers seems always to be futile.

Added to the uncertainties that teachers face daily in their workplaces, the teaching role, according to Dwayne Huebner is uncertain because teachers are enslaved by the teaching images generated by society. Teachers must become what society wants them to be; the teaching images they adopt are dependent on public policy.

Teachers and teaching are thus defined by everyone other than teachers, and changes in the lives and workplaces of teachers appears orchestrated by forces seemingly beyond their control. The teaching role is placed in a very precarious position and teachers can never be certain of when the next role upheaval will occur, changing the way they do what they do.

Besides adhering to public images, teachers must also work within the constraints set by societal norms, constraints such as the law status of their position and a general lack of respect for the teaching profession.

As a result of this enslavement, teachers seem to have lost their voice when it comes to setting or influencing public policies that affect them professionally or vocationally. The "shadowed social standing" of teachers allows the voices of politicians and administrators to dominate education, while the voices of teachers have been silenced.

Given these understanding, what vocational choices do teachers have? Currently, the choices are limited. One is either a teacher or not. For those who wish to advance within the teaching field, few options are available. Usually the only option is to leave the classroom.

The educational reports attempted to address this issue by proposing that teaching should cease to be an unstaged profession, and should become instead a profession where capable teachers are recognized for their excellence and rewarded within teaching field. The feeling is that if classroom teachers are presented with more vocational choices that will professionally boost teaching, they will be enticed to remain in the classroom where they are most needed.

That teaching is an uncertain activity and that teachers are vulnerable as a result of the uncertainties is established. Unless we are able to magically make all students, all schools and all teachers exactly the same, we will not be able to escape the fact that teaching cannot be made a finite activity. Effective staff development efforts may not reduce the uncertainties that teachers face, but they can give teachers vocational choices that enhance the way teachers view themselves.

Good staff development can affect teachers from the inside

out rather than modify the framework within which they practice their vocation. It can help counterbalance the uncertainties that teachers faced by connecting them to other teachers and breaking the loneliness and lack of support they experience; by allowing them the rewards that come from recognition, accomplishment and professional control; by enabling them to acquire and generate new knowledge; and by encouraging them to take charge of their own professional development.

Though the approaches used were very different, the end products of the two staff development projects are very similar—the increase in teacher self-esteem, the acquisition of new skills by teachers, the development of teacher networks, and most important, the involvement of teachers in educational change within their workplaces. The staff development efforts serve to point out the road staff development could take and to unequivocally underline the understanding that staff development should be more than yet another in-service course on yet another classroom management techniques. They demonstrate clearly that staff development possibilities are really endless and could do much toward empowering teachers by beginning where teachers are and by acknowledging that teachers have expertise and can acquire the control to effect change rather than merely to allow change to affect them.

QUESTIONS FOR ANSWER

1. Write a note on U.N. and International efforts for better education.
2. Write a note on the importance of "Exchange of Experiences Among Teachers" for better education.
3. Write short notes on:
   (*a*) Teaching a Comprehensive Technology
   (*b*) Hindrances to Good Teaching
   (*c*) Metaphors of Teaching
   (*d*) Teachers as Technique Makers.
4. Write a note on Fallibility and Insecurity of Teaching Vocation.
5. Write short notes on:
   (*a*) Need for Career Development for Teachers
   (*b*) School as a Community
   (*c*) Teacher Education

6

Teaching Strategies

Teaching Strategies is a phrase used to indicate applications of various methods and techniques of teaching to achieve the objective of teaching in a given situation. Therefore, the teacher has to decide which one or combination of more methods and techniques of teaching need practical application in a given situation. These strategies may be defined as "Broad Method Instruction".

Remember that there is a lot of difference between a method and a technique. Teaching methods are directly linked with teaching objectives. Hence, each teaching method decides the direction and speed of the teaching. Contrary to this, the teaching technique is not directly linked with the teaching objective, but it is linked with the teaching method.

In spite of this, in teaching method, the feeling of "how" works, but the main spirit of teaching technique is—"with what". Not only this, teaching method also emphasizes proper and systematic planning of the content, while technique emphasizes psychological and logical aspect and hints those ways by which the teaching can be made impressive.

Meaning of Teaching Strategy

According to the Collin's English Gem Dictionary, 1968 the strategy means the art of war or the skill of war. In Encyclopaedia too, its meaning has been given as an art of deploying army so that a specific goal can be achieved. Hence, according to Encyclopaedia, "Strategy is the science or art of planning and directing large military movements and operations".

It is very clear that the strategy is such planning or line of action which is related to the working system. In other words, strategy is that skilful planning of a working system by which the objective can be achieved conveniently. Remember that the strategies are never the same. These change according to the changing situations.

The word strategy is also being used by the social scientists in social planning, human dynamics and teaching areas B.O. Smith writes about strategy as, "The term strategy refers to pattern of acts that serve to attain certain outcomes and to guard against certain others. It is clear that the word strategy means the determination of some policy by planning before presenting the contents with the help of which the student's force is faced and the teaching objectives are achieved."

In this way, the pre-planning of the lesson is key to success. Hence, every teacher should be skilled in this art of pre-planning.

Making clearer the meaning of strategy, Stones & Morris have written that, "Teaching strategy is a generalized plan for a lesson which includes structure, desired learner behaviour in terms of goals, instruction and an outline of planned tactics necessary to implement the strategy."

Attention should be paid that the teaching strategies are more comprehensive than the teaching methods. It is because the teaching methods include only the presentation of contents. Contrary to this, teaching strategy includes all the aspect like contents, task analysis, teaching objectives, the expected changes in the behaviour of the pupils their interests, attitudes, capacities, abilities, needs, mental level and entering behaviour etc.

In the words of I.K. Davis "Strategies are broad methods of teaching". Their construction includes educational philosophy, teaching objectives, learning principles, desired activities, feedback and motivating tactics.

Difference between Teaching Method and Teaching Strategy

Usually, people consider teaching method and teaching strategy as one and the same thing. But this is not true. Both have important differences in their meaning and these are as follows:

1. In the teaching methods, the main aspect is the way of presentation and the contents. The teaching method is determined according to the nature of the contents. There can be three methods of presentation:
   (a) **Telling Method**—Such as lecturing, questioning etc.
   (b) **Doing Method**—Such as Project Method.
   (c) **Showing Method**—Such as Demonstration, Observation.
2. In teaching method macro approaches are followed. But in teaching strategy micro approach is followed.
3. The teaching methods are based on classical Human Organization Theory, while teaching strategies are based on Modern Human Organization Theory.
4. The norm or criterion for evaluating the teaching method is the mastery on contents while in teaching strategy, the norm of evaluation is the acquisition of objectives.
5. It is the assumption of teaching method that the teaching is an art while the teaching strategy considers teaching as a science.
6. In teaching method, the task and its presentation are considered important but in teaching strategies, the behaviours and the relationship are considered more important.
7. In teaching method, the teaching objectives are not considered very important while these are considered important in teaching strategy.
8. The main objective of teaching method is the impressive presentation while in teaching strategies, the main objective is to create complete learning situations.

Sometimes, some educationists name the teaching method as teaching strategies. But in that case, the objective of the teaching strategy also changes. For example, lecture is considered as teaching method, but when the lecture is used to achieve some specific objective, it comes under the teaching strategy. In teaching methods, help is sought from techniques while in teaching strategies, help is sought from teaching tactics.

Meaning of Teaching Tactics

The success of the teaching depends on its planning. A skilled teacher, while planning thinks carefully about the teaching system, its structure, strategy and tactics, before presenting the contents to the pupils.

Now we are explaining the meaning of teaching tactics. Remember that the teaching tactics means that method with which new knowledge is marked in the minds of pupils permanently. Hence, for qualitative development of teaching, keeping in view the structure of learning and by using proper teaching strategy and tactics, he changes his behaviour in such a way, according to the changed conditions during teaching, that he may achieve the teaching objective as a result of verbal and non-verbal ones and maximum interaction.

From this point of view, teaching tactics are more comprehensive than the teaching strategies. In other words, under a single teaching strategy, by using one or more teaching tactics, the lesson can be made easy, clear and understandable.

For example, while using a lecture strategy, various teaching tactics are used in order to achieve the objective. While explaining the meaning of teaching tactics, Stones & Morrison write, "Teaching tactic is goal linked influencing the behaviour of the teacher. It includes the way he behaves in the instructional situations and how he fulfils various instructional goals with the students of the class and how the teacher, the students and the subject-matter interacts."

Pre-application Considerations. Before opting to apply particular strategy, tactics or method of teaching teacher should give full consideration to the following aspects.

Task Structure Approach

In determining the teaching tactics, the task analysis and task structure are given more importance. Norms and tactics are also determined on the basis of task structure. We can say that the basis of teaching tactics is the task structure. The utility of task structure is as follows:

Utility for Pupils

(i) The pupils can select themselves the learning tactics on the basis of their class and the task structure.

(ii) In the structure of the task, pupils gain deep understanding and they can get the benefit of change

in their behaviour while learning.

(iii) The pupils can understand the relationships of learning objectives and nature of classes by gaining the knowledge of task-structure.

(iv) The pupils can retain in memory the learnt material for a longer time which they learnt on the basis of the knowledge of task-structure.

Utility for Teachers

(i) On the basis of task structures, all the teaching tactics can be selected.

(ii) The pupils can be provided with deep knowledge by knowing the task structure.

(iii) The teacher can present the informations and data in such a way that the pupils may remember them for a long time.

(iv) Various learning objectives and various learning patterns of different classes can be made better understandable.

Teaching Strategy and Pupil Ability

In the teaching-learning process, the teaching strategy and an interaction of pupils' abilities are essential. The pupils possess various abilities. It is not essential that all teaching strategies suit all pupils with various types of abilities. In this connection, following are some facts:

(i) It has generally been observed that the talented pupils like democratic teaching strategies.

(ii) Contrary to this, non-talented pupils like autocratic teaching strategies.

(iii) The pupils with limited talent can gain the benefit from autocratic teaching strategies.

(iv) Similarly, the talented pupils can gain benefit from democratic teaching strategies.

Hence, it is very important that which teaching strategy has been selected for pupil having what type of ability.

Types of Teaching Strategies

Teaching Strategies are used for achieving the teaching goals and objectives. Keeping in view the class-room environment and the teacher's attitude, teaching strategies can be divided

into two categories—
1. Autocratic strategies
2. Democratic strategies.

1. Autocratic Strategies. Autocratic strategies are traditional teaching strategies. These are content centred and teacher-centred. While using these strategies, the teacher's place is primary and the pupil's is secondary. The teacher determines the content himself and by considering himself an ideal and by suppressing pupil's interests, attitudes, capacities, abilities and needs, he tries to impose knowledge forcibly from outside in the minds of the pupils.

In such a situation, pupil don't have any freedom for their expressions. Hence, in these autocratic strategies, only mental development is emphasized, for achieving cognitive objectives and group development is not cared for at all. Autocratic teaching strategies include (1) Lecture (2) Demonstration (3) Tutorial (4) Programmed instruction etc.

Some Autocratic Teaching Strategies

Lecture

When a teacher takes the help of a lengthy short explanation in order to clarify his ideas or some fact, that explanation is termed as a lecture or lecture method. Actually the lecture method is not a new method, but it is a traditional autocratic method. Some scholars feel that the lecture can be made lengthy or short as the situation is. Hence, the lecture is the easiest method of imparting knowledge to the pupils. Teacher makes use of it very conveniently, therefore this method is more popular as compared to the others.

Remember that the lecture is a one channel method. In this, presentation is more emphasized, but the pupils function as passive listeners. This creates dullness in the class-room as interaction between the pupils and the teacher ceases to occur. With this, pupils get no motivation for acquiring knowlege.

The lecture method can be used in the following three situations:

(a) To achieve the lowest objective of the cognitive aspect.
(b) To achieve the highest objective of the cognitive aspect.
(c) To achieve the "affective" objectives.

It is a matter of experience that in lecture method, the main teaching aspects are not included carefully. Therefore, most of the teachers usually remain unsuccessful in achieving these objectives. This is the reason of accepting the lecture method as communication strategy only.

Precautions while Using Lecture Strategy

The following precautions should be observed while using the lecture method.

1. Lecture is an art and continuous efforts are needed in order to gain success in it.
2. The person delivering his lecture should know the subject fully.
3. An easy language, meaningful and interesting illustration should be used in lecturing.
4. While lecturing an effort should be made to avoid non-relevant references.
5. The contents of the lecture should be organized systematically according to the interest and mental level of the pupils.
6. Important points should be emphasized during lecturing.
7. An appropriate teaching material should be used while lecturing.
8. The lecture should follow an interaction between the teacher and the pupils.
9. The lecture should not be so lengthily and formal that the pupils start feeling boredom.
10. The lecture should be interesting. The book or the notes should not be used while delivering a lecture.
11. The lecture method should be accompanied by some other methods so that the pupils may follow the lecture properly.
12. The lecture should be delivered for the prescribed time.

Demonstration

A demonstration method is that method in which a verbal interaction between the teacher and the pupils is encouraged. As a result of this interaction, pupils acquire new knowledge very conveniently. Since the demonstration method is used in the teaching of science subjects, but this method can also be used successfully in the teaching of art, craft and various experimental subjects. While using demonstration method successfully the teacher should also use essentially the techniques like verbal presentation, exposition and the description etc.

In order to make success of demonstration method, following three things are necessary:

(i) The objects, being displayed during demonstration, should be of such size that all the pupils may see without any difficulty.

(ii) There should be no use of tough language and difficult words while demonstrating, but such a simple clear interesting language should be used that the pupils may understand the contents very easily.

(iii) The pupils should be allowed to remove their difficulties by independent questioning with the teachers.

If the teacher follows these three points, his teaching will be effective and the pupils will follow the subject-matter very easily.

Tutorial

It is the fundamental right of every person to get education in democracy. Therefore, instead of individual teaching, group-teaching is emphasized so that the large group may be educated at the low rate of expenditure. But it is also true that in group-teaching, a general teacher cannot solve the 'personal' problems of every pupil. Its reason is that if he does this, he cannot finish his fixed syllabi in a time-bound manner.

To remove this drawback of group-teaching, pupils are divided into small groups so that the personal problems which came across during group teaching may be solved successfully. Hence, a tutorial is a sub-part of the class in which a teacher tries to solve the problems of the small groups of the pupils through individual teaching. Tutorials are of three types :

1. Group Tutorial
2. Supervised Tutorial
3. Practical Tutorial.

Group Tutorial. Group Tutorials are conducted to solve the problems of the grown up pupils of average level. It should be remembered that the group tutorials can only be organized successfully by a teacher who possesses the full knowledge of

Group Dynamics and Social Psychology.

Supervised Tutorial. In the supervised tutorials, the talented pupils and the teachers discuss the problems time to time. The pupils put up their difficulties. Then the teacher tries to solve those problems. In this way, after a discussion between a teacher and the pupils, the solutions to some problems come up.

Practical Tutorial. Practical tutorials are conducted to develop the physical skill and to achieve the objectives of psychomotor skill. Pupils have to work in the laboratory for this. Such tutorials are more useful for youngers and pupils of lower-classes.

Some people consider the teacher as primary and pupils as secondary in conducting the tutorials. In such a situation, if a tutorial acquires the form of a lecture, then this will be considered as autocratic strategy. Contrary to this, if the pupils are more active instead of the teacher, then it will definitely occupy its main place in democratic strategies. Prof. Bloom's view is that the discussion should be based on the problem and the teacher should help the pupil to the maximum to solve the problem.

Programmed Instruction

Programmed Instruction was indoctrinated by the famous educationist of America. Prof. B.F. Skinner and Norman A. Crowder for individual teaching. Remember that this method has various forms. These are—(1) Linear, (2) Branching, (3) Mathematics, and (4) Teaching Machines etc. All these forms provide new knowledge to the pupils by individual motivation and providing feedback by reinforcement after getting correct responses.

This method has five principles. These are—(1) Principle of small steps, (2) Active Responding, (3) Immediate confirmation, (4) Self-pacing, and (5) Student testing.

In America, various programmes have been developed by using programmed instruction method in the field of language, art and medical. In our country too, by accepting this method, important for individual teaching, an appreciable effort has been made in NCERT, Baroda, Meerut and H.P. universities for its development. We can achieve cognitive objectives of lower level and by more trials, we can also achieve middle order cognitive and affective objectives.

Some Democratic Strategies

Democratic strategies are child centred. The pupils determine themselves the content. In the use of these strategies, the pupil's place is primary and that of teachers is secondary. As a result of its use, maximum interaction occurs between the pupils and the teacher. This develops their constructive capacities in accordance to their interests, attitudes, capacities, abilities, need and mental level of the pupils. Democratic strategies are objective. Hence, the genius pupils like them and gain advantages to the maximum. The following strategies are included in the democratic category of strategies.

1. Discussion

In discussion method, the teacher motivates the pupils to think over some problems by the way of questioning. After gaining motivation, the pupils answer certain questions of the teacher or respond in some or the other way. In this way, the teacher develops his lesson by discussions, answers and some responses of the pupils.

As the need arises, the teacher helps himself the pupils for solving the problem. As a result of this interactions, a change occurs in the attitude, feelings and motivation of the pupils along with the acquisition of knowledge. Hence, psychologically and sociologically, discussion is an appreciable method for social learning and development of the pupils.

Discussion is of two types—1. Formal, and 2. Informal. Formal discussion is adopted to gain pre-determined objectives. Hence, its principles are also pre-determined. It is essential to follow these principles in any condition.

In informal discussion, there is nothing like pre-determined, but oral actions and reactions and there is no need to follow any principle to participate in informal discussion. It is evident that the class-room discussion is an informal discussion.

2. Discovery

The discovery means to find out that object which has novelty. Hence, the discovery means to disclose a new fact. In other words, discovery is that method in which a new fact is searched out.

In the field of education, the discovery is termed as Problem Method. A teacher makes its use when he wants a pupil to be known as an original discoverer.

The discovery method is being used in all the dynamic schools and colleges of western countries like America, England and Russia. In India the progressive teachers use this method to make their teaching effective in science, mathematics, philosophy and other social sciences such as sociology, political science and economics etc. Both, pupils and the teachers have to work hard for the success of this method. Also its use needs time and money.

The discovery method is quite useful for the development of both pupils and the teachers. Its reason is that if we want to bring any change in our country's examination-centred education, that can be done by making use of this method. Hence, there must be some application of this method in some special situation.

3. Heurism

The word "heurism" has been derived from Greek word "Heurisco" which means "I discover". In this view, heurism or heuristic method is that method in which the pupils search out the knowledge themselves by keeping themselves physically and mentally active or they learn themselves.

In this method, the teacher creates such an environment that a problem arises before the pupil. All the pupils think about the problem, observe and in the end they conclude some result. In this way, all the pupils find out truth by their own way. In short, in this method the teacher—

1. creates problem before his pupils,
2. presents suitable material in order to solve the problem, and
3. as the need arises, provides necessary guidance so that they may search out new knowledge by solving the problem as a result of making use of books, devices and other resources of his choice.

Armstrong developed inductive method for science subjects only by keeping in mind the basic principles of inductive method, but this method can also be used in teaching History, Geography, Mathematics and Grammar etc. The teaching order of the heuristic method can be divided into the following steps—

1. *Creation of Problem.* In this step, the teacher presents a problem to the pupils in such a way so that every pupils may come to know about that.

2. *Discovery of Facts.* In this step, the teacher presents various books, devices and necessary equipments in order to solve the problem. Not only this, he also guides them so that they may collect the problem-related facts.

3. *Formation of Hypothesis.* In this step, the pupils forms various hypothesis for solving the problem after collecting the facts.

4. *Testing of Hypothesis.* In this step, the pupils collect facts by experiments in favour of or against the hypothesis. In other words, they test the hypothesis by considering many false facts as the basis.

5. *Drawing Conclusion.* In this step, the pupil accepts only true hypothesis and leaves the false one. This conclusion is known as their discovered knowledge according to which the principles and laws are formulated.

Merits of Heurism or Heuristic Method

The following are the merits of heuristic method—

1. In this method, pupils realize the problem, think about it, observe it, test it and conclude about it. This creates scientific attitude in pupils. Hence, this method is a scientific method of teaching.
2. In heuristic method, pupils learn by doing themselves. Hence, it is a psychological method of teaching.
3. In heuristic method, in addition to the mental and reasoning powers, development of self-confidence and intellectual inter-dependence etc. also occurs gradually. This prepares them to solve any problem likely to arise in future life.
4. In heuristic method, the entire task is completed in laboratory. This solves the problems of home work automatically.
5. This method motivates pupils for doing more difficult tasks. This also avoids the hindrance of individual

differences in learning.

6. In this method, pupils work themselves and consult themselves. This coordinates their physical and mental powers.
7. This method does not allow the pupils for cramming of ready-made knowledge.
8. Many maxims of teaching are used in heuristic method. For the very same reason, great educationist like Rousseau has emphasized the use of this method in "Emile".

Demerits of Heurism or Heuristic Method

The following are the demerits of heuristic method—

1. Heuristic method is useful only for the pupils of higher classes and not for lower-class pupils. This method cannot be used in nursery and primary classes.
2. The modern culture and civilization has become so much complicated that every pupil acquire knowledge by doing research himself. The teacher has to provide its knowledge directly.
3. In higher classes too, this method can be used only by the talented pupils. The average or backward pupils get frustrated.
4. The knowledge of all the subjects of a curriculum cannot be imparted to the pupils for examinations by heuristic method. Hence, this method is not appropriate.
5. In searching out the knowledge by this method much time is consumed. Hence, it is impossible to search out the knowledge as a result of pupils' self-efforts for a period of thirty or forty minutes according to the school time-table.
6. While using this method, the teacher prepares everything before-hand which deprives the pupils of the opportunities of self-thinking. This also deprives them of the training of self-discussion.
7. Heuristic method is also not suitable for those classes in which the pupils are out-numbered.
8. For this method, special books, devices and trained teachers are needed. In the schools of poor countries these if not impossible, but are difficult indeed.

4. Project Strategy

W.H. Kilpatrick, an eminent American educationist was the main brain behind the project strategy. Kilpatrick was the favourite pupil of John Dewey. He was deeply influenced by John Dewey's pragmatism. They wished Education should enter the depth of real life.

They were provided with such an artificial education according to the individual difference of the pupils which resulted in their mental development but they got frustrated due to their failures in their practical life.

Hence, Kilpatrick indoctrinated a new teaching strategy on the basis of his teacher's pragmatic principles according to the interests, attitudes, capacities and abilities of the pupils in order to acquire practical knowledge. This system was called as project strategy.

Meaning of Project Strategy. That strategy is called a project strategy in which the pupils perform such constructive activities in natural conditions so that they may learn to lead best possible social life without any difficulty. The reality is that each activity in this strategy has necessarily one or the order objective. The plan is made according to the objective.

In order to complete the plan, a working system is devised. Then all the pupils evaluate the utility of the results for the society after completing the task in natural conditions according to their interests, attitudes, capacities and abilities.

Thus, the project strategy is such a plan which is used to complete some other plan. For this, the teacher creates some problem before the pupils. Then, all the pupils acquire knowledge in different subject according to their interest in a natural way.

Definition of Project Strategy. Some definitions are given below in order to clarify the meaning of project strategy.

Kilpatrick: "A project is a whole-hearted purposeful activity processing in a social environment."

Thomas and Lang: "Project is a voluntarily undertaking which involves constructive effort or thought and eventuates into objectives results."

Prof. Stevenson: "A problem is a problematic act carried to completion in its natural selection."

Types of Project

Projects are of the following two types—

1. *Individual Project:* Individual projects are such projects which every pupil completes in his own way. By completing them, social qualities do not develop in the pupils.

2. *Social Projects:* Social projects are those projects which are completed by the students of a class collectively. Such projects develop feelings of citizenship and sociability in the pupils.

According to W.H. Kilpatrick, projects are of following four types—

1. *Constructive Projects.* In constructive projects, the nature of the work is physical, such as—letter writing, digging of a well, making models and playing a drama etc.

2. *Aesthetic Projects.* In aesthetic projects, some artistic or aesthetic feeling is aroused, such as—presenting a music programme, recitation of poems etc.

3. *Problematic Projects.* In problematic projects, some intellectual problem is solved, such as—why tide occurs in a sea?, why it rains? etc.

4. *Drill Projects.* In drill projects, the working efficiency and capacity of the pupils are increased such as—drawing a map and a sketch.

According to some other scholars, the projects are of the following two types:

1. *Simple Projects.* In simple projects, only one activity at a time is given for completion, such as—to produce a one-act play, compiling the collection of poems etc. Since, only one task is given to the pupils for completion, they acquire knowledge in one field only.

2. *Complex Projects.* These are such projects in which more than one activities are to be carried on for their completion, such as—constructing a house, sending a parcel etc. Since, various activities are unified in these projects, pupils acquire the knowledge of various aspects of the projects.

Principle Underlying Project Strategy

Project strategy is based on the following principles:

1. *Principle of Purposiveness.* According to this principle, there must be some objective of the project. Its reason is that the pupils do that work with more enthusiasm which have definite and clear objectives.

2. *Principle of Utility.* According to this project, the project must possess the quality of utility. It is because the pupils do the work with more interest which are useful for them.

3. *Principle of Reality.* According to this principle, the project should be real. Only then, the pupils would be able to complete it naturally and in real conditions.

4. *Principle of Activity.* According to this principle, the project should be activity-centred. Its reason is that the knowledge gained as a result of activity is stable and useful.

5. *Principle of Freedom.* According to this principle, the pupils are free to select the project. They select the project according to their will and they execute it with the advice of the teachers.

6. *Principle of Social Development.* According to this principle, the project should be such that the social development of the pupils may occur by social attributes and social contacts.

Essential Steps of Project Strategy

Following are the steps of project strategy—

1. *Creating the Situation.* To create the situations by the teacher is the first step of project strategy. In this step, it is the pupils themselves who put up the proposals regarding some problems and not the teacher. Since, the pupils cannot define a problem completely themselves after selecting the problem. Therefore, the teacher must guide them.

In this connection, the teacher should create such a condition by mutual conversation so that it may create interest in the pupils for solving daily life problems. In short, as a first step of project strategy, a teacher encourages the pupils to such an extent that they put a proposal themselves, regarding some problems, before the teacher.

2. *Choosing the Project:* To choose a project is the second step of project strategy. Since all the projects, chosen by the pupils, cannot be accepted. In such a situation, the teacher helps the pupils in choosing such a project which meets their real needs. Hence, the teacher initiates discussion in the class. Take care that the teacher should participate in the discussion

with such an efficiency and skill that the proposed projects and plans may be made clearer to the pupils.

They should be prepared to choose those projects, after evaluating their merits and demerits, which carry some social and real value. In this regard, Kilpatrick says, "The part of the pupils and the part of the teachers in most of the school work depend on largely as who does the proposing. It is practically the whole thing."

3. *Planning*. Planning is the third step of project strategy. After choosing the project, teacher prepares the programme for accomplishing that project from the pupils themselves. It is not an easy job.

Hence, the programme should be prepared in such a way that it can be completed in natural conditions. From this point of view, the teacher should create such an environment that each pupil can express his opinion with freedom regarding the programme when the debate is over, the teacher should write the programme on black-board.

Not only this, he should divide the programme in many parts and each pupil should be provided with some task immediately according to his interest, ability and capacity so that each pupil of the class may become curious to finish the project work.

4. *Execution of the Programme:* Execution of the programme is the fourth and important step of project strategy. Remember that when the task is distributed, then all pupils start doing their task happily. In other words, they are to collect the facts about many things by supervising and testing and then they are to write all those facts.

But, since learning by doing is more stable and effective than forced knowledge, the teacher should provide more opportunities for doing their task according to their speed. If need arises, the teacher should provide necessary help to the pupils while supervising the task.

5. *Judging or Evaluating the Project.* Judging the accomplished task is the fifth step of project strategy. In other words, the pupil decides whether the pre-determined objectives have been achieved or not.

All the pupils express their ideas with freedom, before the teacher and they tell about the drawbacks—1. Planning,

2. Selecting a project, and 3. Preparation of a programme and its execution regarding a project. All the above things are discussed collectively and the results are drawn. In short, all the pupils repeat the knowledge acquired by self-criticism.

6. *Recording*. Recording is the sixth and last step of project strategy. All the pupils keep their individual project book. In these project books, all the pupils write in detail about all the five steps of a project with the mention of consulted books, aids, detail of tasks provided to the pupils, the people contacted and the methods used to accomplish the project. Such type of recording conveys the pupils and the teachers about the amount of the task done and the balance of the task remained undone.

Practical Working of Project Strategy

Human life is full of projects. Since, the pupil gains a variety of experiences while solving his life's various problems in natural conditions with a practical approach in project strategy, therefore, not only learning by doing, but also learning by living is emphasized in this strategy.

C.W. Stone has tried to explain the principles and the working of project by mentioning a complex project of sending a parcel. With this example, the readers will understand easily that how the pupil acquire knowledge in a project strategy. According to this project, the pupils of fourth class acquire the knowledge of various subjects while registering a parcel through postal system for their far-off friends in the following way:

1. *Discussion*. Initially, the pupils decide to send a parcel to their far-off friends. Then they discuss mutually how that parcel should be sent. This involves logic and reasoning. As a result of this, their pronunciation gets corrected. Also, their thinking, reasoning, logic and decision-making powers get developed.

2. *History*. When the history-period starts, then all the pupils think that when and how a post-office came into existence. When, there were no such post-offices, then what the difficulties people used to face in sending their dak?

After establishing post-office, how the provision of the stamp was made and of what value the parcel is to be stamped? etc. After giving a thought to the above aspects, the pupils acquire the knowledge about the stamps and citizens of various countries very easily.

3. *Hand Work.* In the period of hand work, pupils make envelopes. This teaches them folding, cutting and pasting of the paper. Not only this, they also learn through conversation how the paper is made. What are the types of paper? And of what type of paper is used for making a parcel?

4. *Language.* In the period of language, the address of the receiver is written. This teaches the pupils writing of letters to their friends.

5. *Geography.* In the period of Geography, pupils look at the map where the parcel is to be sent. They also acquire the knowledge about the mode through which the parcel will be sent and the places which will come in its way. In short, the study of Geography provides the knowledge of various means, places and their distances.

6. *Arithmetic:* In the period of arithmetic, pupils weigh the parcels themselves and they put the stamps according to the weight of the parcel. From this they learn to keep the accounts of expenditure along with subtraction, multiplication and division etc.

7. *Excursion.* After preparing the parcel, pupils go to the post-office. This provides them the knowledge of standing in the queue, getting the weight of the parcel from parcel clerk and getting its receipt from parcel clerk as a token of its booking.

It is very much clear from the above description that the pupil acquires practical knowledge of various subjects while solving the real life's problems through this projects method.

Important Things about the Selection of a Project

The following points are to be kept in mind while selecting a project:

1. The project should have an academic value.
2. The essential materials should be arranged before starting or executing a project.
3. The materials to be used in a project should be cheaper.
4. A project should take so much time for its completion that it may not become an obstruction in the completion of curriculum.

Merits of Project Strategy

The merits of project strategy are as follows:

1. *According to the Laws of Learning.* The project strategy is based upon all the laws of learning. Remember that there are three laws of learning—*(a)* Law of Readiness, *(b)* Law of Exercise and *(c)* Law of Effect.

According to law of readiness, the pupils are made ready before starting the lesson in this project strategy. This law is used especially in the second phase of the project.

According to the law of exercise, the conditions are created to practise the acquired knowledge for the pupils.

Lastly, according to the law of effect, the pupils feel satisfaction and enjoyment when they complete the project. This has pleasant effect upon them.

2. *Psychological.* In the project strategy—

   1. Teaching activities are made meaningful. This makes education effective.
   2. Teaching activities are purposeful. This increases curiosity for learning.
   3. The learning laws are used properly. This keeps the pupils happier.
   4. Various basic instincts of pupils like curiosity, construction, pugnacity and self-assertion are used.
   5. The inferiority complexes formed unconsciously in the pupils are removed. Hence, this strategy is psychological.

3. *Respect for Dignity of Labour.* The project strategy develops respect for dignity of labour among pupils. It is because in this strategy, all the pupils have to work physically along with mental work. By doing with their own hands, they don't consider it as their result. This arouses the feeling of importance of handicraft among the pupils and they meet the labourers with respect in their daily life.

4. *Related with Real Life.* A relationship of school with the real life gets established by this project strategy. This makes education meaningful and purposeful. All the pupils solve the real life's problems practically. Pupils use this new knowledge in the new situations of future life and spend a successful social and enjoyable life.

5. *Connection between Life and Work.* In the project strategy, while working in natural conditions and working in reality, a

relationship of pupils life is established with the task.

Hence, the pupils do their respective tasks with interest. This, on one side, provides knowledge of various subjects in a play-way manner, they become efficient in doing every responsible task of the life on the other side.

6. *Training for Democratic Way of Life.* The project strategy is a democratic way of learning. Its use involves all the pupils to think and work collectively to complete a project. This develops the social values like cooperation, politeness, sympathy, tolerance and social service on one hand and makes them aware about their rights and duties on the other hand very conveniently. In short, project strategy prepares the pupils to live democratically.

7. *Correct Use of Time.* In the project strategy, the selection of a project and the preparation in its outline is carried out by the pupils themselves. They understand it properly that it is their personal project. Hence, they work hard with involvement in order to complete it. They learn to utilize the time properly from this strategy.

8. *Economical.* By the project method, the pupil acquires only that knowledge which is required in his present and future life. He acquires such knowledge in a very short time. In this way, this strategy includes the characteristic of being economical.

9. *Helpful in Character Building.* The project-strategy causes an all-round development of the pupils. Its use develops the various attributes like self-dependence and self-confidence among the pupils. As it is the collective responsibility of all the pupils to complete the project, therefore, they become resourceful, efficient and perfect in making decisions.

10. *Facility for Correlation.* The pupil is considered more important than a teacher in the project strategy. Also, the pupils are not to study all the subjects of the curriculum side by side. Since, all the subjects are correlated with this project through activity, therefore, all the subjects get correlated with each other in a natural manner. In short, the unity of the lesson increases through this project strategy and all the pupils acquire knowledge through activity as a complete unit.

11. *A Source of Bliss for the Retarded.* Project strategy is a source of bliss for the retarded pupils. Psychological research has provided that some pupils lag behind in their class-room

tasks with regard to intellectual achievements or due to some other reasons.

Such backward pupils either become problem-students or inferiority complexes develop in their unconscious mind. Since the project strategy provides opportunities for all pupils to work collectively in a group, this strategy is a source of peace and pleasure for these backward pupils.

Demerits of Project Strategy

Following are the demerits of project strategy:

1. *Teaching Haphazard and Discontinuous:* The project strategy can not provide knowledge of all the subjects of the curriculum to the pupils. Actually, the objective of education is to cause an all-round development of the pupil. A project with a limited scope being used in the school can not help in achieving this great objectives.

Not only this, there are still some topics which can not be taught through any project. Hence, in project strategy teaching becomes haphazard and discontinuous. In such a situation, there should be a provision for a systematic study of all the subjects along with use of project strategy.

2. *More Handwork But Literary Aspect Neglected.* According to some people, it is the main defect of project strategy that its use neglects literacy aspect. Hence, according to them, there should be a separate provision in the school for literary education.

3. *Balanced Learning of all Students not Possible.* In the project strategy, clever pupils often lead other students while doing the project work. This makes the retarded pupils passive and they imitate them blindly. Not only this, the specific tasks are assigned to the main students also. This leads to the disinterest of all the pupils in completing the project. Hence, the teacher should encourage all the pupils to participate in the conversation and he should motivate them to do the tasks according to their abilities.

4. *Selection of Suitable Project Difficult.* Some scholars believe that the selection of a project, if not impossible, but is difficult for young students. Its reason is that the views which pupils present before the teacher are not alike. But this demerit does not belong to the project-strategy. Its responsibility goes on to the teacher. The teacher should guide the pupils at every step of the project with patience, tolerance and intelligence.

5. *School Teaching Disorganised and Irregular.* Some educationists are of the opinion that education can not be provided with this project-strategy according to the time table, because the project needs freedom and flexibility. Both these requirements disturb the school programme. In other words, pupils cannot be provided with education in accordance to the prescribed curriculum. The only remedy to avoid this demerit is that the first four hour of the school should be given to the classroom study and the rest four hours to the project strategy.

6. *Encouragement of Indiscipline.* In the project-strategy, freedom and responsibility are emphasized. It is often observed that the students of the school misuse their freedom and try to escape from their responsibilities. This encourages indiscipline.

7. *Difficulty of Text Books.* Its defect is also accounted for its need of some special text-books, but in market, books are available which are written for traditional schools only. Efforts of teachers can eliminate this defect too.

8. *Costly Method.* According to some people, the major defect of this project method is its cost. It is a costly method. It needs costly books, apparatus or devices and some other materials. Hence, this method can not be used in poor countries and normal schools. These people, perhaps, forget that such projects should be completed in natural environment. Hence, this needs only local materials. If we make provisions of education through productive projects, then this project strategy will become not only self-supporting, but also profitable.

9. *Difficulty of Examinations.* While using the project-strategy, it is very difficult to examine the pupils. If education is to be provided through this strategy, then we shall have to change examination system which is impossible.

10. *Change of School Difficulty.* It is the opinion of the scholars that if a pupil transfers from a school offering project-strategy to a non-project strategy school, then the adjustment of that pupil if not impossible, will become very difficult. Remember that such incidents take place in the beginning only, later on these eliminate.

5. Brain Storming Strategy

Brain storming is a democratic strategy. This method is based on the principle that the pupils can be provided with more and more knowledge through interaction. Hence, while using this strategy, such means are used which create movement in the minds of the pupils of the class for mutual consultation, logic or reasoning and discussion in order to solve some problems. It is evident that brain-storming is a problem-centred method.

A teacher assigns some problems to all the pupils while using it. All the pupils think over the problem independently, they arrange a debate and express their respective views frankly. It makes no difference whether these views are meaningful or not.

The teacher writes pupils' views on black-board. At last, that movement comes when the problems get solved. In this way, when the brain-storming method increases the knowledge of pupils, it also encourages them to think collectively sitting in a group.

It is the view of the experts that the pupil's group can present more valuable ideas than a teacher. Hence, the teacher must use brain-storming method time-to-time so that the attributes like self-confidence, originality, farsightedness and creativity etc. may develop in the pupils and they can lead a successful life in a democratic age.

With this method, cognitive aspect of the pupils can be developed very easily. Also their objective domain can be made stronger.

6. Role Playing Strategy

Role playing is that strategy in which four or five pupils of the class or a small group of pupils is allowed to imitate the experiences of others. The pupils express their views in a natural manner through the various roles.

Hence, role playing is a formal method in which pupils are assigned roles without any practice and the pupils play those roles happily in the class.

It is to be cared that through the use of role playing method, recreation of the pupils takes place on one hand and expression of their emotions takes place on the other hand.

As a result of it, their attitudes develop in a natural way. In the teaching of subjects like civics, history, literature and science etc., by using this method successfully, the cognitive objectives can be achieved.

7. Strategy of Independent Study

In the past years, it was the firm belief of educationists that through the traditional teaching methods and techniques, the natural development of the pupils was not possible by forceful inculcation of knowledge into the brains of the pupils. Hence, a new method got developed which is termed as independent study or self-study. It is not essential that the teacher must be present in the class while using this method and the teaching task should be organized regularly.

Actually, this method is pupil-centred method. It is expected from the teacher while using this method that he should create so much capacity in the pupils so that they may carry on their self-study or they may solve the problem as a result of independent study.

While using independent study method, pupils either study individually or they do self-study in small groups. They do their task independently by preparing the outline of their study themselves. In the modern age, the independent study method is gaining success in various forms.

The pupils take interest in their respective tasks on one side while they solve any problem without any difficulty on the other hand by using this method. This creates self-confidence among them.

In the independent study method, the teacher acts like a guide only. Hence, it is essential for a teacher that he should provide opportunities of independent study in a systematic way.

8. Sensitivity Training Strategy

A sensitivity training method is that method by which mutual relations of the pupils are developed and they are made sensitive in respect of some problem. In other words, in this teaching method, by awakening the sensitivity among the pupils, their ego is awakened. As a result of which, they get motivated for solving the problem with their full energy.

This method is used for training the small groups of the pupils. Such group meets once a week or thrice a month at the most. A programme of participating all the pupils of the group in the debate is determined. Teacher does not participate in the debate. But he guides the pupils, as the need arises, keeping in view the activities of the group. Hence, the use of this method has many advantages, which are as follows:

1. The pupils' behaviour can be analysed easily.
2. The social capabilities of the pupils can be developed.
3. The tolerance and adjustment capability among the pupils can be developed.
4. By appreciating the pupils, they can be motivated for doing a task.
5. The behaviour efficiency of the pupils can be enhanced.
6. A diagnostic understanding takes place as a result of interaction between the pupils and a teacher.
7. By mutual consultations of the pupils the problem can be solved conveniently.

9. Recapitulation Strategy

Recapitulation means repetition. Hence, the objective of this method is the repetition or recapitulation of the lesson. Remember that the lesson is recapitulated in order to consolidate the new knowledge, taught to the pupils in their minds. It is remarkable that while using this technique, the teacher does not re-teach the lesson.

He gives such tasks to the pupils or asks such questions with which the recapitulation of the lesson becomes easy.

This recapitulation has so many advantages. First, the revision of the lesson takes place. Second, it becomes easy to know about the limit to which the pupil has acquired new knowledge. Third, it becomes also clear the parts which a pupil could not understand or what a teacher should teach again. Fourth, how a teacher is successful in achieving his teaching objectives. Hence, recapitulation repeats the lesson on one hand and it tells how much the teaching is successful on the other hand.

10. Drill Work Strategy

The meaning of drill work is to apply the learnt tasks or skills or to read material in novel situations. Drill work tells the teacher whether the teaching objective has been achieved or not. In other words, the knowledge gained by drill work gets consolidated. In short, the pupils perform drill of acquired knowledge and the teachers supervise their tasks or methods of doing so. He rectifies their errors and provides personal assistance to them.

While performing drill, the teacher should keep certain precautions in his mind. For example, first, the teacher should start drill of that content only which all the pupils have learnt by heart. Otherwise, they will take this drill as merely a burden. Second, the drill work should go only for that duration till the pupils enjoy it, otherwise it becomes mechanical for them.

Third, the specific and difficult points of the learnt knowledge or skill of a lesson should be emphasized specifically. Fourth, drill work should be related to the actual life. The knowledge learnt from this relationship gets consolidated in the brains of the pupils.

Fifth, while performing drill work, if pupils commit certain errors, the teacher should rectify them by providing essential assistance. Sixth, the teacher should have patience while the drill work is being performed. The hurry-up tendency may cause erroneous drill or practice and faulty or bad habits among pupils.

11. Review Strategy

'Review' means to think over certain main points regarding teaching. For example, initially, which lesson should be considered more important and which one is less. Second, to see how many lessons have been taught and how many lessons left. Third, to see errors in teaching and how those errors can be rectified.

Fourth, what the important points were included in the lesson and the points which were missed. Lastly, what the points should be kept in mind so that the teaching objectives can be achieved.

After reviewing all the above points, a teacher succeeds in achieving the objectives of teaching on one hand, a feeling to criticize also develops in the pupils on the other hand.

Hence, the teacher and the pupil should both participate activity in reviewing. In short, the content gets consolidated in a systematised way in the brains of the pupils.

12. Assignment

Meaning of Assignment. The assignment means the task to be done at home by the pupils. It has already been mentioned that the main facts and questions of the lesson are repeated. Already learnt knowledge is repeated through drill. In review also, the content is got repeated in a new way.

Similarly, through home assignments, the acquired knowledge is made permanent. In short, in home assignment, the knowledge acquired in school is given to the pupils to read, write and learn by heart.

Importance of Assignment

In the teaching process, the home assignment is important in a special way. Its importance is as follows:

1. *Development of Self-Study Habit.* While doing the home assignments, the pupils have to write the answers of the questions themselves. Hence, they bring books of various subjects at home from the library to study them. This study of the books develops the habit of self-study among the pupils. As a result of this, attributes like self-confidence and self-reliance also develop among them.

2. *Motivate.* In class, pupils get hardly any opportunity to utilize the new knowledge. The home assignment provides maximum motivation to use the acquired knowledge.

3. *Encouragement to Self-Activity.* The pupils get opportunities to express their views by self-activity. This develops their powers of expression.

4. *Time Saving.* The lesson given as home assignment does not require its re-teaching. This saves time.

5. *Guidance in Learning.* Properly planned assignment helps in guidance. The pupils and the teacher gain success in achieving educational objectives.

6. *Help in Fixation.* Psychological researches have proved that for fixation, not only school's environment but also home's environment should be academic. Otherwise, it would be impossible for the pupils to memorize the knowledge learnt in the class. As the home assignment provides special assistance in making the home environment academic, therefore some part related to the lesson must be given for memorization at home. This makes the acquired knowledge permanent.

Types of Assignment

The classification of home-assignments is done invariably. Some of these classifications are being given in the following lines:

1. *Study Type.* This assignment is too easy. In this, pupils are asked to prepare a note on some topic.

2. *Memorization Type.* It is such a home assignment in which the pupils try to cram the already read lesson, e.g., the pupils should be directed to learn any poem of the book by heart.

3. *Informative.* It is such a home assignment in which the pupil collects various types of information, such as, the pupils should be ordered to reply the following questions—

(*i*) What are the main industries of Saharanpur?

(*ii*) At what places the sugar mills are located in Meerut commissionary?

(*iii*) who founded Anup City?

4. *Problematic.* It is such an assignment in which the pupils search out the solution of some problems themselves.

According to another classification, the home assignments can be divided into two parts:

1. *Average.* It is that assignment which any student can attempt. In other words, average home work has to be done normally by each and every pupil.

2. *Achievement Level Type.* This type of assignment is given to the pupils according to the individual variations of the pupils. In other words, more problematic and sufficient home assignment is given to the pupils having sharp intelligence and simpler and limited home assignment is given to the mentally retarded pupils.

According to the third classification, the home assignment is divided into three parts:

1. *Unit Assignment.* It is that type of assignment in which pupils are assigned those activities in which pupils' real life needs are fulfilled.

2. *Problematic Assignment.* In this assignment, either a problem from the book or from the real life is given to the pupils for solving it.

3. *Practice Assignment.* In this assignment, pupils are made aware of their previous knowledge. In such assignments, pupils are given such questions, to which they are to write answers at home.

Characteristics of Good Assignment

The following are the characteristics of a good assignment:

1. *Motivative.* A good assignment motivates the pupils to acquire new knowledge. Hence, the home assignment should be such that the pupils, get motivated themselves for accomplishing that assignment. They should not take up it just to avoid punishment or to get some reward.

2. *Interesting:* A good assignment is according to the interests, attitudes and the natural tendencies of the pupils. Hence, while providing home assignments, the interests, capabilities and tendencies of the pupils must be looked after, otherwise they won't show full interest in completing that home assignment.

3. *Definite and Clear.* A good assignment is definite and clear. At the very first sight, it becomes clear to the pupils what they are to do and how much they are to do. Unless and until they get clear and definite idea of the home task, they do not like to do it. Hence, it must be made easy and clear to the pupils the home task given to the pupils.

4. *Stimulative.* A good assignment creates curiosity among the pupils. Under the influence of this curiosity, the pupils become active and they accomplish the assignment.

5. *Purposeful.* A good assignment has one or the other purpose: Purposeless assignment fails to make the pupils interested in doing that task.

6. *Relevant.* A good home task is related to the learnt lesson. Not only this, home task makes the main points permanent. From this angle, the home assignment should be useful and appropriate in the practical life of the pupils.

7. *Based on Individual Differences.* A good home task is based on individual differences. Hence, the intelligence quotient interest and aptitudes of the pupils should be considered while assigning the home task. If the home task will not be according to the mental level of the pupils, they will not be able to finish it. As a result, the objective of the home task will not be achieved. From this point of view, sharp-minded pupils should be assigned comparatively more complex and sufficient home task.

8. *Related with Previous Knowledge.* A good home task is related to the previous knowledge and experiences of the pupils. Remember, if the home task is not related to the previous knowledge of the pupils, they cannot acquire the new knowledge

conveniently. Hence, the pupil-teachers should be conscious about this.

9. *Accurate.* A good home task is accurate and real with regard to the language, subject and validity. Hence, all these things should be cared while framing the home assignment.

10. *Challenging.* A good home task is always challenging for a pupil. Hence, the achievement level of the pupil should be considered at the time of assigning the home task so that they can utilize their mental ability to the maximum.

11. *Economic.* A good home task is in short but the pupils gain much knowledge from this.

12. *Sequential.* A good home task is presented in graded manner from simple to complex. In other words, every home task should be related to each other. This helps in acquiring the new knowledge from the acquired knowledge.

13. *Related to Life.* A good home task is related to the real problems of the pupils' life. Hence, while assigning the home task, it should be cared that the home task must be related to the real life of the pupils, otherwise they won't like to finish it.

14. *Necessary Direction.* The teacher issues instructions to do a good home task. In other words, the teacher makes the pupils familiar with the possible difficulties so that they may not loose the heart.

15. *Time Factor.* In a good home task, time factor is kept in mind. Since the grown up pupils can work for a longer time as compared to the younger pupils. Therefore, the grown up pupils should be assigned with the home work of longer duration and the younger pupils should be assigned with the home work of shorter duration. From this view-point, the younger pupils should be given the interesting home tasks.

The pupils, aged 11 to 13 years, should be provided with the home task which can be finished in one and half an hour. Similarly, so much home task should be given to the pupils aged 13 to 16 years, which takes about 3 hours for its completion. It needs attention that the above planning can only succeed when the different teachers of different subjects mutually decide beforehand the amount of home task to be assigned to the pupils.

16. *Evaluation.* A good home task is evaluated properly. Hence, the teacher should evaluate that task which the pupils

do at home and their mistakes are removed. Hence, they move gradually towards correctness.

Precautions in the Planning of Assignments

It is often observed that the different subject-teachers assign so much home task of their respective subjects to the pupils that they are unable to finish that home task. This encourages the bad habits of copying, telling a lie and bluffing among them. Sometimes, they lose their interest in a particular subject as a result of home task's burden and its resultant frustration.

Consequently, they cease their schooling and if they go to school, they remain absent from the class. Therefore, some educationists oppose home task. But, since the home task is a connecting link between the teachers and the parents with which the pupils plan their future for their progress by learning that home task by heart. Therefore, education is incomplete without home task.

Accordingly home assignments cannot be neglected in any way. But, if we want to protect the pupils from the adverse effects of home assignment, we shall have to plan the home assignments properly by controlling them properly. Hence, the teachers, especially pupil-teachers should keep in mind the following precautions:

1. *Based on Previous Knowledge.* The home task should be selected on the basis of pupils' previous knowledge. In other words, the home task should be related to that lesson which the pupils already have studied in the class. This facilitates the pupils for completion of the home task without anybody's help.

2. *Stimulating.* The home task should be such that the curiosity of the pupils may get aroused and they become themselves active for completing their home task.

3. *Interesting.* While planning home task, the interests, attitudes and natural tendencies of the pupils should be looked after. In other words, the home task should not be similar for all the pupils.

4. *Motivative.* The home assignment should be motivative. This motivates the pupils for its completion.

5. *Definite and Lucid.* The home task should be definite and lucid. This makes the pupils aware of what and how much they are to do.

6. *From Simple to Complex.* While planning the home task, a teaching maxim 'from simple to complex' should be used. In other words, the pupils should be given first easy task and then he should advance towards difficult tasks. In short, the home task should be given while progressing from simple to complex.

7. *Integrated.* The home assignments should be coordinated. Hence, one home task should be closely related to the other home task.

8. *Utility.* In the home task, the content should be focussed which is useful and essential for pupils, otherwise they will not complete it considering as useless.

9. *Variety.* The home assignment should have variety. It is because the pupil feels boredom by doing one type of home task.

10. *According to Difficulty Level.* The home assignment should be planned according to the difficulty level of the pupils. If this is not followed, the pupils will lose interest in finishing it.

Bloom's Mastery Learning Strategy

If it is clear from the name, this strategy was developed by B.S. Bloom. With this strategy, mastery learning is developed. This strategy includes reinforcement technique, remedial and individual learning errors. For example, an extra time is provided to a pupil weak in some subject. In this strategy, the following steps are followed—

1. First of all, the teaching content is divided into learning units.
2. In every learning unit, the instructional objectives are identified or it is determined that what objective is to be achieved in which learning unit.
3. Level of mastery is determined keeping in view each learning unit and objective. To achieve this level, 80 to 85% marks are to be secured.
4. After this, the teaching task of every teaching unit is done in normal class-room teaching. Such teaching occurs in a group. This step is just like traditional teaching.
5. In this step, performance test is given. Then, it is observed whether the pupil has achieved mastery level

or not. Those pupils who do not achieve this, they are given diagnostic tests. This informs about the difficulties of the pupils.

6. On the basis of step No. 5, remedial instructions for the pupils are arranged. It also includes the extra time for study. Suggestions for books are also given and tutorial classes are also organised. After this, re-testing is again done.
7. After remedial teaching and instructions, the pupils are given performance test. Then the gradation of the pupils is done.

If we differentiate traditional teaching and mastery learning strategy, we will observe that the traditional teaching emphasizes the presentation of the content only while in mastery learning strategy, the weakness of the pupils are focussed and their elimination is tried.

QUESTIONS FOR ANSWER

1. Define the term 'Teaching Strategies' and explain with examples any three important Teaching Strategies.
2. 'Teaching Strategies help the teacher in organizing effective teaching". Justify this statement.
3. Define and distinguish between Autocratic and Democratic Teaching Strategies.
4. Write short notes on:
   (*a*) Difference between Teaching Method and Teaching Strategy.
   (*b*) Characteristics of Good Assignment.
   (*c*) Bloom's Mastery Learning Strategy.
   (*d*) Practical Working of Project Strategy.
5. Write a brief note on various types of Democratic Teaching Strategies.

7

Teaching Models

Meaning and Definition

Teaching models act as the basis for the indoctrination of teaching theories and, thus, considered as hypothesis for teaching theories, therefore, teaching model contribute to make the teaching effective and interesting because development of teaching models is brought about by keeping in view the learning theories so that the teaching theories may be indoctrinated by using these learning theories. In this way, the teaching models are the basis and the first step for the indoctrination of the theory of teaching. In every model, such situations are created in which an interaction of pupils occurs causing the achievement of the objective by bringing about changes in the behaviour. It is to be observed that in each teaching model, a comprehensive and specific outline of teaching is prepared. Its principles are based upon the verified results. In teaching models, the following six activities are included:

(i) To give practical shape to the learning achievement.

(ii) To select stimulus so that pupil may give expected response.

(iii) To specify such situations in which the response of the pupils may be seen.

(iv) To determines such criterion behaviours so that the performance of the pupils may be seen.

(v) To specify the specific teaching strategies for achieving the desirable educational objectives by analysing the

interaction in the class-room situations.

(vi) To modify the teaching strategies and tactics if the expected changes in the behaviour do not occur.

According to Joyce and Weil, "A Model of teaching is a plan or pattern that can be used to shape curriculum (long term courses of study), to design instructional materials, and to guide instruction in the classroom and other settings."

According to Hyman, model is a way to thinking. According to him, "The model is a way to talk and think about instruction in which certain facts may be organized, classified and interpreted."

Again, according to Joyce and Weil, "Teaching models are just instructional designs. They describe the process of specifying and producing particular environmental situations which cause the student to interact in such a way that specific change occurs in his behaviour."

Main Features of Teaching Models

Mr. Bruce R. Joyce emphasising the importance of teaching models says, "School Facilities and individual teachers create life in schools by models they choose and create." The main feature of teaching model is that they bring about the qualitative development of teacher's personality. Fundamental characteristics of these teaching models are as follows:

1. *Some Assumptions.* Each teaching model has certain basic elements which are kept in mind while these models are developed. These basic elements—*(a)* Creation of appropriate environment for learning, *(b)* Occurrence of an interaction between a teacher and the pupils, *(c)* Using proper teaching strategies and tactics for making the teaching easy, clear and understandable. Remember that each teaching model acts as an outline for creating the environment.

2. *Presenting Appropriate Experiences.* The second characteristic of a teaching model is that it provides proper experiences to both, teacher and the pupil. Remember that selecting the content and presenting it for learning before the pupils is the main problem of teaching. This difficulty is verified when a teacher presents appropriate experience before the students.

3. *Answer to Fundamental Questions.* The third characteristic of a teaching model is that it provides answer to all the

fundamental questions. For example—*(a)* How a teacher behaves?, *(b)* Why he does like this?, and *(c)* What would be effects of his such behaviour on the pupils? In short, in every teaching model, answers to all the fundamental questions pertaining to the behaviours of teacher and pupils are received.

4. *Based on Individual Differences.* The fourth characteristics of a teaching model is that it is constructed on the basic of individual differences and according to various assumptions. For this reason, we see that some teachers formulating different models of teaching under the influence of their own philosophies of life. Under this influence, they either give importance to rote memory or to the clarification of concepts.

5. *Use of Student's Interest.* The fifth characteristic of teaching model is to use the student's interest. Herbart's five-step pattern is still an importance base of teaching because its all the five points look after the interests of the pupils.

6. *Influenced by Philosophy.* The sixth characteristic of a teaching model is that each teaching model is influenced by the philosophy of life. We often observe that a teacher constructs a teaching model to change the behaviour of the pupils according to the philosophy of which he is a follower. For example, an idealistic teacher develops the pupil as an idealist and a pragmatist teacher develops a pupils as pragmatist and for this, teachers develop the teaching models according to their philosophies.

7. *Maxims of Teaching.* The seventh characteristic of a teaching model is that the basis of a teaching model is the maxim of teaching. In other words, the maxim of teaching functions as the foundation in each teaching model and these maxims develop those powers which help in organizing the personalities of the pupils. The readers are requested to read the sixth unit of this book to gain the proper knowledge of maxims of teaching.

8. *Practice and Concentration.* The eight characteristic of a teaching model is that the development of a teaching model takes place as a result of continuous practice and study. Hence, its base is thinking. The development of a teaching model is possible only when the assumptions are made clear by thinking and necessary use of the problem.

9. *Development of Human Ability.* The ninth characteristic of

a teaching model is that it helps in developing the human abilities. Also, it increases the teacher's social competency.

10. *Teaching as an Art.* Its tenth characteristic is that the teaching is known as an art. A teaching model encourages the art of teaching.

Four Fundamental Elements of Teaching Models

1. *Focus.* Every teaching model has one or the other objective which is called its focal point. A teaching model is developed by keeping in mind this focal point. In other words, the focus of a teaching model is that for which a teaching model is developed. Remember that the model has various phases. Hence, for this, some particular types of competencies are developed.

2. *Syntax.* The syntax of teaching model means those points which produce activities focussed on educational objectives at various phases. In this way, under syntax, the teaching tactics, teaching activities and interaction between a pupil and the teacher are determined in such a sequence that the teaching objectives are achieved conveniently by producing desirable situations.

3. *Social System.* A social system is according to the focus of a teaching model. Since every teaching model has separate objective, therefore, every teaching model will have separate social system. The real situation is that the every class is a society which must has some system or administration. This system is made by the pupil, teacher and the curriculum. The society makes this system active by educational interaction so that the behaviour of the pupils may experience desirable changes. In this way, under the social system, the activities of pupils and the teacher and their mutual relationships are discussed. Hence, the social system occupies an important place in making the teaching impressive.

4. *Support System.* In this support system, it is evaluated by oral or written examination, whether the teaching objective has been achieved or not. In other words, teaching was successful or not. On the basis of this success or failure, a clear idea is achieved regarding the effectiveness of those strategies, tactics and techniques which were used during teaching. Remember that since each teaching model has a separate focus, therefore,

the support system for every teaching model would also be separate.

Classification of Teaching Models

Teaching models are of three types:

1. Philosophical Teaching Models

Israel Saffler had mentioned following types of philosophical teaching models—

(a) The Impression Model of Teaching. It is a common assumption that at the time of birth, the child's brain is blank or empty. Whatever experiences are provided through teaching they go on learning the impressions on the child's brain. These impressions are termed as learning. In this process, the feelings of the sense organs and principles of language are given more importance. The success and effectiveness of entire teaching process depends upon the teacher's ability and capability to communicate.

(b) Insight Model. The developer of this model was Plato. His belief was that the knowledge cannot be provided merely by speaking the words or by merely, listening them. Mental processes and language both work together. This model is an answer to the impression model. This insight model discards the assumption of impression model that the meaning of a teaching model is merely to deliver the knowledge or ideas through teaching to the mental domains of the pupils. It is the belief of insight model that the knowledge cannot be provided merely through the expressions of sense organs, but knowledge of the content is also essential for this.

(c) The Rule Model. Kant gives importance to logic power. In logic, certain rules are followed. The main function of education is to develop the character. The objective of rule model is to develop the capacities of the pupils. The impression model and insight model have their own limitations. Their drawbacks have been removed by the rule model. In this model, more importance is given to the logic power.

For this function, some particular rules are followed, such as planning of teaching, organization and interaction occur under specific rules. Cultural and moral values are developed with this model.

2. Psychological Models of Teaching

It is the assumption of psychologists that the teaching models can acquire the place of teaching theories. In short, it can be stated that the teaching models are the primitive form of teaching theories. In the psychological teaching models, the relationship of teaching objectives and teaching-learning activities are explained. John P. Dececco has given the following psychological teaching models:

(a) A Basic Teaching Model. This model was developed by Robert Glaser. He has used psychological laws and principles in this model. This model has the following elements:

(i) Instructional Objectives.
(ii) Entering Behaviour.
(iii) Instructional Procedure.
(iv) Performance Assessment.

(i) Instructional Objectives. These objectives mean those activities which a teacher has to do before teaching. In other words, the objectives of teacher and pupils are called instructional objectives. This process is also known as task description. By this element, we can differentiate the objectives of schools, teachers and pupils.

(ii) Entering Behaviour. Entering behaviours mean those abilities or behaviours of the pupils which are necessary for the understanding of contents. In simple words, in order to acquire the level according to teacher's expectations, in future, the present level of pupils' knowledge and skills is the entering behaviour. Entering behaviour exists where the instructions start.

(iii) Instructional Procedure. This element means those teaching activities which are used for the presentation of the contents. Instructional process is known as the practical aspect of teaching. In this aspect, various methods, techniques, strategies etc. are used.

(iv) Performance Assessment. This step means those tests on the basis of which a teacher takes decisions. He decides the limits upto which a pupil has acquired the efficiency in the contents.

In this step, performance may be measured by any method, but it should be valid, reliable, objective and efficient. Hence, the tests which are used in this step should be objective and efficient.

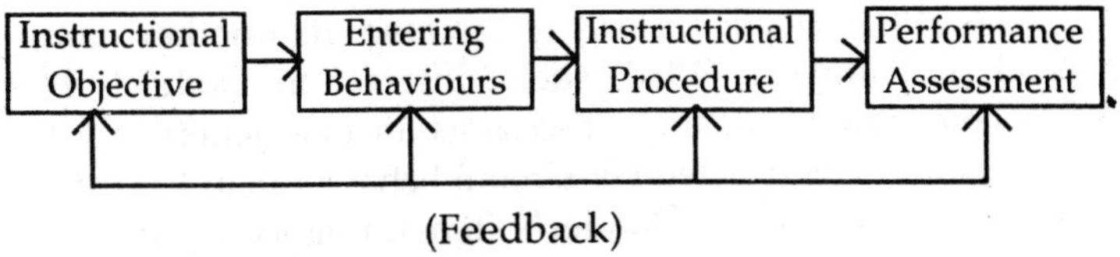

Glaser's Basic Teaching Model

(b) A Computer based Teaching Model. The teaching model was developed by Lowrence Stuloro and Daniel Davis in 1965. This is the most complicated model. This model has the following elements—

(i) Entering behaviour of the pupil.

(ii) Determination of Instructional objectives.

(iii) Teaching aspect—In this element, computer teaching is selected according to the entering behaviours of pupils and instructional objectives. The performances of the pupils are evaluated. If the evaluation is satisfactory, then another teaching plan is presented. In this model, the teaching and diagnosis go side by side. On the basis of diagnosis, remedial teaching is provided. In this model, individual differences are also given importance.

(c) A Teaching Model for School Learning. This model was developed by John Carol. His assumption was that the time according to the needs of the pupils are considered as important and essential component. This model has the following important elements—

(i) Definition of objectives in behavioural terms.

(ii) More importance to intelligence and performance or achievement in entering behaviours.

(iii) The level of instructions should be according to the pupils.

(iv) To provide appropriate time for learning according to the needs of the pupils.

(v) For achievement, the pupils should have mastery.

In this model, in the process of instruction, the pupils are provided with full opportunities. They are provided with time according to their needs in order to control the individual differences. Its main drawback is that the achievement tests cannot be administered in a systematic way.

(d) An Interaction Model of Teaching. Its another name is—Neel A. Flander's (1960) social interaction model-1. Flander has considered teaching process as an interaction process.

Flander has divided class-room behaviours in ten categories. It is also known as Flander's Ten Category System. In this model, the behaviours of teachers and pupils are analysed. This model has the following elements or aspects—

(i) Objectives or Focus—The nature of interaction between a teacher and pupils is determined.

(ii) Entering Behaviours—It includes pupil's feeling ideas and current information.

(iii) Presentation—Verbal interaction occurs between a teacher and pupils which extends to the indirect effect.

(iv) Evaluation—In this, the achievement or performance are evaluated by tests and the effectiveness of the interaction is decided.

It is evident in this model, an interaction between a teacher and the pupil is more emphasized. In this model, the analysis or observation of non-verbal interaction cannot be made. Another drawback of this model is that no decision can be taken regarding the contents in this model.

3. Modern Teaching Models

Bruce R. Joyce has divided all the teaching models, under the title "Modern Teaching Model", in the following four categories—

(a) Models based on Social Interaction Source.

(b) Models based on Information Processing Source.

(c) Models based on the Personal Source.

(d) Models based on Behaviour Modification as Source.

(a) Models based on the Social Interaction Source. In the models based on the social interaction source, the social aspects of human beings are kept in mind and their social development is more emphasised. As the human nature emphasizes the social relations more, therefore, its analysis comes under this teaching model.

Remember that the use of models based on the social interaction sources can be used successfully in democracy. The social interaction source includes the following four types of models—

(i) Group Investigation Model.
(ii) Juris Potential Model.
(iii) Social Inquiry Model.
(iv) Laboratory Method Model.

(b) Models based on Information Process Source. In the information process source, the pupils are provided with the knowledge of the facts and necessary informations. In these models, the solution of the problem and knowledge of stimuli are provided by creating effective environment.

These models have proved useful for developing intellectual competencies of the pupils. This information source includes the following six types of models:

(i) Concept Attainment Model.
(ii) Inductive Model.
(iii) Inquiry Training Model.
(iv) Biological Science Inquiry Model.
(v) Advanced Organizational Model.
(vi) Developmental Model.

(c) Models based on Personal Source: In the models based on personal source, the personal development is essentially emphasized. In such models, more emphasis is given to the development of internal and external powers of the pupils by developing their affective domain which facilitates the development of self-imagination and self-understanding.

The following five are the personal source dominated models—

(i) Non-directive Teaching Model.
(ii) Class-room Model.
(iii) Synatics Teaching Model.
(iv) Awareness Model.
(v) Conceptual System Model.

(d) Behavioural Modification Model. In these models, the desirable changes are emphasized with the help of reinforcement and learning activity in the behaviour of the pupils. The following model is included in the behavioural changes based models—

(i) Operant conditioning Model.

of Teaching Models

:ty of teaching models is as follows:

Classification of Teaching Models

Class	*Teaching Model*	*Innovator*	*Aims and Application*
1. The Social interaction source	*(i)* Group Investigation Model	*(i)* John Dewey *(ii)* Herbart	Development of democratic capacities, use of knowledge and skills in life, Dev. of person and Society.
	(ii) Juris Potential Model	*(i)* Donald Oliver *(ii)* James P. Shaver	Solution of problems on the basis of informations and Dev. of reasoning power.
	(iii) Social Inquiry Model	*(i)* Benjamin Cox *(ii)* Byron	Dev. of competencies of solving problems and adjustment.
	(iv) Laboratory Method Model	*(i)* Bethal *(ii)* Maine	Group Skills, Dev. of individual capacities and adjustment.
2. The Information Processing Source	*(i)* Concept Attainment Model	*(i)* J. Bruner	Dev. of Inductive reasoning.
	(ii) Inductive Model	*(ii)* Hilda Taba	Dev. of Mental inductive process and understanding of concepts and principles.
	(iii) Inquity Training Model	*(iii)* Richard Suchman	Dev. of individual competencies to achieve the social objectives.
	(iv) Biological Science Inquiry Moldel	*(iv)* Joseph J. Schwab	Understanding of research method, to think over social problems logically.

	(v) Advanced organizational Model	*(v)* David Asubel	To understand concepts and facts, to establish the relation in the knowledge and to make the content interesting and purposeful.
	(vi) Developmental Model	*(vi)* Jean Piaget	Dev. of general intelligence for the logic, social and moral development.
3. The Personal Source	*(i)* Non-directive Teaching Model	*(i)* Carl Rogers	Self-Learning by auto-instructions, self-research and development of self-understanding.
	(ii) Classroom Model	*(ii)* William Glasser	Dev. of skills of self-understanding and capacities of dutifulness.
	(iii) Synectics Teaching Model	*(iii)* William Gordon	Dev. of Creative competencies for problem solving.
	(iv) Awareness Model	*(iv)* W.S. Fietz	Dev. of individual competencies and mutual relations.
	(v) Conceptual System Model	(v) David. F. Hunt	To adjust in the environment by developing flexibility in the personality.
4. Behaviour Modification as a Source	*(i)* Operant Conditioning Model	*(i)* B.F. Skinner	To achieve the objectives of lower level of cognitive domain on the basis of individual differences.

(i) A teaching model helps in achieving some specific objectives.

(ii) The nature of a teaching model is practical. Also it makes possible to achieve learning.

(iii) Specification in the field of teaching is possible by a teaching model.

(iv) A teaching model helps in making the teaching more effective.

(v) A teaching model helps in selecting such stimulating situations which cause the desirable changes in the behaviour of the pupils.

(vi) Under a teaching model, such teaching strategies and tactics are used which help in fringing change in the behaviour of the pupils.

(vii) A teaching model can bring changes and rectifications in teaching.

(viii) A teaching model evaluates the behaviour of the pupils For this important task, it presents such a specific criterion with the help of which the changes in the pupils' behaviours can be easily evaluated.

QUESTIONS FOR ANSWER

1. Define 'Models of Teaching' and explain their fundamental characteristics.
2. Write a note on classification of Teaching Models.
3. Write a note on Philosophical and Psychological Forms of Teaching Models.
4. Write a note on Psychological and Modern Forms of Teaching Models.
5. Write short notes on the following:
   (a) Meaning and Definition of Teaching Models.
   (b) Four Fundamental Elements of Teaching Models.
   (c) Utility of Teaching Models.

8

Three Levels of Teaching

Teaching is a purposeful process which has close relationship with learning. Therefore, in the modern age, teaching-learning are accepted as one concept. Remember that the content has its own nature by which various learning levels can be effected with the acquisition of various teaching objectives. It is to be observed that a teacher can present the content at three levels, from thoughtless to thoughtful situations. These levels are—

1. Memory level,
2. Understanding level,
3. Reflective level.

It depends upon the teacher's competency that to what extent he succeeds in reaching upto reflective level starting from memory level on the basis of his efficiency and experiences. It is a common observation that the normal teaching corresponds to the memory level teaching. Such learned and efficient teachers who succeed in upgrading their teaching from memory level to reflective level-teaching are lacking.

Memory Level of Teaching

Meaning of Memory

Memory is a mental process which occurs essentially in some quantity in every living being. Actually, when a person sees some object, thing or place, then the engrams of the object, thing or a place are formed in his mind. To memorize these engrams or pre-learnt things is called memory. We recall these accumulated past experiences when required and we recognize them by bringing them into our conscious mind, then that is called memory.

Definition of Memory

Ideas of following scholars make clear the meaning of memory:

Woodworth—"Memory is the direct use of what is learned."

J.S. Ross—"A memory is a new experience determined by the dispositions laid down by a previous experience, the relation between the two being clearly apprehended."

Mcdougall—"Memory implies imagining of events as experienced in the past and recognizing them to one's own past experience."

Stout—"Memory is the ideal revival in which the objects of past experience reinstate as far as possible in the order and manner of the original occurrence."

Phases of Memory

The following are the phases of memory:

(i) Learning. Memory depends upon the engrams of experiences. Hence, the first phase of memory is the learning of some facts. Learning task is done by the conscious mind. In this phase, the life-experiences get engrammed in the brain in the form of mental impressions and these can be made conscious as and when needed. Hence, the pupils should acquire direct knowledge. Repeat it again and again. They should search out the meaning of that knowledge. Memorize that knowledge by linking it with other objects or subjects.

(ii) Retention. To make the contents permanent in the minds is called retention. Remember that the retention power occurs differently in the different individuals. A memory is said to be good if a person can retain something in his mind for a longer duration. The pupils and adolescents have more retention power as compared to the adults. It is for this reason that they memorize rapidly. In the opinion of psychologists, the retention power reaches at its peak at the age of 25 years and after this it starts reducing. Remember that the retention power depends mainly upon four conditions, which are—*(i)* brain, *(ii)* health, *(iii)* interest, and *(iv)* thinking.

Every experience learns impressions in the brain. Our brain not only protects these impressions, but also arranges them in a sequence. Retention power is also closely related to the structure of the brain. Due to the differences in the structure of the brain of every person, variations in the retention power occur.

Physical health is also deeply related to the retention power. Our nervous tissues function very conveniently when we have sound health. Consequently, we learn anything very easily. It is the reason that in the morning, i.e. with complete sound health, when we learn something, it gets memorized very rapidly. It is the only reason that our nervous tissues don't work properly when we have ill-health. Hence, our retention power lowers down.

Retention power is also related to the interest and thinking. We remember rapidly in which we have interest. Due to our interest, we think about that thing again and again and we establish relationship with other things resulting in our rapid learning.

(iii) Recall. The learnt experiences when brought to conscious mind is called recall. Recalling of past experiences is responsible for a person's good or bad memory. If he fails to recall when needed all goes in vain even in spite of his superb learning. When a person fails to recall the retained material, that enhances the chances of forgetting. Psychologists have emphasized on certain laws in order to bring learnt material at the conscious level. These laws are Law of Contiguity, Law of Similarity, Law of Contrast, Law of Continuity of Interest, Law of Primacy, Law of Recency, Law of Frequency, Law of Vividness.

(iv) Recognition. If we see an object or a person and we can say that we have seen before that object or a person is termed as recognition. In other words, recognition is that mental process by which we can tell, by coming in contact with an object or a person what a thing is, who is the person and when we were introduced? Remember that the recall and recognition have the similar relationship as that of brain and the body. Recalling becomes difficult when the association among objects does not occur and consequently we are unable to remember them. Contrary to this, we recognize them quickly when our

association among those objects and persons becomes strong.

Characteristics of Good Memory

Characteristics of good memory are as follows:

(i) Rapidity in Learning. The first characteristic of good characteristic is its rapidity and simplicity in learning. Hence, the memory of those pupils can be said as good who learn rapidly.

(ii) Stability of Retention. Another characteristic of good memory is retention of learnt material for a longer duration. The pupils are said to have a good memory if they retain for a longer time what they have learnt.

(iii) Rapidity in Recall. In addition to rapid learning and stability of retention, the third characteristic of good memory is rapidity in recall. Those pupils are said to have good memory who can bring anything to their conscious level very rapidly. Only those pupils are said to have good memory who can recall anything according to the needs and at proper time.

(iv) Serviceableness. The fourth characteristic of good memory is its score ability at some occasion. There are some pupils who possess much but when needed, they remember only irrelevant material. Contrary to this, there is no dearth of the pupils who bring only desirable at the conscious level. Only those pupils are said to have good memory who can recall the appropriate material according to the need.

(v) Forgetting Irrelevant Things. A good memory requires forgetting of irrelevant things. The recalling of irrelevant things at the time of examination does not benefit the pupils. Similarly, recalling the painful events of life struggle does not prove advantageous in any way.

Classification of Memory

Persons differ in ability to memorize. Some persons don't forget after a single reading. Contrary to this, people forget frequently even after repeated learning. On the basis of their different abilities memory can be classified as follows:

1. *Immediate Memory.* Immediate memory is that when a person recall immediately after learning something. This type of memory has the following two characteristics—*(a)* It is

temporary. It is possible that the learnt material may not retain for a longer period, *(b)* Its development occurs along with age. In an infancy period, the development of the pupil is slow and somewhat faster during childhood. During adolescence, this rate of development acquires its maximum limits.

2. *Personal Memory.* While recalling past experiences, we remember our personal past experiences.

3. *Permanent Memory.* The recalling of learnt material for a longer time is known as permanent memory. In other words, the things with which our association is strong, are remembered for a longer duration.

4. *Logical Memory.* To learn something by using intellect and its recalling when needed is called logical memory. Burgson has termed this memory as true memory.

5. *Rote Memory.* Rote memory is that memory in which the facts are crammed without any understanding. Such type of memory is very sharp during childhood. It is the reason that counting and tables etc. are crammed very rapidly. However, the memory is not considered as very good memory.

6. *Mechanical Memory.* Mechanical memory is also known as physical memory. When our body becomes habitual of doing any task repeatedly, then our body has no need to recall that task again and again. For example, a swimmer swims without any major recalling.

7. *Active Memory.* The recalling of past experiences needs some efforts, for example the candidates sitting in examination hall have to make efforts to recall the answer to the questions again and again.

8. *Passive Memory.* In passive memory, we recall the past experiences without any effort.

9. *Impressional Memory.* The recalling of the material learnt from the books and companions is called impersonal memory. There is no place of personal experiences in such types of memories.

Memory Level of Teaching

Remember that the memory level teaching is thoughtless. In this level of teaching, emphasis is laid on the presentation of facts and informations and its cramming. It is a matter of observation that the cramming of facts of the contents has no relation with intelligence. Its reason is that the mentally handicapped children can also cram. Yes, it is something else that if the content is purposeful, then it can be crammed very conveniently and also can be retained for a longer duration. Hence, memory level teaching lacks insight.

Almost all the pupils cram the contents unwillingly. They succeed in the school examination on the basis of scores secured by cramming but they seem to fail in the lengthy examination of the life. In short, memory level is the level of cramming.

In reality, there is a definite pattern of memory level teaching. In this type of teaching, the teacher is like a dictator who suppresses the independence, interests, attitudes and competencies of the pupils and tries to impose the facts and information upon the pupils. Hence, in this level of teaching, the teacher remains active but the pupils go on learning by heart in strict discipline as a passive listener. In short, no inter-action occur between the teacher and the pupils.

In the memory level teaching, signal learning, chain learning and stimulus-response learning are emphasized. In the end, both essay type and objective type examinations are used to evaluate the learnt contents. The above description shows that the memory level teaching is teacher-centred. Pupils have secondary place in this level of teaching. As a result, the teacher goes on imposing facts and information externally by keeping them in the strict discipline in order to develop the pupils mentally, neglecting their interest, attitudes, abilities and needs. This makes the pupils as crammers but they cannot be an intelligent learned person. The teaching of this level has the maximum level of motivation.

The evaluation of the acquired knowledge is done by traditional methods. In spite of many drawbacks, the memory level of teaching has some special importance. Its reason is that the teaching at understanding and reflective levels can be successful only when the teaching at memory level occurs. In other words, understanding and reflective level teaching cannot take place unless and until memory level teaching has not been managed.

Model of Memory Level of Teaching

Herbart is considered exponent of memory-level teaching. He has described the following steps while presenting the model of memory level teaching:

(a) Focus: According to Herbart, the focus of memory level teaching is the emphasis on cramming of facts and development of the following capacities—

(i) Training of mental aspects.
(ii) Providing knowledge of facts.
(iii) Retaining the learnt facts.
(iv) Recalling and re-presenting the learnt facts.

(b) Syntax: Herbart has divided the memory level-teaching into five steps which are known as Herbart's Five Formula Steps. By following these five steps, the teacher can create learning situations for memory-level teaching. The following is the sequence of Herbart's five steps—

(i) *(a)* Preparation,
(b) Statement of Aim.
(ii) Presentation.
(iii) Comparison of Association.
(iv) Generalizations.
(v) Application.

(i) (a) Preparation. Preparation is the first step of teaching method. In this step, some questions are asked to test the previous knowledge of pupils so that the curiosity to learn new knowledge may be aroused in them. In other words, in this step, the pupils are prepared to acquire new knowledge by testing their previous knowledge.

(b) Statement of Aim. This step is the part of the first step. Here the topic becomes clearer to the pupils and the teacher himself writes the topic on the black-board.

(ii) Presentation. In this step, the lesson is developed with the help of the pupils. In other words, by stimulating their mental activity, the pupils are provided with opportunities for self-learning. The teacher tries to derive most of the information from the pupils so that a relationship may be established between the new and the previous knowledge.

(iii) Comparison and Association. Herbart has named this step as association. Here, the mutual relationship is established among

facts, events and experiments by comparisons which clarifies the learning material in the minds of the pupils.

Hence, the teacher should establish a relationship between two subjects and between the facts and events of one subject and other facts and events of the same subject and make their comparison so that the new knowledge may be clarified and made permanent in the minds of the pupils.

(iv) Generalization. Herbart named this step as a system. After explaining the basic lesson, the pupils are given the opportunities to think in this lesson. After this, they formulate some such principles and laws which can be used in the future life situations.

(v) Application. It is the last step of teaching. In this step it is observed whether the new learnt knowledge can be used in new situations or not. This can be verified by the principle through questioning or he can provide new opportunities to make use of learnt knowledge. This makes the knowledge permanent and the laws can be verified.

(c) Social System: The process of teaching is social and professional. The members of this social system are—*(i)* pupil, and *(ii)* the teacher. At this level, the behaviour of the teacher is dominating based upon the dictatorial and authoritarian tendencies. As a result of this, the pupil functions as a passive listener.

Hence, the function of the teacher is—*(i)* presenting the contents, *(ii)* controlling the pupils' activities, and *(iii)* providing motivation to them. All the activities are performed by the teacher and the pupils follow considering them ideal.

(d) Support System: In the examination system of memory-level teaching, cramming is stressed. Hence, while evaluating the teaching of this level, both oral and written examinations are used. Remember that while the teaching of this level is evaluated, essay type examination is considered more useful, but the steps like recall and recognition are also used successfully through the objective type examination.

Guidelines for Memory Level of Teaching

Memory level teaching provides help to the teaching at understanding and reflective levels on one side while it provides basis for the success of these two. Hence, the following suggestions are being given to make the memory-level teaching effective—

(*i*) The teacher should try to achieve the cognitive objective.
(*ii*) The content to be presented should be purposeful.
(*iii*) The teaching points should be presented as a whole or in toto.
(*iv*) The content should be presented in a sequence.
(*v*) There should be no teaching when the pupils are tired.
(*vi*) Only whole-method should be used.
(*vii*) A definite reinforcement system should be used.
(*viii*) Recall should be grown through practice.
(*ix*) Recapitulation should be done in a rhythm.

Understanding Level of Teaching

Remember that in the understanding level of teaching, the teacher tries to present his instructions and stresses to make understand to the pupils the generalizations, principles and facts.

It results in turning the teaching thoughtful. In other words, in understanding-level teaching, the teacher tries to provide more and more opportunities to develop the intellectual behaviours of the pupils.

This develops the essential competencies for generalizations, insight and solving the problems. In this way, both pupils and teachers participate in developing the lesson while teaching occurs at the understanding level.

Model of Understanding Level of Teaching

The model of understanding-level teaching was indoctrinated by Morrison. Hence, it is named as Morrison's Teaching Model. Morrison has described the structure of this model in the following four steps—

(*a*) *Focus.* According to Morrison, the focus or objective of the understanding-level teaching model is that the pupil should achieve the mastery of the concept. In other words, the teacher stresses upon the mastery of the content so that a desirable change may occur in he personality of the pupils.

(*b*) *Syntax.* Morrison has divided the syntax of understanding-level teaching in to five steps and a teacher can create teaching and learning situations following them. The order of five steps of this model is as follows—

(i) *Exploration:* Morrison has included the following activities under this step—

(a) Previous knowledge testing by questioning.

(b) Analysing the contents, the elements are arranged in a logical sequence from psychological point of view.

(c) Determining how the units of contents or new knowledge should be presented.

(ii) *Presentation:* At this stage, the teacher remains more active. He performs the following activities for the presentation of the contents—

(a) The teacher presents the content in small units. Also, he tries to maintain the sequence of these units and a relationship with the pupils establishers.

(b) While presenting the contents, the teacher also diagnoses whether the contents have been understood by the pupils or not. If not, how many pupils could not acquire this understanding.

(c) The teacher recapitulates the contents till most of the pupils acquire the understanding.

(iii) *Assimilation:* After presenting the contents, the teacher reaches at the conclusion that most of the pupils have gained the new knowledge, he provides pupils opportunities for assimilation. It has the following characteristics—

(a) The pupils are provided with occasions for generalization through assimilation so that they get the mastery of the concept.

(b) Assimilation-opportunities are provided in order to stress upon the depth of the content.

(c) At the time of assimilation, every pupil studies in accordance with his requirement. Hence, the teacher should provide maximum opportunities of performing individual activities.

(d) In assimilation, the pupils work themselves in laboratories and libraries. Hence, home assignments are also given.

(e) In the assimilation period, supervised study occurs. During this period, both pupils and the teachers remain active. The pupils perform individual activities and the teachers guide them according to the need during supervision.

(*f*) During the assimilation period, the teacher tests whether the pupils have achieved mastery over the contents or not. If this does not happen, the teacher should provide re-opportunities for assimilation after observing precautions during supervision.

(*iv*) *Organization:* The period of assimilation is of mastery test. After succeeding in the mastery test, the pupils enter the period of organization or recitation according to the nature of contents. According to Morrison, during organization, the pupils are provided with the occasions for re-presentation. All the pupils write contents in their own language. From this, the teacher comes to the conclusion whether the pupils can write the contents without anybody's help or not. Hence, the pupils enter into recitation rather to the organization.

(*v*) *Recitation:* Recitation is the last step of understanding level teaching. During this period, the pupils present the contents orally before the teacher and his mates.

(*c*) *Social System.* In the understanding level of teaching, the various steps of social system go on changing. In presentation, the teacher controls the behaviour of the pupils like memory-level by keeping himself more active and he also provides necessary motivation. In assimilation-period, both pupils and the teacher remain active. The teacher imparts necessary instructions to the pupils they work themselves with full involvement.

(*d*) *Support System.* In uderstanding-level teaching, the support system does not remain static, but it goes on changing. The pupils have to pass the examination of presentation in order to perform experiment in assimilation. Similarly, they have to pass assimilation test essentially for their entry into organization and recitation. At the end of organization period, a written test takes place. Similarly, recitation is followed by an oral test. Hence, both oral and written tests (essay type and objective type) occur during the various steps of understanding-level of teaching.

Features of Teaching at Understanding Level

The following are the limitations and characteristics of understanding-level model given by Morrison—

(i) The main problem of this teaching system is its stress upon the mastery of the content. Human behaviour is over-looked.

(ii) Morrison has considered teacher's involvement in the content as motivation for the pupils, while psychological motivation can prove more effective.

(iii) Mastery of the contents restricts the development to the cognitive aspect only and it does not help in developing affective and psychomotor aspects.

(iv) Psychologically, this model of teaching given by Morrison is considered more effective.

(v) With the teaching model, a deep study of the contents can be carried out by the pupils. Hence, this model causes complete learning.

Guidelines for Understanding Level of Teaching

Morrison has provided the following suggestions to make the understanding level of teaching more effective:

(i) The pupils should be allowed to enter the understanding level of teaching unless and until they pass out the tests of memory-level teaching.

(ii) Every step of understanding level of teaching should be followed in a proper sequence.

(iii) The pupils should be promoted to the new step unless they pass the tests of previous stage. For example, pupils should be allowed to enter assimilation when they pass the tests of presentation.

(iv) The teacher should provide psychological motivation from time to time in spite of his involvement in the content. Also he should raise the aspiration level of the pupils.

(v) The teacher should make efforts for solving the problems related to understanding level of teaching.

Reflective Level of Teaching

Remember that the reflective-level teaching means 'problem-centred' teaching. In this, the class-room environment is open sufficiently. The teacher creates such a problem before the pupils which arouses so much mental tension in the pupils that they start solving their problems by formulating and testing their hypothesis as a result of their own motivation and activeness. At last, a time comes when the problem is solved. In short, the teaching of reflective level cooperates in developing creative capacities by providing pupils with the opportunities of developing intellectual behaviour.

The real situation is that the human life is a struggle. He has to do his best for achieving his aims of life. Sometimes, the achievement of the aims occurs, without any obstruction, in a natural way. But sometime, human beings have to face numerous obstacles in order to achieve his aims. From this point of view, the provision of the teaching of reflective level is essential for the pupils. It is this teaching level which develops the reflective power of the pupils. As this power develops when they grow up, they can solve their problems of iife by reasoning, logic and imagination and they can lead a successful and happy life. M.L. Bigge has rightly written about reflective level of teaching while clarifying it, "Reflective-level of teaching tends to develop the class-room atmosphere which is more alive and exciting, more critical and penetrating and more open to fresh and original thinking. Furthermore, the type of enquiry pursued by a reflective class tends to be more rigorous and work producing than pursued at an understanding learning situation."

Model of Reflective Level of Teaching

The credit goes to Hunt for developing reflective level of teaching. Therefore, this teaching model is named as Hunt's Model of Teaching. Hunt has described the structure of reflective level model in the following steps—

(a) Focus. The reflective level of teaching has the following three objectives—

(*i*) To develop problem-solving competency among the pupils.

(*ii*) To develop critical and constructive thinking among pupils.

(iii) To develop independent and original thinking power among the pupils.

(b) Syntax. The syntax of reflective level teaching is designed in the following four steps, keeping in mind the individual and social nature—

(i) In the first step, the teacher creates a problematic situation before the pupils.

(ii) In the second step, pupils formulate hypotheses for testing. Remember that more than one hypotheses may be formulated for the solution of a problem.

(iii) In the third step, to verify the hypotheses, pupils collect data. On the basis of these collected data, it is decided whether these hypotheses may help in the solution of the problem or not.

(iv) In the fourth step, hypotheses are tested. Results are derived on the basis of these tests which are original ideas of the pupils.

(c) Social System. In the reflective level of teaching, the classroom environment is open and independent. In such environment, the pupil occupies primary places and the teacher's place is secondary. At the stage, the teacher has three main functions—

(i) To present some problem before the pupils.

(ii) To use discussion and seminar during teaching.

(iii) To raise the level of aspiration of the pupils. All the pupils become active and sensitive for solving the problem. Hence, at this level, both self-motivation of the pupil and the social motivation have importance.

(d) Support System. For reflective level of teaching, objective type tests are not useful. The proper evaluation of the pupils' competencies can be done correctly by easy type tests. While examining reflecting level—

(i) the attitudes and beliefs of the pupils should be evaluated,

(ii) their involvement in the learning activities should be evaluated,

(iii) it should be evaluated that how much development of the critical and creative competencies of the pupils have taken place.

Features of Reflective Level of Teaching

The following are the limitations and characteristics of reflective level of teaching as described by Hunt:

(i) In reflective level of teaching, no definite programme is followed as in the case of memory and understanding levels of teaching.

(ii) This level of teaching is required for the pupils of higher classes. It is because this level of teaching carries much importance for age and maturation.

(iii) The teaching at reflective level is problem-centred.

(iv) In this level of teaching, only group-discussion method is considered effective.

(v) Reflective level of teaching cannot be restricted only to the curriculum, contents and text-books.

(vi) In the reflective level of teaching, pupils can criticize their teachers openly.

Guidelines for Reflective Level of Teaching

Hunt has presented the following suggestions to make the reflective level of teaching more effective—

(i) Teacher should allow those pupils' entry into the reflective level of teaching who succeed in the tests of memory and understanding levels of teaching.

(ii) In the reflective level of teaching, the teacher should follow all the four steps of his level observing the precautions.

(iii) The teacher should raise the level of aspiration of the pupils to make the teaching at reflective level a success.

(iv) In order to eliminate the weaknesses of the teacher, cognitive field psychology should be stressed.

(v) The teacher should create such problematic situations before the pupils in which original and creative thinking may develop in them.

(vi) At the time of teaching, there should be a free and open environment so that the pupils may participate actively in discussion in order to solve the problem.

(vii) The teacher should present the problem before the pupils so that they may formulate the hypotheses after realizing the problem.

The table on the next page clarifies the relationship of teaching and learning concept and verifies its meaningfulness.

Comparative Study of Memory, Understanding and Reflective Levels of Teaching

Levels of Teaching Headings	*Memory Level*	*Understanding Level*	*Reflective Level*
1. Exponents	Herbarts	Morrison	Hunt
2. Nature of Teaching	Thoughtless	Thoughtful	More thoughtful
3. Focus	Cognitive objective	Understanding and application objective	Analysis, synthesis and evaluation objective
4. Effect of Intelligence	Helpful in development	Direct relation with teaching	Dev. of original and creative capacities
5. Class-room Environment	Passive (Not-critical)	Critical and without criticism (Pupil can seek clarification from the teacher)	More critical (use of discussion)
6. Teacher and Pupil	Control of the Teacher on pupil's behaviour is passive (Not-critical)	Democratic (Both Active)	Pupils is free and more active.
7. Learning of Theory	Stimulus-Response Theory	Reinforcement-in light Theory	Problem solving, cognitive aspect and psychological Maxim
8. Learning Method	Signal and Chaining	Verbal relationship differential, conceptual	Principle and problem solving
9. Content	Factual	Explanatory	Reasoning
10. Strategies	Lecture	Question-Answer	Discussion and consultation
11. Motivation	External	External and Internal	Internal
12. Testing	Oral and Written	Oral and Written in description step only oral	Essay Type

Also, it presents an outline about the activities of testing and teaching-learning while throwing light on the new concepts of teaching-learning and testing so that an effective teaching may be managed.

QUESTIONS FOR ANSWER

1. Make a comparative study of the three levels of teaching.
2. Distinguish between Memory Level and Reflective Level of Teaching.
3. Write a note on Classification of Memory.
4. Write a note on Models of Memory Level and Understanding Level of Teaching.
5. Write short notes on:
   (a) Guidelines of Reflective Level of Teaching.
   (b) Model of Reflective Level of Teaching.
   Meaning and Definition of Memory.

9

Educational Technology Resources

With the development of human civilization, technology had developed but the development of science led to faster development of technology in all walks of human life, including educational technology. Educational Technology is not a substitute to teacher it aims at making the process of teaching effective and process of learning much easier and interesting and thus, it is of great help both to the teachers as well as to the students.

Viewed in its broadest sense, educational technology is simply an attempt to apply technology know-how to improve education. Ideally, this effort starts with an analysis of the learning of the desired, determination of the experiences that are likely to be effective in helping students learn, and development and use of these experience followed by an evaluation to determine whether they have indeed been effective. Teaching has, for years, used a more and more extensive educational technology, but the development has been so gradual that most teachers have not been fully aware of it.

The teacher, educated in a discipline and viewing competency in that discipline as the major requirement for effective teaching, may react negatively to the use of educational technology, forgetting, for the moment, that pencils, pens, paper, and books are part of that technology.

A major reason for this reaction is a lack of understanding

about what educational technology is and a suspicion that it is merely time-consuming gadgetry introduced to enliven the classroom or to replace it.

In modern educational system there is a wide range and significance of the various types of educational experiences appropriate to available technology and the nature of the learning desired. This is done by proposing a new conception of the teacher's role in relation to such technology.

History and Nature of Development of Educational Technology

Certain forms of educational technology have long been used in education. Indeed, some are employed so widely that they are not recognized as adaptations to technology development to educational use. At present, technological developments provide for a much wider range of educational usage than is apparent in most classrooms.

Cost and availability are part of the problem, although the costs of science laboratories have long since been incorporated into educational budgets. Most programmes are not flexible enough, and facilities and equipment needed are not yet widely available. Relatively few teachers have as yet experienced as students the fullest educational potential of these developments.

Besides, many institutions have neither the appropriate facilities nor the technical assistance, sometimes, required for the use of such new technology. Tightly scheduled programmes and lack of cooperation may forbid the use off-campus facilities such as museums and art-galleries. The failure to use existing technology certainly cannot be blamed on the teachers alone.

Paul L. Dressel of Michigan points out in his book on Teaching and Learning in College that before the spoken language evolved, teaching was done by demonstration and imitation. At a later point, much of teaching was, and had to the oral, simply because writing developed much later than speech. Even today, we may use a stick to draw a picture or figure in the sand or soil to illustrate a point. Marks on clay tablets unearthed in the Near East indicate that they must have been used by students learning how to write in cuneiform Where baked clay, papyrus, and slates were used in the past, today chalkboards and easels with paper pads are used for writing and for the temporary exhibition of materials to be assimilated by students.

Long-hand Written Copies. In the days before printing was developed, materials were written out in longhand and laboriously copied in order to make them available to others and to preserve them for later generations. And, for many years, these copies formed the major source of knowledge for teachers and students.

When printing first came into use, it is said that many masters were outraged because lectures could now be made generally available. This availability constituted a threat to the professorial role of lecturing that had formerly been the only way anyone could get the benefit of the professor's learning.

Sound and Visual Recording. In the present day of sound and visual recording and rapid copying, we have effective means of educating people without having to bring large groups together in a single classroom by a professor. Indeed, as some wit was pointed out, a professor's tape recorder could deliver a lecture to the student's tape recorders, with neither professor nor students present.

Spectacles, Telescopes and Microscopes. But these are by no means the whole of educational technology. The development of spectacles, telescopes, and microscopes effectively extended the vision of man and thereby vastly expanded the range of phenomena to be investigated. And, in turn, these instruments became essential for the educational process.

These extensions of vision, conjoined with the camera, the X-ray, and, more recently, the making of holographs that incorporate three dimensions, have provided ways of recording expanded vision and enriching the classroom and laboratory learning process as never before possible.

Man has long since learned to make sketches, drawings, paintings, and rubblings that preserve the essence of certain visual experiences and permit them to be transferred to others. The development of photography allowed even more accurate reproduction. Black-and-White film permitted the recording of motion, and colour film added to this the preservation of the colour components of the objects in motion.

More recently, videotapes have enabled us to unite sound, colour, and motion and to present them to others at different places and times. What we once could experience only by being present at an event or by travelling to the site of a building or picture is now readily transferred in time and space to enrich the education of students.

Museums, Libraries, Art-Galleries, Planetoriums. For many years, man has engaged in the accumulation or collections of objects, art works, and the like in museum, libraries, parks, art-galleries planetoriums, horticultural gardens, zoological gardens, and country, state, and world fairs.

The educational experience possible in each of these is, in many respects, far richer than that provided in most schools, but the costs of travel or reproduction and the time thereby consumed have forced many teachers and schools to undersue or to ignore them.

Collections of rocks, insects and animals have also provided at least a visual enrichment beyond pictures in textbooks, but the tendency for these mounted specimens to deteriorate with time and handling had greatly limited their use in student learning.

Models, Mock-ups, Diagrams. Models, mock-ups, and diagrams have been effectively used in museums to bring out inter-relationships among objects and to present the third dimension clearly. Assembled models of planes, steam engines, and cars—particularly if the parts are movable—provide an experience in understanding these technological developments far beyond what a picture can supply.

The military students who has at hand plastic soldiers, horses, guns, and models of all the accoutrements of war can lay out and sense strategy and tactics far better than he can with a map dots and crosses on it.

If, further, a model of the terrain is provided, the visual components of learning are expanded to the point where reliance on the verbal is reduced greatly.

Graphs, diagrams, maps, and globes also constitute ways of presenting data or aspects of reality so that students may grasp ideas not well understood before.

The use of a globe and light source to present the sun can enable a child to understand the reason for night and day more easily than can any verbal statements or two-dimensional picture.

In the average school of even twenty years ago, teachers

were already surrounded by an extensive technology. Accordingly, there has been a great reliance on listening as the principal mode of learning, and on reading, writing, and viewing along with it. Other than with exotic foods and drinks, taste has been largely ignored, although people learning to cook find that taste is an admirable check on whether the ingredients have been well chosen and mixed in the right proportions.

Taste is sometimes used as a particle means of identifying various substances. Touch is seldom used except in the education of the blind, although the sense of touch is an excellent way of learning something about the texture of cloth, metal, or rocks, or of determining how paint has been applied to obtain certain effects in a picture.

Smell is almost totally ignored, although a sensitivity to odors can be useful in cooking, cleaning house, identifying plants, or working in the laboratory. These remarks about the sensory aspects of learning suggest that one of major purposes of educational technology should be to make known the sensory realities of those substances students confront in the learning process.

Purpose and Benefits of Educational Technology

It is fitting to open a discussion of the purposes and uses of educational technology by identifying the wide range of educational experiences and opportunities it can provide. Quite obviously, the first comprehensive purpose in the use of technology would be to improve and extend learning or understanding. Increasingly, motivation, interest, convenience, and realism of experiences are also purposes; and they are meritorious purposes, though they should be subsidiary to the major ones.

No matter how well chosen are the words describing a building or the comfort achieved in an automobile by the use of a new spring design, words will never provide the insights that seeing the building or riding in the automobile will readily yield. A textbook picture or a slide of the building cannot provide an equivalent of the experience available through the use of film or videotape.

Film, videotape, computer-assisted instruction, laboratories, work-sample kits, and other educational technologies offer an enormous range of learning experiences well beyond those of the lecture or recitation in a classroom.

It is important to understand that this increase in range of experiences, even when available, may only increase the insights and understanding achieved by students about concepts and principles initially presented in textbooks and lectures.

The students is provided with a wider range of sensory involvement and a better sampling of materials and experiences but uses them only to master traditional objectives largely limited to acquiring factual knowledge and the simpler skills.

From our observations of the use of available educational technology, we conclude it is still highly underemployed. For example, many history classrooms have an extensive range of excellent maps; yet in some classrooms, the maps are seldom used and then for a very limited purpose, such as locating a city.

Much of computer-assisted instruction turns out to be little more than drill on vocabularies, definitions, principles, and simple problem solving. Many teachers, indeed, have apparently not given careful attention to the effective use of textbooks and library resources.

Although many course syllabi contain an extensive list of resources, the list frequently seems appended more to impress fellow teachers than to encourage students or to ensure that they have a planned sequence of encounters with the best writers and researchers in the field.

Deeper, Richer, More Complex Experience. Educational technology can be used to extend the range of educational objectives by bringing into the student's environment much more potent—deeper, richer, more complex, more realistic—experience than could otherwise be had.

The *Ramayana* can be read in a classroom over a period of weeks accompanied by lectures by the professor and the reading of various commentaries. If it happens that the play is being presented on television with an excellent cast, watching that broadcast, preceded by some introduction and followed by some discussion, should be a richer experience than simply reading and discussing the play.

Various forms of educational technology also provide the possibility of preserving peak and unique experiences. These would include films or videotapes of the performances of great musicians, of surgeons or of natural events that are unusually picturesque or cataclysmic.

Technology can also make learning much more individualized. Some slides used in the typical classroom situations are exhibited for only a few seconds, others for lengthly intervals. The exhibit time may be more than adequate for some students but grossly inadequate for others; it depends largely on what is said about the slide. Lectures, too, are given in a certain span of time, and people vary in how far they are able to capture the essence of these in notes.

Computer-assisted instruction provides the opportunity for individuals to work through various programmes repeatedly or to accelerate their learning.

Motivation. Educational technology has numerous advantages in facilitating and motivating learning. The non-English-speaking person who hears a television commercial in English about the comfort of a new car may have learnt of nothing from the statement, but after riding in the car for ten minutes he will have arrived at a conclusion about its comfort. By direct experience using other senses than hearing, this person will have easily learned how comfortable the car is.

Educational technology may also provide learning experiences that are more pleasant and convenient than the traditional lecture, textbooks or classroom discussion. For example, educational television can bring significant learning into the home. Without time-consuming travel, an individual can sit in a comfortable chair on a stormy night and learn as much as in an uncomfortable classroom.

Educational technology can also provide learning experiences that are less dangerous than the reality might be. The use of trainer equipment with realistic film for the education of pilots is effective and does not endanger their lives or risk an expensive plane.

A film or videotape of a complicated laboratory experiment may give students insights into all aspects of the experiments while avoiding the possibility of accidents or explosions or the waste of materials.

Laboratory Experiment—Computer Etc.

In the case of an elaborate laboratory experiment carried out over several weeks, the use of film also illustrates the possibility of providing superior educational experiences at less cost. Film of the experiment can be shown many times in many different classrooms and institutions, and on television to an extended audience.

Although expensive, the film, by eliminating space requirements, instructor supervision time, and the costs of raw materials and equipment for all the times and sites at which it might instead be used, may make for a far lower total cost and greater understanding than engaging all students in the actual laboratory experiment.

Some use of educational technology permit the student to engage in more complicated tasks, and therefore, in a larger number of similar tasks, than otherwise possible, with the probability of gaining new insights and competencies.

The computer is one example. So long as all computations had to be carried out by hand, the time involvements and the possibility of error in any long sequence effectively forbade asking students to carry out complicated computing tasks. Even so, almost as much time was spent in developing shortcuts as in developing an understanding of the problem itself. For example, in the case of statistics, only a few years ago it took a long time to teach students how to compute by using deviations from some central item rather than the actual numbers in the frequency distribution.

With modern computers, even with some of the pocket miniatures, individuals can perform in seconds computations that would have taken many hours. The engineer who for years depended on the slide rule for quick but approximate calculations now gets quicker, easier, and much more accurate with the hand computer.

In addition, this ease of computation makes it possible for students to engage in a series of computation using many different types of data and distribution. It also permits them to carry out multiple correlations and regression and a variety of other complex analyses that only a few decades ago could be done only with a great expenditure of effort, time, and money.

This technological improvement lets the student engage in a greater variety of analyses and have a more extensive range of contacts with various types of data and the problems of interpreting them.

Computer programmes have been developed for use in equipment design courses so that students can, within a very short, while, try out a number of different designs to meet certain requirements, and compute various coefficients that characterize the design. Students thereby achieve a sense of the role of various quantities, materials, and variables in developing effective designs.

Thus, today, the individual can compress into a few weeks or even hours experiences that past designers of equipment have had only over years.

Diverse Aspects Need Realistic Integration

It should not be assumed that the major purpose of educational technology is always that of providing a more realistic experience. It is true that the realistic integration of various separately discussed aspects of a complex experience is desirable.

Field trips have been introduced into educational programmes simply because they do provide an on-site experience in which the various facets of that experience are brought together in a realistic way not possible in a classroom.

A film depositing various stages in the painting of a picture may be highly effective in generating an understanding of the creative act. Some one seeing a steam engine running may have not noticed how the steam engine works until a stripped-down model, a film, or a simplified diagram highlights the essential principles of its operation.

A combination of enactive, iconic, and symbolic learning experiences will usually increase motivation, ease the learning task, and improve the quality or learning.

Simulation. Another aspect of technology is that of simulation. Usually, a simulation is an attempt to set up an operating but simplified model of a complex situation or interaction. Such complex situations must be simplified by establishing certain assumption and interacting principles that may not be revealed to those engaging the simulation.

Simulation has obvious deficiencies and is distasteful to

some people. In counselling simulations, for example, in which one person assumes the role of a client and the other that of a counsellor (possible videotaped for repeated use), one person plays a role and the other attempts to act in a reasonably realistic way in situation in which each knows that the other is pretending. Simulation requires a pretence of what is not and, hence, is not far removed from dissimulation or a concealment of what is.

The simplification, analysis, and differentiation that are required for simulation are useful and necessary techniques in achieving and understanding of components of a complex situation to avoid generating erroneous conceptions. Thus, the distinctions made among drama, novels, biographies, autobiographies, history, and "real" experiences are subtle, unclear, and somewhat artificial, for many people are "acting" in real life. Individuals designated as administrators may simulate the role rather than execute it.

The purposes of educational technology can be viewed through the range of experience that may be provided. One purpose may be to integrate a number of separately identified and discussed stimuli.

In other words, we may use educational technology to achieve greater experience or we may use it for the purpose of differentiation through simulation that inevitably involves simplification.

One of the major accomplishments of effective use of educational technology is an increase in the active involvement of the students as against the passive receptivity observable in most classrooms, where the larger part of the activity, both mental and physical is of the professor's.

Educational technology whether used to provide an integrating or differentiating experience, provides for adaptability to the individual learner. Some people may have no difficulty in putting, it all together, others, intrigued with a complex operation, may not be able to single out the significant components.

Practical Classroom Technology

In the usual classroom, a very high level of verbalization is employed. The rigidity of that pattern may, in fact, not convey full understanding to anyone. The effective use of educational technology can give the individual students practice.

No one would argue that a prospective physician in training should be limited to observing other physicians operate. It seems perfectly obvious that each physician in training should have an opportunity to deal with human models and then engage in simple manipulations and interactions with patients under close supervision, before taking full responsibility for the patient.

Even an extremely limited and conservative conception of what constitutes a liberal education must accept the obligation to move the student from passive receptivity and verbal proficiency to self-initiated, though, valuing and action.

To the extent that people very in how easily they learn by various experiences (cognitive styles), the greater the range and variation of experiences provided, the greater the likelihood that a combination will be found that will motivate them.

Furthermore, if the experience is provided with a feedback evaluation (as in programmed materials or computer-assisted instruction) that enables the individual to become self-critical about his or her performance, then insight and improvement become directly possible, without constant mediation by the teacher and without the risk of failure or ridicule.

Learning Aids

As already noted, educational technology can provide greater convenience in learning. Learning experiences may be carried to where an individual lives and, at times, be more suited to his or her schedule and moods. In fact, the typical approach to scheduling educational episodes is predicated upon the professor's and institution's convenience instead of the student's.

At one time, learning in medicine and law was almost entirely a matter of serving at extended internship with a practising professional. As we have moved to centralizing and closely controlling educational preparation of prospective professionals, we frequently subject them for long periods to the tutelage of professors.

The students must then engage in learning completely separated from the situation in which that learning will be applied. Recalling and using that information at a later date is surely not expedited by this separation.

This discussion should not be construed as support for the idea that all learning should take place in practical situations. Rather, it is meant to reinforce our earlier assertion that the major purpose of educational technology is to provide, at a given time, an educational experience that enhances and enriches the learning of the student, and that this learning should be transferable to situations in which the individual will ultimately live and make decisions.

Teacher's Role Modified

Educational technology has often been looked at as merely a set of aids to be used by teachers. Those taking this point of departure argue that the teacher is the ultimate manger of the classroom, and that every additional item or aid that is brought to the classroom must be determined and introduced according to a plan developed by the teacher. This is a erroneous view.

Teachers are mediators between the best products of the human mind and those who cannot be directly in touch with these minds and their products because of barriers of time, distance, language, or incapacity to assimilate the ideas without help.

Teachers who ignore this mediating role and overestimate their potential for significant personal impact may interfere with learning. In fact, teachers who persist in inserting themselves and their views between great minds and great works do both the students and the authors, artists, and writers an injustice, for their intervention denies the possibility of direct communication and, especially, denies the students the opportunity to reach their own individual judgments.

Hence, it seems inappropriate to suggest that every aspect of direct student experience with outstanding personalities or their works should be dominated by a teacher, who offers only a second-hand critical scholarship applied to the creativity of others.

We fully realize that teachers may add some insights for all students and provide essential guidance and direction for many; this is the mediating role we have emphasized here. Our contention is that, through technological advance, it may be possible to bring to the classroom or the individual's living room a teacher or learning experience superior to what a student typically experiences at school.

In talking about technology and the best use of it, we refer to resources used by students in learning, not solely to aids used by teachers. And, in some cases, the best learning may be achieved through self-teaching that uses media offerings not generally available on a campus.

This possibility leads to the need for developing an evaluation system whereby the educational accomplishments of individuals can be recognized apart from the deficiencies, rigidities, and biases of individual departments and disciplines.

In fact, it is entirely likely that enrichment of the learning experience of students by the fullest use of educational technology would force professors to engage in an expansion of their own learning and thus improve not only the quality of their teaching but also of their own insights and understandings of the discipline. Scholars tend to view their fields of specialization from a limited perspective and thus, may have serious deficiencies in presentation of these materials to students.

Need for Co-ordinated Use of Hardware and Software Educational Technology

Educational technology is often thought of only as hardware, though what is, in fact, basically important is the software—that is, the materials and the procedures that determine the way the hardware is used and the ends to which it is directed. For many years, the undergraduate science laboratory (especially in the introductory courses) has been much criticized as being expansive and time consuming and as emphasizing manipulator operations that yield little insight into the essential nature of science.

This is a clear example of the commitment to hardware rather than the well-planned utilization of it to achieve understanding of the fundamental nature of scientific modes of thought. The use of textbooks as a backdrop of lectures is another example of misused hardware. Side projectors, overhead projectors, and language laboratories have also been misused in this way. Teachers become enthusiastic about the availability of hardware without having thought through how it might best be used.

A teacher who is well grounded in the topics, covered in a particular course may view that further range of learning experiences provided by educational technology as distracting and irrelevant. This narrow reaction may result from either of two circumstances.

A teacher of drama may not realize that a purely verbal approach, however excellent, does not invoke the sensory experiences that result when a student both sees and hears a play and when the roles of the actors are reinforced by their motions, by their dress, and by the staging and scenery. In brief, a teacher who has preferred ways of approaching topics and knowledge may not be able to judge the effect of a variety of different experiences on the relatively naive student.

Teachers may learn much more about computer-assisted instruction, programmed learning, or some other variety of technological presentation if their initial experiences with it are directed to a field not previously studied or to one that caused difficulty earlier.

The potential of a particular experience for learning may be far better realized if that experience is in a field in which the individual is naive rather than proficient.

It is not unreasonable to expect that every teacher preparing to instruct in schools at any level have an awareness of a full range of learning experiences that can be provided to students. Basically, this requires the teacher to become acquainted with available technological apparatus useful for teaching.

QUESTIONS FOR ANSWER

1. Write a note on the history and nature of educational technology.
2. "The purpose and benefits of educational technology are explanatory." Justify.
3. Write a note on the modified nature of Teacher's Role in the developed age of educational technology.
4. "Educational Technology is no substitute to teacher but a positive and effective aid to teaching and learning." Justify.
5. Write a note on the need for Co-ordinated use of Hardware and Software Educational Technology.
6. Write short notes on:
   (a) Practical Classroom Technology.
   (b) Learning Aids.
   (c) Utility of Laboratory Experiments and Computers in Education.

10

Seven Teaching Techniques—1 (General Techniques)

Teaching techniques are such aids which are used for making the pupils interested in the lessons, explaining the contents and remembering it by heart during teaching. From this point of view, in order to achieve the teaching objective, the teacher not only seeks the help of a teaching method or teaching strategy, but also it is essential to seek help of a teaching technique in order to mark the knowledge in the brains of the pupils. Following teaching techniques are used in order to make the lesson interesting, effective and a success.

Explanation Technique

Meaning of Explanation Technique

Explanation is that technique in which every idea regarding the content is made clear. In other words, explanation is that technique in which a difficult thing is simplified. In short, by explanation, every problem, confusion and difficulty of the lesson is analysed and explained in such a simple language that every pupil of the class may pick up very easily. This explanation technique is used in the factual and informative lessons of social subjects but this method is especially needed in teaching the difficult words of language and sentences. For example, when a teacher tells the meaning of some difficult words, he tries to make clear its meaning by its origin, opposite word, use in sentences etc. In other words, during language teaching, explanation technique is used in the following forms—

(i) *By Acting*—Explaining the difficult words by acting.

(ii) *Using in a Sentence*—Using difficult words in sentences.

(iii) *Stating Synonyms*—Explaining difficult words by such simple words which carry the same meaning.

(iv) *Stating Opposite Words*—Difficult words are interpreted by telling opposite words of the difficult words.

(v) *By Analysis*—Difficult words are explained by analysing.

(vi) *By Telling Origin*—To clarify the words by telling their origin.

(vii) *By Defining*—To explain by defining the words.

Precautions while Using Explanation Technique

The teachers, especially the pupil-teachers, should observe the following precautions—

1. Before explanation, all the confusions should be eliminated just to avoid any obstructions while explaining.
2. Explanation should be simple, correct and in clear words. Use of difficult words makes the explanation a failure.
3. Explanation should not be stretched. This makes the lesson dry. As a result, the pupils start feeling boredom. Hence, the explanations should be relevant.
4. The teacher should have the complete knowledge of the subject-matter. In its absence, the explanation would be erroneous and irrelevant.
5. Explanations should be according to the level of the pupils.
6. Explanation should occur for only those points which a student can understand with his own efforts. It is a great mistake to explain meaningless things.
7. Explanations should be started when the pupils are absorbed in the lesson and they are very curious. In other words, without any need, explanation should not occur.
8. While explaining, the full cooperation should be sought from the pupils. For this, both teachers and the pupils

should be free for questioning. He should repeat whatever the pupils fail to understand.

9. Explanation should not be in the form of advice, because pupils don't like such advice. The teacher should carry on maximum explanation in higher classes and minimum in lower classes.
10. Examples, illustrations and pictures should be used according to needs in order to make the explanation more concrete.
11. Before explaining, the object or thing should be shown to the pupils for which the explanation is to occur.
12. In explanation technique, various techniques like narration, description and questioning etc. are included.

Exposition Technique

Meaning of Exposition Technique

Exposition is also known as guidance or inauguration. This technique means the presentation of facts of a lesson in a definite, logical manner, understandable and simplified way that all the pupils may learn the most difficult things very easily.

This exposition technique is used in the teaching of all the subjects but it is more beneficial in language-teaching. In order to make this exposition technique effective the following points should be observed specifically—

1. The correct exposition of any subject is possible only when the teacher is fully familiar with all parts of that subject. Hence, the subject should be presented properly, before the pupils.
2. The subject to be expositioned should be according to the interest and the mental level of the pupils. In other words, the exposition should be appropriate.
3. While exposing, the difficult parts, facts and various aspects of the lesson should be carefully elucidated.
4. While exposing, the teacher should use simple, clear and interesting language.

Precautions while Using Exposition Technique

The teachers, especially pupil-teachers, must observe the following precautions—

1. The teacher should present the lesson before the pupils after determining the objectives of the lesson.
2. While exposing, the teacher should try to maintain the interest of the pupils.
3. The teacher should have sufficient knowledge about the attitudes of the pupils.
4. A simple, clear and effective language should be used while exposing.
5. In order to make the exposition effective, the entire lesson should be divided into clear and natural units. Then, the first unit should be made clear to the pupils and then next.
6. Exposition should be clear and definite.
7. Before exposition, the teacher should eliminate the errors committed by himself and he should think over the subject-material and also, he must remove the doubts of the pupils.
8. While exposing, only those main things should be stressed specifically which are directly related to the lesson. It can also be written on blackboard for clarification if it is considered necessary.
9. The rapidity and slow rate of exposition should be according to their intelligence and their power of understanding.
10. While exposing, the teacher should use all the techniques like narration, description, explanation etc. and as the need arises, he should allow the pupils to ask the questions. Not only this, when the exposition is over, the teacher will have to inquire by questioning the limit upto which the explanation succeeded.
11. In order to make the exposition best, interesting and understandable, examples, illustrations, pictures and devices should be used frequently.

Narration Technique

Meaning of Narration Technique

Narration is also termed as statement which means an interesting oral presentation of some reference, object or an incident in such a way that a mental picture is formed in his mind, i.e., he understands clearly. Hence, narration is a form of story. Remember that narration is an art. In order to be efficient in this art, the teacher presents with the help of his imaginative power, the description of an object or some incident with such an enthusiasm and in an effective manner that all the pupils of the class gain the full knowledge very conveniently.

However, this narration technique is used in science subjects successfully, but it is also used especially in subjects like history, geography, civics and economics etc.

Characteristics of Narration Technique

The following are the main characteristics of narration technique—

1. Narration provides so much knowledge to the pupils that they need not to read various books.
2. Pupils enjoy listening narration more than reading the books. It is the reason that the narration leaves permanent effect upon pupils' mind.
3. Pupils gain knowledge in lesser time through narration as compared to books.
4. A complete review can occur by throwing light on all the aspects of the subject through narration.
5. Narration can guide the pupils properly. This makes them interested in solving various problems of life.

Precautions while Using Narration Technique

The teacher should especially observe the following precautions while using the narration technique—

1. The teacher should have the knowledge of those objects and places which are to be narrated.
2. The teacher should awaken the imaginative power of the pupils through narration.
3. In order to make the narration interesting and effective, the teacher should also use his imagination.
4. Narration should occur with patience and self-confidence.
5. The narration should be in accordance with the need.
6. During narration, the teacher should not talk irrelevant.
7. While narrating, the teacher should speak clearly with fluctuations.

8. The language of narration should be easy, clear and understandable that the pupil may pick-up it easily.
9. Narration should neither be long nor too short. A lengthy narration puts the pupils in doubts and too short narration cannot benefit them more.
10. The provision of narration should be according to pre-planning. This will leave a permanent effect upon pupils.
11. A continuous narration makes the pupils passive. This encourages boredom. Therefore, the teacher should present in a sequence the subject-matter by dividing it in units. Not only this, after each unit, questions should be asked from the pupils. This keeps the class alive and the teacher gets reinforcement regarding the understanding of the contents.
12. For a successful narration, the teacher should draw an actual picture in the minds of the pupils so that the emotions get aroused after witnessing an actual incident. For this, the teacher should narrate the real incident with proper gestures and proper acting. This makes the narration alive.
13. Narration should reach its climax gradually along with a curiosity to know further details.
14. The speed of the narration should be according to the class-level. Too fast or too slow narrations cause partial learning.

Description Technique

Meaning of Description Technique

That technique is called description in which a verbal picture of some matter or an incident is presented before the pupils. Sometimes, situations arise in the class when some things are to be described essentially. For example, sufficient knowledge about 'Quit India Movement' can be imparted to the pupils by this method.

Attention is to be paid that in this description technique, the teacher presents some illustrations or some incidents in such an effective and encouraging way by using the help of his own imaginative power, that all the pupils acquire essential knowledge about them very conveniently.

This technique has been proved very useful in teaching, therefore, experts have considered it the alternative version of lecture technique.

This technique can be used in the teaching of science but in teaching social subjects and languages, this technique is especially used.

Precautions while Using Description Technique

The pupil-teachers should observe the following precautions:

1. Before using the description technique, the teacher should arrange his ideas in a sequence and these should be described in the same order.
2. The description should be in clear, simple and interesting language according to the mental level of the pupil.
3. The style of the description should be interesting, alive and attractive. This makes the pupils absorbed listeners.
4. The description should be according to the age and interest of the pupils, otherwise they won't be benefited.
5. The teacher should pre-determine the points when the description is to be given, while preparing lesson-plan. The inclusion of irrelevant things and incidents wastes the time and energy.
6. The lengthy and the short nature of the descriptions delimits the interest of the description. Hence, the teacher should not present too lengthy or too short descriptions.
7. The teacher should have full knowledge about those persons, objects and incidents which are to be described.
8. While giving description of some persons related to some incidents and names of places, date etc. should be written on blackboard. Also the teacher should use models, pictures, maps, specimens and other aids accordingly. This forms the proper memory images in the pupil's mind.

Difference Between Narration and Description

Both, narration and description have many similarities. The

effectiveness of both depends upon the language and style. Both the techniques are used with the aim of presenting all-round description of the subject. Verbal pictures are presented in the minds of the pupils by these both techniques. Both these techniques leave a permanent effect upon the pupils. Still, these techniques show some differences, which have been made clear in the table given hereunder.

Narration Technique	*Description Technique*
1. Narration is brief.	Description is detailed.
2. Narration presents facts in a logical sequence.	Description Presents facts in both logical and psychological points of view.
3. Narration is used casually for clarification.	Description Technique is used continuously for presenting all sound verbal picture
4. Narration is presented usually in the oral form	Description can be presented both in oral and written form
5. Narration is more analytical.	Description is more synthetic.

Story Telling Technique

Meaning of Story Telling Technique

Story-telling means to recite or to tell a story. Through story telling, the complicated and minute details of a subject are made so easy that all the pupils understand it very easily. Psychologically, young pupils don't have so much mental development that they can acquire minute and complex ideas very easily. But, as they show natural interest in listening a story, therefore, they grasp very easily the knowledge presented in the form of a story.

Through a story, the imaginative and reasoning powers of the pupils are developed in such a way, by awakening their interests and aspirations in a recreational way, that their moral and social qualities get developed. Also, they assimilate very easily the knowledge of any subject.

Story-telling technique is generally used in the lower classes in a special way. But this, technique can be used successfully in the higher classes.

Remember that story-telling is an art. Some people are expert in this art by birth, but these are such skills which can be acquired and expertise can be achieved by learning those skills. Those skills are as follows: Each and every pupil-teacher should take care of them.

1. The story-teller should prepare a complete mental-picture of the various elements of the story. Then, its theme and ideas should be presented in a logical manner.
2. While telling a story, the mental stage, interests and emotional characteristics of the pupils should not be over-looked.
3. The characters of the story should be according to the characters of the close surroundings of the pupils.
4. Before telling a story, the important elements of the knowledge should be understood by learning them.
5. The story-telling should occur when the pupils are interested in it and the class-environment should be completely peaceful.
6. There should be a direct relationship of the story with the subject.
7. The story teller should develop the imagination, curiosity and motivating tendency of the pupils more and more by using his own imaginative power.
8. The language of the story should be easy, correct and clear.
9. The story-teller should have fluctuations in his voice. Also, the method of the story should be natural, emotional and attractive.
10. While telling a story, the teacher should exhibit gestures according to its theme and incidents.
11. The story-teller should tell the story in such a lively and natural way that he should forget himself and become a story himself.
12. The story-telling should be continuous. Any interruption in its flow and change in the reference will spoil its enjoyment.

13. The story should not be told by reading.
14. The story should not be too lengthy.
15. After telling the story, questions should be asked from the pupils. This will lead us to know whether they have learnt the subject-matter or not.

Supervised Study Technique

Meaning of Supervised Study Technique

Supervised study technique is based on the principles of individual differences and activity. The birth of this technique took place in the form of a reaction to the traditional techniques. In this technique, keeping in view the individual differences, every pupil is provided with an opportunity to do his respective task and study, and the teacher solves his individual problems by supervising his tasks as a friend, helper and a guide. Hence, in supervised study technique, both pupil and the teacher are active.

Whatever it is, this technique is used keeping in view all the pupils of the class especially backward pupils. Remember that the supervised study technique has various forms, which are as follows—

1. *Double Period Plan.* According to this plan, two periods are provided to the pupils to study the same subject-matter. In the first period, pupils are instructed to study after presenting the background of the decided subject. In the second period, pupils study that subject and the teacher supervises their activities. Mabel E. Simpson has divided two collective periods of 90 minutes by using this plan in a very appreciable manner—

Review	25 minutes
Assignment	25 minutes
Physical Exercise	25 minutes
Study of the Assignments	35 minutes
	Total 90 minutes

2. *Divided Period Plan.* In this plan, two teachers supervise the tasks of the pupils in the duration.

3. *Periodical Plan.* In this plan, pupils are instructed to do predetermined tasks. After some definite period, their progress

is supervised. Hence, the teacher performs the function of supervision and guidance weekly, fortnightly or monthly.

4. *Special Teacher Plan.* In this plan, specialized teachers remove the difficulties, errors and mis-conceptions of the pupils.

5. *Conference Plan.* According to this plan, conferences are organised time to time. In these conferences, the problems of the pupils are sorted out by mutual consultations.

Precautions while Using Supervised Study Technique

Following precautions should be observed to make the supervised study technique a success:

1. To make this technique a success, a teacher must possess insight and resourcefulness.
2. A habit of working in a friendly way should be created by this supervised study technique.
3. Self-confidence and self-dependence should be developed by using this technique.
4. While using this technique, the teacher should plan in such a way so that a scientific attitude may developed.
5. The tasks assigned to the pupils should be according to their mental and physical abilities and interests.

Illustration Technique

Meaning of Illustration Technique

Illustration means that material with the help of which the contents are made interesting, understandable and clear. Since the instructing material is used in the form of illustrations, hence, that is termed as an illustration. In short, knowledge of new objects is imparted to the pupils by using solid or physical objects in this technique of illustration.

Advantages of Illustration

Advantages of illustrations are as follows:

1. Illustrations develop the curiosity and interest of the pupils.
2. By using an illustration, the attention of the pupils can be attracted towards the main lesson very easily.
3. With the use of illustrations, good habits are formed in the pupils. Its only reason is that when a teacher presents

a variety of illustrations, then the pupils also become efficient in using those illustrations.

Kinds of Illustration

Illustrations are of two types which are as follows—

1. Verbal Illustration
2. Visual Illustration

Verbal Illustration

Meaning of Verbal Illustration. The illustrations which are presented verbally are called verbal illustrations. In such illustrations, hearing and understanding activities are essential. Hence, by using these illustrations, pupils get training in hearing and understanding. In verbal illustrations, examples, story, idioms, moral verses, similes, drama and metaphor *(utpreksha)* etc. are included.

By using these illustrations, the teacher draws such a verbal picture of difficult facts and ideas of the contents before the pupils that all the pupils understand the lesson easily.

It is the only reason that the verbal illustrations are openly used to make the interpretation and description effective.

Use of Verbal Illustrations

The value of illustration depends upon the skill of their presentation. Hence, the teacher should keep in mind the following things while using verbal illustrations—

1. The teacher should decide, while preparing a lesson plan, those points and the illustrations which are to be used. With this, the teacher remembers these illustrations and he will not commit any mistake regarding an illustration at the time of teaching.
2. Illustrations should be such that even a dry and dull lesson becomes interesting and alive.
3. Illustrations should be easy, correct and in clear language, otherwise pupils will make the problem complicated instead of solving it.
4. Illustrations should be based upon their previous knowledge according to the mental level, ability and need of the pupils. In other words, illustrations should

be such that the pupils may understand easily.

5. Illustrations should be such that the attention of the pupils may be drawn towards the main lesson by awakening the interests of the pupils.
6. Illustrations should be used at proper time. Excessive and without any reason, its use spoils the value of the illustrations.
7. Illustrations should be related to the main lesson.
8. The teacher should present the illustrations in a proper standing posture and in audible voice.
9. In illustrations, the teaching maxims like 'from simple to complex', 'from known to unknown' and 'from concrete to abstract' etc. should be used.
10. Young pupils, as compared to the adult pupils, have limited experience and knowledge. They cannot grasp the lesson without illustrations. Hence, illustrations should be used more frequently in lower classes than the higher classes.
11. Illustrations should be presented just after the abstract ideas. It maintains the understandability.
12. The young pupils have young world. They posses the knowledge about domestic environment only and the things related to it. Hence, in the beginning classes, such illustrations should be presented which are related to the domestic environment only.
13. The teacher should not present unreal, false and personal-attacking illustrations before the pupils. It affects pupils badly.
14. While presenting the illustrations, the teacher should not make any change in the language of idioms and phrases.
15. The illustrations should be of various types. Similar illustrations make the pupils disinterested in the lesson.

Visual Illustration

Meaning of Visual Illustration. Visual illustrations are termed as objective illustrations. These illustrations attract the pupils. These include essentially the activity of looking and understanding. Hence, with these, pupils get the training of visualising and understanding. In other words, visual illustrations activate the sense organs and acting organs of the pupils. This makes the teaching interesting and effective. These illustrations include the devices like models, pictures, maps, sketches, charts, graphs etc. When all these devices are used during teaching, the whole lesson becomes clear to the pupils.

Use of Visual Illustrations

The following points should be observed while using visual illustrations—

1. It is necessary to select visual illustrations before using them. Therefore, the teacher should decide, during lesson planning, the stages which need illustrations and how these are to be used.
2. Visual illustrations should be used only when the need arises. Without need, a teacher using visual illustrations looks like a magician.
3. The pupils should be provided with full facilities to observe visual illustrations.
4. Visual illustrations should facilitate the achievement of the teaching objectives.
5. The size of the visual illustrations should be such that these are visible to each and every pupil while he is in his seat.
6. Visual illustrations should be attractive.
7. Visual illustrations should be used properly. For this, the placement of the object or its model should be conveniently visible to every pupil of the class while he is in his seat. Similarly, pictures and maps should be displayed on the wall so that every pupil can have a look of these pictures and maps properly.
8. The presentation of visual illustrations should not be repeated again and again.
9. Visual illustrations should be used for the clarifications of the lesson and not for recreation.
10. While using visual illustrations, too much time should not be consumed.
11. The pupils should be provided with opportunities of asking questions after observing visual illustrations.
12. If two visual illustrations are to be used, the first one

should be shifted safely at some other place before using the second visual illustration.

13. Visual illustrations should be used more in lower classes instead of higher classes.
14. Visual and verbal illustrations should be used alternatively.

NOTE

1. Questioning and Receiving Answer Techniques, which are also Teaching Techniques, are mentioned in the next chapter because they need much more details for better understanding.

QUESTIONS FOR ANSWER

1. Define Teaching Techniques. How these are useful for a teacher?
2. What are the differences between Narration and Description Teaching techniques? Explain.
3. Write short notes on:
   A. Explanation Teaching Technique.
   B. Supervised Teaching Technique.
   C. Meaning and Use of Visual Illustration.
   D. Precautions while using Explanation Technique.

11

Teaching Technique—2 (Questioning and Receiving Answer)

Thring has rightly said, "Teaching means skilful questioning to force the mind to see, to arrange and to act."

Questioning enjoys special importance in clarifying and simplifying the subject-matter. In ancient times, 'give and take' process of the knowledge happened to take place only through questioning, i.e., Gurus éducated their pupils through questioning and pupils also used to remove their doubts only through questioning. Socrates, a famous thinker and philosopher of Athens City, also organised the unorganised knowledge of the people only through questioning. In the present age, a teacher comes in contact with the pupils through questioning. The questioning is an art. To gain skill in this art, the teacher must know some important points. The fresh teachers, especially pupil-teachers should pay special attention to these points. These points are: (1) What are the aims of questioning? (2) Classification of questions? (3) What are the characteristics of good questions? (4) Which questions are defective? and (5) How the questions are asked?

Aims of Questioning

The following are the aims of questioning—

1. To motivate the pupils, so that their attention may be drawn tow the original lesson.
2. To create i e..st and curiosity in the pupils so that the task of teaching may go on smoothly.
3. To test the previous knowledge and mental state of the pupils, so that on the basis of acquired knowledge, new knowledge may be disseminated.
4. To develop the lesson with the cooperation of the pupils so that they remain mentally active and their ideas and powers of imagination, thinking, observation, supervision and analysis get developed.
5. To link the previous knowledge of the pupils with the new experiences.
6. To give a definite speed and direction to the mental achievements of the pupils.
7. To know the difficulties of the pupils.
8. To concentrate the attention of the pupils and the teachers on the original lesson so that the lesson can be developed in an organised way.
9. To create self-confidence by removing the hesitation of the pupils so that their power of expression may be developed.
10. To revise and apply the knowledge which pupils have learnt.
11. To evaluate the comprehension of the pupils, which can aware us how much they have learnt and how much they have not learnt. And whatever they have not learnt, what are the causes for that? To eliminate these causes, the strategy of teaching can be modified.

Classification of Questions

On the basis of mental processes, two classifications of the questions may be presented. According to the first classification, Risk has divided the questions into the following two classes :

1. Memory Questions.
2. Thought Questions.

1. Meaning of Memory Questions

Memory questions are those questions which the pupils answer on the basis of their own memory. Such questions are used to test the previous knowledge of the pupils and to revise their acquired knowledge. Remember that the memory questions start generally with 'How', 'When', 'Who' and 'How many'. Some examples of memory questions are being given below—

1. What was the name of the father of Smt. Indira Gandhi?
2. Which animals are found in forests?

2. Meaning of Thought or Thoughtful Questions

Thought or thoughtful questions are those questions which the pupils answer with the help of the ideas, and powers of imagination and reasoning. Examples of such questions are as follows—

(i) Why mangoes do not grow in England?

(ii) Why Pakistan invaded India?

We can conclude from the above descriptions that in answering memory questions, memory is much used and for answering the thoughtful questions, much is to be thought. Here, attention is to be paid that without thinking, the learnt knowledge cannot be memorized. Similarly, without memory, it is difficult to answer the thoughtful questions. It clears that in answering memory questions, thinking is necessary and to answer thoughtful questions, help of the memory is to be sought.

According to the second classification, questions are divided mainly into the following two classes—

(a) Training Questions.

(b) Testing Questions.

(a) Meaning of Training Questions: Those questions are called training questions with the help of which, the pupils are motivated to derive the results by imagination, thinking and reasoning so that they may acquire the new knowledge conveniently. In short, while using training questions, the pupils have to seek the help of their imagination, thinking and reasoning powers etc. The example of such question is as follows—

(i) What steps we should take to grow more grains in India?

(b) Meaning of Testing Questions: The testing questions are those which test the knowledge and memory of the pupils. Through these questions, teachers come to know very easily

whether their teaching is successful or not. In nut-shell, with the help of testing questions, pupil's previous knowledge and achievement are tested and their mastery on the subject can be ascertained. The examples of such questions are being given below—

(i) Explain the functioning of an air-pump.
(ii) Tell the name of the person who climbed the Mount Everest for the first time.

Questions Based on Size and Type of Answers

The various types of questions on the basis of size and type of answers are as follows:

1. Essay Type Questions.
2. Short Answer Type Questions.
3. Objective Type Questions.

1. Meaning of Essay Type Questions

Those questions are known as essay type questions which are answered in the form of an essay. Such questions can be used for home assignment. Essay type questions have both advantages and disadvantages. Answering such questions—

1. Expression of the pupils develops;
2. They learn to organise the subject-matter in a logical sequence; and
3. Their language style gets refined.

Contrary to these, such questions have disadvantages, such as—

1. Lesser knowledge is tested in much time;
2. Answers to such questions are generally indefinite or uncertain for which evaluation is difficult; and
3. The acquired knowledge of the pupils cannot be tested completely.

The examples of the essay type questions are as follows—

Compare Jain and Buddha religions and explain how Buddha religion spread?

2. Meaning of Short Answer Type Questions

Short answer type questions are those which are answered in a very short form. Such questions can be used successfully in both teaching of social sciences and home assignments. Their answers are more clear and definite as compared to the answers of essay type questions. The examples of short-answer type questions are being given in the following lines—

(i) Who wrote the 'Ram Charitamanas'?

(ii) How much salary gets the President of India?

3. Meaning of Objective Type Questions

Objective type questions are those which have small and definite answers. Through these questions, expression power and linguistic style cannot be evaluated, but still these can be used in teaching, home work and at the time of testing. Examples of objective type questions are given below—

If the following items are true, then mark the 'true', and if these are false, then mark the 'false'—

1. Delhi is the Capital of India. [True/False]
2. Mahatma Buddha was born in Japan. [True/False]

Kinds of Questions

Questions are used from the very beginning of the lesson till it is over. But it is necessary, for the help of fresh teachers and pupil-teachers, that at various stages, which type of questions are to be asked while lesson is being developed. From this point of view, we present the different kinds of questions hereunder:

1. Introductory Questions.
2. Developing Questions.
3. Thought Provoking Questions.
4. Problem Questions.
5. Comparison Questions.
6. Comprehensive Questions.
7. Recapitulatory Questions.

1. *Introductory Questions.* Introductory questions are asked at the introduction stage. In other words, such questions are asked before starting the main lesson so that the pupils may be motivated for new knowledge after testing the previous knowledge of the pupils. Remember that the introductory questions are smaller and three or four in number. Also, the last question is such that it links the previous knowledge of the pupils with the new knowledge.

2. *Developing Questions.* The developing questions are used at the developing stage of the lesson. By such questions, with the help of pupils, new knowledge is developed in a logical sequence. Such questions provide an opportunity to the pupils for using their own intelligence, logic and decisions by stimulating their mental processes.

In short, by developing questions pupils are provided with more opportunities of acquiring knowledge by self-thinking. From this point of view, developing questions have their own importance whatever the teaching method is.

3. *Thought Provoking Questions.* Those questions are called thought provoking questions with the help of which powers of imagination, logic and decision making of the pupils are developed and their brain is made thoughtful and active after awakening it. It is a matter of experience that during teaching, some pupils sometimes look physically present in the class-room but mentally they are somewhere else. In such a situation, the teacher should go asking thoughtful questions like 'Why' and 'How' from whole of the class. Since answering of such thoughtful questions needs pupils' own intelligence, reasoning and decision-making powers, therefore, while asking questions, the teacher should take care of the age, experience, previous knowledge and level of the pupils.

4. *Problem Questions.* Those questions are termed as problem questions by which such a problem is presented before the pupils either in the beginning or in the end or at both the stages of the lesson and the pupils assimilate new knowledge while solving those problems by using their own previous knowledge. In nut-shell, problem questions keep the pupils mentally active.

5. *Comparison Questions.* Comparison questions are those in which the facts or events are compared. Such questions are generally used in the lessons of History, Geography and Science. Remember that comparison questions can be used at the both stages, i.e., in the beginning and in the end of the lesson. But, normally it is appropriate to use in the middle of the lesson.

6. *Comprehensive Questions.* Those questions are called comprehensive questions by which the teacher comes to know whether the pupils have acquired the knowledge of the subject-

matter or not. It is observed that all the pupils listen to the teacher but when the questions are asked regarding the taught subject-matter they get up silently without giving any answer. In such condition, the teacher should repeat all those things which have already been taught. It means that the teacher must ask comprehensive questions. If the pupils answer these questions, it is alright, otherwise re-teaching should take place.

7. *Recapitulatory Questions.* Those questions are called recapitulatory questions by which the main factual points of the lesson are revised. The aim of these questions is to substantiate the knowledge by organizing it properly. From this point of view, these questions should be based on the taught knowledge. Such questions should be asked at the end of the lesson but in the social subjects, these can be used at the end of each unit. These questions should be asked very quickly, only then they may prove useful.

Characteristics of Good Questions

Good questions have the following characteristics:

1. *Realization of Aim.* The questions should be such with the help of which teaching aims can be achieved. Teacher's objective of asking a question should be absolutely clear. This makes the class alive.

2. *Language.* The language of the questions should be simple, correct and clear so that all the pupils in the class may understand them easily. The teacher should keep in mind the intelligence level of the pupils and simplicity and clarity of the language while framing the questions.

3. *Pointed Questions.* Questions should be so much pointed that all the pupils get ready to answer them. In this light, the questions should neither be so simple nor too difficult but their construction should be done keeping in view the ability and mental level of the pupils.

4. *Thought Provoking.* The questions should be thought provoking so that the mental activities of the pupils may get alerted and awakened and they get motivated for memorizing, observation and thinking.

In nut-shell, the questions should be thought-oriented and problem-centred.

5. *Brief and Direct Questions.* The questions should be brief

and related to the subject. In other words, the questions should be so much easy and short that they can be answered in small sentences. The pupils can understand such questions very conveniently and they can answer them easily.

6. *Definite Answer.* The questions should bear a definite answer so that the pupils of the class may respond correctly. For example, what was the economic policy of Allauddin Khilzi? It is a definite question. All the pupils will respond in a similar way. In short, the teacher should ask the pupils those questions which bear definite answer so that the teaching may go on lively.

7. *Proper Distribution.* The questions should be asked from every part of the lesson. It is not fair to ask questions either from one or the other part of the lesson. Similarly, all the pupils should be allowed equal opportunities to understand and to answer the questions.

8. *Systematic.* The questions should be classified and systematic. It leads to the natural advancement of the lesson. Hence, the teacher must organise the questions in such a logical sequence that one question should get automatically linked with the other.

9. *Variety in Form and Difficulty Level.* There should be a variety in the form and difficulty level of questions. In other words, all the questions should not have the same method and difficulty level.

Defective Forms of the Questions

The defective form of the questions turn the teaching activity ineffective. In other words, the pupils will not be benefited by asking defective questions. We are throwing light on some defective forms of the questions in the following lines for fresh teachers and especially for pupil-teachers in order to be vigilant.

1. *Echo Questions.* When the questions on the stated material are asked immediately after making the statement, then such questions are termed as echo questions. For example, first of all the teacher should tell the pupils that Anupshahar was founded by Raja Ani Rai. Then, immediately a question is asked that who founded Anup Shahar? Remember that such questions are considered to be useless. Therefore, the teacher should not ask pupils these echo questions.

2. *'Yes' or 'No' Type Questions.* 'Yes' or 'No' type questions are also known as "Two Answer Type Questions". Such questions can be answered only in Yes or No. For example, Was Bulban a great administrator? The pupils answer such questions on the basis of guess and without any thinking. This fails to arouse their curiosity and they don't get opportunity to ascertain their view by thinking at their own. This spoils class-room discipline.

3. *Elliptical Questions.* In elliptical questions, the last word of the sentence remains hidden, such as Lucknow is U.P.'s .... What's that? In such questions, pupils complete the sentence by telling the last word. Remember that the mental process of the pupils does not get any encouragement from such elliptical questions. Hence, the teacher should not ask such questions.

4. *Rhetorical Questions.* Those questions are called rhetorical questions which are asked during teaching as a challenge to put emphasis on certain point, such as, who can be greater sacrificing personality than Lal Bahadur Shastri? Such questions using the ornamental language, make the statement effective, but pupils are not made mentally active. Hence, asking the pupils such questions is mere wastage of time.

5. *Suggestive Questions.* The suggestive questions are those which suggest or prompt pupils regarding the answer. Such questions carry their answers too, such as—Was Morarji Desai Prime Minister of India? Answering such questions, pupils are not to think even for a moment. Hence, pupils are not benefited by asking suggestive questions.

6. *Indefinite, Ambiguous and Irrelevant Questions.* Indefinite questions are those which make the pupils confused while answering. Ambiguous questions are those which arouse doubts in the minds of the pupils. Irrelevant questions are those which are not related to the subject. Remember that the pupils cannot respond clearly to all these three types of questions. Such questions are considered as defective.

7. *Questions Requiring More than One Answer.* There are some questions which require more than one answer. Such questions are considered as defective. The teacher should ask such questions after bifurcating it.

How to ask Questions?

In order to achieve teaching objectives, whichever method or technique is used, seeking assistance of questioning technique is must. From this point of view, the teacher should use direct, brief, easy and thought provoking questions with clear language and definite answers. Hence, in the following lines, we are thrówing light on all those important points which the teachers are to keep in their minds while questioning the pupils:

1. The teacher should speak the question so loudly that every pupil of the class may hear it conveniently.
2. The teacher should ask the questions standing amidst the pupils. He should seek the answer first from those pupils who seem to be less interested in the lesson.
3. The teacher should ask the questions quickly. This keeps the class alive and the pupils maintain their attention in the lesson. The teacher should manage appropriate duration for the pupils in order to answer the questions after proper thinking keeping in mind their ability and mental level.
4. While asking questions, the teacher should avoid his random movements in the class-room.
5. The teacher should not use unnecessary sentences before or after the questioning, such as "Who will tell"? or "Who can tell amongst you"? This wastes the time.
6. There should be equal distribution of the questions in the class. If a teacher asks questions continuously from one or two or front-line benchers (pupils), then the other pupils cease to show any interest in the lesson. This will spoil the class-room order and the teaching will become bore.
7. The teacher should remember the names of the pupils of the class. Not only this, he should call the pupils while asking questions. This facilitates the participation of the pupils in the development of the lesson as a result of their alertness.
8. The teacher should follow, while asking questions, the principle of variety. In other words, a teacher should not ask the pupils questions of the same type.
9. The teacher should not change again and again the language of the questions. This develops the

understanding in the minds of the pupils that the teacher has asked some other question. Hence, they sit silently.

10. The teacher should be cheerful while questioning is in progress. This mobilizes the life in the pupils when they look at his face.
11. While asking questions, the teacher should behave affectionately and sympathetically with the pupils. It is because that in the fearful environment, the pupils cannot answer properly after thinking independently. Hence, at the time of questioning, the class-room environment should be independent, affectionate and sympathetic.

Receiving Answers Technique

Davis has rightly said, "It is by means of children's answers that you can get an insight into the working of child's mind."

Through an answer, a teacher comes to know about the mental activity, energy and development of the pupils. In other words, a teacher comes to know very easily from the answer whether the pupils got the understanding of the subject-matter or not. From this point of view, for a successful teacher, both the arts, i.e., all the points regarding answering along with asking questions, have special importance.

Importance of Answers

Since the success of teaching depends upon the answers made by the pupils, therefore answers have importance as follows:

1. A rapport is developed between pupils and the teachers through answers.
2. The answering develops the thinking and imaginative powers of the pupils and their memory stabilizes.
3. The answering systematizes the ideas of the pupils.
4. The answers convey the teacher regarding how much the pupils have gained the knowledge of taught-matter.
5. A teacher comes to know about the mental level of the pupils through answers.
6. With the repetition of the answering exercise, pupils' hesitation eliminates. Also, courage and self-confidence develops among them.

7. Through answers, the teacher makes the language of the pupils refined and increases their knowledge.
8. An answer provides the opportunity to rectify the mistakes and errors of the teachers and the pupils.
9. Through answer, all those pupils come in light who don't concentrate in studies.
10. The answering facilitates recapitulation of the taught lesson.
11. The answers evaluate the teaching.

Characteristics of Good Answers

The following are the characteristics of good answers—

1. The answers should be in one language only. These should not be in more than one languages. Its reason is that the use of single language develops the thinking and descriptive powers of the pupils. Also, they become habitual of using correct language.
2. The answers should be in the terms accepted by civilized society, not in domestic words. Hearing general words of daily talk, pupils will laugh. This also creates a problem of discipline.
3. In answers, the clarity and systematization of ideas should occur. The answers which lack these qualities are termed as inappropriate and irrelevant answers.
4. Answers should be spoken loudly sweetly and with speed. Those answers spoken slowly and in low pitch are not audible to all the pupils of the class. Hence, the pupil-teachers should be alert on this account.
5. The answers of the questions should not be in bookish language, but these should be in simple, correct and clear language of the pupils.
6. The answers should be in complete sentences. This develops power of expression of the pupil and they will be efficient in the art of speaking.
7. In an answer only required number of words should be used. Use of excessive words wastes time. Also it distracts the pupils.
8. Answers should be full of ideas. Expression of incomplete ideas is not a good habit.

Receiving Answers

As every teacher is not an expert in asking question, similarly, correct answer cannot be received from every pupil. Therefore, fresh teachers and pupil-teachers must pay attention to these points:

1. *Proper Distribution of Questions.* First of all, the teacher should present his question before the whole class in easy language and louder voice so that all the pupils become thoughtful and active to give answer. Then some one should be instructed, calling by his name, to answer.

2. *Discouragement to collective Answers.* Sometimes, some pupils just after getting a question from the teacher, start answering, without teacher's permission, either individually or collectively. In such situation, the teacher should restrict such tendency and try to receive answer from that pupil only to whom he points out.

3. *No immediate Answer just after the Question.* The teacher should not try to receive answer immediately after questioning. It is because no pupil is so much mentally matured that he can answer immediately after receiving the question. Therefore, the teaching should allow some time to the pupils to think properly after asking a question.

4. *Patience for Answers.* Some pupils become so much excited to answer a question which disturbs the class-room discipline. In such situation, the teacher should not feel nervous. He should instruct the whole class to keep quiet and ensure them with an opportunity to everyone to answer the question. The teacher should make clear to the potential answer tellers not to stand up again and again crying "should we tell?", rather they should raise their right hand. Still if some pupils make a noise by raising their hands, then for some time he should not encourage such pupils. This will facilitate auto-correction among them.

5. *Encouragement to Shy Students.* The teacher should not accept the answers in low pitch, in shyness and in a sitting posture. Such pupils should be encouraged to answer in a standing position and louder voice.

6. *Asking Answer by addressing Names of Students.* The teacher should instruct that pupil to answer who has raised his hand

calling by his name. This learns the impression in the minds of the pupils that the teacher knows all the pupils of the class personally. This enables the pupil's active participation in the development of the lesson.

7. *Analysis of Wrong Answers.* The teacher should not laugh at the pupils' wrong, inappropriate and foolish answers rather he should rectify such answers with patience in a civilized way after analysis.

8. *Encouragement for Answers.* The teacher should appreciate the answers made by intelligent pupils. He should encourage the weak pupils to answer correctly. But at the same time, the teacher should show whatever appreciative he can. The child needs encouragement.

9. *Teacher's Sympathetic Behaviour.* Those pupils who keep on sitting passively in the class, avoiding face to face encounter with the teacher, should be awakened and they should directed to answer the question. If such pupils are afraid of answering, they should not be reprimanded. The teacher should try to make them active and thoughtful by affection and sympathetic behaviour.

10. *No Help in Answering.* The teacher should provide no help to the pupils for answering a question. But fearful, weak and shy pupils should be incited to answer the questions after providing necessary help.

11. *Equal Opportunities for All to Answer.* It is not appropriate to receive answer repeatedly from intelligent pupils only. This makes the weak and mentally retarded pupils so passive that they neither listen the teacher's questions nor they think to answer his questions. Thus, a situation arises when the teacher allows sometimes such pupils to answer, they start answering either in a very obsurd way or they stand up silently. Hence, to make all types of pupils active and thoughtful, all the pupils should be provided with equal opportunities from time to time to answer the questions.

12. *Repetition of Correct Answers by Defaulters.* The teacher should receive answers from the intelligent pupils. But every correct answer should be repeated by the defaulters of incorrect answers.

13. *Answer in Full Sentences.* Some experts are of the view that while teaching science and maths, pupils should not be

forced to answer in complete sentences. Since, we want to develop power of expression of the pupils so that their ideas may be well organised and skill of speaking is acquired, therefore, in our view, habit of answers in complete sentences should be created in the pupils.

14. *Only Necessary Encouragement.* Some teachers make excessive use of appreciative words like 'Well done', 'Beautiful', 'Most Beautiful',—which is not appropriate. There is no doubt that the pupils should be encouraged by their appreciation, but remember that excess of everything is bad. With excessive appreciation, pupils start either laughing at the teachers or they underestimate them. Hence, the teacher must appreciate good answers but appreciative words or sentences should be used at appropriate occasions only.

15. *No Repetition of Student's Answers.* The teacher should not repeat the answer made by the pupils This wastes the time and pupils also avoid to listen the answers given by their class-mates. It's reason is that all the pupils are confident that the teacher will repeat the correct answer. It is a bad habit. Hence, pupil-teachers should be alert on this issue.

16. *No Satisfaction by One Student's Answer Only.* If an answer to some problematic question is received in the beginning, the teacher should not feel satisfied. He should try to receive the answer from other pupils too. This creates a habit of thinking. instead of guessing in the pupils.

17. *Telling the Reason of Wrong Answers.* The teacher must explain the reason of wrong answers. Otherwise, this will create confusion in the minds of the pupils and they would be unable to eliminate their errors.

Method of Correcting Wrong Answers

The answers provided by the pupils generally carry linguistic and factual errors. To correct these erroneous answers, the teachers should keep in mind the following points:

1. The teacher should explore the causes of the error. Without knowing the causes, if it is not impossible to correct the incorrect answers, it is essentially difficult to do so.
2. Often the answers carry errors regarding language and object. The teacher should, first, rectify linguistic errors

and then the object. Its reason is that through language, pupils express their ideas. If the language is incorrect, his ideas would certainly be vague and overlapping. Therefore, the teacher should rectify the mistakes regarding grammar and pronunciation of the pupils at first priority so that they may express their ideas in correct language conveniently.

3. In order to correct pupils' incorrect answers, the teacher should be affectionate and sympathetic.
4. If a pupil is unable to answer the question, the teacher must receive the correct answer from the other pupil first. This correct response should be repeated by the pupil and then he should be asked to sit down.
5. When the teacher thinks that the pupil is repeating the correct answer mechanically, then in such situation, the teacher should receive correct response by asking 'What' and 'How'.
6. Sometimes the pupils cannot give answers due to the complexity and vagueness of questions. In such situation, the teacher should divide his main question into sub-questions so that the pupils may answer easily.
7. The teacher should never accept completely incorrect answer. If he does so, then the pupils will be confused and they will go on repeating their incorrect answer.
8. The teacher should not reject pupils' answers outrightly. It would be better if the teacher accepts the correct part of the answer and rest incorrect should be rectified.
9. If the answer is completely incorrect, the teacher must tell clearly where the answer is incorrect and how much. This facilitates the pupils to correct the answer.
10. If none of the pupils is able to answer the question, then, in such a situation, the teacher should give the answer himself in order to avoid boredom in the class.
11. Help of a black board should be sought to correct the incorrect answers of the pupils.

Answering the Questions of Students

A teacher's success depends on two things—(1) How much the teacher motivates the pupils to ask questions? (2) What the attitude of the teacher towards the pupils' questions is?

Psychology suggests that the instinct of curiosity among the pupils is innate. 'Suspense' or 'Surprise' has an active role in keeping the pupil active. Therefore, while describing the knowledge, the teacher should arouse 'surprising moments or suspense' in the pupils.

In order to know the causes of these surprising moments, pupils will be motivated to ask questions regarding 'What', 'Why' and 'How'. In short, in order to make the teaching successful, the teacher should provide maximum opportunities to the pupils of the class to ask the questions. In this regard, two questions arise before us—(1) How the pupil should ask a question? and (2) How the answers are provided to the questions of the pupils?

So far as the first question is concerned, the teacher should make clear to the pupils that the question should be related to the subject and the pupil who wants an answer to a question must raise his hand. Then, he should ask the question in a straight, standing posture and in sweet voice along with proper speed. Now comes the point how pupils' questions are to be responded? In this context, following points deserve consideration.

1. The teacher should try to get solved the questions, asked by some pupil, with the help of some other pupils. Remember that when a pupil succeeds in answering the questions asked by some other pupils, he enjoys happiness. Also he develops a feeling of self-confidence in him.
2. The teacher should make answers to those questions of the pupils which benefit maximum pupils of the class. If any pupil has some individual difficulty, it must be removed after the period is over.
3. When no pupil is able to give answers of the questions asked by a pupil of the same class, then the teacher should not waste his time. He should respond himself.
4. The teacher should discourage asking irrelevant questions by the pupils. It is because while it destroys the whole time on one side, the teacher also deviates from the objective of the main lesson on the other side.
5. It can also happen that the teacher is unable to get answer to the questions of the pupils. In such a situation,

he should not entertain the pupils by presenting false answers. He should promise to give answer after consultation and put it pending for the next day. But the next day, he must present the correct answer. The pupils disown any respect for those teachers who are in the habit of avoiding the answers. Hence, the fresh teachers, especially pupil-teachers need to be alert in this regard.

QUESTIONS FOR ANSWER

1. "The success of teaching depends upon the answers made by the pupils." Justify.
2. "If the art of framing a question is so much important, the method of receiving an answer is also important in the same way." Explain this statement.
3. What are the characteristics of good answers?
4. How and when incorrect answers are corrected?
5. What is the importance of asking questions in teaching? Explain.
6. What are the main characteristics of good questions?
7. "Good Questions have importance in an effective teaching. A person learns properly from them and the lesson too goes on logically." Explain this statement by giving examples.
8. How the questions should be asked? Write a short note on it.

12

Management of Teaching and Learning—1 (Basic Concepts and Planning Aspects)

In earlier times all over the world the teacher himself managed all affairs concerning teaching-learning but now a complexity has developed in the teaching process, therefore teaching-learning management has developed as a specialised skill. Therefore teacher has to be trained in this art to achieve the real objectives of education and for this purpose we first define management as hereunder.

The collective use of human means and resources, which he possesses is called management, i.e., the way of using human means and resources to achieve definite aims is called management. The following tactics are used in the management:

(i) Tasks and activities are divided.

(ii) Hierarchy of rights and duties is determined.

(iii) Coordination is established between efforts, means and resources.

On the basis of management, a statement regarding real outcomes and educational achievements is given and means and tactics for learning structures are determined. Since, the management is directly related to the human being, therefore assumptions of human nature affect this concept. Assumptions about human nature are as follows as per Mach and Simon:

1. Task Centred Classic Theory of Organization

In the field of Education, the pupil acts like a machine only. No place is given to his interests, capacities and aptitudes in educational management. The teaching-management is task-centred and teacher-controlled. In the class-room, the presentation of the content is emphasised only. In this teaching management, the pupils are to cram more, i.e., only memory-level teaching occurs. In this, only cognitive objectives are achieved.

2. Human Relation Theory of Organization

Relationship Centred. This theory can be explained in this way— that the members of the management bring their attitudes, aptitudes, values and aims with them. They should be encouraged and motivated.

In the present teaching system, this theory is being followed. This theory is contrary to the task-centred theory. According to this theory, the teaching is managed in such a way so that an all-round development of the pupils may take place. This is managed in accordance with the interests, aptitudes and abilities of the pupils.

The teacher performs the role of counsellor in such type of management and he encourages the pupils to remain active. The use of teaching material is more emphasized.

According to this theory, the content is managed in such a way that the learning process may become interesting and motivating. Cramming is not emphasized.

3. Modern Theory of Organization—Task and Relationship

This theory means that the members of the management are competent for solving any problem and able to take any decision. In this, presentation and thinking are more emphasized. A difference occurs among the objectives of these three theories. Actually, these theories are being used successfully in the field of education.

In the modern approach of management, task and human relations are also included. According to this theory, a coordination is established among the teacher, the pupils, the task and the management variables. This theory is related to the independent study, instruction, system and instructional technology.

Management of Learning

First of all, I.K. Davis presented the teacher as a manager. In the teaching process, the planning of tasks and processes and their management occur. In the teaching-learning management, the activities of teaching and learning are to be managed. Then, the process takes place by means of teaching and learning.

Davis has described the following four main tasks of the teacher in the teaching-learning management:

(i) Planning
(ii) Organizing
(iii) Leading
(iv) Controlling

With the help of above four tasks, a design of a learning system is prepared.

Features of Management of Teaching-Learning

In a teaching process, the teaching-learning management has the following characteristics:

1. Through management approach, the teacher is made more conscious and encouraged towards his duties.
2. Through this management approach, a coordination between all the teaching activities can be established.
3. Teaching activities can be made purposeful.
4. Teaching theories can be developed through this approach.
5. With the help of this approach, a relationship between teaching and learning can be established.
6. The pupils are provided with complete opportunities of all-round development through this approach.
7. Teaching and training can be made objective-centred.
8. In the teaching-learning management, help is sought in the selection and development of teaching aids.

Teacher's Role in Managing Teaching-Learning

Two functions of a teacher have been considered—*(i)* to manage learning means, *(ii)* to execute those learning means. From this point of view, I.K. Davis has reminded us the following four types of responsibilities in order to establish the teacher as a manager:

1. *Planning of Teaching*. Under this responsibility, the teacher has to determine and define the objectives. The teacher also plans the curriculum in a sequence after analysing it. In spite of this, the responsibilities of a teacher also include the selection of teaching aids for teaching. It is the very same phase in which the teacher gets an opportunity to apply his imagination and creative powers.

2. *Organisation*. Achieving the objectives is the main aim in teaching-learning management. Hence, in this phase teaching-learning conditions are developed in order to achieve objectives. These teaching-learning conditions are developed keeping in view the individual differences.

3. *Leading to Teaching*. The fundamental duty of a teacher is—to encourage pupils, to supervise their functions and to provide them necessary guidance. All these duties of a teacher help him in achieving the objectives.

4. *Controlling of Teaching*. The last duty of the teacher is controlling of teaching. It is the most difficult task for a teacher. In this, the teacher evaluates all the pupils in the light of objectives. The teacher evaluates this through tests.

As a result of these duties of a teacher, we can hope that a laborious teacher can make the teaching-learning process successful and effective.

Aspects of Teaching-Learning Planning

Ivor K. Davies defines modern concept of teaching-learning as follows:

> *"Teaching is a highly skilled professional activity and a great deal of what teachers and instructors do, both within and outside the class-room, involves making decision of one kind or another."*

I.K. Davies has divided the functions of the teacher as a manager into the following four steps as discussed earlier:

1. Planning
2. Organization
3. Leading
4. Controlling

"In teaching planning is the work a teacher does to establish learning objectives." —*I.K. Davies.*

"Organization is the work a teacher does to arrange and relate learning resources, so as to realize learning objectives in the most effective, efficient and economical way possible." —*Ivor K. Davies*

"Leading is the work a teacher does to motivate, encourage and inspire the students, so that they will readily achieve the learning objectives." —*Ivor K. Davies.*

"In teaching controlling is the work a teacher does to determine whether his plans are being carried out effectively, organization is sound, realizing is in right direction and that how far these functions are successful in realizing the set objectives." —*I.K. Davies.*

Planning of Teaching

Planning is the first important phase or step of teaching-learning management. Therefore teaching's base is planning. Remember that in the task of planning, only those teachers get success who possess qualities like clarity and efficiency.

I.K. Davies, in his book "The Management of Teaching", has written about the following three activities which are to be followed by the teacher during planning teaching:

1. Task Analysis
2. Identification of Teaching Objectives
3. Writing the Teaching Objectives in Behavioural Terms

1. Task Analysis

In task analysis, the activities related to the contents are analysed. If task analysis is not carried out properly, expected achievement is not possible. Hence, task analysis has special importance. According to I.K. Davies, four activities are included in task-analysis—

(i) Description of activities which are to be learnt by the pupil.

(ii) Identification of expected behaviours.

(iii) Identification of those stimuli and conditions with the help of which pupils may show expected behaviours.

(iv) Determination of norms for expected performance or achievement.

Remember that through task analysis, proper decisions are made regarding learning objectives, teaching strategies and tactics.

Types of Task Analysis

Task analysis is of the following three types:

(i) Content Analysis or Topic Analysis
(ii) Job Analysis
(iii) Skill Analysis

(i) Content Analysis or Topic Analysis. In content analysis, the content or topic is analysed on educational and intellectual basis.

(ii) Job Analysis. This step is concerned with 'what is to be done in the task.' Hence, in this phase, physical and psychomotor activities are determined and sub-processes are analysed.

(iii) Skill Analysis. The skill analysis is the next stage of job analysis. In this step, it is emphasized how the work is accomplished. It includes all those tasks which need skill, but the skill analysis is done only for questioning and diagnosis activities.

Meaning and Definition of Content or Topic Analysis

In the words of I.K. Davies, "It is the analysis of topic or content unit to be taught into its constituents or elements and synthesize into logical consequence."

Since many techniques are used for content analysis but matrix techniques of I.K. Davies is considered most useful. According to this technique, content is divided into sub-topics first of all which are meaningful and completely separate from each other. Then, these sub-topics are psychologically arranged in a sequence.

Then, each sub-topic is divided into its elements and arranged in a sequence. Remember that each element of the sub-topic is meaningful, complete and separate from each other like sub-topics of the content are arranged in a sequence on the basis of certain laws and maxims of teaching.

Hence, in content analysis, both activities of analysis and synthesis are included. We can represent the content analysis in the chart given on page 255 according to I.K. Davies matrix technique.

Arrangement of Topic Elements in Logical Sequence

In the above lines, we have made it clear that each sub-division's elements should be arranged keeping in view certain laws. Here, it is important to tell the pupils to follow the following maxims of teaching which have already been described in this book:

(*i*) From simple to complex
(*ii*) From known to unknown
(*iii*) From concrete to abstract
(*iv*) From whole to part
(*v*) From Psychological to Logical

Sources of Topic Analysis

Teacher should follow the following sources to present the content or topic by analysis:

(*i*) Study of Standard Text-Book
(*ii*) Knowledge of Student's Needs
(*iii*) Understanding Educational Needs
(*iv*) Utility of Teaching Aids
(*v*) Possibilities of Examination System

Identification of Teaching Objectives

Teaching is a purposeful and meaningful process. Hence, after the content analysis, the teacher should determine the teaching objectives in the same phase. But before determining the teaching objectives, it is necessary to understand the meaning of teaching objectives, their need and importance and difference between teaching and educational objectives.

(a) Meaning of Teaching Objectives. According to NCERT's Evaluation and Examination issue, "An objective is a point or end in view of some thing towards which action is directed, a planned change sought through any activity what we set out to do."

According to this definition, teaching objective includes three things; (*i*) Direction, (*ii*) Planned Change, (*iii*) Activity. It is a reality that the objective has such a power, due to which all the teaching activities of the pupils are managed towards a definite direction. Due to this, desirable change goes on occurring in his behaviour.

(b) Need of Teaching Objectives: Through teaching, we wish to bring change in the pupils by developing their personality. Definite and clear objectives bring the expected changes in the pupils in the following areas—*(i)* In the area of knowledge *(ii)* In the area of application, *(iii)* In the area of skill, *(iv)* In the area of interest, *(v)* In the area of attitudes, *(vi)* In the area of appreciation, and *(vii)* In the area of personality.

Remember that education increases the new knowledge of the pupils. This develops ability and efficiency of solving complex problems in them. They modify their attitudes towards life and society by showing new interests.

This is clear that teaching process can bring changes in the various areas like knowledge, application, interest, ability, efficiency, attitude, appreciation, personality and character etc. of the pupils.

(c) Importance of Teaching Objectives. Teaching objectives occupy important place in the teaching process. It's only reason is the revolutionary changes which have occurred in the nature of teaching, functions of the pupils and the teachers and the traditional training attitudes.

According to the new attitude, learning experiences of the pupils are being more emphasized, so that expected behavioural changes in them may be brought about.

Thus, during planning of teaching, after topic analysis, learning objectives are specifically defined. Not only this, now strategies of teaching, tactics and teaching material aids are decided keeping in view the learning experiences. And, in the end, the evaluations and measurement of the behavioural changes by learnt experiences are carried over.

(d) Difference between Teaching Aim and Goal. According to B.S. Bloom, teaching objectives means forming those clear plans which make possible behavioural changes in the pupils. According to this definition, teaching objective is definite and clear. It provides concrete help to the pupil and gives direction for action.

In this way, teaching objective is directly concerned to that content which a teacher intends to teach the pupils through teaching. In short, being definite and clear, teaching objectives may be achieved conveniently.

Contrary to this, goal is the general description of some task. It is not a definite and clear. Not only this, goal neither helps in determining strategies of teaching nor in evaluation. Hence, goal helps in no way in the teacher's task. Since the nature of a goal is comprehensive, therefore, it is merely an 'ideal' which is difficult to achieve.

Why Specify Objectives

The following are the reasons for specifying objectives:

1. The specification of the teaching objectives facilitates restrictions. Also, all the uncertainties regarding interpretations eliminate.
2. The specification of the teaching objectives presents the complete level of the curriculum. The level of the curriculum functions as conceptual management and future management in learning.
3. Specifying teaching objectives helps in making the learning objectives definite by turning the curriculum effective.
4. Specifying teaching objectives helps pupils and teachers in differentiating various behaviours. It helps in determining strategies of teaching.
5. Specifying teaching objectives helps in measurement and evaluation of teaching.

Difference Between Educational and Teaching Objectives

The objectives are mainly divided into two parts—*(i)* Educational Objectives, and *(ii)* Teaching Objectives. Remember that both types of objectives are very much different. We are making clear these differences in the following table.

	Educational Objectives	*Teaching Objectives*
(i)	Expect more the philosophical basis.	Expect more psychological basis.
(ii)	These are concerned with entire education.	These are restricted to the class-room and these are used for teaching various subjects.

(Contd.)

Educational Objectives	Teaching Objectives
(iii) These are broad and general.	These are narrow and specific.
(iv) These are formal.	These are functional.
(v) These are theorietical and indirect.	These are direct. These are concerned with class-room teaching. Hence, these help in changing the behaviour by providing speed to the learning process.
(vi) Their acquisition needs long duration i.e., these can be achieved from primary to University-level education.	These can be achieved in short duration i.e., only in the period of 40 minutes only.

The above table makes clear the difference between educational and teaching objectives. From this, we conclude that teaching objectives are specific, direct and practical. Remember that the Teaching objectives are directly concerned with learning objectives. According to I.K. Davies, "Learning objective is a statement of proposed change". It has two advantages—*(i)* It helps in selecting the activities which create the learning experiences for pupils, and *(ii)* It helps in collecting those evidences on the basis of which it can be proved whether the class-room activities have achieved the desired objectives or not. This helps the teacher in conducting his teaching task smoothly.

Classification of Learning Objectives

Although Mager and Krathwohl have done appreciable work regarding classification of learning objectives, Prof. B.S. Bloom's contribution in this direction has special importance. Its main reason is that Bloom's classification is directly related to the problems of curriculum and evaluation and this has proved more helpful in formulating the techniques of communication, evaluation and the development of the curriculum. According to Bloom's hierarchy of educational objectives, learning objectives are as follows:

(*a*) Cognitive Objectives
(*b*) Affective Objectives
(*c*) Psychomotor Objectives

(a) Cognitive Objectives

Cognitive objectives stress more that the pupils should acquire more and more knowledge. Since in the behaviour related to cognitive aspect psychological processes like recall and recognition remain active, efforts are made to develop this aspect more through various school subject.

Remember that Bloom has suggested in his book "Taxonomy of Educational Objectives of Cognitive Domain", that it is essential to cross the six stages of cognitive domain in order to develop cognitive domain by cognitive objectives.

These classes or stages are—

1. Knowledge,
2. Comprehension,
3. Application,
4. Analysis,
5. Synthesis, and
6. Evaluation.

In the following lines we are throwing light on the six categories of cognitive domain.

1. *Knowledge Objective*. The cognitive objectives are concerned with the development of recall and recognition activities of the pupils with the help of terms, facts, informations and theories. Remember that from content's viewpoint, following are the three levels in the knowledge category.

(i) Knowledge of Specifics. Knowledge of specific means recalling of specific terminology, facts and information. The knowledge of specific is also divided into two: (1) Knowledge of terminology, and (2) Knowledge of specific facts.

Remember that the knowledge of terminology is the knowledge of verbal and non-verbal references. These have normal signs and these include defining specific terms, description of their qualities, relationships and their parts so that the general meaning of the various terms may be acquired.

Contrary to this, the specific facts means the knowledge

of events, dates, places and the persons.

(ii) Knowledge of Ways and Means—Dealing with Specifics. In this, appropriate decisions are taken and the criticism is carried out by studying systematically the various ways and means of the knowledge. Bloom has divided the ways and means dealing with specifics into the following five categories—

(a) Knowledge of Conventions
(b) Knowledge of Trends and Sequences
(c) Knowledge of Criteria
(d) Knowledge of Methodology
(e) Knowledge of Classification and Categories

(iii) Knowledge of Universal and Abstractions. The knowledge of universals and abstractions is concerned with laws and principles. Prof. Bloom has given two forms of knowledge of universals—*(a)* Knowledge of principles and generalization, and *(b)* Knowledge of theories and structures.

2. *Comprehension.* Comprehension means understanding of new knowledge to the pupils. The pupils who have comprehension of the contents, i.e., the recalling and recognition abilities can carry on the activities of translation, interpretation and extrapolation on the basis of comprehension objective. In short, comprehension activities have three levels—*(a)* Translation, *(ii)* Interpretation, and *(ii)* Extrapolation.

3. *Application.* After knowledge and comprehension, application is followed. Remember that the application objective has also three levels—*(i)* generalization of laws and principles, *(ii)* diagnosis of pupils' weaknesses, and *(iii)* use of contents or terms and laws by the pupils in their own statements.

4. *Analysis.* After knowledge, comprehension and application, analysis is followed. The analysis objective includes division of the contents into its elements and these are mutually related. Remember that the analysis objective has three levels—*(i)* analysis of elements, *(ii)* analysis of relationships, and *(iii)* analysis of organized principles.

5. *Synthesis.* Synthesis is termed as the creative objective. Its reason is that the elements analysed in this step are assembled to give a complete picture and a new format is prepared. This develops the creative abilities of the pupils.

Remember that the synthesis has also three levels—

(i) production of unique communication, *(ii)* production of a plan or proposed set of operations after synthesizing the elements, *(iii)* derivations of a set of abstract relations.

6. *Evaluation.* Evaluation is the highest level of the cognitive domain. It is a continuous process. In this, after making critical decisions regarding the laws of contents, principle and facts, it is explored by tests or other types of norms that *(i)* whether the determined teaching objectives have been achieved or not, if yes, to what extent, *(ii)* whether the learning experiences created in the classroom proved effective or not amongst pupils? and *(iii)* how fairly the teaching objectives have been achieved?

(b) Affective Domain

Affective objective is concerned with the interests, emotions, mental tendencies and values of the pupils. The development of affective domain is not an easy task. These are first concerned with a particular person and then with other persons. It is not an easy task to understand their nature and determined elements.

Since our interests, sentiments and mental tendencies are taken as the criteria for our personality, therefore, in education these occupy important place. It is the duty of the teacher to develop maximum the affective domain of the pupils by affective objectives i.e., their interest, emotions, mental tendencies and sentiments.

Bloom has divided affective objectives into the following categories in order to develop the affective domain of the pupils:

1. Receiving
2. Responding
3. Valuing
4. Conceptualization
5. Organization
6. Characterization of a Value System

1. *Receiving.* Receiving means pupils' will to receive. Receiving is directly concerned with the sensitivity of the pupils which occurs in the presence of some activity or stimulus. Receiving has the following three levels:

(i) Awareness of the phenomena
(ii) Willingness to receive phenomena

(iii) Controlled or selected scheme

2. *Responding*. Responding is the next stage of the receiving stage. In this, pupils actively receive new knowledge under the influence of motivation. Responding has three levels:

(i) Acquiescence in responding
(ii) Willingness to respond
(iii) Satisfaction in response

3. *Valuing*. Valuing means those values in which the pupils have their belief and they give special importance to those in their life. Valuing has three levels. These are—

(i) Acceptance of a value
(ii) Preference for a value
(iii) Commitment

4. *Conceptualization*. As the conviction regarding those values starts forming in the pupils, such situations also arise where more than one value is appropriate. In such situation pupil thinks which value he should retain.

5. *Organization*. When such a situation changes before the pupils in which there is more than one value is appropriate, then they organize these received values in an order or sequence.

6. *Characterization of a Value System*. Characterization of a value system is that level in which the consistency in the hierarchy of values of the pupil occurs. At this level, the teacher can characterize the knowledge of the value system of the pupils very easily. The characterization of a value system has two levels. These are—

(i) Generalized set, and
(ii) Characterization.

(c) Psychomotor Objectives

The psychomotor objective is concerned with the training of the pupils' physical activities and the development of the skills. The main levels of psychomotor domain are—*(i)* Impulsive, *(ii)* Manipulation, *(iii)* Control, *(iv)* Coordination, *(v)* Naturalization and *(vi)* Habit formulation.

Remember that like Prof. Bloom, E.J. Simpson has divided the objectives of psychomotor domain in the following five levels—

1. Perception
2. Set
3. Guided Response
4. Mechanism
5. Complex Overt Response

1. Perception. Perception is the process which gets alerted on the basis of interest and motivation regarding the external objects by sense organs. Perception has following levels—*(i)* Descriptive, *(ii)* Condition of Transition Period, and *(iii)* Interpretive Level.

2. Set. Set means that initial adjustment which occurs for some specific activities and experiences. Set has three aspects—*(i)* Mental, *(ii)* Physical, and *(iii)* Emotional.

3. Guided Response. Guided response is the initial stage of developing a practical skill. It is the external behaviour of a person under the guidance of another person. In the guided response, abilities with more complex skills are stressed.

4. Mechanism. Mechanism is said to be that level at which self-confidence and skill for doing some task gets developed in the pupils. Hence, mechanism is that condition which helps the pupils for responding properly.

5. Complex Overt Response. Complex overt response is said to be the highest level of psychomotor domain. At this stage, the pupil acquires so much efficiency and skill that he can accomplish the most complex task with minimum energy and time.

Writing Teaching Objectives in Behavioural Terms

From the above lines, it has been made clear that the teacher must have identified or determined the teaching objective after the content analysis. It is also essential to define them. Since, changes are brought in many aspects of pupil's behaviour, therefore, only then, any 'teaching objective' is said to be meaningful or attainable when it is defined completely which behavioural change in the pupils is to be brought and in what aspect. From this point of view, making clear the specifications of teaching objective in simple language is defining the objective. It will benefit in many ways. For example:

1. All the uncertainties and confusions will be removed.

2. It will help in advance study. For the convenience of the pupil-teachers, we have explained the characteristics of teaching objectives in the fourteenth unit of this book. All the readers are advised to study that unit and be benefited.
3. A comparison between the class-room behaviours of teachers and pupils will be established.
4. Measurement of performance and other activities would be possible.

While writing and defining the learning objectives, the following points should be kept in mind—

1. Learning objective should indicate desired behaviour.
2. The level of the objective achievement should be described in clear terms.
3. The learning objective should be described with reference to pupil's achievement.
4. Mastery on the subject must be there in order to achieve the objective.
5. The description of the objective should be in accordance with the learning.
6. Achievement of a single learning experience should be possible from each objective.

Need for Writing Objectives in Behavioural Terms

In the modern teaching process, the following is the need or importance of writing teaching objectives in behavioural terms:

1. Writing objectives in behavioural terms help in making certain and specific the teaching activities.
2. The teacher gets help in selecting teaching strategy, because once after such objectives are fixed, we can find out the differences between the various types of behaviours of the pupils and teachers.
3. It helps in selecting the questions for testing.
4. With the help of these objectives, the characteristics of learning experiences can be determined and measurement is also possible.
5. A balance between teaching and learning can be maintained.
6. It helps in selecting audio-visual aids.

7. The objectives written in behavioural terms help in managing an examination for the achievement of objectives relating to all the aspects.

1. Mager's Scheme

Mager has made the Bloom's taxonomy as basis for writing the objectives in behavioural terms. In Mager's scheme of writing objectives in behavioural terms 'Action Verbs' are used. A list of action verbs is prepared for every objective suggested by Bloom. A teacher selects action verbs and then writes objectives in behavioural terms. Various action verbs have been suggested for each objective. A list of these action verbs is given below:

A List of Action Verbs Cognitive Objectives

Objectives	*Action Verbs*
1. Knowledge	Define, Select, State, Measure, Recall, List, Recognize, Write.
2. Comprehension	Explain, Illustrate, Indicate, Present, Formulate, Classify, Judge, Select, Interpret, Translate.
3. Application	Predict, Assess, Compute, Construct, Use, Find, Demonstrate, Explain.
4. Analysis	Analysis, Divide, Conclude, Compare, Differentiate, Criticize, Separate, Justify.
5. Synthesis	Argue, Select, Discuss, Conclude, Organize, Predict, Generalize, Summarise.
6. Evaluation	Judge, Identify, Evaluation, Avoid, Criticize, Defend.

Robert Mager has gives a list of 'Action Verbs' for writing Bloom's Affective Objectives into behavioural terms. The list is given hereunder in the form of a table—

A List of Action Verbs Affective Objects

Objectives	Action Verbs
1. Responding	Listen, Receive, Accept, Perceive, Prefer, Select.
2. Receiving	Answer, Develop, State, Receive, List, Write.
3. Valuing	Accept, Influence, Participate, Recognise, Increase, Indicate, Decide.
4. Conceptualization	Differentiate, Relate, Analyse, Demonstrate, Indicate, Compare.
5. Organization	Organise, Correlate, Judge, Select, Relate, Determine, Form, Revise, Develop.
6. Characterization	Change, Demonstrate, Accept, Identify.

Limitations of Robert Mager's Scheme

Robert Mager's scheme has many drawbacks too, which are as follows—

1. In this Mager's scheme, activities have been given more importance. Mental reactions have not been considered.
2. Mager has given the list of action verbs for writing cognitive and effective domains of objectives in the behavioural terms. Many verbs have been included in the tables of cognitive and affective objectives. Therefore, a clear differentiation cannot be made in writing cognitive and affective objectives in behavioural terms. The objectives in behavioural terms must be more specific and definite.
3. Many action verbs determined for objectives of cognitive domain by Mager have been included in many objectives which create confusion in the minds of the teachers. Therefore, the use of one action-verbs in many objectives is not proper.
4. Mager's this scheme is more useful in programmed learning.

5. Mager's this scheme cannot be used for writing objectives of psychomotor domain in behavioural terms.
6. Mager has expressed learning through stimulus and response. But all human learning cannot be expressed through stimulus and response.

Examples: Following are some examples of writing objectives in behavioural terms—

(a) Example of Cognitive Objectives

1. *Knowledge—(i)* The pupils can define photosynthesis. In this, the term 'define' is used as action verb.

(ii) The pupils can list audio-visual aids. In this objectives, the action verb is 'List'.

2. *Comprehension—(i)* The pupils can explain the 'teaching'. In this, 'interpret' is the action verb.

(ii) The pupils can classify teaching models. In this, 'classify' is the action verb.

3. *Application—(i)* The pupils can demonstrate the method of preparing oxygen gas. In this, 'demonstrate' is the action verb.

(ii) The pupils can compute mean of the given scores. In this, 'compute' is the action verb.

In this way, we can write other objectives in behavioural terms.

(b) Examples of Affective Objectives

1. The pupils can select adjectives in the given lesson. In this, 'select' is the action verb. (Responding Objective)
2. The pupils can list verbs. In this, 'list' is the action verb. (Receiving Objective)
3. The pupils can decide appropriate adjectives in specific conditions. In this, 'decide' is the action verb. (Valuing Objective)
4. The pupils can relate teaching and learning. Here, 'relate' is the action verb. (Organization Objective)

Schemes of Writing Learning Objectives in Behavioural Terms

Various educationists have presented schemes of writing or defining learning objectives. In this context, the scheme of both

Mager and Miller for writing or defining objectives proved more useful. In the following lines, we are throwing light on the other than Mager and Miller Schemes:

Mager's Scheme

In 1962, Robert F. Mager has suggested by developing his scheme that all the cognitive and affective objectives should be written according to the following plan—

(i) The teacher should describe those specific behaviours after the identification of the terminal behaviours which prove as an evidence of achieving the objective.

(ii) After identifying terminal behaviours, the teacher should describe all those important conditions in which the pupil's behaviour is expected to occur. Hence, the teacher should define the desired behaviour later on.

(iii) After defining the desired behaviour, the teacher should specifically describe the criteria for expected achievement.

Miller's Scheme

In 1962, Dr. Robert B. Miller suggested by developing his scheme that the psychomotor objectives should be written in the following way—

(i) The teacher should describe indicator at first. This indicates the essential activity.

(ii) After describing the indicator, the teacher should describe the stimulus so that the responding may occur.

(iii) Then, after this, the teacher should describe that controlling thing which is to be activated.

(iv) The teacher should write that activity which is to be performed.

(v) In the end, the teacher should give importance to the adequacy of indication of the response or reinforcement.

From the above description, it becomes clear that Dr. R.F. Mager has given clear schemes of writing cognitive and affective objectives, while Dr. R.B. Miller has given the scheme of writing psychomotor objectives and by describing this, it is explained how learning objectives should be written.

The pupil-teachers should write the learning objectives in simple and clear language, keeping in view, both the above schemes, which may lead them towards next phases of the teaching-learning management.

The R.C.E.M. System

As it has already been mentioned that Robert Mager's scheme of writing objectives in behavioural terms has some limitations. Keeping in view the limitations of Mager's scheme, Regional College of Education, Mysore (R.C.E.M) developed its own scheme which is known as R.C.E.M. System.

In Mager's scheme, more emphasis is laid on the product, while process is more important in R.C.E.M. system. In this system, mental abilities are also considered more important. Mysore's this institute of Mysore adopted Bloom's Taxonomy as its base.

Bloom has divided cognitive objectives into six objectives, but R.C.E.M. system has changed Bloom's six cognitive objectives into four objectives only. The later three objectives of Bloom, i.e. analysis, synthesis and evaluation have been named as 'creativity', in R.C.E.M. System.

All the mental abilities, involved in these four objectives, have been placed into 17 categories. Hence, we see that all the activities of human learning have been divided into 17 mental abilities. These mental abilities are used in writing objectives in behavioural terms. The objectives and mental abilities used in this system are described in the table given on the next page.

Classification of Objectives according to the R.C.E.M. System

Example: Following are some examples of writing objectives in behavioural terms according to R.C.E.M. System—

1. *Cognitive Objective.* The pupils have the ability to recall the definition of the term 'Motivation'.

2. *Understanding Objective.* The pupils have the ability to differentiate 'teaching' and 'training'.

3. *Application Objective.* The pupils have an ability to infer results on the basis of presented data.

4. *Creativity Objectives.* The pupils have an ability to analyse the characteristics of 'teaching'.

Characteristics of R.C.E.M. System

R.C.E.M. system has some characteristics which are as follows:

1. Writing or converting objectives into behavioural terms is easy.
2. The construction of test-items is convenient.
3. This system lays more stress on mental activities.
4. This system has been developed in and according to Indian conditions.
5. All the educational objectives can be written in behavioural terms in this system.
6. The objectives in behavioural terms are more specific and definite.
7. R.C.E.M. system gives more importance to the learning process than learning outcome.

Limitations of R.C.E.M. System

R.C.E.M. system has some limitations which are as follows:

1. If we see the table of objectives, it would be clear that there is no balance between the various mental activities for different objectives. In cognitive objectives there are two, in understanding objectives, there are seven, in application objective, there are five and in creativity objective there are three mental activities.
2. It is a difficult task to associate various elements of the content with the various mental activities.
3. Guilford has suggested 120 mental abilities, while this system has suggested only 17 mental abilities.
4. This system is more useful for cognitive objectives only because use of a single design for cognitive, affective and psychomotor objectives does not seem to be appropriate.

QUESTIONS FOR ANSWER

1. What do you mean by ' Managing Teaching- Learning'? Describe the characteristics of Teaching- Learning Management approach.
2. Describe the various phases of teaching-learning management as suggested by I.K. Davis.
3. Write notes on the following:
   (*i*) Task Analysis

Management of Teaching and Learning

4. Sub-topic (1)	Sub-topic (2)	Sub-topic (3)	Sub-topic (4)
Planning of Teaching	Organization of Teaching	Leading the Teaching	Controlling Teaching
Elements 1. Task Analysis	Elements 1. Structure of Learning	Elements 1. Harnessing Students Motivation	Elements 1. Evaluating the Learning System
2. Identification of Teaching Objectives	2. Selecting Appropriate Teaching Tactics	2. Selecting Appropriate Motivational Strategies	2. Measuring Learning
3. Writing the Learning Objectives	3. Selection of Appropriate Communication Strategies		3. Managing by learning objectives
	4. Selection of Appropriate Audio-visual Aids		

(ii) Identification of Teaching Objectives

(iii) Writing Teaching Objectives

4. Describe the Educational objectives of Cognitive, Affective and Psychomotor objectives as suggested by Bloom. What precautions should be observed while writing instructional objectives?
5. Describe Bloom's Educational objectives of Cognitive, Affective and Psychomotor domains.
6. Explain the importance of planning in Teaching-Learning Management. What activities are considered essential for this task?
7. What do you mean by writing Educational objectives in behavioural terms? Describe various schemes of writing Educational objectives in behavioural terms.

13

Management of Teaching and Learning—2
(Organizing Teaching and Learning)

After planning the teaching, the next phase is organizing the teaching-learning, I.K. Davies has defined organisation in the following words:

"Organizing teaching-learning is the work a teacher does to arrange and relate learning resources, so as to realize learning objectives in the most effective, efficient and economical way possible."

Davies suggests that a teacher must perform the following four activities while organizing teaching-learning:

1. Selecting an appropriate teaching tactics.
2. Selecting appropriate audio-visual aids.
3. Selecting appropriate class size.
4. Selecting appropriate communication strategies.

Selecting Appropriate Teaching Tactics

Meaning of Teaching Tactics. When teaching is organized, the teacher should, at first, select appropriate teaching tactics. So far as teaching tactics are concerned, they are more comprehensive than the teaching strategies that is why a teaching tactic can be used in many teaching strategies.

It means to say that the teaching tactics make the knowledge stable. Hence, for the qualitative progress of teaching, we use various tactics according to the conditions or learning structures.

Remember that the each element of the subject-matter has its own structure. The teacher selects teaching strategies, tactics and aids on the basis of the structure of each element of the subject-matter. In other words, the structure of each element of the subject-matter acts as the norm or a criterion in the selection of teaching strategy, tactic and aid.

Hence, the teacher should keep in mind the learning structure, while selecting the teaching tactic. Since, the knowledge of learning structure is essential in order to select appropriate teaching tactic, we are throwing light on the types of learning structures and the tactics to be used in them.

1. Signal Learning Structure and Teaching Tactics.
2. Chain Learning Structure and Teaching Tactics.
3. Multiple Discrimination Learning Structure and Teaching Tactics.
4. Concept Learning Structure and Teaching Tactics.
5. Principle Learning Structure and Teaching Tactics.

1. Signal Learning Structure and Teaching Tactics

Signal Learning Structure is termed as stimulus response. It is because its basis is stimulus response. The main feature of this structure is that the pupils continuously carry on the practice while organizing the stimulus and the response and this consolidates the relationship of stimulus and response.

In this learning structure, it's the teacher's duty to compel the pupils first of all respond to the stimulus. Then, they are motivated to give correct answers overlooking their wrong answers. In the end, they should be put gradually to the exercise relating to the response through reinforcement.

Hence, in the signal learning structure the following teaching tactics should be used—

(i) Establishing contiguity,
(ii) Constant Practice and Rehearsal,
(iii) Reinforcing the correct Response.

2. Chain Learning Structure and Teaching Tactics

The Chain Learning Structure is the sequence of facts and symbols learnt before. Remember that the chain sometimes is formed from the verbal activities such as, poetic-recitation and sometimes motor activities are included in it such as, cycling. This chain is of the types—

(i) Progressive Chain
(ii) Rote Learning
(iii) Retrogressive chain

In the progressive chain, starting from signals, we reach upto the end of the chain. In the rote learning, the chain is acquired by cramming. In the retrogressive chain, we start from the last activity and then reach to the beginning of the chain.

Out of these three tactics, retrogressive chain is more effective. It has two reasons—*(i)* it functions as reinforcement, and *(ii)* it makes possible to acquire efficiency in the task. Hence, the teacher should use the chain learning structure.

3. Multi Discrimination Learning Structure and Teaching Tactics

In this multi discrimination learning structure, both the signals and chains are included. The real situation is that in this type of learning, facts are separated from each other and the comparisons are made clear.

For this, pupils should take care of two thing. These are—

(i) stimulus and response should be clear
(ii) all the things should be presented simultaneously

Hence, pupils should proceed from simple to complex, so that they may understand the difference. In this multi discrimination learning structure, the teacher should use the following two tactics—

(i) Distinctive Conditions
(ii) Simultaneous Presentation

4. Concept Learning Structure and Teaching Tactics

In the concept learning structure, capacities of generalization of those groups of actions are created in the pupils which look different externally. Remember that such groups are different from each other but they have similar peculiarity which makes it easy to identify their basic concept.

Attention is to be paid that the pupils may identify or understand the concepts by trial and error method. But they must know the signal and chain structures. Only in that situation, they would be able to generalize. In the concept learning structure, the teacher should present various stimuli so that all the pupils may generalize something regarding that concept.

Then, he should create such situations before the pupils so that they may differentiate two confusing concepts. Hence, in the concept learning structure, the teacher should use two tactics—

(i) Generalization within the class
(ii) Discrimination between classes

5. Principle Learning Structure and Teaching Tactics

In the principle learning structure, a chain of two or more concepts is included. In this chain, the concepts of a principle have the relationship. Hence, to know each principle, concepts relating to it should be clear to the pupils. For example, consider one principle—"Solid objects expand in heat." It has three concepts:

(i) object or matter
(ii) heat
(iii) expand

These three concepts have been placed in one chain which looks like one principle. Remember that in order to provide knowledge of principle learning structure, he should try let the pupils recall the concepts and make a chain of these concepts. He should use the following two tactics in the principle learning structure—

(i) Recalling the concept
(ii) Chaining the concepts

Learning Structures and Learning Objectives

The learning structures are directly related to the learning objectives. Hence, by using different teaching tactics in various learning structures, various learning objectives can be achieved.

For example, by using tactics of signal learning structures, we can achieve knowledge objectives, by using the tactics of chain learning structures, we can achieve the comprehension objective and by using the tactics of multi-discrimination learning structures, we can achieve application objective and by using the tactics of concept learning structure and principle learning structure, we can achieve creativity objectives.

Since the learning structure is made precise from task analysis, therefore, while selecting teaching tactics, the teacher should keep in mind the task analysis, learning structures and learning objectives. It means to say that the teacher should determine the learning structure by task analysis. Then, the teaching tactics should be selected in accordance with the type of learning structure.

Selecting Appropriate Teaching Aids

Meaning of Teaching Aids

The teaching aids are also known as the audio-visual aids. Remember that the 'audio-visual' means all those sources which make the audio and visual sense organs of the pupils activated and they understand minute and difficult ideas of the lesson very conveniently. In other words, audio-visual aids include all those sources which make the pupils interested in the lesson and the learning objectives are achieved very easily. It is termed as 'Educational Technology' and the use of audio-visual aids is termed as the 'Hardware Technology'

Importance and Functions of Audio-Visual Aids

In managing teaching, audio-visual teaching occupies an important place. The use of audio-visual aids is advantageous for all the pupils. In the following lines, we are throwing light on the need and importance of audio-visual aids:

1. *Motivation.* Audio-visual aids present the knowledge in the concrete form by attracting the attention of the pupils. This provides motivation and curiosity to the pupils in the learning activity.

2. *Principle of Activity.* The pupils get various opportunities of doing various activities by using audio-visual aids. When audio-visual aids are used while teaching a lesson, the pupils talk, ask questions and discuss. This stimulates their various sense organs. As a result of this, their interest in the lesson prevails and they learn the most difficult things in a natural way without any difficulty.

3. *Meaningful Experience.* With the help of audio-visual aids, lesson is taught to the pupils in a concrete form. Every

pupil tries to understand correctly by seeing and touching an object. This makes the lesson easy, interesting and entertaining and all the pupils acquire it happily. In other words, the use of audio-visual aids makes the experiences of the pupils meaningful.

In short, the symbolic representation of direct experience is possible by means of audio-visual aids.

4. *Clarification:* The use of audio-visual aids clarifies the most difficult contents. Its only reason is that whatever the pupils hear, they also see it with their own eyes. After seeing with their own eyes, all the confusions are eliminated and they acquire the knowledge with precision.

5. *Discouragement to Cramming.* By using audio-visual aids, the pupils take interest in the development of the lesson and they acquire the knowledge by doing themselves. This makes the learnt knowledge definite and stabilized. There is no need of cramming anything.

6. *Efficiency in Teaching.* The use of audio-visual aids causes efficiency in teaching. Also, the teaching becomes more effective. In other words, those minute things and difficult ideas which a pupil is unable to understand with chalk and talk, are followed easily by using audio-visual aids. It means to say, dry and dis-interesting subjects and topics can be made easy, interesting and precise by using audio-visual aids.

7. *Increase in Vocabulary.* The use of audio-visual aids increases vocabulary of the pupils. Its reason is that while using radio, telephone, television and cinema, new terms are used and they acquire them.

From the above description, the audio-visual aids make teaching and learning effective. Its use helps the pupils in learning with low I.Q. From this point of view, it has an important place in the education of the pupils.

Characteristics of Audio-Visual Aids

I.K. Davies has suggested the following five characteristics of audio-visual aids:

(i) Audio-visual aids help in developing perception.

(ii) It helps in developing understanding. Its use enables the pupils to acquire correct knowledge.

(iii) Audio-visual aids help in transfer of training.

(iv) These are helpful in acquiring knowledge and providing reinforcement.

(v) Audio-visual aids help in developing retention. Its use facilitates assimilation of the knowledge.

Audio-Visual Aids

Equipments for Audio-Visual Aids

Presentation Equipment	*Materials*	*Production Equipment*
Sound		
Record players	Records	Tape recorders
Tape recorders	Tapes	
Radio		
Still pictures	Slides	Cameras
Slide projectors	Filmstrips	Photoraphic equipment
Filmstrip projectors	Transparencies	Graphic equipment
Overhead projectors	Photographs	Heat copies, etc.
Epidiascopes	Wall charts	
Micro-Projectors		
Still pictures with sound		
Record/Filmstrip system		
Slide/Tape systems		
Motion pictures with or without sound		
Loop projectors	Film loops	Cine-cameras
(8-mm and super 8-mm)	Silent film	
cine-Projectors	Sound film	
(8-mm and 16-mm)		

It is the planned use of audio-visual resources which is most likely to improve quality and most of the planning and preparation time will have to come from the faculty concerned. Without adequate faculty, planning usually increases the cost of teaching without increasing its effectiveness.

The purpose of feedback device is to supply knowledge of results, when a student or a group of students are questioned on what they have learned. When the question is also presented by the device it is called a 'teaching machine'; but when a question is posed by a teacher it is usually referred to as a feedback classroom. The feedback classroom gives knowledge of results to the teachers as well as to students.

Teaching Machines

Teaching machines are normally divided into three categories—adjustive, linear and branching. The adjustive machines developed by Pressey and his co-workers provide knowledge of results to students answering multiple-choice test questions. Methods of giving feedback include lighting a bulk allowing a punch in the correct answer space to penetrate more clearly and having chemically treated paper change colour. The term adjunctive is used because these machines are adjuncts to the main teaching-learning process. They only contain tests and they are used to test and revise material which the student has already encountered elsewhere.

"A teaching machine or auto instructional device is a piece of apparatus designed to be operated by an individual student." This apparatus has following features:

1. There is a device for displaying the question or problem on the machine.
2. The student in response must do something overtly about the problem such as writing an answer or pushing a button to indicate answer.
3. The student is informed by the machines through some device whether his answer is correct or incorrect and sometimes, why he is right or wrong.

New Resources for Learning

Norman Mackenzie, Director of the Centre for Educational Technology and Hywel C. Jones of University of Sussex observe; "It is a reflection of the state of innovation in education that the phrase new resources for learning is normally considered to include resources such as film (first used regularly in education in about 1910) and slides (first used in education in about 1890). Nevertheless it is true that for most colleges and universities teachers, the use of any resource other than chalk, talk and book is regarded as something special if not as novelty.

There is no obviously convenient or generally accepted

system for classifying learning resources, so we shall use one which is based primarily on information sources. The authors list the following as new resources for learning:

1. Television
2. The Language Laboratory
3. Teaching Machines
4. Computer
5. Programmed Learning

Television

The glamour of television as an entertainment medium has at least brought it to everybody' notice and it has probably received more attention in education during the last decade than any of the other new media. Its potential for education lies in three main directions:

(*a*) it can show things that would otherwise be difficult to see because they are of an inconvenient size, too far away or too complex;

(*b*) it can transcend the limits of space and time either by open broadcast, closed circuit or recorded transmission;

(*c*) it can be used for evaluation of performance; for instance an athletic, an actor or a teacher can be recorded as he performs and his performance can then be viewed in a replay by himself and others.

Computer as a Learning Resource

It is certain that the use of computer education extends most rapidly and extensively in dealing with problems that are common to education, science business and public administration; that is, for high-speed computation and data processing. Already, the use of computer in higher education for the purposes of administration and research is becoming a major item in a university budget and before long it may be the single most costly item next of faculty salaries. But the proposition that a computer could also become a potent new vehicle for teaching and learning is more recent, though, it is being taken up with considerable enthusiasm. Serious research programmes are now underway, not only in the United States, but also in Belgium, Canada, France, Japan, the Netherlands and the U.S.S.R.; some sponsored by commercial enterprises producing computers and associated software, some underwritten by state agencies. Computer Assisted Learning (CAL), in which the computer is used as a highly sophisticated teaching machine which can replace and sometimes surpass many but not all of the function of a human tutor is the natural focus for the educational futurists. The use of computer in tutorial mode will undoubtedly accelerate research into the learning process but it can never replace it.

Programmed Learning

Programmed learning is potentially one of the most confusing of recent innovations because it is difficult to define. Early definitions divided programmes into linear programmes and branching programmes and listed the salient characteristic of each. Schramm in 1952 for example, wrote as follows (with a footnote to the effect that it only applied to linear programmes): To sum up, these are the essential elements of programmed instruction:

- *(a)* an ordered sequence of stimulus items,
- *(b)* to each of which a student responds in some specified way,
- *(c)* his responses begin reinforced by immediate knowledge of results,
- *(d)* so that he moves by small steps,
- *(e)* therefore, making few errors and practising mostly correct responses,
- *(f)* from what he knows, by a process of successively closer approximation towards what he is supposed to learn from the programmes.

Continuing Education

Education is a continuous process and an individual needs a lifelong education to understand the changing of the community in which he lives and works. It is very essential for him to comprehend the nature of the changes brought about by the rapid technological developments in various areas by:

- *(i)* Undertaking literacy programmes through the use of machine controlled programmes, teleboard and computer terminal media.
- *(ii)* Facilitating learning of numeracy through electronic calculators.
- *(iii)* Facilitating professional development through close

circuit television. Thousands of surgeons can conserve a special performing an intricate operation.

(iv) Facilitating vocational development and retraining.

(v) Personal and social development through radio and T.V.

Resources Based Learning

The technique of resource based learning was initiated in England in 1975 at the Red Fort Sheet, Bristol. The Resource-based learning involves two activities:

(i) Material production

(ii) Material effectiveness

Resources based learning is based on the idea that the pupils should be involved in devising and monitoring relevant activities for themselves rather than to bolster up the teacher centred approach. The simplest form of resource-based learning is the expansion of the existing school library services into the audio-visual field usually without an education technologist. W.J. Carr has stated seven hypotheses which may be examined in this context.

Education Technology and Programmed Learning

Science and technology has almost revolutionized human life and have touched almost all aspects of human behaviour. Education can hardly afford to remain aloof from their rich contributions. Terms like 'education technology', 'educational engineering'... are not new now-a-days and it is in this context that Programmed Learning has come as an application of behavioural sciences and technology together to the field of education. According to G.B. Shan and O.S. Dewal (1970) "Educational Technology refers to the development of a set of systematic methods and practical knowledge of designing, operating and testing schools as educational systems. Educational technology, in this sense, is educational engineering. It draws upon many disciplines. In the new environment which technological advancement has brought to education, much remains to be done to help teachers adopt new goals and become familiar with new techniques of teaching.

Satellite Instructional Television Experiment (SITE)

The Satellite Instructional Television Experiment (SITE) has heralded advent of television for development and education in India. Also, by adopting this satellite system, India will have overtaken the developed nations in using advanced communications technology. The rationale behind SITE is harnessing the visual impact of TV for social and economic progress. According to the agreement signed by the Government of India, Department of Atomic Energy and the United States National Aeronautics and Space Administration (NASA) in 1969, when SITE came into being, education was a secondary objective of the project. Yet now, of the four hours of transmission time, one and a half hours will be devoted purely to education for 6 to 12½ years old and their teachers priorities have been mixed up because time had to be utilized in the morning. There will be four 22½ minute sessions in four languages (Hindi, Oria, Telegu and Kannad): children will not be confused with two audio channels. Educational TV experiment for the under- privileged/rural children are being conducted in the US Rocky Mountains on the Ivory Coast and in the Samoa Islands. In the evaluation of the Samoa project learning gains by children were found to be minimal. However, significant gains were observed in their ability to handle the English language. This learning gain was attributed to the fact that the medium of TV instruction was English. The idea is that if we have an insight from these failures, why not examine them to our advantage?

Utility of Audio-Visual Aids

(a) Audio-Aids

Audio-aids mean those sources in which only hearing organs are used i.e., knowledge gained mainly through the ears. In the following lines, the main audio-aids are given:

Radio. The story of the radio's birth started from 1885. In the modern life, radio has developed so much that now it has become our need. Radio provides knowledge of latest events and informations simultaneously to all the pupils living at far off places. This arouses curiosity of learning new things in the pupils. Radio provides various tasks and speeches of eminent educationists to the pupils on national and international problems to hear. This develops international feeling among them.

The programmes of famous artists and musicians are also broadcast from the radio. These programmes provide them with education in music. In short, radio creates interest in the pupils regarding every nation and the activities of the people of that nation. It broadens their general knowledge. In nut shell, radio has special importance in the field of modern education. Therefore, almost all the schools have their own individual radio-sets.

Gramophone and Linguaphone. Like radio, gramophone and linguaphone are also important teaching devices. Pupils are given training for speech and music by gramophone while language is taught by correcting their pronunciation with the help of linguaphone. Hence, the teacher should use both the devices during teaching as the need arises.

Tape-recorder. Tape-recorder is new instrument. In this, anybody can hear his recorded voice. From this point of view, tape-recorder is used to hear the ideas of great men, speeches of leaders and music and poems of famous artists on one side, while on other side, the pupils and the teachers can also hear their recorded voice. This helps in improving their pronunciation and removal of errors regarding effects of the voices.

Remember that by using audio-visual aids, only knowledge and affective objectives can be achieved. Psychomotor objectives cannot be achieved by using them.

(b) Visual Aids

Meaning of Visual Aids. Visual aids means those sources in which only visual organs are used or applied i.e., knowledge is mainly achieved through visual organs. Some visual aids are as follows:

Real Objects. The actual objects means original objects. These real or actual objects motivate the sense organs of the pupils and develop their power of observation by providing the opportunities of supervision and testing.

When the pupils see real objects, touch them and taste them, their visual, taste, touch and hearing powers develop.

These powers or talents help in developing their power of

imagination. It means to say that by using the real objects pupils acquire various types of experiences which are more superior to those experiences provided by others. Hence, the teacher should collect real objects in the school museum so that these can be exhibited to the pupils as the need arises.

Models. Models are the miniature forms of real or original objects. These are used when the real objects are either beyond availability or these are of such huge size that these are impossible to be exhibited in the class, for example, an elephant, horse, railway engine, aeroplane etc. These are of such size that these cannot be presented actually in the classroom.

Hence, models are presented to the pupils for the knowledge of such objects. Remember that the models should be the exact copy of the real objects irrespective of their size. If the models are very close to the real objects in structure, it would help the teacher to achieve the objective by developing the power of imagination of the pupils.

From this point of view, models are mainly advantageous in providing the knowledge to the pupils regarding historical, geographical and scientific facts. Hence, the models presented before the pupils should be very attractive.

Since, in models, length, breath and height are clearly visible, hence, these are more useful than the pictures.

The teacher should make aware the pupils regarding the actual dimensions of the real objects while presenting the models. This will avoid the formation of misconceptions regarding real objects.

Pictures. The pictures are used when neither the real objects nor their models are available. In other words, when the availability of the real objects and their models becomes difficult, then in such a situation, pictures are used. Remember that in the picture, the real touch of the real object does not occur. Still these pictures are useful in teaching.

These pictures are, however, cheaper than the models and real objects and these are easily available in the market. When the teacher imparts knowledge with the help of pictures, the pupils' attention remains focussed on the lesson. This enables the teacher to achieve the objectives successfully.

Remember that though the pictures should be used in teaching all the subjects, but these should be used especially in the teaching of geography, history, science, language, gardening and observation of nature etc. The teacher should follow the following points while selecting the pictures—

(a) The pictures should be so precise, coloured and attractive that the pupils become familiar with the size and shape of the real objects.

(b) In pictures, only relevant things should be shown, otherwise the main points will be side-tracked and the pupils will get confused.

(c) The size of the picture should be so large that every pupil sitting in the class may have its look clearly without any difficulty and can secure the benefit.

Maps. The use of maps is essential to study the main historical events, geographical facts and places. Though the ready-made maps are available in the market, yet it is better if the teacher prepares them himself and mark only those things beautifully which are required.

Remember that the teacher must write the name, heading, direction and symbol etc. on the maps and the colours should be used with imagination, experience and artistic sense. Otherwise the maps would be useless.

Sketches and Diagrams. Sometimes, the teacher fails to acquire real objects, models, pictures and maps. Then, in such a situation, the teacher should draw sketches and diagrams on the black-board with the coloured chalks to make the sense distinct.

Sketches and maps can be used for language, geography, history, mathematics and science etc. Hence, the teachers must possess the ability of drawing sketches and diagrams very quickly.

Since, there is no expenses on drawing the sketches and diagrams, every teacher should practise the drawing of sketches and diagrams in an attractive way.

Graph. Graph has its own importance. By using graph, knowledge regarding subjects like geography, history, maths and science etc. can be imparted conveniently. Remember that with the help of graph the knowledge of climate, cultivation and population etc. in the lesson of geography can be imparted.

In history, it can be used in imparting the knowledge of the progress of freedom-struggle and development in the religious and political fields. Similarly, many problems can be solved by using graphs in the subject of mathematics and science. Hence, the teacher should draw graphs himself as the need arises while teaching various subjects. Also, he should get these graphs drawn from the pupil.

Chart. The use of charts helps in achieving the teaching objective. The charts can be used successfully in all the subjects like geography, history, economics, civics, maths and science etc.

Hence, keeping in mind the needs of the lesson, the teacher should prepare himself large-sized charts and he should use them properly. The content presented in the charts should be so beautiful, bold and large-sized that every student may get attracted towards that chart and the teacher may clarify his point easily.

Black-Board. Black-board means a black wooden piece of large size. Its size is 48" × 36". It is used in the classroom at the time of teaching. Also, it can be shifted out of the class-room as the need arises.

In this modern age, a board of 72" × 48" size is also made of cement on the wall. Sometimes, a wooden board of the same size is fixed on the wall. In short, this black-board is very useful for a teacher whether it is wooden or cemented.

Importance and Advantages of Black-Board

The black board is the cheapest instrument of modern education. In past, black-board was used to teach mathematics only. But in modern age, its application has increased so much that it is not possible to teach any part of the content conveniently without the help of black-board.

Now, the psychological researches have proved that each pupil will get definite and stable knowledge if he uses maximum number of senses. From this point of view, if the teacher writes important points on the black-board while teaching orally, then along with the sense of hearing, the sense of sight of the pupil also becomes active.

Therefore, in the modern age, the black-board is considered an important device in the teaching of all the subjects like language, economics, civics, history, geography, mathematics and science etc.

We see that in the teaching of a language, the learning of

meanings of difficult words, the teaching points to develop the lesson in economics, civics, history, geography and to write the summary, and to draw the diagrams and maps etc. to solve the mathematical questions, to make angles and triangles in geometry, and to draw the pictures in science i.e., beaker, thermometer, burette and pipette etc. black-board is used. Hence, by using black-board, all the pupils understand the terms, facts, events, pictures and summaries etc. written on the black-board very easily.

Also, the teachers feel comfort in assigning the home work and teaching the whole class at a time with the help of black-board. In other words, both the pupils and the teacher are benefited. Since the pupil considered the written matter on the black-board as a model and he follows it and gets impressed from this, therefore, the teacher and the pupil-teacher must use black-board while teaching.

How to Write on Black-Board

Following points be kept in mind while writing on the black-board:

1. Writing should be neet, clear and beautiful and letter be bright.
2. Large-sized letter be written in straight line.
3. Write systematically and use one language only as far as possible.
4. Write rapidly and keep distance between black-board and yourself.
5. While writing on black-board keep on talking about written words and sentences.
6. Make proper use of duster. Do not use finger to rub the written words.

Importance of Drawing Pictures, Sketches and Maps on Black-Board

Generally, the teacher is unable to secure real object in order to make the lesson effective. In such a situation, he tries to complete his task by drawing pictures, diagrams, maps and sketches on the black-board. Hence, every teacher, especially pupil-teacher, should acquire a skill in the art of drawing pictures on the black-board along with beautiful writing. The advantages of pictures, sketches and maps drawn on the black-board are as follows:

(i) Essential Help in the Development of Lesson. The pictures, sketches and maps drawn on the black-board help surprisingly in developing the lesson. In the pictures the teacher presents only needful and according to the pupil's abilities. This develops the lesson easily and the facts of the subject also become definite and stable in the pupils.

(ii) Concentration of Student's Attention. When the teacher develops the lesson by drawing a picture on the black-board, then the concentration of student's attention is focussed on the lesson. The pictures drawn on the black-board motivate the pupils to acquire new knowledge by creating interest in the studies amongst the pupils.

(iii) Clarification of Subject Matter. When the teacher tries to draw pictures on the black-board with the skill of his figures and develops the lesson, the most difficult subject-matter becomes easy and clear for the pupils. This leaves the impression of teachers' ability, efficiency and skill upon the pupils.

(iv) Effective: The pupils are very much impressed by the pictures drawn on the black-board. They witness the drawing of these pictures. Hence, they start believing on the shown facts. Sometimes, the pupils are so much impressed that they also succeed in making such drawings. Hence, every teacher should be expert in drawing pictures on black-board.

(v) Economy of Time and Money: The drawing of pictures and maps at home takes much time. Also it costs more. But drawing of pictures and sketches on black-board is economical in terms of money and time.

How to Draw Sketches and Maps on Black-Board

The teacher should keep in mind the following points while drawing pictures on a black-board:

1. Draw necessary details only
2. Use coloured chalks
3. Draw correct and beautiful

Black-Board as a Friend

According to Davis, black-board is a real friend of the teacher. It is always ready to help every teacher. Hence, every teacher must make the best use of such a self-less friend. A teacher who does not make the proper use of black-board cannot be a good teacher. So every teacher should seek the help of the black-board while teaching. Only then, he would be able to succeed in achieving his objectives. From this point of view, all the teachers, especially pupil-teachers, must use black-board. But how? In this connection, the following points should be kept in mind—

1. Clean the black-board if it is not so and clean it before leaving the class.
2. Make proper black-board entries—date, class, subject, topic, period etc. with white chalk.
3. Place the black-board at such a place where the pupils feel convenient to read the written matter on it.
4. Write on black-board from left to right and avoid your central position.
5. Write rapidly, facts and events much be written on black-board in all the subjects.
6. Keep on talking while using chalk about the written matter.
7. Keep an eye on the class while using black-board.
8. Make use of pointer to point out the matter written on black-board.
9. Ask students to use black-board.

Bulletin-Board. Bulletin-board is a useful instrument of education. On this, the information regarding country's political, economical and social problems along with pictures, graphs, diagrams, articles and necessary information are displayed and the pupil's curiosity is aroused in order to increase their knowledge. Hence, the bulletin-boards are very useful for teachers. To benefit from bulletin-boards, the teacher should keep in mind the following points—

1. The material being displayed on bulletin-board should be in accordance with the interest, mental level, age and ability of the pupils.
2. Bulletin-board should be fixed at some higher and appropriate place in the school so that all the pupils of average height may benefit conveniently from the displayed material.
3. The informations to be displayed on the bulletin-board

should be managed in a definite order or sequence.

4. The material to be displayed on the bulletin-board should be large enough that the pupils may see it from a distance.
5. Bulletin-board should be so beautiful that the pupils are attracted automatically.
6. The pupils also must have the opportunity of displaying their collected material.

Flannel-Board. In the modern are, flannel-boards have special importance. These are prepared by mounting a flannel cloth very tightly on a 36" × 48" piece of plywood or hard board. Then, on it, various pictures, maps, sketches and graphs etc. related to different subjects are displayed.

In order to display on the flannel-board, sand papers are pasted on the back of the pictures and maps etc. This makes these pieces sticking to the flannel-board. After using them, these can be removed very easily.

These flannel-boards can be used very conveniently for teaching language and mathematics to the lower classes and history, geography, civics, economics, maths, and science etc. to the higher classes. Hence, every teacher should use this instrument as the need arises.

Museum. Museum is also an important device of education. It includes all the collected objects. The lesson becomes alive and interesting with the help of these objects and the pupils understand easily.

Hence, the teacher should encourage the pupils to collect postal stamps, coils, traditional arms, insects and instruments for the school museum. This will enable the school to collect many objects without spending any money.

Magic-Lantern: The magic-lantern is a picture exhibiting device. This device has proved so much useful and successful in making the teaching alive and effective that almost all the educationists have accepted its utility. Its use needs slides.

Hence, after providing knowledge regarding various subjects to the pupils in the morning, they should be shown slides relating to those subjects in the evening. This makes easy to acquire knowledge and forgetting would be minimized.

While using magic-lantern, the teacher should observe the following precautions—

(i) Before showing slides, the teacher should present some background regarding the subject.

(ii) While showing slides, the teacher should provide some interpretations or inferences.

Epidiascope. Epidiascope is more effective device than magic-lantern in order to make the lesson precise and interesting. Its reason is that the magic-lantern needs the preparations of slides before showing pictures. But it is not in the case of epidiascope we can project small maps, pictures, posters and pages of books on a screen in the dark room without preparing any slide.

In other words, these small pictures which cannot be magnified even by an artist, epidiascope magnifies that micro-picture very easily. It is the reason that this device has made its important place in the modern education system in teaching civics, history, economics and geography etc.

In rich countries like America and England, the epidiascopes are too much in order to make the lesson interesting and precise. But due to financial restrictions in our country, the pupils are devoid of its benefit. While using epidiascope, the teacher should observe the following precautions:

(i) Before using epidiascope, screen should be arranged.

(ii) The room should be darkened where it is to be used.

(iii) The size of the pictures to be projected should be according to the epidiascope.

(iv) The classroom environment should be peaceful.

(v) While using epidiascope, notes should be given so that the pupils gain clear knowledge about the subject.

Slides, Film Strips and Projector. With the help of slides the micro informations can be magnified on the screen. While showing slides, the teacher clarifies very minute points by his statements. This simplifies the lesson and makes it interesting. Pupils acquire it very conveniently. These slides are made on glass.

Hence, these are very delicate. Also, these are heavy. Now slides are being produced on films. This film is projected with the help of a projector in the class-room on a screen. This makes the lesson alive.

Hence, projector becomes more important than epidiascope. Its reason is that with epidiascope only individual objects can be shown separately while the slides of the pictures or film strips can be shown in a sequence.

In short, as in cinema hall, advertisements are shown to the public, pictures relating to different subjects can be shown at different intervals of time with the help of a projector as the need arises.

Soundless Motion Pictures. Soundless picture is the primitive form of a motion picture. In this, complete activities are shown but it lacks sound. In other words, different activities like methods of cleanliness, preventive measures of various diseases, natural scenes and descriptions can easily be clarified by silent or soundless pictures. Hence, it is also important in teaching. Remember that by using visual aids, only cognitive objectives are acquired. Affective and psychomotor objectives cannot be achieved.

Procedure of Multi-media Approach

It is essential to follow the following aspects for using it effectively in teaching and learning:

(i) Determining and defining the terminal behaviours.
(ii) Managing the content or strategy.
(iii) Applying teaching method or organised strategy.
(iv) Passing through the process of evaluation.
(v) Managing remedial instruction on the basis of diagnosis of the pupil and providing feedback.

Principles of Using Multi-media. It is essential to use the following principles in order to apply teaching approach to the class-room teaching:

(i) To prepare the pupils to use the medium in the class
(ii) To prepare physical conditions.
(iii) To conduct a continuous evaluation so that the effectiveness of the medium may be known.
(iv) To select a teaching medium keeping in view the objectives.
(v) To provide guidance to the pupils for imitation so that they may succeed in acquiring the experiences.

Computer Assisted Instruction: Amongst the important hardware devices of educational devices, computer occupies an important place. Computer is used for individualized instruction. It is based on self-instructional system.

The use of the computer has increased not only in education, but it has also affected the trade, industry, war, administration and research work etc. In the field of education, the influence of computer can be seen maximum in research work, examination system and instructional system.

Hence, it is also known as electronic brain. By considering entering behaviours by the computer, instruction has to be selected.

Functions of Computer. In teaching process, the computer has the following functions—

1. Instructional material can be collected by a computer. It can have 32 types of instructional material for a single topic.
2. Informations on cards can be collected by the computers.
3. Computers can communicate the informations.

Computer and Teaching Process. In 1965, Lorence Stoluro and Daniel Davis developed most complicated teaching processes in which computer was used for presenting instructions in place of teacher. They divided the teaching process of the computer in two parts—

1. Pre-tutorial phase.
2. Tutorial Phase.

In the first phase, computer assisted instruction is given to the pupils to achieve the specific objectives on the basis of his entering behaviour. In the second phase, the instructional material is presented accordingly. The pupil studies it. Then, the achievement of the pupil is evaluated. After presenting the instruction, computer also controls it. It also provides reinforcement to the pupils.

Uses of Computer. In the present modern age, the use of computers has revolutionized every field. In the field of education, it is used in the following areas:

(i) All the researchers do all analytical tasks with the help of computer in the research work.

(ii) Computer is also used in educational guidance and counselling.

(iii) Computer's help is sought for preparing the results of the examinations.

(iv) Remedial teaching of the pupils is also done by the computer.

Multi-Media Centres. Multi-Media centres are also known as instructional material centres. In addition to this, these are also called as 'Multi-Media Library', 'Reading Material Centre' and 'Learning Resource Centre'.

These types of multi-media centres provide the facility to teaching-learning material to the teachers and pupils according to their needs. In multi media centres, programmed instruction material, audio-visual material, and other materials for multi-media approach are collected and the training regarding their use is provided to the teachers. In these centres, provision is made for personal or institutional use. The behavioural technologists are also appointed in these centres.

Organization of Multi-media Centres. Multi-media centres must have organizers or coordinators. An organizer in a multi-media centre has the following functions—

(i) To provide help in using audio-visual aids to the teachers.
(ii) To organize a workshop for the training of in-service teachers and training of instructional technology to them.
(iii) To organize a library of audio-visual material.
(iv) To help the teachers in preparing instructional material.
(v) To maintain audio-visual and other materials.
(vi) To provide training regarding audio-visual material and instructional material to in-service and pre-service teachers.
(viii) The organizer of a multi-media centre should be aware of the development of the latest instructional technology.

(c) Audio-Visual Aids

Meaning of Audio-Visual Aids

Audio-Visual material means those sources in which both audio and visual senses are used, i.e., in which the knowledge is acquired by both audio and visual sense organs. In the following lines, we are throwing light on some main aids by which pupils acquire knowledge by using both audio and visual sense organs side by side. Cinema documentary films, television and drama are audio-visual aids.

Qualities of Audio-Visual Aids

Audio-visual aids should have the following qualities—

1. A.V. aids should help in achieving the teaching objectives.
2. A.V. aids should be beautiful and attractive. But it does not mean that the pupils get absorbed in its beauty and they deviate from the main lesson.
3. A.V. aids should neither be large nor so small. But it should be of such size that every pupil sitting in the class may see it conveniently.
4. A.V. aids should be useful. Irrelevant material wastes the time and creates indiscipline in the class.
5. A.V. aids should arouse the curiosity of the pupils instead of their entertainment, otherwise pupils will divert towards entertainment only.
6. The pictures, maps or charts which are displayed before the pupils should not bear unnecessary information. It decreases their influence.
7. The visual aids which are presented before the pupils should accompany the actions also. Such materials will provide some signals to the pupils and the teacher can also prove his desire successfully.

Where to Use Audio-Visual Aids

The A.V. aids should be used in the following situations--

1. When the object is of such huge size, that its shifting to the class-room is impossible, such as Taj Mahal, Birla Mandir, Elephants, Horses etc.
2. When the object is too small that it is not possible to see it easily, such as atoms, amoeba etc.
3. When the object is not available, e.g. old coins, arms and dresses.
4. When the objects are very fast, e.g. train, aeroplanes etc.
5. When there is need of developing continuously certain living things, e.g., flies and mosquitos.
6. When the object's speed is not observable e.g. electricity.
7. When the internal activities are needed to be shown, e.g., blood-circulation and digestion etc.
8. When the knowledge of distant objects is to be given,, e.g., the traditions and customs of various countries.

When and How to Use Audio-Visual Aids

Sometimes, many fresh and pupil-teachers collect in plenty the audio-visual aids to teach science, language and social subjects, but they can not make use of these aids properly. Hence, in the following lines, we are throwing light on those rules and principles which make us aware of the fact that when and how there audio-visual aids should be used.

1. A.V. aids can be used in the three phases of the lesson—*(i)* Introduction, *(ii)* Presentation, and *(iii)* Recapitulation. In introduction, A.V. aids are used to create interest in the pupils for their lessons, in presentation, A.V. aids are used to make the minute and difficult facts and ideas of the lesson more precise while in recapitulation, these are used to evaluate the lesson.
2. A.V. aids should be used only when the need arises. When it is used excessively, it looks like a juggler's show. In such a situation, teaching flops. Hence, the pupil-teacher should remember that the success of teaching does not depend on the plenty of material, but depends on its proper use.
3. While using A.V. aids, the teacher should remember whether a desirable impression can be left on the pupils by clarifying the ideas of the lesson in a simple, interesting and entertaining way.
4. Before presenting the A.V. aids, necessary background should be prepared. It saves the time and the pupils understand the necessary things quickly.
5. Some questions must be asked about the displayed material. This simplifies and clarifies the sense of the lesson.
6. A.V. aids should not be presented before the pupils merely for an bird's eye-view only. It causes no benefit to the pupils. Hence, the teacher should present the material for so much time that the pupils may have sufficient time for observation and thinking.
7. A.V. aids should be shown by placing it on the table or by hanging on the wall. Some pupil-teachers show these aids by holding them in their hands, which is not correct. This restricts the movement of teacher's body parts.

8. A.V. aids should be immediately removed after their presentation. Otherwise, pupils will deviate from their lesson. Therefore, after displaying a picture chart, it should either be placed at some safer place or it should be reversed on the wall.
9. A.V. aids are means to achieve the teaching objectives, not the ends.
10. After using A.V. material, the teacher should come immediately on his lesson. Its reason is that the teacher's main aim is only the development of the lesson, not showing the material.

Selecting Appropriate Audio-Visual Aids

In managing teaching, audio-visual aids occupy an important place as we have mentioned in the above lines. But the question is how the audio-visual aids should be selected? Its answer is that the various bases and principles are kept in mind when audio-visual aids are selected.

(i) Kinds of Learning Objectives. The first criterion for selecting the audio-visual aids is objectives of learning. The teacher should select those audio-visual aids according to those learning objectives which he determines and defines during the planning phase.

In this connection, we want to make clear that:

(a) Cognitive objectives can be achieved successfully by using every type of audio-visual aids,

(b) Affective objectives are achieved by using gramophone, radio, tape-recorder, television, pictures, cinema, laboratory and excursions etc.,

(c) Psychomotor objectives are achieved by using language, tape-recorder, gramophone, laboratory and models etc.

(ii) Types of Learning Structures. The second important criterion in selecting audio-visual aids is types of learning structures. In the following lines, we are clarifying what audio-visual aids should be selected for various learning structures.

(a) Signal Learning Structure: Signal learning structures can be presented successfully with the help of gramophone, tape-recorder, pictures, sketches, language, laboratory and models.

(b) *Chain Learning Structures:* Chain learning structures can be presented by using gramophone, radio, tape-recorder, television, picture, cinema, language, laboratory and models.

(c) *Multiple Discrimination Learning Structures:* These can be presented with the help of language, laboratory, sketches, gramophone and tape-recorder.

(d) *Concept Learning Structure:* Concept learning structure can be presented by pictures, sketches, cinema and television.

(e) *Principle Learning Structure:* These can be presented by picture, sketch, cinema etc.

This shows that the audio-visual aids are closely related to learning objectives and learning structures. Hence, the teachers and pupil-teachers should select the audio aids considering both the criteria as basis.

Selecting Appropriate Class Size

For a desirable communication and achieving learning objectives appropriate class-size or group of learner is needed. Seats in the class-room should be as per the pupil's numbers. The pupil-teacher ratio should also be appropriate so that the teacher is able to pay attention to each pupil, but in India alike many other developing countries due to financial problems this aspect is overlooked, hence in small room without proper seating arrangement large number of pupils are made to sit which creates communication problems for the teacher and effects the learning objectives. In America and England pupil-teacher ratio is 1:24 and class-room having seats and learning facilities as per number students. I.K. Davies thinks that for achieving objectives of cognitive effective domains the pupil-teacher ratio should be 1:7 at the most, because the criterion for class size in the number of students a teacher can effectively manage in a learning situation.

Selecting Appropriate Communication Strategies

Teaching has two elements— *(i)* content, and *(ii)* communication. The teacher should analyse the content at first. Then, he should think over which communication strategies should be selected in order to present the content so that the objectives may be achieved. I.K. Davies has divided the strategies into two categories in order to solve the communication problems.

In the first category, those communication strategies are included which do not guarantee the selection of correct solutions in order to acquire necessary information. In the second category, those strategies are included which guarantee the correct selection of solutions.

The first category includes two strategies—

(i) Continuous prose, and

(ii) Heuristics.

Similarly, the second category includes

(i) Algorithms, and

(ii) Decision tables.

Hence, according to I.K. Davies, communication has following four strategies:

(i) Continuous Prose. Continuous prose is the most simple, useful and general method of communication. The understanding objective is achieved by imparting knowledge of various facts and information to the pupils by this strategy.

There is no doubt that in the complex instruction, we cannot depend on this strategy only, but it is also not possible that without continuous prose, there occurs no other communication. In this strategy, language and style have special importance.

Hence, while using this strategy, the words and sentences which are used in it, should be so simple and easy that the pupils may pick up them easily. The teacher should take care of the following points while using this strategy—

(a) The prose should be structured in simple and easy language.

(b) The excessive use of the words should be avoided.

(c) Smaller sentences should be used for complicated facts.

(d) The use of negative sentences should be avoided.

(e) The sentences should be in active voice.

(ii) Heuristics. Polya and Duncker used this communication for solving the problem. This strategy is an experimental method. In it, discovery is made on the basis of alternates. No doubt, it is an expensive and fast method but its application fails sometimes. Sometimes wrong solutions are also accepted. Not only this, by using this method, discovery of drawbacks also

becomes difficult.

(iii) Algorithms. Algorithms is a word from Arabian language which means the order of counting. Therefore, this communication is used in mathematics. In algorithms, the informations are organized in such a way to achieve the objective and are executed which makes possible solving of the problem.

This strategy was developed by Wason and Jones in London University in order to interpret government rules. I.K. Davies has thrown light in detail on the peculiarities of this strategy. He believed that this strategy presents easily the tasks of problem-solving on one side and logical presentation of the rules or laws in the minimum time occurs on the other side.

Hence, this strategy is very comprehensive and effective communication. But the application of this strategy is not an easy task. This strategy is not successful in multiple discrimination structure but it can be used successfully in chain structures.

(iv) Decision Tables. Decision tables are also called as logic tables. This communication was developed by Grad in 1961. It is being used in computer programme since then. In 1969, Packer and Davies used this communication in addition to the computer to communicate complex rules and instruction.

Remember that the decision tables are used in problem solving, question-answer and informations. Informations are of two types—

(i) Those questions which are to be responded by the pupils, and

(ii) The decisions to be made on the basis of these questions. When the pupils compare their answers with the correct answer and they find it correct, they feel pleasure.

Hence, decision tables are more useful as compared to continuous prose and algorithms. When these decision tables help to establish cause and effect relationship by defining the problems, between the directions and tasks on one-side, these are also successful in interpreting completely each event.

This avoids any fear of error. Since the decision tables proved useful in expressing complex rules successfully, therefore, in the modern age, these should be used as a teaching strategy.

Selecting an Appropriate Strategy

In the above lines, we have made clear that the communication has four strategies. These are—

(i) Continuous Prose,
(ii) Heuristics,
(iii) Algorithms, and
(iv) Decision Tables.

Out of these four strategies, none is a complete strategy. Their selection should be made according to the condition and nature of the task. Remember that some tasks are easy and some are difficult.

I.K. Davies has classified the nature of the tasks—

(a) Some tasks are risky,
(b) Some are non-risky.

According to the first classification:

(i) If the task is simple, continuous prose should be used.
(ii) If the task is difficult and diagnostic, heuristic communication should be used,
(iii) If the task is difficult and cannot be presented in steps, then algorithms communication should be used

Contrary to this, according to second classification—

(i) If the task is diagnostic, decision tables should be used, and
(ii) If it is difficult to present the task in steps, then algorithms should be used.

Selection of Teaching Strategy

Communication and teaching strategy are closely related. Hence, it is essential for a teacher that he should select an appropriate teaching strategy for communication. We have discussed various teaching strategies earlier in this book.

Here, it is necessary to explain that at the time of selecting appropriate teaching strategies, the nature of task and learning objectives are considered criterion. From this point of view, in order to achieve knowledge objectives, these strategies should be used—

(i) Lecturing,
(ii) Discussion,
(iii) Lecture and Discussion,

(iv) Demonstration,
(v) Tutorial or Individual Education,
(vi) Brain Drain or Brain Storming,
(vii) Role Playing,
(viii) Independent Study,
(ix) Programmed Learning,
(x) A group without guide,
(xi) Sensitivity teaching, etc.

In order to achieve affective objectives, we should use these strategies—

(i) Lecturing,
(ii) Demonstration,
(iii) Individualized education,
(ix) Role playing,
(v) Brain storming,
(vi) Independent study,
(vii) A group without a guide and sensitivity training etc.

To achieve psychomotor objectives, we should use strategies such as—

(i) Demonstration,
(ii) Role playing, and
(iii) Sensitivity training etc.

From the above description, it is very clear that while managing teaching, an efficient teacher should know, as a manager, how to select—

(i) Proper teaching tactics.
(ii) Appropriate audio-visual aids.
(iii) Appropriate class size.
(iv) Proper communication strategies.

Only then he can succeed in achieving the learning objectives in an effective and economical way by creating proper environment for teaching learning.

QUESTIONS FOR ANSWER

1. Write a note on the importance of learning structures in the selections of appropriate teaching tactics. Explain teaching tactics too.
2. Explain in detail I.K. Davies' theory of 'steps in managing teaching-learning'.

3. Write short notes on the following:
   (*a*) Utility of communication strategies.
   (*b*) Utility of Audio-visual aids.
   (*c*) Computer as a learning resource.
   (*d*) Satellite Instructional Television Experiment (SITE).
   (*e*) Multi-media Approach.
4. Write a note on the importance of black-board in class-room teaching.
5. Write short notes on:
   (*a*) Use of Epidiascope in Teaching.
   (*b*) Qualities of Audio-visuals Aids.
   (*c*) Types of learning structures.

14

Management of Teaching and Learning—3 (Leading and Controlling Teaching and Learning)

Leading and controlling are the third and fourth phases of the management of teaching and learning technology. I.K. Davies has rightly written as follows:

"In teaching leading is the work a teacher does to motivate, encourage and guide students so that they will readily realise the agreed learning objectives." In short, as an efficient manager, the teacher should follow the following two things for *leading the teaching*—

1. Harnessing students motivation.
2. Selecting appropriate motivational strategies.

Harnessing Students Motivation

Meaning of Motivation

Unless the ability and motivation, both the components function equally, the quantity of work done is affected. Woodworth has made clear this equation as follows:

Achievement = Ability + Motivation

Remember that the human motivation may be due to his love

for his wife and children or in order to attain a special status in the society. In other words, if his ideas motivate him, he will go on moving ahead, facing the most difficult situations unless he attains his goal. Contrary to this, if his mental and physical conditions do not arouse tension in him, he will not concentrate his mind in any task.

It is applicable completely on pupils also. It is generally observed that in a same class, some pupils of same age and ability are more lazy and disappointed. They don't have interest in doing any work happily, if the interest happens to occur, then it is negligible. As a result of it, due to frustrations, they run away.

Contrary to this, there are some pupils who have many hopes. They face the adverse conditions present in the environment with hard work till they acquire their objectives.

Take the case of an optimistic adolescent of a poor family. He wants to marry a beautiful girl, who belongs to a family with sound financial background. The poverty of that adolescent is a barrier to fulfil his this need. He starts loving music. After some days, he feels that he has done remarkable progress in singing songs. He works very hard so that he may become a famous singer and by earning money he may marry that girl and may lead family life. His thoughts, feelings and conditions motivate him in this task so that he may acquire his goal.

In this way, we can say that every person is active according to his psycho-physical condition. As his needs increase to achieve some goal, he goes on getting motivated.

In other words, motivation is a psychophysical and intrinsic process which activates an individual in order to fulfil his need till he attains the goal.

Definition of Motivation

We are giving the following definitions in order to make clear the meaning of motivation—

1. *Thomson.* "Motivation is the art of stimulating interest in the pupils where there is no such interest."

2. *Lovell.* "Motivation is defined more formally as a psychophysiological or internal process initiated by some needs which lead to activity which will satisfy that need."

3. *Woodworth*. "Motivation is a state of the individual which disposes him for certain behaviour and for seeking goals."

4. *Johnson*. "Motivation is the influence of general pattern of activities indicating the behaviour of the organism."

5. *Mcdougall*. "Motivations are conditions physiological and psychological within the organism that dispose it to act in certain ways.

Difference between Need, Drive, Incentive and Motive

In order to understand the meaning of motivation, it is essential to learn the meanings of need, drive, incentive and motive. All these terms have the feeling of motivating force. If observed carefully, all these terms depend on each other and all these have the relation of cause and effect. In the following lines we are clarifying the differences in each other.

Need

Every individual has some needs. He has various types of psychological and physiological needs. He feels the need of food when he is hungry, feels the need of water when he is thirsty, wants clothes when he feels cold, needs medicines when he is ill. As soon as one need of an individual is fulfilled, another need arises.

Hence, the cycle of the needs goes on. It is essential that all needs of an individual should be fulfilled but out of these, his physiological needs like air, water, food, and sex etc. are main.

As long as their physiological needs are fulfilled, their balance is maintained. But as soon as any one of his physiological need is not fullfilled or he feels lacking something in himself, his physiological balance disturbs, he feels restlessness. This cycle goes on till he regains his such balance. Thorndike has proved this fact by conducting an experiment on a cat.

According to the eminent psychologist Soreeson, "A need indicates a lack of something which a person should have." According to Boring, Langfield and Wield, "A need is a tension within an organism which tends to organise the field of the organism with respect of certain incentives or goals and to incite activity directed towards their attainment."

Drive

The origin of drive is needs. The drives lacking needs cannot originate. Hence, the drive of thirst originates from lack of water, drive of hunger originates from lack of food. In daily life, when essential things like air, water and food are not available, a tension arouses which forces to act. The force or internal power is termed as 'drive'. Sorenson has defined the drive as "Urges and drives are impelling forces that impel to action."

Incentive

All those objects found in environment which satisfy all these drives are called incentives. For example, the drive of hunger is satisfied by food. Hence, the food will be termed as incentive. Actually incentive is a goal-object which attracts an individual towards some particular direction by influencing the individual.

In this situation, we can say that the needs and drives are the only internal powers on one side while on other side, incentives include all the objects and living things which satisfy the drives of the human being.

Boring, Langfield and Wield have presented the definition of an incentive—"An incentive may be defined as object, a situation of an activity which excites, maintains and directs behaviour."

Motives

Every behaviour of an individual has some objectives. In order to obtain his objectives, whatever he performs is due to his intrinsic condition. This intrinsic condition due to which activity of an individual occurs is called a motive.

In other words, a motive is that thought, feeling or condition which activates the behaviour of the individual by influencing him till the time he attains his objectives.

The motive has two main functions—

1. To produce activity on the individual,
2. To carry on the activity till the acquisition of the objectives. While defining motivation, Woodworth has written, "A motive is a state or set of the individual which disposes him for certain behaviour and for seeking certain goals."

In the above lines, it has been said that motivation is a psycho-physiological or internal process which keeps an individual activated till some need arises. The most important factor of human motivation is his needs.

Hence, we are to understand completely how the pupils can be motivated. For this, the knowledge of human needs is must. In this connection, Maslow's hierarchy of needs has much importance.

Maslow's Hierarchy of Human Needs

The famous educationist Maslow has explained in his Theory of Motivation, that motivation includes feeling and satisfaction of needs. He divided the needs in five categories in a definite order. Since this motivation is directly related to the needs of the pupil, therefore, we are describing them in detail as follows:

1. *Physiological Needs.* Physiological needs are those primary and basic needs which an individual wants to satisfy naturally. Among these needs, main are air, water, food, sex etc. Maslow has described physiological needs as of lower level. He has told that unless he satisfies physiological needs, needs of higher level do not arise.

2. *Safety Needs.* As an individual satisfies physiological needs, safety need arises. In other words, he manages proper safety arrangements just to survive. Maslow has considered safety need as important but it is also of lower level.

3. *Needs of Belongingness.* When physiological and safety needs are satisfied, an individual feels the need of belongingness. Maslow has described this need too as of lower level. These needs include friendship, love, recognition in society etc.

Remember that the pupils also want other persons to know them, to recognize them and to accept them. Therefore, they become member of some group and participate actively in various school functions so that they may have maximum number of friends. They want to love society and they want people's affection. They want to make some place in the society.

4. *Esteem Needs.* Maslow told that when lower level needs are satisfied, then needs of higher level like esteem-need arises.

In other words, when physiological and safety needs are satisfied along with an individual's need of belongingness, then he wants that other persons should accept him, respect him and he should have some power in his hand so that he may provide leadership to others. He wants all this in order to gain a high place in the society.

5. *Needs of Self-actualization.* Needs of self-actualization are last and of highest order needs. Maslow says that if an individual wants self-satisfaction, he should be made what he can be. In the words of Maslow: "A musician must make music, Artist must paint and a poet must write, if he is, ultimately, to be at peace with himself. What a man can be, must be."

Types of Motivation

Maslow has categorized motivation into the following three categories according to various needs—

1. *Extrinsic Motivation.* Extrinsic motivation means to present such an environment before the pupils by the teacher which motivates them to behave. According to Maslow, extrinsic motivation is effective in the case of first three lower-level needs. He has also suggested that praise and reward techniques can be used to motivate mentally retarded pupils. Similarly, talented pupils can be motivated by techniques of punishment and blame.

2. *Intrinsic Motivation.* Intrinsic motivation means motivating pupils by contents of study or activity itself. Remember that the intrinsic motivation is concerned with the internal condition of the individual. It is present in the individual itself. Hence, by internal motivation, the pupils are motivated to discover the facts by doing himself.

According to Maslow, intrinsic motivation is effective for higher order needs like esteem needs and actualization needs. He further explained that to provide intrinsic motivation, techniques like knowledge of progress, novelty and level of aspiration can be used successfully in the higher classes, not in the lower classes. Based on democratic system, intrinsic motivation is considered as the best.

3. *Intrinsic-Extrinsic Motivation.* Intrinsic-extrinsic motivation is concerned with both environment and contents. Maslow has considered it as middle order motivation.

It is effective for safety, belongingness and esteem needs. It is used to develop social competencies in the pupils. The teacher should use the techniques like success and failure, competition and co-operation to develop the pupils socially.

Techniques of Motivation

How the pupils should be motivated, for this, the teacher should select and use properly the following seven techniques of motivation according to the maturation, aims, needs of pupils and keeping in mind the learning structures and on the basis of contents, knowledge of the child psychology and personal experiences—

1. *Reward and Punishment*. Reward and punishment have their own importance in motivation of the pupils. In order to gain the reward each pupil tries to perform appreciably. Its only reason is that the pupil feels delighted as a result of reward and they have their enthusiasm boosted. This motivates them to do work. While rewarding the pupils, the following three things should be observed—

1. Reward should be according to the performance of the pupil.
2. Pupils should know the importance of reward.
3. The distribution of the reward should not occur at general level, hence, its importance should not be minimized.

Punishment is also an important technique to motivate the pupils. It is an experience that if the pupils are punished for some undesirable task, they won't repeat the same in future. It means the fear of punishment sometimes gets the work done from the pupils which they don't perform in normal conditions. It would be unpsychological to punish the pupils unnecessarily or in excess. This will hamper their development and growth. Reward and punishment are included in extrinsic motivation.

2. *Praise and Blame*. Naming praise and blame as natural motivations, Morgan and King have told that praise in the success of pupils and blame in their failure must be used. The teacher should use praise and blame techniques adequately.

Hence, while using these two techniques, the teacher must consider the mental level of the pupils. Praise and blame also belong to category of extrinsic motivation.

3. *Success and Failure*. Although the use of success- technique

is desirable for all the pupils, but this technique is important for normal pupils. According to Bernard, success develops self-confidence in the pupils, on the basis of which they acquire the goals of life successfully.

Like success, sometimes failure also becomes the important source of motivation. This is true, especially in the case of gifted pupils. When a talented pupil is unsuccessful, then he takes this failure as a challenge and tries for a succe

Therefore, it is true that failure is the key ιω -uccess. The teacher should use both of these techniques keeping in view the child-psychology, otherwise it can damage instead of benefit.

4. *Competition and Cooperation.* In the class, almost all the pupils are in race to score more. In other words, every pupil has a tendency of competition. The teacher can motivate the pupils to acquire more scores by using competition technique. Remember that the competition is in two forms—

(i) individual, and

(ii) group.

Through individual competition, pupils can be motivated to score more than before. Contrary to this, through group competitions, the pupils of two or more sections can be motivated to score more. The competition should be in good shape otherwise it can lead to some damage.

Cooperation is also an important technique to motivate the pupils. Its reason is that the pupils can progress to the maximum by cooperating mutually. The teacher should motivate the pupils to work with cooperation. It will benefit in two ways—

(i) Socialization of the pupils will occur, and

(ii) They will develop to the maximum.

5. *Knowledge of Progress.* To what extent the pupils can be motivated in a subject depends upon their knowledge regarding their progress. As they go on getting the knowledge of their progress, they work with more enthusiasm. In other words, pupils get reinforcement as a result of getting the knowledge about their progress. This helps them in determining their objectives and they become active after getting motivated in accordance with their objectives.

Since the pupils get more motivation to work hard more, therefore, teachers provide periodic informations to them on one side regarding their progress and on the other side they prepare progress charts regarding their monthly tests.

6. *Novelty.* It is a psychological fact that the pupils get motivation as a result of novelty. They take natural interest in doing novel task. Hence, the teacher should use the technique of novelty to motivate the pupils. For this, it is the duty of the teacher to present the content in such an interesting way that all the pupils get motivated to learn new knowledge. In doing so, the teacher should keep in mind the previous knowledge of the pupils.

7. *Level of Aspiration.* The level of aspiration is linked with the goal of the life. From this angle, the aspiration level of the pupils should be according to their capabilities and their physical and mental powers.

Remember that if the aspiration level of pupils is according to their capability, they can be made active to acquire their goals. Contrary to this, if their aspiration level is higher than their capacity or capability, they will face disappointment in place of motivations.

Also, if their aspiration level is lower than their capability, a feeling of inferiority will arise among them. Hence, keeping in mind the achievement of the pupils, they should be guided properly so that they may get motivated in order to acquire the objectives of their life according to their levels of aspiration.

Leading Theories of Motivation

The leading theories of motivation are as follows:

1. *Instinct Theory.* This theory of instinct, was indoctrinated by a famous English Psychologist McDougall. Scholars like Burt, Ross, Hughes and Hughes and Valentine etc. pleaded this theory throughout the world. McDougall has made clear that every human being has some innate powers of basic instincts. They considered these basic instincts as motives and they have told that these basic instincts influence human thoughts and functions.

They further told that when a relationship is established between any basic instinct's emotional aspect and an individual, object and thought under the influence of intelligence and experience, then the sentiments come to existence. These sentiments organize an individual's emotional life and cause stability in his behaviour, McDougall has also explained the importance of self-respect regarding sentiments, because an individual's character is evaluated in terms of stability of his self-respect.

2. *Social Theory*. Social theory is of following two types—

(i) Culture-Pattern Theory.

(ii) Field Theory

(i) Culture-Pattern Theory. The supporters of this theory agree that the behaviour of the children is influenced by learning techniques which occur in their various cultures.

Hence, the social anthropologists like Mead, Gorer and Benedict etc. have described similarities in various rearing techniques and interpreted the behaviour influenced by those techniques.

They have told that the children of those castes who are under strict control, not looked after properly and are frequently snubbed. They become foolish, dry and short-tempered when they grow up. Contrary to this, the castes in which the children are behaved affectionately, they exhibit affectionate behaviour when they grow up.

Hence, some sociologists have accepted many sub-cultural models in an entire culture. In their view, these sub-cultural models depend on two things—(1) That social group of which the child is a member, and (2) Type of that task which he undertakes. In this way, the motivation and the children's behaviour is affected by their social status.

(ii) Field Theory. This theory i.e., field theory was indoctrinated by Kurt Lewin. The nature of an individual's behaviour is determined in some specific situation by all those forces or components which act between that individual and environment. These forces or components are needs of other individual's groups, mental tendencies and needs etc.

Hence, it can be said clearly that there is a close relationship between an individual and environment. As the behaviour of an individual is affected by his characteristics on one side, environment also forces an individual to behave specifically. It becomes clear from the above description that the motivation is determined by the mutual action of an individual and environment.

3. *Learning or Behaviour Theory.* This theory was indoctrinated by eminent psychologist of Yak University, Clark Hull. He told that every individual's behaviour depends on the satisfaction or dissatisfaction of his needs. When his needs are satisfied, his psychophysiological tension reduces and he retains the reactions of his behaviour or learns them. Contrary to this, if his needs are not fulfilled due to some reason, he does not retain or learn those reactions relating to his behaviour.

It is Hull's view that the needs of the child arise out of experience when his organic needs are satisfied, he learns to link the social conditions with his primary needs which become needs themselves. This theory has not been accepted entirely. Its critics view that even in the absence of any reward, an individual learns.

4. *Maslow's Theory of Motivation.* Maslow divided the motives in two categories: (1) Inborn motives, and (2) Acquired Motives. Maslow has stressed motives like hunger, thirst and sex etc. in the inborn motives category. He classified acquired motives in two categories: (1) Social, and (2) Individual.

In the social category of the motives, socialization, combat, and self-assertion motives etc. are included. Individual motives include interests, attitudes, habits and unconscious motives. Remember that Maslow has presented a hierarchy of needs.

5. *Psychoanalytic Theory.* To discuss human motivation, Frend, Young and Adler have indoctrinated psychoanalytic theory. According to these three psychologists, unconscious mind play main role in controlling an individual's behaviour. To understand this theory, it is essential to understand the meaning of repression and unconscious mind. Repression means the elimination of painful and unhealthy experiences from the conscious mind.

As the child grows, his needs, feelings and especially sex-needs are disliked by elders. Hence, he eliminates unhealthy experiences and needs from his conscious mind. These go on collecting in his unconscious mind. According to this theory, needs assembled in unconscious mind affect human behaviour without coming to his conscious mind's level. According to Freud, the unconscious feelings are founded in childhood which always try to become conscious. This causes many changes in human behaviour. Young, Adler and Freud differ on unconscious mind. But these three experts are of the opinion that the human behaviour is influenced by such motives about which he is totally unaware.

6. *Motivation Hygiene Theory.* Fredrick Herzberg interviewed farmers, accounts officers, nurses and house-wives in Pittsburg University in 1966 and indoctrinated this new theory of motivation. This theory was indoctrinated in the fields of industry and commerce and this was observed what factors can influence the behaviour of the workers.

But it was also felt that this theory is also useful for a teacher in the case of pupils. In other words, on one side, motivation hygiene theory organizes the teachers functions properly, on the other side, this theory stresses the teacher to create proper conditions to motivate the pupils. Herzberg also interpreted the needs and presented the following clauses—

1. Motivation.
2. Hygiene Factors.

(1) *Motivation:* According to motivation hygiene theory, motives enhance the efficiency by providing comfort and satisfaction to the pupils. This enriches the learning. Since the effect of motives is positives and it persists for a long time, therefore, the motives develop the following feeling in the pupils.

(i) Achievement
(ii) Recognition
(iii) Responsibility
(iv) Advancement
(v) Personal Growth

(2) *Hygiene Factors:* According to this theory, these hygiene factors affect directly the achievement of the pupils and their attitude of doing work. The hygiene factors are as follows—

(i) Method of supervision
(ii) Conditions of work
(iii) Interpersonal Relations
(iv) School Policy and Administration
(v) Status
(vi) Security

If the level of these factors is lower, the pupils become unhappy. They are not satisfied in any way. As a consequence, the learning outcome decreases. Also, negative attitude of the pupils develops. The hygiene factors function as a basis for effective motivation. These are concerned with school environment

In other words, these factors are directly concerned with organizational climate of the school. A good organizational climate of the school will lead towards appreciable emotional climate. Consequently, learning outcomes would be satisfactory.

Since the organization of the school affects the achievements of the pupils directly, therefore the teachers and administrators should care for hygiene factors. In short, the superiority of school organization and administration is essential for the alround development of the pupils.

Therefore, the relations between teacher and pupils should be such that they always gain motivation for learning. Not only this, the teachers should apply democratic strategies during teaching so that the learning experiences may get increased. In the end, the organization and administration of the schools should be superb so that maximum development of the pupils may occur.

Selecting Appropriate Motivational Strategies

While teaching, the teacher should present before the pupils such an effective environment that the desired behavioural changes may occur in their behaviour by gaining maximum learning experiences. Remember that pupils respond physically and mentally in the teacher-made environment and in intensifying these reasons, the motivation has its own importance.

Hence, it is duty of an efficient teacher to select such appropriate teaching strategies that all the pupils may show maximum learning outcomes. In this context, we consider it necessary to suggest the teachers that while selecting appropriate strategies of teaching and techniques of motivation, they should keep in mind the following criteria—

1. **Objectives to be realized.**
2. **Needs of students to enrich learning experiences.**

3. Ability of students involved in the task.

1. *Objectives to be Realised.* An individual's behaviour has three aspects (a) Cognitive, (b) Affective, and (c) Conative. Remember that to acquire objectives of all these three aspects, the teacher should apply following different teaching strategies and techniques of motivation—

(a) Cognitive Objectives. To achieve the higher order of cognitive objectives, the teaching strategies like lecturing, demonstration, tutorials, programmed study, group-discussions, role-playing, project strategy and independent study etc. can be used. But to achieve lower level objectives of this aspect, lecturing, demonstrations, programmed study etc. teaching strategies and reward and punishment, praise and blame, success and failure, competition and cooperation etc. techniques of motivation should be applied.

(b) Affective Objective: To achieve the objective of affective aspect, almost all the teaching strategies can be used, but to achieve the higher order objectives, the teacher should use tutorial, discussion, individual study, role playing, brain-storming, computer assisted instruction, sensitivity training and independent study etc. teaching strategies and techniques of motivation like competition and cooperation, knowledge of progress, success and failure, praise and blame, reward and punishment etc.

(c) Conative Objectives: To achieve objectives of conative aspect, the teacher should use various teaching strategies like demonstration, tutorial and independent study and techniques of motivation like novelty and aspiration level etc.

2. *Need to Enrich Learning Experiences.* The need of qualitative growth is directly related to the motivation. Remember that the motivation is concerned with the needs of the pupils. Unless and until their needs are satisfied, their balance is maintained. Just opposite to this, as some need is not satisfied, a tension arouses in them. They perform various activities to remove this tension. This also increases qualitatively their learning experiences. Remember that the pupils go on doing these activities till their tension decreases i.e. they become balanced.

Hence, in order to satisfy these needs, such a motivation

should be selected which can help in developing their performance or achievement, acceptance, responsibility, progress and individual development. To accomplish this important task, the teacher should apply all the democratic strategies of teaching and techniques of motivations according to the needs.

3. *Ability of Students Involved in Task.* The ability of the students and the teaching strategies are closely related. Hence, the teacher should select the teaching strategies keeping in view the age, level, interest, ability, capacity, attitude and needs of the pupils.

I.K. Davies had told in very clear words that the able and ablest pupils like democratic teaching strategies. Hence, they take interest in completing the teaching task by democratic teaching strategies. Contrary to this, the pupils with lower ability and mental retardation, prefer to use authoritarian teaching strategies.

Hence, the teacher should motivate the pupils to achieve the objectives and keeping in view their abilities, he should use such motivational strategies of teaching which cause desired behavioural changes by bringing about qualitative growth in the learning objectives.

Controlling of Teaching-Learning

Controlling is the fourth and last important phase of management of teaching-learning. Regarding this phase, I.K. Davies, rightly observes as follows:

"In teaching, controlling is the work a teacher does to determine whether his plans are being carried out effectively, organisation is sound, leading is in right direction and how far these functions are successful in realizing the set objectives."

The controlling activities help in making the teaching successful by modifying planning, management and leading. These activities also help in modifying the curriculum, teaching strategies, techniques and tactics.

Steps in Controlling

In controlling teaching, the following three steps are followed:

1. Evaluating the Learning System
2. Measuring Learning

3. Managing by Learning Objectives

1. Evaluating the Learning System

Till recently, essay type examinations were popular in examination system. By conducting these examinations, the style, thoughts, language, reasoning, criticism etc. of pupils can be evaluated easily but the other aspects of their personality such as interests, attitudes, emotions, habits and behaviours cannot be tested. In order to eliminate these defects of examination, a new testing method was developed in America which was termed as Evaluation. In our country too, a new evaluation method was used in 1958.

Meaning of Evaluation: Evaluation is such a social and psychological process which is used in every field of life day by day. We observe that an individual evaluates the behaviours of other individuals on one side, he also evaluates his own actions at regular intervals.

For example, a gardener evaluates his plants considering their beauty, and a doctor evaluates his medicines by observing the behavioural changes in the patients.

Similarly, a teacher also evaluates his teaching on the basis of the behavioural changes occurred in the pupils. In the field of education, the evaluation is linked with the learning objectives. Therefore, every teacher observes while evaluating his teaching that whether the behavioural changes which have occurred in the pupils are with reference to the pre-determined learning objectives or not.

In this way, the teaching and testing going on side by side according to learning objectives is known as evaluation. Kothari commission has defined the evaluation as "Evaluation is a continuous process. It forms an integral part of total educational system and thus is intimately related to education objectives."

Features of Evaluation

1. *Comprehensiveness.* All changes which occur in all the aspects such as the physical aspect concerning pupil's personality, mental, social and moral aspects. Hence, evaluation is a comprehensive method to test the pupils. It includes both measurement and evaluation.

2. *Continuous Process.* Evaluation is a continuous process which is closely related to the learning objectives. In this, in accordance with educational objectives, the desirable learning experiences are created in the pupil and the behavioural changes which occur day-to-day are recorded. On the basis of this record, the ranking of pupils is done and they are sent to the next higher class.

3. *Cooperative Process.* Evaluation is a cooperative process. In evaluation, the necessary material is collected by seeking essential cooperation of all the sources like teacher, pupils and parents. Then his progress is evaluated.

4. *Social Process.* Evaluation is a social process. In this all the aspects of personality are evaluated on one side, it is also evaluated whether the teaching has been conducted according to the needs, ideals and norms of the society or not on the other side.

5. *Descriptive Process.* Evaluation is a descriptive process. In this, the progress which occurs in all the aspects of the pupils is given.

6. *Decisive Process.* Evaluation is a decisive process. After this, it is decided that—

(i) whether any object or process is useful or not,

(ii) to what extent the teaching is successful according to the determined educational objectives,

(iii) whether the learning experiences provided to the pupils in the class are effective or not.

(iv) how fair the teaching objectives have been achieved. If not achieved then whether the remedial instruction should be given or the teaching strategies are to be modified.

In short, evaluation measures the educational achievements. It also improve the teaching process.

Steps in Evaluation

Evaluation is a continuous process. In it, following are the three steps—

1. *Formulation of Educational Objectives:* Teaching objectives are key to teaching. Hence for successful teaching, teaching objectives are determined while keeping five points in mind,

otherwise the possibilities of failure of teaching enhance. These points are—

(i) Teaching objectives should be determined keeping in mind the interests, attitudes, tendencies, abilities, needs and physical, mental, emotional and social aspects of personality of pupils,

(ii) Keeping in view the social needs and ideals while determining the teaching objectives,

(iii) Keeping in sight the nature and areas of contents while determining the teaching objectives,

(iv) Take care of nursery, primary, middle and high levels of education while determining teaching objectives, and

(v) Having knowledge of educational psychology while determining educational psychology.

When the above five things are achieved, then the teacher should make it clear the areas in which what changes are to be brought about in the pupils in order to achieve teaching objectives.

2. *Creating Appropriate Learning Experiences through Educational Activities.* It is the responsibility of the teacher to create such teaching materials or conditions after determining and defining the teaching objectives so that the pupils get appropriate experiences of learning and in the end by those teaching experiences, the teaching objectives are successfully achieved. In other words, the teacher should create such an environment while selecting such activities and experiences so that the pupils get appropriate experiences of learning from his own activities while living in that environment.

Remember that after selecting learning experiences, creation of appropriate educational environment is not an easy task. For this, the teacher should take care of the following points:

(i) The learning experiences should be directly related to the teaching objectives.

(ii) The learning experiences should be meaningful and satisfactory for the pupils.

(iii) The learning experiences should be according to the interests of the pupils so that they may achieve determined objectives by keeping them maximum activated.

(iv) The learning objectives should be adequate.

(v) The learning experiences should be according to the maturity of the pupils.

(vi) The learning experiences should be the integral part of the behaviour of the pupils.

3. *Evaluating on the Basis of Behavioural Changes.* The ultimate aim of education is to bring a change in the behaviour of the pupils. The change in the behaviour occurs by teaching the pupils various school subjects and this change occurs in the various aspects of the personality of the pupils. These aspects are—*(A)* Cognitive, *(B)* Affective, and *(C)* Conative or Psychomotor.

All the three aspects are tested by evaluation. Remember that these three aspects of behaviour are related to each other. From this angle, all the three aspects are included in every behaviour, whether it is external or internal. In the following lines, we are explaining all the three behavioural aspects.

(A) Cognitive Aspect. Cognitive aspect is the first aspect of pupils' behaviour. By this, pupils acquire knowledge regarding new things, informations, facts, events and theories. Since the cognitive aspect includes psychological process like recall and recognition, this aspect is developed to the maximum with the help of school subjects.

According to Prof. Bloom, in cognitive aspect, the knowledge acquired includes—

(i) Knowledge of specific facts,

(ii) Knowledge of ways and means of dealing with specifics,

(iii) Knowledge of conventions,

(iv) Knowledge of actions and events,

(v) Knowledge of criteria,

(vi) Knowledge of classification and criteria,

(vii) Knowledge of methods and techniques, and

(viii) Knowledge of principles and generalization.

Remember that to develop the cognitive aspect of behaviour, different levels will have to be crossed. These levels are—

(i) Recall and recognition,

(ii) Comprehension,

(iii) Analysis,

(iv) Synthesis, and

(v) Evaluation.

(B) Affective Aspect. Affective aspect is the second aspect of pupils' behaviour. It is concerned with the interest, emotions

and mental tendencies of the pupils. In other words, the occurrence of interest or attitude towards some subject in the pupils and other changes relating to other mental tendencies and emotions come under the affective domain. It is nct an easy task to develop affective aspect of the pupils. These are concerned to an individual first and other people afterwards. It is easy to understand its nature and determining elements. Since our interests, sentiments and mental tendencies are criteria of our personality, therefore, these occupy important place in education. It is the main duty of the teacher to develop maximum the affective aspect of the pupils. For this, they are to pass through many levels. These levels are—

(i) Receiving,
(ii) Response,
(iii) Valuing,
(iv) Organization, and
(v) Characterization of a value system.

(C) *Conative Aspect*. Conative aspect is the third important aspect of pupils' behaviour. It appears in such actions for which muscular and physical or motor activities are needed. The appropriate examples of conative aspect are—vocational and technical education. In such education, the conative aspect of the pupils occupies primary place.

The main levels of this aspect are—

(i) Impulsion,
(ii) Manipulation,
(iii) Control,
(iv) Co-ordination
(v) Habit or Skill and
(vi) Evaluation.

The continuous process of evaluation has three aspects. These three aspects are closely related to each other. Teaching objectives are the starting point of teaching process. As soon as the teaching objectives are determined and defined, the teacher creates such an effective environment that each pupil gets activated and achieves various experiences. It is the purpose to say that for achieving determined and defined objectives, the teacher presents the contents with the help of such strategies of teaching, tactics and material aid that appropriate learning experiences are created in the pupils.

These learning experiences cause desirable behavioural changes. The interests, attitudes, emotions and thinking and working styles of the pupils present basis for behavioural changes. These changes occurred in the cognitive, affective and conative aspects are called as behavioural changes. In this way, in order to explore the behavioural changes correctly, evaluation is must. Now the question arises how this evaluation is done? For this, the teacher should know two things—

(i) What are the techniques of evaluation? and

(ii) What is the procedure of evaluation?

Techniques of Evaluation

Those techniques are called evaluation techniques by which not only factual knowledge of the pupils is tested but their behavioural changes are also evaluated. Hence, in order to evaluate behavioural changes, various techniques are used, such as, written (essay type and objective type) oral and practical examinations, interview, questionnaire, check list, interest inventory, attitude scale, rating scale, values test, records, students' products, observation and criterion power test etc.

For example, for evaluating behavioural changes in cognitive aspect, written (essay and objective type), oral and practical examination and observation techniques are used. To evaluate behavioural changes which occur in affective aspect, observation, rating scale, aptitude test, attitude scale, values testing and partially essay-type examinations can be applied. In order to evaluate behavioural changes in psychomotor aspect, practical examinations can be used successfully.

Remember that in the evaluating techniques, criterion power tests are much important. It is because such tests are objective-centred. Hence, the evaluation of behavioural changes can be carried out very conveniently and successfully. These Criterion Power Tests should have three qualities. These qualities are—

(i) Appropriateness,

(ii) Effectiveness; and

(iii) Practicability.

In other words, Criterion Power Test should be reliable and valid and which can be administered easily.

Procedure of Evaluation

While evaluating, the following points should be paid attention.

1. *Determination of Teaching Objectives.* Before conducting evaluation, the teaching objective to be evaluated should be determined.

2. *Defining Educational Objectives.* After determining teaching objectives, the teacher should define them clearly. The teaching objectives should be defined with reference to the behaviours.

3. *Identification in New Situations.* The teacher should keep the pupils in new environment just to see whether the pupils have experienced behavioural changes as a result of their learning experiences or not. The pupils are to be kept in new situations just to allow them to express desirable behaviour. In other words, the novel situations should be related to the teaching objectives and awareness should be sought regarding the attainment in those new situations.

4. *Creating and Selecting Learning Experiences.* After determining and defining the teaching objectives, the teacher should select or determine appropriate learning experiences. In other words, the teacher should create such an environment that the pupils do get appropriate learning experiences.

5. *Selection to Tests.* To edit the procedure of evaluation, proper selection of a test should have occurred. The teacher should be extra cautious in this regard.

6. *Construction of Devices.* In order to evaluate such techniques should be developed which may collect directly or indirectly the evidences in connection with the behavioural changes. The teacher should ask himself the following questions in this regard—

   A. What objective is to be evaluated with the ready-made techniques?
   B. Is it possible to collect evidences regarding desirable behaviours with the help of ready-made techniques?
   C. Is it possible for the two persons to come to the same conclusion with the application of the similar technique?
   D. Is the application of the technique simple?

7. *Applying Devices and Recording the Evidences.* After developing the technique, the teacher should use it in the testing situation. Also, the evidences regarding the behavioural changes should be recorded.

8. *Interpretation of Evidences:* When the teacher receives evidences in support of behaviour of the pupils, he should then analyse the evidences and should conclude whether the gained changes are in accordance with teaching objectives or not. Hence, the teacher should take care of the following points while interpreting the market evidences with reference to the teaching objectives—

(i) What are the maximum marks in the examination?
(ii) What are the maximum marks obtained in the class?
(iii) What are the minimum marks obtained in the class?
(iv) What are the average marks obtained in the class?
(v) What is the rank of individuals?
(vi) Has the pupil got his best of his ability?

Keeping in view the above things, the summary of the result should be prepared with reference to each objective. Then the present result should be compared with the previous one. But the result should be presented in such a way that the strengths and weaknesses of each pupil may come to light.

2. Measuring Learning

Meaning of Measurement

Measurement is a process by which the developed abilities of the pupils are expressed in the quantitative form. By measuring, the content, skill and the results of abilities are expressed in numbers, scores, percentage and average, so that the provision of education of the pupils may be made according to their present achievement.

Remember that by measurement, the variables, groups, capacities, time and distance etc. can be tested very conveniently. In short, according to Campbell, "Measurement is the assignment of numerals to objects or events according to rules."

Difference between Evaluation and Measurement

Sometimes teachers, especially student-teachers feel some doubts regarding the meanings of measurement and evaluation. Therefore, the difference between measurement and evaluation is being clarified in the following table:

Evaluation	*Measurement*
1. Evaluation is a new concept.	Measurement is an old concept.
2. Evaluation is a technical term.	Measurement is a simple word.
3. The scope of evaluation is wider. In this, the measurement of pupil's qualitative progress and behavioural changes are tested.	The scope of measurement is narrow because in this, only quantitative progress of the pupils can be explored.
4. In evaluation, the learning experiences provided to the pupils in accordance with pre-determined teaching objectives are tested.	In measurement, the content, skill and achievement of the ability are not tested on the basis of some objectives. Merely, the result of the testing is expressed in numerals, scores, average and percentage.
5. The qualities are measured in the evaultion as a whole.	In measurement, the qualities are measured as separate units.
6. Evaluation is that process by which the previous effects and hence caused behavioural changes are tested.	Measurement means only those techniques which are used to test a particular ability of the pupil.
7. In evaluation, various techniques like observation, hierarchy, criteria, interest and tendencies measurement etc. used for testing the behavioural changes.	In measurement, personality test, intelligence and achievement test etc. are included.
8. Evaluation is that process by which the interests, attitudes, tendencies, mental abilities, ideals, behaviours and social adjustment etc. of pupils are tested.	By measurement, the interests, attitudes, tendencies, ideals and behaviours cannot be tested.

(Contd.)

Evaluation	*Measurement*
9. The evaluation aims at the modification of education system by bringing a change in the behaviour.	Measurement aims at measurement only.

Functions of Measurement

Functions of measurement are as follows:

1. *Comparison.* Measurement compares various pupils, various classes and different strategies of teaching. The teacher too finds out what progress his pupils have made by doing year to year comparison.

2. *Diagnosis.* Measurement diagnosis the weaknesses of the pupils. Also, it manages the remedial teaching to eliminate those weaknesses.

3. *Prediction.* Measurement predicts the future of the pupils in the following way—

(i) The placement in a proper class and gradation of the pupils is done in accordance with the planning of the pupils by measurement.
(ii) Measurement classifies the pupils by testing their performance or achievement.
(iii) Measurement helps the pupils in selecting their subjects.
(iv) Measurement explores the pupils of high, normal and lower classes or levels.
(v) Measurement awares the teachers whether the pupils could understand what they have taught or not. If learnt, then how much change in their behaviour has occurred.
(vi) Measurement can predict, by exploring the intellectual level of the pupils, how much they can make progress in future in comparison to other pupils.
(vii) Measurement also predicts how the pupil will behave in future if he secures below norms.
(viii) Measurement promotes the pupils from one class to the next.

4. *Research.* Measurement is very essential for psychological and educational research. With the help of this, the researcher

collects data by using research tools. Then, by interpreting the collected data, he can reach to some conclusion by generalizing that interpretation and reaching some valid and reliable conclusion.

Scales of Measurement

Stevens and Coombs presented following four measurement scales in 1946.

1. *Nominal Scale.* Nominal scale is the primary stage or level of measurement, because this level provided minimum information. At this level, some fact is divided into two or more categories, but their results are not known. For example, the pupil-teachers are divided on the basis of teaching subjects or sex etc. This level can be used for educational measurement up to 40% approximately. In order to analyse these data, various statistical methods are used such as mode, percentage, chi-square and contingency etc.

2. *Ordial Scale.* This scale is more correct than nominal scale. At this level, the pupils of every category are arranged in a sequence and they are provided with ranks. In other words, at this level of measurement, the pupils are provided with a level of sequence on the basis of observation.

The nature of this level is comparative. Its measurement is placed in the quantitative category. This level is used for measurement in education upto 50%. For measuring at this level, various statistical techniques are used such as rating scale, observation technique, median, rank-difference correlation and chi-square etc.

3. *Equal Interval Scale.* This scale has similar characteristics as nominal and ordial scales have. But this level is concerned with intervals or distances. In other words, equal interval scale presents the distance between two persons. At this level, zero is to be supposed, because education is measured in comparison. In teaching, this level is taken as the most correct level or scale because this scale presents the most correct and appropriate information.

Hence, this scale is used in maximum. At this level, the data can be analysed without any difficulty. For this, various statistical techniques are used such as median, standard deviation, correlation, training etc. For this level, criterion tests are used and the decision are made regarding objectives on the basis of obtained scores.

4. *Ratio Scale.* This scale is also the most correct scale of measurement, because in this scale, absolute zero is also included. This scale provides more informations as compared to other scales. Hence, this scale is more used in science than education. In other words, in scientific research, ratio scale is an ideal method of measurement.

For the above four levels, the observations techniques, rating scale questionnaires and achievement tests are used. Remember that the techniques or tests for measuring bearing are of two types—

(i) Essay Type tests, and

(ii) Objective tests.

Characteristics of a Good Measuring Techniques

The following are the main characteristics of a good measuring techniques:

1. *Objective.* The leading characteristic of a good measuring technique is its objectivity. Remember that the test is said to be objective when from its repeated administration, the same scores are obtained. A good test is said to be a good one which has no influence of neither tester's subjectivity nor pupil's mental state. In short if a test is successful in measuring pupil's achievement independently, then that is a good technique or a test.

2. *Validity.* Validity is the second characteristic of a good measuring technique. If a test measures for what it is constructed, then definitely test is a valid test. Kolesnik has rightly written that "A valid test is one which measures the traits and qualities it is intended to measure."

3. *Reliability.* Reliability is the third quality of a good technique. Reliability means similar effect of a test of the pupils and that of pupils on the test. In other words, when the repeated administration of test to a group causes consistent scores, that test is termed as a reliable test.

Freeman has rightly written, "The reliability of a test is its ability to yield consistent results for one set of measures to another".

4. *Usability.* The fourth characteristic of a test or a technique

is its usability. Usability means no difficulty should come across while using a particular test, scoring and interpretation of the obtained scores. Remember that every test is constructed so that the learning outcomes of the pupils may be measured easily. From this point of view, a good test is that which is convenient and usable for both the teacher and the pupil.

3. Managing by Learning Objectives

In 1950, Peter Drucker presented a new concept of management by objectives. Since then, in industry and commerce, this idea is being used widely.

According to Peter Drucker, the manager of every organization should control the management keeping in view the objectives. Like industry and commerce, Peter Drucker's new concept of managing by objectives can be applied successfully to the teaching area too, because in teaching too, planning, organization and leading phases have importance.

In addition to teaching, a teacher has to face many other responsibilities. For example, a teacher has to be alert regarding the expectations from him in relation to the pupils. Second, he has to provide learning opportunities. Third, it is his most important duty to inform the pupils, regarding their progress. In order to meet out his responsibilities, the teacher provides necessary guidance to the pupils periodically and measures their achievements.

The teacher is to perform the following four functions while managing by objectives (M.B.O).

(i) To determine the objectives of the topic after determining the objectives and goals of the organization.

(ii) To prepare learning guide for informations and achievements.

(iii) To prepare a plan for modifying the learning of each pupil.

(iv) To guide every pupil according to his achievements and to measure his achievements or performance.

From the above description, it becomes clear that managing by learning objectives is an impressive method of individualized instruction while functioning as an important strategy, technique or tactics.

Tests for Measuring Learning

In order to measure learning, various types of achievement tests are used. In the following lines we are throwing light on some main achievement tests—

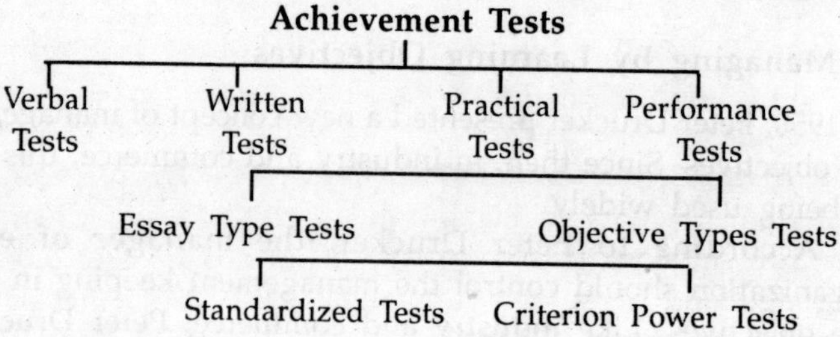

Verbal Tests

The aim of verbal tests is to evaluate immediate verbal expression and activeness of the pupils by verbal questions. These tests were used initially for the pupils of the lower classes, but now these are also used for admissions, interviews, in higher classes.

These tests have the following demerits—

(*i*) The shy pupils are unable to exhibit their knowledge and ability by these testing system.

(*ii*) These tests contain sufficient quantity of subjectivity.

(*iii*) These have no written record or evidence. Hence, the teacher can use his discretion for assigning the scores.

(*iv*) These tests are not full of justice for many pupils.

Written Tests

Written tests are of two types—(*i*) Essay type, and (*ii*) Objective type.

Practical Tests

In practical tests, pupils accomplish some pre-fixed task through some experiment. Such type of tests are used in Chemistry, Physics and Geography etc.

Performance Tests

In performance tests, the pupils do not respond in writing.

They exhibit their skill by doing some task. Such tests are used in music, art and science subjects.

Essay Type Tests

Meaning of Essay Type Tests. The essay type test means such an examination system in which the pupils give responses to many questions of the curriculum in some fixed duration in the form of an essay. The answers to questions in this type of tests are so lengthy that the tester can measure very easily the powers of thinking, comparison, expression, reasoning and criticism along with the ability of organisations of thoughts, language and style etc. Remember that at the recall and recognition level, the achievement of the pupils can be measured by objective type tests, but at the levels of interpretation, application and evaluation, the use of essay type tests is essential.

Merits of Essay Type Tests

The following are the merits of essay type tests:

1. *Easy Construction.* The question papers of essay type tests are too short. These can be prepared in a very small duration and at low cost.

2. *Suitable for All Subjects.* These tests can be used for measuring every subject.

3. *Development of Good Study Habits.* These tests encourage such tendencies in the pupils which establish relationship between the various parts of the knowledge and the preparation of an outline of each lesson, which prove advantageous for them. This develops good habits in the pupils.

4. *Measurement of Mental Abilities:* The mental abilities like thinking, reasoning, expression and criticism etc. can only be measured by essay type tests. It is clear that these tests are useful in measuring the mental abilities and power of the pupils.

5. *Test 'Application of Knowledge' in Different Spheres.* In these tests, the questions start from 'describe', 'elaborate,' 'discuss' 'criticise' and 'reason out' etc. In this, the pupils describe the facts on one side, they also learn to use them in other situations.

6. *Definite Improvement in Language and Style.* In these tests,

pupils are stressed to write language. This definitely improves the language and style of the pupils.

7. *Measurement of Teacher's Efficiency.* These tests measure the mental powers of the pupils on one side and measure teachers' teaching, planning and efficiency very comfortably on the other side.

8. *Convenient.* These tests do not possess any special instructions which the pupils fail to understand. From this point of view, the essay type tests are convenient to both pupils and teachers.

9. *Freedom of Response.* In these tests, the pupils are free to express their ideas in a logical way.

10. *Economy of Time, Labour and Money.* Thousands of pupils are examined at a time in these tests. Their answer-books are also evaluated simultaneously. Also, success and failure can be predicted without any difficulty. All these things lead to economy of time, labour and money.

Demerits of Essay Type Tests

The demerits of these tests are:

1. *Lack of Clearly Defined Objectives.* The essay type tests lack clearly defined objectives. The pupils fail to understand till last what the tester wants to measure?

2. *Lack of Proper Sampling.* In these tests, five to ten questions are asked from some portions of the curriculum. This improper sampling fails to evaluate properly the development of the pupils.

3. *Emphasis on Cramming.* In these tests, some specific questions are asked. Hence, pupils do not prepare the entire curriculum, but they try to cram a few main portions. It is the major demerit of this test.

4. *More Emphasis on Speed and Style.* In these tests, speed and style are emphasized more. The pupils score more who can answer in a good handwriting and with a higher speed in an effective manner. Contrary to this, the pupils score less who cannot write beautifully and in high speed in spite of their complete knowledge of the facts.

5. *Subjectivity in Awarding Marks.* These tests carry higher subjectivity. Hence, uncertainty and variation occur in scores. Since, in these tests, the interest, ability, mood and mental

attitude of the tester affect deeply.

6. *Lack of Validity*. These tests measure the language, style, speed, writing and cramming power of the pupils, therefore, these tests cannot be designated as valid tests.

7. *Lack of Reliability*. The scores of these tests show variations and the results are also not consistent. Therefore, these tests lack reliability.

8. *Lack of Predictability*. In essay type tests, obtaining scores depends upon the cramming power of the pupils. Hence, on the basis of results of these tests, the first divisioner cannot be predicted to be superior in general knowledge and behaviour too.

9. *Interference in Mental and Physical Health*. These tests interfere in the mental and physical health of the pupils, because the pupils start their studies one or two months before the commencement of the examination.

10. *Difficulty in Evaluation*. Proper evaluation is not possible by these tests. No such definite norm has been made which may evaluate properly the progress of the pupils.

11. *Costly and Time Consuming*: It costs more in preparing question papers, their printing and arrangement of answer books in essay type tests. Also, it takes months to measure the achievements of the pupils by these tests. Hence, these tests are more expensive and more time consuming.

Essay Type Tests and Learning Objectives

The essay type tests are devices of measuring learning objectives. Every individual depends upon this device to measure educational achievement because objective type tests measure the achievement of the pupil at recall and recognition levels, but these tests are also important at interpretation, application and evaluation levels for measuring high learning objectives. In other words, these tests cannot be eliminated even in the presence of many limitations.

Remember that in this connection, many researches have been conducted. These are conducted only in positive direction. A few are attracted towards making these measuring devices more accurate, valid and reliable. To accomplish this great task, improvements in the following areas are essential:

(a) In the construction of Test Papers.

(*b*) In the Examination System.
(*c*) In the Evaluation of Scripts.

Objective Type Tests and Learning Objectives

Meaning of Objective Type Tests. The objective type tests mean those good techniques or tests of measurement which are constructed to eliminate the defects of essay type tests. In these tests, variation of scores is controlled by avoiding subjectivity.

In other words, in objective type tests, the achievement of subject-knowledge of pupils, their aptitudes, attitudes, interests and intelligence etc. are measured by receiving answers of 150 to 200 short and pointed questions based on the entire curriculum in a very short duration.

These tests have objectivity. This measurement cannot be supported by any type of partiality. Also, there can not be any type of difference regarding answers among the examiners. This will not affect the scorability of the pupils.

The objective type test was first of all constructed by Horace Mann in 1854 in black and white. After this, George Fisher, J.M. Rice, Starch and Thorndike prepared many objective tests for measuring educational achievements. Even at present, various types of objective tests are being used to measure every aspect of the pupils.

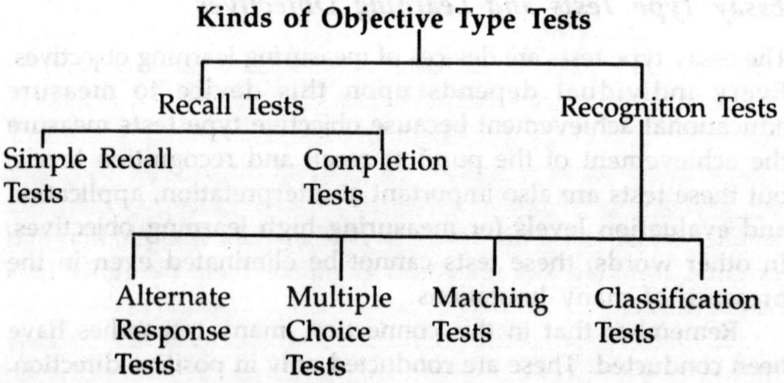

Merits of Objective Type Tests

The following are the merits of objective type tests—

1. *Objectivity.* These tests are objective. The subjectivity of

the examiners does not influence these tests.

2. *Comprehensibility.* These tests measure the entire subject area. Hence, these tests are more useful than the easy type tests.

3. *Validity.* The objective type tests measure for what these are made. Hence, these tests are valid.

4. *Reliability.* These tests are reliable. In these tests, if their administration is repeated on a pupil or a group of pupils, the results obtained every time show relationships.

5. *Administrability.* The administration of these tests is very simple for teachers. Also, since their directions are easy to understand, hence, pupils follow them very easily.

6. *Utility.* Objective type tests are more useful because these are constructed to achieve some objective. After achieving the objectives, on the basis of the results, the pupils can be guided easily.

7. *Easy Scorability.* In essay type tests, evaluation of scripts takes much time, but objective type tests take a few hours to score them.

8. *Practicability.* These tests consume less time. The pupils and the teachers both like them. Hence, these tests are practicable.

9. *Discrimination.* These tests discriminate both foolish and intelligent pupils. Hence, objective type tests are also known as discriminatory tests.

Demerits of Objective Type Tests

The following are the demerits of objective type tests—

1. *Difficult Construction.* The number of questions in the objective type tests ranges from one hundred to two hundred. These questions can only be constructed by experienced, competent and efficient teachers. In other words, the construction of questions in these tests is very difficult.

2. *Lack of Organization of Thought.* In these tests pupils answer smaller questions. This develops neither their imagination and original thinking nor they can organize their thoughts in a sequence.

3. *Over Simplification.* Sometimes, these tests are so easy that even very weak pupils do write correct answers of such questions. This does not guide the pupils' future properly.

4. *Partial Information.* These tests carry very small questions.

Their answers are shown either in symbols or in one or two words. This keeps the teacher away from full information regarding a pupil.

5. *Standardization of Instruction.* These tests try to bring similarity in the teaching strategies instead of developing thinking, reasoning and logic powers of the pupils. This violates the principle of individual differences which results mental activity into a mechanical activity.

6. *Difficulty of Measuring Mental Abilities.* In essay type tests, it is easy to measure the thoughts, logic and criticism powers of the pupils. In objective tests, the measurement of these abilities cannot be done.

7. *Guessing and Cheating.* While answering questions in these tests, pupil seeks the help of guessing. Sometimes, they bluff the teachers and copy the script of other pupils.

8. *Very Costly:* The preparation and printing of question papers of these tests is very costly. The financial position of our country is not satisfactory. Hence, such expensive tests cannot be used easily.

QUESTIONS FOR ANSWER

1. Define motivation. Write a note on its importance, 'Need' while explaining Maslow's 'Theory of Motivation'.
2. Write a note on the relationship between the techniques of motivation and effective teaching while explaining the criteria for selecting appropriate technique of motivation.
3. Define 'Evaluation'. Write the characteristics of Evaluation while describing its utility in controlling teaching.
4. Write short notes on:
   (*a*) 'The Motivation Hygiene Theory.'
   (*b*) Functions of Motivation.
   (*c*) Evaluation techniques.
   (*d*) Main Functions of Measurement.
   (*e*) Methods of measuring learning.
5. Write a note on the merits and demerits of objective type and essay type tests. Explain why even being defective essay type tests cannot be eliminated.

15

Fundamentals of Lesson Planning

When the students (pupil-teachers) go to the training colleges or departments to gain training in teaching, they are first given theoretical knowledge of all the concepts which have been discussed in previous chapters of this book. Before, they are sent to various schools for teaching practice, they are given instructions in the art of lesson planning or training of writing lesson plans so that they may achieve the teaching objectives by making the teaching effective.

Instructions about lesson planning contain various approaches to lesson planning and as a prelude to the concept of lesson planning of various approaches they are instructed to understand the teaching of objectives of various subjects at secondary stage of education. Therefore, hereunder an idea is given about the teaching objectives of various subjects at secondary stage of education.

Teaching Objectives of Subjects

Edwin Wandt and G.W. Grown have rightly observed:

"The process of education involves three steps—(1) determining objectives, (2) providing experiences designed to achieve the objectives, and (3) measuring and evaluating the results to determine if the objectives have been achieved." Therefore, in the earlier chapter concerning planning aspects of teaching and learning, it has been clearly stressed that teaching and learning objectives should be clearly determined and written in clear terms after the task analysis. Therefore, for the convenience of trainee-teachers in particular and teachers in general, we are presenting some subjects and the lists of their characteristics to be taught at the secondary stage. The pupil-teachers can prepare the lists of learning objectives of other subjects adopting the given sample-lists.

Teaching Objectives of Different Subjects at Secondary Stage

Objectives	*Specification of Objectives*
HINDI	
1. To enable the pupils to understand the language orally, completely and clearly.	(1) He will be able to identify the sounds and their groups clearly.
	(2) He will be able to differentiate the sounds.
	(3) He will be able to understand the meaning and relevant idea of the words, idioms, phrases and tactics.
	(4) He will be able to understand the variations in the words having similar meanings.
	(5) He will be able to differentiate the words with similar sounds.
	(6) He will be able to receive the meaning and idea of the words according to the context.
2. To develop the ability in the pupils to understand completely and clearly the written or non-verbal from of the language.	(1) He will be able to understand the meaning and feeling of written words, idioms, phrases in accordance with the context.
	(2) He will be able to understand the importance of words and statements.
	(3) He will be able to understand their mutual relationships.
	(4) He will be able to understand important ideas, facts and theme.

(Contd.)

Objectives	*Specification of Objectives*
	(5) He will be able to receive the central idea of the read portions. (6) He will be able to understand the mental state of the author. (7) He will be able to read written portions with proper speed and understanding. (8) He will be able to analyse and evaluate the read portions from the linguistic, subject and style point of view.
3. To acquire the skill of presenting orally the ideas and feelings of the pupils.	(1) He will be able to use properly the feelings, idioms and phrases. (2) He will be able to pronounce the words and idioms correctly. (3) He can use correctly the language and style. (4) He can present the desired material.
4. To create efficiency of expressing the ideas and feelings in the written form amongst the pupils.	(1) He will be able to write with proper speed. (2) He will be able to write beautifully, boldly and legibly. (3) He will be able to use the words and idioms properly in the written form. (4) He will be able to construct correct sentences. (5) He will be able to use correct translation. (6) He will be able to use punctuation properly. (7) He will be able to use effective language and style. (8) He will be able to bring a sequence in the ideas. (9) He will be able to make paragraphs in the writing work

(Contd.)

Objectives	Specification of Objectives
	properly.
5. To create interest in the pupils in language and literature.	(1) He will be able to read interesting stories, plays, novels and poems in addition to the text-books. (2) He will be able to enjoy and study the literature according to his own level. (3) He will be tempted to read the creations of other writers. (4) He will be able to participate all the cultural programmes of outside and inside the school. (5) He will be able to collect the literary creations. (6) He will be able to memorize beautiful and effective poems. (7) He will be able to write a story, essay and poem. (8) He will be able to contribute to the school and class magazine.
6. To develop the ability of creating Hindi literature.	(1) He will be able to increase his powers like imagination, observation, logic and intellect etc. (2) He will be able to express effectively his ideas and feelings on the basis of his mental powers. (3) He will be able to express his ideas and feelings in an original way.
SCIENCE	
1. To provide knowledge to the pupils regarding facts, steps, concepts, principles and reactions of science	He will be able to— *(i)* memorize, *(ii)* identify, *(iii)* differentiate, *(iv)* classify, *(v)* establish mutual relationship, *(vi)* present oral and exhibitable examples, *(vii)* infer,

(Contd.)

Objectives	*Specification of Objectives*
	(viii) manage systematically, *(ix)* find out mistakes, of facts of science, steps, concepts, principles and reactions.
2. To create the capacity of applying the knowledge of science to the new situations in the pupils.	(1) He will be able to select the material and the principles related to the problem. (2) He will be able to verify the facts and steps. (3) He will be able to find out the sufficiency of the facts. (4) He will be able to generalize on inappropriateness of the facts. (5) He will be able to select appropriate methods, laws and processes to solve the problems. (6) He will be able to find out the solution of the problems in a logical way. (7) He will be able to generalize after concluding. (8) He will be able to predict on the basis of the given facts.
3. To develop expected skill for mathematics in the pupils.	(1) He will be able to use tables and devices relating to mathematics. (2) He will be able to prepare graphs, charts and diagrams. (3) He will be able to interpret all of them. (4) He will be able to count orally and in written form with speed and accuracy. (5) He will be able to do the written work in a well organised way.
4. To create interest in the pupil for mathematics.	(1) He will be able to study the literature regarding mathematics. (2) He will be able to discuss mathematical problems.

(Contd.)

Objectives	*Specification of Objectives*
	(3) He will be able to take interest in solving the mathematical problems. (4) It will be able to solve the questions of other books in addition to the text-books.
5. To develop attitude of the pupils towards mathematics.	(1) He will like to live with famous persons related to mathematics. (2) He will be able to feel proud of being a student of mathematics. (3) It will be possible to develop mental set to analyse the questions of mathematics. (4) He will be able to appreciate the tasks related to mathematics.
6. To develop personality traits among pupils.	(1) He will be able to follow regularity and time. (2) He will be able to do his task in a well-organized way and legibly. (3) He will be able to express precision, exactness and compactness while presenting his oral and written works.
SOCIAL STUDIES (History, Geography, Civics and Economics)	
1. To impart knowledge to the pupils regarding the relevant steps, facts, concepts, events, time cycle, directions, principles and processes related to the subjects.	Regarding steps, facts, concepts and events, he would be able to— (1) recall, (2) identify, (3) analyse, (4) interpret, (5) understand sequential importance, (6) collect informations through pictures, maps and charts, (7) compare and contrast, (8) derive results.

(Contd.)

Objectives	*Specification of Objectives*
2. To develop the capacity of the pupils to apply the knowledge of facts, events, principles and processes related to the subjects in the new situations.	(1) He will be able to apply the steps and concepts in the new situations. (2) He will be able to identify the problem. (3) He will be able to apply the acquired knowledge in order to analyse and evaluate the situations of life. (4) He will be able to formulate hypothesis to solve the problem. (5) He will be able to collect evidences relating to the hypotheses. (6) He will be able to indoctrinate new results and principles.
3. To develop skills in the pupils related to the subject.	(1) He will be able to prepare pictures, figures, maps, graphs and charts related to the charts. (2) He will be able to prepare the models of historical buildings, forts, utensils, coins, ornaments, arms and other things of the past. (3) He will be able to use properly the pictures and charts etc. (4) He will be able to make decisions in a logical way after logical analysis. (5) He will be able to understand the new situations. (6) He will be able to derive cause and effect relationship. (7) He will be able to express properly the laws and principles. (8) He will be able to understand properly the social situations. (9) He will be able to study the reference books.
4. To create interest in the pupils regarding the subject.	(1) He will be able to study the books related to the subject.

(Contd.)

Objectives	*Specification of Objectives*
	(2) He will be able to collect the coins and pictures.
	(3) He will be able to take interest in visiting the places of economic, geographical and historical importance.
	(4) He will be able to discuss the problems related to the subject.
	(5) He will be able to write the articles related to the subject.
	(6) He will be able to participate in the exhibitions of the objects related to the subject.
	(7) He will be able to participate in the games related to the subject.
5. To create proper mental tendencies in the pupils.	(1) He will be able to develop impartial attitude.
	(2) He will be able to express open ideas.
	(3) He will be able to possess the patriotic feeling.
	(4) He will be able to have belief in human values.
	(5) He will be able to adopt a critical attitude.
	(6) He will be able to respect his own country's culture along with the culture of other countries.
	(7) He will be able to express his belief in the development of international understanding.

Lesson Planning

After clear understanding of the teaching objectives of the subject concerned, lesson planning has to be done and for this the trainee-teacher (pupil-teacher) or teacher must know various aspects concerning the actual concept of lesson planning, an outline of which is as follows:

Origin of Lesson Plan. The development of the lesson-planning occurred as a result of Gestalt Psychology. According to Gestalt Psychology, when we perceive a figure, our attention goes first to its 'whole' form. Then, we analyse its different parts. In other words, learning is considered as 'unit'. Hence, to understand 'whole' pupils seek the help of 'unit' and the 'whole' is communicated by the 'unit'. Remember that in an unit, the meaningful activities are established in which a way that the desired behavioural changes may take place by creating appropriate learning experiences in the pupils. In this way, Gestalt Psychology gave to the concept of unit plan.

Gestalt divides the unit lesson plan in two ways. First, in an unit plan, content and information occupy an important place. This is known as "Herbart's Approach". Second, in an unit plan experiences are given preference. This is known as "Dewey and Kilpatric Approach".

Meaning of Lesson Planning. The lesson Plan is that small unit or units of subject-matter which a teacher teaches in a definite period.

Hence, the lesson-planning means that detailed description which a teacher completes in a definite period. This duration varies from school to school and college to college.

The duration of a period may be smaller or longer, but in all the lesson-plans, all the teachers have to give similar description of the things. These are—(1) General aims, (2) Specific aims, (3) Previous knowledge of students, (4) Appropriate strategies of teaching, (5) Tactics of teaching, (6) Techniques of Teaching, (7) Teaching aids, (8) The correlation between the new knowledge of the pupils and other subjects, (9) What are the various teacher's activities, (10) While helping personally the students what activities to be performed. (11) How the evaluation of the knowledge acquired by the pupils to be done?

In other words, a lesson plan is said to be that pre-determined plan according to which the teacher presents the unit or units of the content regarding new knowledge or experiences by appropriate methods, strategies, tactics, techniques and instruments before the pupils in a particular period, in order to achieve the objectives of the lesson.

Need of Lesson Plan. The lesson plan does not allow the

teacher to deviate but it keeps him on the way. Not only this, in the process of teaching, lesson-plan is needed due to the following reasons—

1. A lesson-plan develops the possibilities of adjustment in the class-room situations. This makes the teaching effective.

2. Through lesson plan, the teacher achieves regularly the teaching objectives and processes in the form of complete objectives and processes.

3. A lesson plan helps in recalling every step of curriculum unit.

4. A lesson plan helps in planning the process of teaching on the basis of class-control, motivation and individual differences.

Types of Lessons

The psychological researches have proved that the basis of learning is mental activity which is a complete unit in itself but it has three aspects—*(i)* Cognitive, *(ii)* Affective, and *(iii)* Conative. The lessons can be classified into the following three categories on the basis of above three aspects of mental activity—

1. *Knowledge Lessons.* In the knowledge lessons, the learner's cognitive aspect of his mental activity is more active which results an increase in his knowledge. In short, the pupils acquire the knowledge of various facts and events through the knowledge lessons. The lessons of History, Geography, Economics, Civics, Mathematics, Science and Grammar are knowledge lessons.

2. *Appreciation Lessons.* Appreciation lessons keep active the affective aspect of learner's mental activity. Since these lessons develop the appreciation of the pupils, they take interest in studying these lessons. The lessons of music and arts are said to be appreciation lessons.

3. *Skill Lessons.* In skill lessons, the conative aspect of the learner's mental activity is more active. In such lessons, the teacher provides some guidance to the pupils in the beginning. All the pupils get involved in accomplishing the task following the teacher's instructions or guidelines. In short, in skill lessons, the creative power of the pupils is more active. This benefits pupils and the society to its maximum. Painting,

handicraft, gardening and agriculture etc. come under the skill lessons.

Classification of Lesson-Plans

Lesson plans are of following four classes:

1. *Macro Approach.* The macro approach to lesson-planning is used in the traditional teaching practice. In this, the basis of the lesson's unit is larger. Hence, in the lesson plan of macro-approach, the activities of forty to fifty pupils in 30 to 45 minutes are asked to develop. The preparation of lesson plans are taught to the student-teachers before beginning the teaching task in the teachers training colleges or departments so that they may accomplish the task of teaching practice under the guidance of some supervisor or a guide.

2. *Micro Approach.* The lesson plans of micro approach are not used for teaching practice but these are used to develop various skills and to bring about the modifications in their behaviour. The lesson-plans under this approach are prepared to teach 5 or 7 pupils in 5 to 10 minutes. When the pupil-teachers teach according to the lesson plan of micro-approach in order to develop a skill in them, their supervisor allows him or some other pupil-teacher to teach the same lesson after imparting proper and urgent instructions. Hence, micro-approach includes teaching, guidance, re-teaching, re-guidance or instructions, reinforcement, feedback etc. and by using these techniques, behaviour of the pupils is modified. This micro-approach has proved very useful in the qualitative improvement of the teachers.

3. *Written Form.* In the training colleges or departments, preparing the written form of lesson plan is taught to the pupil-teachers in the training colleges or training departments. When the pupil-teachers get learnt to prepare the written form of the lesson plan and start their teaching practice, then their supervisors provide them with proper suggestions by comparing the lesson plan and the teaching activities so that they may acquire the objectives of teaching.

4. *Unwritten Form.* Under rules, every in-service teacher has to teach daily 5 to 6 classes. In such a situation, to teach every class, preparation of written forms of lesson-plans is very difficult. Hence, before entering the class, they prepare unwritten

form of the lesson-plan in their minds so that the teaching objective may be achieved by an interaction between a teacher and the pupils.

Advantages of Lesson-Plans

Planning is essential for every aspect of human activities, but for teaching more planning is required, because the entire teaching becomes hotch-potch in the absence of lesson-planning. Hence, the fresh teachers, especially pupil-teachers must get the lesson planned. The following are the advantages of lesson planning.

1. *Suitable Environment.* In a lesson plan, objectives are fixed and the teaching strategies, tactics, techniques and material aid etc. are decided before-hand. This creates interest of the pupils in the lesson and helps in creating proper environment of teaching. When a proper teaching environment is created, the teaching task goes in a very planned way.

2. *Based on Previous Knowledge.* In preparing lesson plans, the teacher presents new knowledge on the basis of previous knowledge of the pupils. This enables the pupils to gain the knowledge very conveniently on one side, the teacher succeeds in acquiring his objective on the other side.

3. *Developing of Teaching Skill.* The lesson plan acts as an important means for developing teaching skills in the pupil-teachers.

4. *Limitation of Subject Matter.* In a Lesson Plan, the subject-matter becomes limited. This enables the teacher to give up irrelevant things. He only remembers definite and limited matter and its presentation before the pupils becomes easy. The pupils also receive the knowledge in a systematic and organized way.

5. *Economy of Energy and Time.* The teachers who start teaching task without preparing any lesson-plan, generally deviate. He has to put more efforts for presenting the subject-matter. It wastes the time. Contrary to this, the teacher who prepares lesson-plan before-hand can present the new knowledge in a proper sequence before the pupils and can remove their doubts successfully.

6. *Determination of Activities.* In a lesson plan, the teacher's and pupil's activities are pre-decided according to the class level. In other words, while preparing lesson-plan, the teacher

decides before hand what he and his pupils are to do in the class. This makes the teaching activities meaningful and purposeful.

7. *Psychological Teaching*. The teacher uses proper teaching strategies, techniques, tactics and instruments keeping in mind the interests, aptitudes, needs, capacities and abilities of the pupils for teaching them, when the lesson-plans are prepared. This makes the teaching more psychological.

8. *Use of Theoretical Knowledge in Teaching*. Whatever theoretical knowledge the pupil-teachers get during their training period, that knowledge can be applied in the class with the help of lesson-plan.

9. *Preparation of Material Aids*. At the time of preparing a lesson-plan, the teacher decides what facts are to be clarified by what strategies, tactics, techniques and instruments and what aid is to be used at what time. This prepares the necessary and effective aids before starting the teaching task.

10. *Orderliness and Development in Thinking*. By preparing a lesson-plan, orderliness and development in the thinking of the pupils occurs. This enables him in achieving the teaching objectives while presenting the contents in an orderly way.

11. *Teaching with Confidence*. The preparation of a lesson-plan makes the subject and other allied subjects more clear to the teachers. This arouses self-confidence among them. When a teacher gets self-confidence, then he presents the new knowledge to the pupils with more enthusiasm and naturality along with pleasure. This makes the class full of life.

12. *Fixation of Knowledge*. In a lesson-plan, the teacher writes summary of the lesson too. The reading of the summary of the lesson helps pupils in the revision of the lesson. Also, the knowlege gets consolidated.

13. *Discipline in Class*. By preparing lesson-plan, the teacher becomes aware of what, when and how much is to be done in the class. This absorbs all the pupils in their respective tasks. Hence, it results in appreciable class-room discipline.

14. *Practical Shape to the Concept of Management of Teaching-Learning*. A lesson-plan can give the practical shape to the concept of management of teaching-learning. Also, the teaching objectives can be successfully achieved by making the teaching impressive. It is very clear that the well organized lesson-plan

occupies important place for the success of teaching.

15. Evaluation Possible. A lesson-plan also has the provision of the evaluation. The evaluation makes the teacher aware of how his teacher has affected the pupils. It also evaluates the strategies, tactics, techniques and aids used by the teacher. If a teacher observes that the teaching strategies, tactics, techniques and instruments used by him have not shown desirable effects, he can modify them accordingly. In this way, the teacher can evaluate the teaching strategies, tactics, techniques and instruments and their effects used by him.

Approaches to Lesson-Planning

According to their assumptions and principles of education various educators have stressed different points to prepare a lesson-plan but the following approaches only are in common use:

Herbartian Four Steps Approach

Herbart has advocated following four things for successful teaching because his educational ideology is based on psychology.

(i) Interest. Herbart advocated that when the interest of pupils is created in some subject, their attention is attracted towards the subject. Therefore, the teaching process should be interesting.

(ii) Apperception. It was Herbart's assumption that the entire knowledge is provided to the pupils from outside. Apperception of this external knowledge in the unconscious mind of the pupils occurs. He further advocated that if the new knowledge to be given to the pupils is related to the previous knowledge of the pupils, their learning will be simplified.

(iii) General Method. Herbart has clarified that the learning activity occurs in a definite sequence. Hence, the activities of the unit should be edited in a definite sequence and in an logical order. For this, we have "Herbart's Five Steps Approach". In our country in most of the training colleges or departments, the pupil-teachers use this approach.

(iv) Correlation. Herbart accepted the entire knowledge as one unit. He stressed on studying all the subjects after correlating each other in the form of one unit. For this correlation, Herbart considered History as important. According

to him, all the subjects of the curriculum should be taught by correlating them with History.

Herbartian Five Steps Approach

Herbart has determined the following steps of a teaching method:

(i) Clarity. In this step, the subject-matter to be taught is broken into various facts so that every pupil can pay attention towards each fact or element. Also, the teacher should present the subject-matter with clarity.

(ii) Association. In this step, the new knowledge of the pupils was related to their previous knowledge.

(iii) System. It was third step by Herbart. In this, the specifies were separated from the generals which may enable the pupils to view the mutual relations between various facts or elements so that they may gain the knowlege of 'whole'. Hence, in this step, new knowledge is organized in a sequence on the basis of logic.

(iv) Method. This was Herbart's fourth and last step. In this step, the pupils used to apply gained knowledge to the new situations.

Remember that Herbart emphasized only four steps while indoctrinating the general teaching method. But with the passage of time, his followers modified the above four steps.

For example, the famous disciple of Herbart, Ziller divided the first step, i.e., clearness, into two— (1) Introduction, and (2) Presentation. Herbart's another disciple Ryan incorporated one more step in between these two which was termed as 'Statement of Aim'. In this way, *five* steps occurred in place of four steps indoctrinated by Herbart. These five steps are termed as Herbartian five steps of teaching. We are describing these steps in a sequence. These steps are as follows:

1. *(A) Preparation.* Preparation is the first step of reading method. In this step, some questions are asked from the pupils in order to test the previous knowledge of the pupils so that curiosity may arouse in them to learn new knowledge.

(B) Statement of Aim. This step is a part of the first step. Here, the topic becomes clear to the pupils and the teacher himself writes the topic on the black-board in clear words.

2. *Presentation.* In this step, the lesson is developed with the cooperation of the pupils. In other words, opportunities

are provided to learn themselves by stimulating their mental activity. The teacher tries to receive most of the points from the pupils by questioning.

3. *Comparison and Association.* Herbart has termed this step as association. In this, the facts, events and application taught are related mutually by comparison which enable the pupils to understand the taught material. Hence, the teacher should establish a relationship between two subjects and also the facts and events of one subject and the facts and events of the other subject. Also, compare them so that the new knowledge may get stabilized and clarified in the minds of the pupils.

4. *Generalization.* Herbart termed this as a 'System'. After explaining the main lesson, the pupils are provided with opportunities to think. After this, they formulate such principles and rules which may be used in various situations of the future life.

5. *Application.* Application is the last step of teaching method. In this step, it is observed whether the acquired knowledge may be applied to the new situations or not. The teacher can verify this by asking recapitulatory questions or by providing opportunities to apply the acquired knowledge in the new situations. This stabilizes the new knowledge and the validity of the rules may also be proved.

Merits of Herbartian Five Steps

The following are the merits of Herbartian Five Steps:

1. *Psychological Method.* It was the belief of Herbart that when the new thoughts related to the thoughts lying in unconscious mind of the pupils are presented, the thoughts of unconscious mind come to the conscious mind, establish relationship with the new thoughts and agains go to the unconscious mind.

Herbart termed this mental process of acquiring thoughts as apperception considering it psychological. From this view point, Herbartian Five Steps approach is a psychological, useful and effective method.

2. *Organized Teaching.* In Herbartian Five Steps approach, each step has been organized in a very logic way. But following this order, the fresh teachers beware of future mistakes. The

competent teachers' originality is never affected and the teaching goes on in a very organized way.

3. *Use of Inductive and Deductive Methods.* While presenting the new knowledge, help of various examples is sought and at 'generalization' step, rules are derived. It is an inductive method. In spite of this, at the step of application, these rules are taught to execute. It is called a deductive method. In short, in five steps approach, both inductive and deductive methods are used.

4. *Correlation Possible.* Herbart has considered entire knowledge as a single unit. From this point of view, the acquired previous knowledge of the pupils is also a single unit. This approach allows to establish a correlation between previous and new knowledge and between all subjects of the curriculum.

5. *Recapitulation.* In this approach, while recapitulating such questions are asked which, on answering, result in the learning how to apply the acquired knowledge in new situations.

The above description makes it clear that Herbartian Five Steps Approach has been organized in a very psychological and logical way.

Demerits of Herbartian Approach

The following are the demerits of Herbartian approach:

1. *Mechanical Method of Teaching.* All the five steps of Herbart have a logical sequence. The use of these steps cuts the independence of the teacher to the extent that he cannot incorporate his independent thoughts in any step. This reduces the originality of the teacher. Hence, this Herbartian approach is a mechanical method of teaching.

2. *No Place for Individual Differences.* While using Herbartian approach, similar questions are asked from the pupils. Even similar activities are asked to do. This overlooks individual differences. Hence, this five step approach is not considered a good teaching method.

3. *Difficulty of Correlation.* Herbart had considered the knowledge as a complete unit. Therefore, they emphasized correlation between different subjects for the unity in the mental life of the pupils. But the real situation is that the teachers impart the knowledge of different subjects to the pupils differently following these five steps. Their notion is that to

establish a correlation between various subjects in order to bring integration in the mental life of the pupils using five steps is essentially difficult, if not impossible.

4. *Teacher More Active.* In this Herbartian approach, the teacher has to be more active than the pupils. But it is more desirable if the pupils remain more active than the teachers. Since, this teaching method is not activity-centred, pupils don't get any motivation for learning. It is because, the new teaching methods do not include Herbartian steps.

5. *Useful in Knowledge Lessons Only.* Herbartian approach can be useful in the knowledge lesson only, not in appreciation and skill lessons. In other words, Herbartian approach can be used successfully in knowledge lessons, but not in appreciation and skill lessons.

6. *Uninteresting.* Some educationists are of the view that this approach stresses upon the teaching of all the subjects of curriculum in a similar sequence overlooking the interests, attitudes, abilities and capacities of the pupils according to their mental development. This makes the entire teaching a traditional one and the pupil does not show any interest in acquiring new knowledge. In short, Herbart's teaching method is not interesting.

7. *No Need of Generalization.* The generalization is the fourth important step in Herbartian approach. While teaching a language, geography, history, music and arts etc. generalization is not needed. From this point of view, all the five steps are not needed while teaching according to Herbartian approach.

Lesson Points

According to the steps indoctrinated by Herbart, every lesson cannot be taught with so ease. Therefore, educational specialists have formulated such lesson points considering the Herbartian five steps as basis which can be used easily in every type of lesson.

Every teacher, specifically pupil-teacher should prepare the lesson-plan according to the lesson-points and the subject-matter should be presented before the pupils. This gives them the knowledge of the subject, topic, pupils' previous knowledge, material aid, questions to be asked and elaboration of the contents. These lesson points are as follows:

1. *Serial Number.* The serial number on the lesson-plan facilitates him and his supervision to know the number of lessons taught and untaught.

2. *Date.* The pupil-teacher should write the date. This will keep the record of teaching the lessons on different dates.

3. *Class.* The lesson-plan must bear the class for which the pupil-teacher has prepared it. It is beneficial in two ways—(1) The pupil-teachers can select the teaching method in accordance with the mental level of the pupils, and (2) The supervisors can also judge whether the content, material aid and teaching method is according to the mental level of the pupils in the class or not.

4. *Subject.* The pupil-teacher should mention the subject on the lesson-plan, because sometimes the same lesson can be taught in the subjects like languages, history and geography etc. The writing of the subject on the lesson-plan is useful in two ways—(1) The lesson-plan will match the subject, and (2) Since the teaching aims of every subject are different, these would be written in the lesson-plan concerning the subject which are to be achieved by the pupil-teachers.

5. *Time and Period.* The pupil-teachers should also be cautious about the time and the period while preparing a lesson-plan. It is useful in two ways—(1) The pupil-teachers would be aware of the time for which they are to teach the lesson. (2) The supervisor would also be able to decide easily whether the lesson is short or lengthy according to the time.

6. *Name of School.* Sometimes, pupil-teachers are to go to many schools for teaching. Therefore, they must write the name of the school where they delivered their practice lessons. This will keep their sympathy for that school. Also, this will keep the supervisor in-touch with the practice-school of each pupil-teacher.

7. *Topic.* In each text book, the subject-matter is divided into many chapters for convenience. The pupil-teachers should determine the topics for each day by dividing each chapter of the text-book into smaller sections considering the mental level of the class and representation of the thoughts as the basis. For example, for teaching history to ninth class, the chapter on "Mohammad Tuglak" can be divided into many topics such as—"Reforms by Mohammad Tuglak", "Administration of

Mohammad Tuglak" etc. Remember that in the lesson of languages, the title of the chapter is topic in itself. The pupil-teachers often commit mistakes in the selection of the topics. Therefore, they are warned to be alert in selecting the topic by well-organizing the contents.

8. General Aims. The teaching of each lesson has two types of objectives—(1) General Aims, and (2) Specific Aims. The general aims are concerned with the subject and the specific aims with the immediate lesson. The general aims can be achieved when the teaching of the subject is completed, but the specific aims can be achieved when the lesson is being taught.

Another difference between these two types of aim is that the general aims are definite aims but the specific aims go on changing from lesson to lesson.

While determining the aims, the pupil-teachers should keep in mind the objectives of education and they must give a thought to the content. Every subject has different general aims. Hence, before preparing lesson plan, the pupil-teacher should know the general aims of the lesson to be taught.

9. Specific Aims. It has been made clear that if a subject has general aims on one side, it has specific aims too on the other side. Hence, the pupil-teacher should write the specific aim of the lesson.

For example, if in a lesson of History, the knowledge about Akbar's administration is to be given, the pupil-teacher should write the specific aims as—'The Administration of Akbar'.

10. Material Aid. Under this point, the pupil-teacher should mention in short that material aid with the help of which the pupils are to learn the lesson. The material aid should be neither too lengthy nor too short. Also, these should be useful from pupil's mental level viewpoint.

11. Previous Knowledge. Previous knowledge means those past experiences of the pupils on the basis of which the teacher wants to develop the main lesson. Some people derive the meaning of previous knowledge from the studied matter. But in reality, it includes all those informations and experiences which the pupils acquire in or outside the class with the help of their parents, neighbours and friends, directly or indirectly. The pupil-teacher should write such previous knowledge after selecting it with which the new knowledge can easily be linked.

12. *Introduction.* Introduction means preparation. Hence, before starting the main lesson, the pupil-teacher should prepare the pupils to acquire new knowledge.

For example, (1) by asking some questions on previous knowledge, (2) by story telling, (3) by interpreting or explaining the subject, (4) by reciting a poem, and (5) by some other methods.

The questions asked by the teacher from the pupils should be three or four in number and these should be in a sequence and very simple. This wll enable the teachers to relate the previous and new knowledge and the statement of the objective will be easy.

13. *Statement of Aim.* As the introducton is over, the teacher should state the objective very clearly. Also, the topic should be written on the black-board. It has three advantages—(1) The pupils will become aware of the objectives of the new lesson i.e., they will come to know what they are going to learn, (2) They will start to participate to achieve the goal, and (3) The teacher will also succeed in presenting the subject-matter in an order.

14. *Presentation.* In this, the teacher should decide by accepting the principle of selecting and division, the amount of knowledge which he is to provide the pupils and which he is to receive from the pupils. Then he should divide the knowledge into two or three units after organising the subject-matter in a natural and logical sequence.

Some lessons can be taught in a single unit. When the teacher divides the subject-matter into two or more units, he should observe these important points. (1) Each unit should be complete in itself, (2) each unit should have the relationship with the other unit so that there is a coordination between them. Each unit should not look like a lesson in itself, (3) each unit should be developed according to the sequence.

The end of each unit should be followed by a test given to the pupils so that it can be ascertained whether the pupils have acquired new knowledge or not. In short, the teacher should present the units as a whole. This will make clear the new knowledge to the pupils.

15. *Comprehensive Questions.* Comprehensive questions are

those questions with the help of which the teacher comes to know whether the pupils gained the understanding of the taught lesson or not. Hence, the teacher should mention some comprehensive questions at the end of each unit. The answers to such questions will indicate the limit of acquisition of new knowledge in the pupils.

16. Black-board Summary. On the basis of comprehensive questions, the black-board summary is prepared. Therefore, the pupil-teachers should not write black-board summary at their own, but they should write the short form of the answers to the questions asked at the end of each unit. These should be clear and in meaningful sentences and the sequence should be such that those sentences present a complete thought.

17. Recapitulation. After presenting each unit, the teacher should mention some recapitulatory questions. It will benefit in three ways—(1) the lessons will be revised, (2) the knowledge acquired by the pupils will be explored, and (3) the teacher would be clear about the limit to which he is successful in acquiring his objective.

18. Home Work. After the recapitulation of the lesson, the home work should be assigned to the pupils by the teachers. This will stabilize the knowledge in the minds of the pupils as well as establish a contact between the teachers and the guardians or parents of the pupils.

Dewey and Kilpatrick Approach

Kilpatrick was the favourite pupil of John Dewey and he was a teacher in Education in Columbia University. He had the deep effects of John Dewey's Pragmatism. Hence, it was his belief that education should penetrate into the actual life. Unfortunately, education was suffering with many drawbacks at that time. The pupils were given artificial education by suppressing their interests, feelings and tendencies and over-looking their individual differences.

In such a situation, Kilpatrick developed a new teaching method, called 'Project Method' to acquire practical knowledge which was based on the principles of John Dewey's Pragmatism and interests of the pupils.

In Dewey and Kilpatrick approach, the basis of learning is a project. Through this method, the pupils gain various experiences while solving their problems of life. This makes the teaching purposeful. By this, the pupils are provided with such experiences which develop social capacities in them in order to be successful in their practical life. In America, this approach is used successfully. Gandhiji, proposed this type of unit approach for the primary level of his basic education.

In a project method, Kilpatrick has mentioned seven steps. These steps are: (1) Creating the situations, (2) Selection of the project, (3) Purpose of project, (4) Planning of the programme, (5) Execution of the programme, (6) Evaluation of the task, and (7) Reporting. All these steps have been discussed in detail earlier.

Morrison's Unit Approach

The advocate of this approach is Prof. H.C. Morrison. In his book, *The Practice of Teaching in Secondary Schools,* he has explained while describing unit method that the unit method is an important method from psychological point of view. It is a student-centred method. It is prepared by pupils and the teachers.

In this approach, the interests, attitudes and needs of the pupils are considered. Also, the learning objectves are made clear to them. Like Herbartian five steps approach, five steps are followed in Morrison's unit approach too. These steps are—(1) Exploration, (2) Presentation, (3) Assimilation, (4) Explanation, and (5) Recitation. In Herbartian five-steps approach, Herbart emphasized more on presentation, while Morrison in his unit approach, emphasized more on assimilation.

Structure of a Teaching Unit

The structure of a unit is based on the nature of the subject-matter and the teaching objectives. Every teaching unit has its own structure. The teaching unit has the following characteristics:

1. *Division of Content.* While using unit approach, the entire subject-matter which is to be taught throughout the session or semester, is divided into smaller units. Pupils understand these smaller units easily by concentrating on them.

2. *Giving Practical Shape of Teaching Process.* After understandng the smaller units of the subject-matter, giving

practical shape to the teaching process is the second characteristic of the teaching unit.

The teaching unit is administered in the following three phases—

A. Introductory Phase. In this phase, the pupils are made clear about the teaching objectives. This makes them curious to gain new knowledge.

B. Presentation Phase. In this phase, the learning experiences are provided to the pupils while presenting the contents.

C. Evaluation Phase. In this phase, pupils repeat the acquired experiences while interpreting them. In other words, in this phase, the acquired knowledge of the pupils is evaluated.

Elements of Teaching Unit

In a good teaching unit the following elements are used in a sequence:

1. *Overview.* The teacher should determine the objectives of the teaching unit in such a way that the needs of the pupils are fulfilled. They should be so much motivated so that they may acquire new knowledge with interest. In order to accomplish this task, the teacher gives the statement of aim after introduction so that the pupils get awareness of the scope of teaching unit.

2. *Previous Knolwedge.* The second important phase of teaching unit is to get awareness of the previous knowledge of the pupils for their new knowledge. For this, the teacher asks questions from the pupils so that he may decide the point to start with after relating the previous knowledge to the new knowledge.

3. *Presentation of New Experiences.* In the third phase of teaching unit, the new experiences and the elements of the contents are presented in a logical order and the lesson is developed with the cooperation of the pupils. For this, the question-answer method is also used. If the pupils fail to answer the questions for some reasons, the teacher interprets the elements himself.

4. *Motivation.* Every activity of the teaching unit is performed for learning. Hence, the teacher should motivate the pupils at intervals of time so that they may show interest continuously in the teaching and get ready to learn.

5. *Summarization.* In a teaching unit, this phase is considered important. It enables the pupils to give the summarized form of the lesson.

6. *Drill and Recapitulation.* To minimize forgetting in learning, drill and recapitulation techniques are important. Hence, the pupils must get the opportunity of drill and recapitulation after presentation so that they may retain the learning experiences for longer duration.

7. *Organization.* The teaching unit has a proper provision for organizing the acquired experiences. For this, the teacher assigns home work to the pupils with time to time instructions which helps them in organizing the acquired knowledge.

8. *Evaluation.* In the teaching unit, there is a provision of evaluating the knowledge acquired by the pupils which makes them aware of the limit of acquisition of the objectives. For this task, oral questions or oral and written tests are used.

Fundamental Principles of Unit Method

The fundamental principles of unit-method are as follows—

1. *Principle of Unit.* In the unit method, the 'whole' is considered important according to Gestalt Psychology. For this the pupil, in the process of acquiring knowledge, the teacher presents the content of an unit before the pupils giving supremacy to the unity or 'Wholeness'.

2. *Principle of Interest and Purpose.* In unit method, the teacher creates interest in pupils in order to achieve the objectives of the unit. This brings the desired changes in their behaviour.

3. *Principle of Child's Supremacy.* In the unit method, the child's supremacy is important. According to this principle, the activities of the pupils are emphasized in the entire teaching while assigning the special importance to the needs and basic instincts of the pupils.

4. *Principle of Dynamism.* According to the principles of dynamism, all the teaching units should be dynamic. This makes the scope of each unit more wider and pupils acquire it easily. Dynamism is the key to teaching. Hence, the teacher should apply the principle of dynamism according to the need.

5. *Principle of Recitation.* From psychological point of view, in order to mark the new knowledge in the minds of the pupils,

recitation is important. Hence, in unit-method, the recitation by the pupils is encouraged more and more and they assimilate the knowledge conveniently.

6. Principle of Organisation. According to this principle, the organization of the content is important in the unit method. Hence, in order to provide complete knowledge to the pupils, various teaching materials should be used.

Merits of Unit Method

The following are the merits of a unit method—

1. Psychological Method. Unit method is based on Gestalt Psychology. Hence, in this method, the importance is given to the 'whole' instead of 'part'.

2. Interesting. In this method, the interest of the pupils is emphasized. Also, the easy acquisition of teaching objectives is preferred.

3. Organized Learning. By using this method, learning occurs in an organized form. Consequently, it becomes the permanent part of the brain.

4. Child-centred Method. The unit method is the child-centred method. In this, the capacities and needs of the pupils are considered supreme.

5. Habit of Healthy Study. The unit method helps in the habit of healthy study. This makes them self-learners.

6. Encouragement to Expression of Ideas. The unit method is a child-centred method. This method encourages the development of social values as well as the capacity to express ideas.

7. Development of Social Values. The unit method is considered an important method of group teaching. It is clear that this method helps desirably in developing social values in the pupils.

8. Use of Appropriate Teaching Aids. In unit method, the knowledge is imparted with the help of appropriate teaching aid. This enables them to learn how to apply properly the teaching aid.

Demerits of Unit Method

The unit method has the following demerits—

1. Mechanical Method of Teaching. While using the unit method, the freedom of the teacher is delimited so much that he fails to present his thoughts before the pupils. In such a situation, the learning becomes lifeless, boring and mechanical.

2. *Limited Scope.* Due to the detailed knowledge provided to the pupils, this unit-method has very limited scope.

3. *Waste of Time.* While using the unit method, the pupils are provided with organized and detailed knowledge. This wastes the time.

4. *Possibility of Gaining Less Knowledge.* In using unit-method, it is possible that the pupils acquire sufficient knowledge in some subjects and insufficient knowledge in others.

5. *End of Originality.* While using unit-method, pupils are to restrict. This finishes the originality of the teaching and learning.

American Approach

American approach aims at *(i)* objective, *(ii)* behaviour, and *(iii)* evaluation. In this approach, by determining and defining the objectives of the content and by using various teaching methods, techniques, tactics and audio-visual aids, the creation of such situations is emphasized that all the pupils participate actively and achieve the (i) learning experiences, (ii) the desired behavioural changes, and (iii) the teaching-learning objectives.

Bloom has stressed upon the writing of objectives in behavioural terms while classifying them in cognitive, affective and psychomotor aspects. Also, he has recommended the use of criterion tests after constructing them to evaluate whether the teaching-learning objectives have been achieved or not as a result of pupils' activities.

British Approach

The contents and the pupils have their own importance in British approach. But being a traditional country, England has still a teacher-centred education. In other words, the central point of entire education is the teacher. Remember that in England, the teachers' activities and the evaluation of the pupils are given equal importance. In short, while preparing lesson-plan with British approach, the teacher's activities and the evaluation of the pupils by achievement tests are specifically emphasised.

Indian Approach

In preparing the lesson, the Indian approach bears the influence of British and American approaches. It is the reason that in India, while preparing lesson-plans, the teaching objectives, teachers' activities and evaluation of the pupils are emphasized. In India, in the beginning of twentieth century, lesson plans were prepared accordng to Herbartian Five Steps of Teaching. Even now, in the old training departments, lesson-plans are being prepared accordng to this approach.

But after 1960, in National Council of Educational Research and Training (NCERT), Centre of Advance Study in Education (CASE) and Regional College of Education (RCE), many experiments were conducted on this unit method and evaluation method. Now, we observe that in the regional colleges of education of NCERT, their own formate of lesson planning was prepared. In these lessons, the objectives and the learning experiences are given the important place.

Features of an Ideal Lesson-Plan

Features or characteristics of an ideal lesson plan are as follows :

1. *Objective Based.* The lesson-plan must be based on one or the other objective. While writing this, objectives should be written and defined clearly because its main objective is to achieve some goal or goals.

2. *Based Previous Knowledge.* An ideal lesson-plan should be based on the previous knowledge to the pupils. This will avoid any difficulty in acquiring new knowledge by the pupils.

3. *Simplicity of Language.* In an ideal lesson plan, the simplicity of the lesson-plan and clarity of thoughts should be according to the mental level of the pupils. In other words, the lesson-plan should be subject-oriented, not language-oriented.

4. *Division of Lesson Plan into Units.* Lessons are of three types *(i)* Knowledge lessons, *(ii)* Skill lessons, *(iii)* Appreciation lessons. In an ideal lesson-plan all the relevant steps of these three types of lesson-plans should be determined. Also, each lesson should be divided into suitable units so that the pupils may understand the lesson gradually.

5. *Decision about Appropriate Material Aids.* The material aid

is an important means of the teacher. Hence, correct decision regarding the charts, graphs, pictures, diagrams and maps should be taken while preparing ideal lesson plans and these should be marked at proper places which a teacher is to use them while teaching.

6. *Use of Strategies, Tactics, Techniques and Teaching Aids.* In order to prepare an ideal lesson-plan, the teacher should gain the knowledge of maxims of teaching and general principles of teaching. Only then, he can use appropriate strategies or methods, tactics, techniques and aids in order to classify the events and facts which occur in different situations.

7. *Determination of Activities.* In an ideal lesson-plan, it should be made clear what activities a teacher and the pupils are to perform. In other words, in an ideal lesson plan, the activities of a teacher and the pupils should be determined before-hand.

8. *Correlation.* In an ideal lesson-plan, a possible balance should occur. This enables the pupils to acquire the knowledge as a whole.

9. *Use of Illustrations.* In an ideal lesson plan, such examples should be used which have the relevance with the daily life of the pupils. This depends upon the comprehensive knowledge and experience of the teacher.

10. *Teaching from Memory Level to Reflective Level.* In an ideal lesson-plan developmental and thought-provoking questions should be asked. Also, there should be an effort to stretch the teaching from memory level to the reflective level.

11. *Individual Guidance.* In an ideal lesson plan it should be indicated how and when the teacher will provide individual guidance to the pupils.

12. *Use of Black-board.* The development of the black-board summary should be proceeded with comprehensive questions. The black-board summary of each and every unit should be written on the black-board immediately after teaching it in small but complete sentences.

13. *Time-sense.* An ideal lesson-plan should be prepared keeping in view the mental level of the pupils and the duration of the periods. It should be made clear in it the time assigned for every teaching step.

14. *Evaluation.* In an ideal lesson-plan there should be a

mention of the method of knowing the influence on the pupils. This also evaluates the methods used by the teacher. Also, the pupils will take interest in learning.

15. *Home Work.* There should be a provision of home work in an ideal lesson-plan. This will enable the pupils to learn the application of the acquired knowledge

How to Prepare Lesson-Plan

The skill of teaching depends mostly on the lesson-plan. Hence, the teachers, specifically pupil-teachers, should keep in mind, the following things while preparing the lesson-plan—

1. *Clarity of Objective.* In a lesson-plan, there should be clarity of objectives. The objectives being clear and well-defined will make the pupils and the teachers both active to achieve them.

2. *Knowledge of the Subject.* The teacher should know his subject for preparing the lesson-plan. Therefore, the teacher, specifically pupil-teachers should be alert in this regard and they should read completely the whole lesson-plan which they have prepared. If possible, the pupil-teacher should not read the text-book only, he should also read other supplementary books and the material concerning the topic.

3. *General Knowledge of All Subjects.* In addition to the knowledge of his own subject, the teacher should also possess general knowledge of all the subjects, because the knowledge is a complete unit and it cannot be divided into different parts. Hence, to teach properly any subject, the teacher must know the other related subjects too.

4. *Knowledge of Student's Nature.* The teaching method will be advantageous only when the nature of the pupils is also know along with the knowledge of the subject-matter. Hence, while preparing a lesson-plan, the teacher must know the nature of the pupils along with the subject-matter.

5. *Knowledge of the Principles and Strategies of Teaching.* In order to prepare a lesson-plan, the teacher must know the principles of teaching, maxims of teaching, teaching methods and techniques. This enables him to mention properly the teaching methods and techniques in the lesson plan.

6. *Knowledge of Class Level.* The teacher should know the class-level for which he is to prepare the lesson-plan which

some fresh teachers overlook. This disturbs the whole teaching and the pupils fail to understand anything. Hence, all the pupil-teachers should be alert in this regard.

7. Clarity about Previous Knowledge. The teacher should know the previous knowledge of the pupils while preparing the lesson-plan, because the new knowledge imparted on the basis of previous knowledge is attained and is stabilized. In other words, lesson can only be developed successfully when the teacher has clarity about the pupils' previous knowledge. Hence, while preparing lesson-plan, the teacher must be clear about the previous knowledge of the pupils in addition to their nature and contents.

8. Division of Units. While preparing the lesson plan, the teacher should divide the topic in one or more units. Also, it should be determined which teaching method or strategy will be used. This simplifies the preparation of the lesson-plan and is acquired easily by both the sides i.e., the pupils and the teachers.

9. Flexibility. The lesson-plan is a slave of the teacher, not the master. Hence, in order to create attraction and interest in the lesson, the teacher is free to make changes in the lesson plan.

10. Use of Material Aids. While preparing the lesson plan it should be decided at what step the material aid is to be used and what is to be clarified with that aid. In other words, the material aid should be used as and when the need arises. This maintains the naturality and interesting feature of the lesson plan.

11. Time Sense. The teacher should have time sense while preparing the lesson-plan. In other words, the teacher should know it clearly how much time it will take to present the lesson before the pupils and how many activities can be performed in the prescribed duration.

Preparation of Lesson-Plan

From the above description, it is very much clear that the teacher, specifically the pupil-teacher, should write the lesson-plan in detail before commencing the task of teaching.

Remember that the pupil-teacher who prepares the lesson plan but does not memorize it, he can neither present the subject-matter in a sequence nor he is able to establish the relationship between various units. Not only this sometimes he becomes nervous and fails to use the prescribed strategy, technique and material aid along with forgetting of facts and events of the lesson.

Hence, in the words of Davies, "Nothing is so fatal for a teacher as unpreparedness". From this point of view, the pupil-teacher should learn by heart the lesson-plan in detail before starting the task of teaching. After preparing and remembering the lesson-plan, the teacher should start the task of teaching.

The teacher should keep in mind that they are not the slaves of the lesson-plan. It is their right to make necessary changes as the need arises, because the teachers may face such problems which they never imagined while preparing the lesson-plan. In such a situation, they should make necessary changes in the lesson-plan using their intelligence and resourcefulness.

In short, every teacher is free to make changes in the lesson plan, because it is better to do the task of teaching properly rather to follow the lesson-plan blindly. But modifications in the lesson-plan does not apply to the pupil-teachers, because, due to lack of experience they cannot make the necessary changes in the lesson-plan successfully. Hence, the pupil-teachers must follow the lesson-plan.

Writing of Lesson–Plan

In order to prepare the written forms of the lesson-plans, the above mentioned approaches are available, but in the modern age, the lesson-plans indoctrinated by Herbart and Bloom are often used. Hence, the description of these two approaches in detail are being given in the following lines:

1. Herbartian Approach

According to Herbart, the knowledge to the pupils is imparted from outside. This knowledge given from outside goes on accumulating in their minds. Hence, if the knowledge being imparted to the pupils from outside is linked with the accumulated previous knowledge of the pupils, then the learning process becomes effective. Herbart further says that this new knowledge should be given in an order.

This relates him to his cumulative knowledge. Hence, he has presented the following format of the lesson-plan by using his five steps approach:

1. Date, Class, Period, Topic
2. General aim
3. Specific aim
4. Material aid
5. Previous knowledge
6. Introduction
7. Statement of the aim
8. Presentation
9. Comprehensive Questions
10. Black-board Summary
11. Recapitulation
12. Home Work

2. Lesson Planning According to Evaluation Approach

Prof. Bloom has developed a new concept in education which is termed as 'Evaluation Approach'. According to Bloom, evaluation is a continuous process. This process has three components—(1) Teaching objectives, (2) Learning experiences, and (3) Behavioural changes. All these three components are closely related. Now, most of the educationists emphasize more on evaluation approach than five steps approach and they are recommending the preparation of lesson-plans based on the evaluation approach instead of other approaches.

According to the evaluation approach, the lesson-plan has eight main points:

(1) Main Thoughts, (2) Content, (3) Aims and Objectives, (4) Method of Teaching, (5) Student's Activities, (6) Aids for Students, (7) Aids for Teachers, and (8) Examination. These eight points are described below in the form of six forms—

1. *Content to be Taught.* In the first column of the lesson-plan, the content to be taught to the pupils should be written. The content should be selected from the prescribed text-books. Then, it should be divided into topics. In this column, the content which is written regarding the topic should not be in detail. However, main facts and thoughts regarding that topic should be very precise.

2. *Objectives with Specifications.* In this column, the general aims of teaching, their classes and characteristics along with relevant and desirable behaviours should be written in short form.

3. *Teacher's Activities.* In the third column of the lesson-plan, the teacher should mention his activities. Under teacher's activities, all those activities are included which are concerned with the content. These activities are—asking questions, statements, to describe, to illustrate, use of material aid, to deliver model lessons and to clarify the terms and concepts. The teacher should also indicate the learning experiences and efforts to be made for them in this column in short form.

4. *Students' Activities.* In this column students' activities should be written.

For example, to listen to the teacher, to tell the meanings of the words, to answer the questions, to participate in discussion, to prepare material and to study it.

5. *Teaching Aids.* In the fifth column of the lesson-plan, that material aid required for teaching is mentioned which makes the contents clear, understandable and alive.

6. *Evaluation.* In this column, those devices of evaluation should be mentioned with the help of which daily evaluation of teaching objectives of each lesson, read material and the learning experiences may occur. This enables the teacher to know about the success and failure of tactics and strategies used by him and he can modify the teaching system.

Model Lesson-Plan According to Herbartian Approach

Date: 18.1.2002   Period: 3rd   Duration: 40 Minutes
Class: 7th
Subject: English (Composition)
Topic: Postman

General Aims:

1. To enable the pupils to understand English.
2. To enable the pupils to speak English effectively.
3. To enable the pupils to read and understand written English.
4. To enable the pupils to develop their feelings and imagination.

Specific Aim:

To enable the pupils to write a composition on POSTMAN.

Material Aids:

A picture of Postman.

Previous Knowledge:

Pupils have seen a postman at their home and they understand his general activity.

Introduction: (Teacher asks question and pupils answer them)

Question—How can we send our message?

Ans. —By telephone, by telegram and by post.

Question—Who brings you the post?

Ans. —A Postman brings the post to us.

Question—What do you know about the postman?

Ans. —(Pupils will be unable to answer it.)

Statement of Aim:

Today we are going to compose a few sentences on 'Postman'.

Presentation:—(By showing a picture of Postman)

1. Teacher's Statement—He is a postman.
   Teacher's Question—Who is that in this picture?
   Pupil's Answer—He is a postman.
2. Tr. St.—Postman is a government servant.
   Tr. Q.—What is a postman?
   Pupil's Ans.—Postman is a government servant.
3. Tr. St.—He wears a Khakhi dress.
   Tr. Q.—What type of dress he wears?
   Pupil's Ans.—He wears a Khakhi dress.
4. Tr. St.—The colour of his turban is red.
   Tr. Q.—What is the colour of his turban?
   Pupil's Ans.—The colour of his turban is red.
5. Tr. St.—He has a long bag.
   Tr. Q.—What kind of bag a postman has?
   Pupil's Ans.—He has a long bag.
6. Tr. St.—He keeps letters in this bag.
   Tr. Q.—What does he keep in this bag?
   Pupil's Ans.—He keeps letters in this bag.
7. Tr. St.—He goes to the post office in the morning.
   Tr. Q.—When does he go to the post office?

Pupil's Ans.—He goes to the post office in the morning.

8. Tr. St.—He goes from door to door to give the post.
   Tr. Q.—Where does he go to give the post?
   Pupil's Ans.—He goes from door to door to give the post.
9. Tr. St.—He gives the people good and bad news.
   Tr. Q.—What does he give to the people?
   Pupil's Ans.—He gives the people good and bad news.
10. Tr. St.—His job is very hard.
    Tr. Q.—What kind of job he has?
    Pupil's Ans.—His job is very hard.
11. Tr. St.—His pay is very small.
    Tr. Q.—What is his pay?
    Pupil's Ans.—His pay is very small.
12. Tr. St.—He is a faithful man.
    Tr. Q.—What kind of man he is?
    Pupil's Ans.—He is a faithful man.

Recapitulation and Black-board Summary: Teacher asks questions and receives answers from the pupil and he himself writes the summary on the black-board.

POSTMAN

1. He is a postman.
2. He wears a khakhi dress.
3. Postman is a government servant.
4. He has red turban.
5. He has a long bag.
6. He keeps letters in his bag.
7. He goes to the post office in the morning.
8. He goes from door to door to give the post.
9. He gives people good and bad news.
10. His job is very hard.
11. His pay is very small.
12. He is a faithful man.

Classwork: Ask the students to write black-board summary on their note-books and supervise them that they are doing so.

Homework: Students will write more sentences on the postman.

QUESTIONS FOR ANSWER

1. Write a note on various approaches to Lesson-Planning.
2. Write a note on the need and importance of Lesson-Plan while explaining the development of Lesson-Plan.
3. Write a note on the characteristics of an ideal Lesson-Plan. Explain how the Lesson-Plan is prepared.
4. Write short notes on:
   (A) Merits and demerits of Herbartian Five Steps.
   (B) Morrison's Unit Approach.
   (C) Prepare a formate of Lesson-Plan according to Herbartian Approach.
   (D) Prepare a formate of Lesson-Plan according to Evaluation Approach.

MODEL LESSON-PLAN ACCORDING TO EVALUATION APPROACH

Date: 18.1.2002

Period: 1st
Subject: Civics
Class: 8th
Topic: Ideal Citizens
Previous Knowledge: Advantages of the Study of Civics are known to the pupil

Duration: 40 Minutes

Contents and Items to be Taught	*Objective and their Specification*	*Teacher's Activity*	*Student's Activity*	*Teaching Aids*	*Evaluation*
Questions based on Previous Knowledge		Teacher will motivate the pupil to learn new knowledge by asking the following question to relate new and previous knowledge 1. What is our country's name? 2. What is our system of government? 3. Who possess the fundamental rights in democracy?	1. Our country's name is India. 2. Our system of government is Democracy. 3. Citizens possess the fundamental rights in democracy.		

		Problematic Question: What are the qualities of an ideal citizen? *Statement of Aim:* We will study about the qualities of an ideal citizen. *Presentation:* 1. Why the pupil go to school? 2. How education effects the pupil?	Pupil will be unable to answer this question. 1. Pupils go to school to learn knowledge. 2. Pupils become educated by gaining education.	
Educated	Interest (Pupils will show interest in acquiring new knowledge)	*Explanation:* An ideal citizen should be well educated. Through education he would be able to solve every problem by adopting scientific attitude and taking his own decision regarding problems of his life. Q. 1. What games pupils play in the playground? Q. 2. How games are useful for the pupil?	Pupils will listen carefully. 1. Pupils play many games in the playground. 2. Playing is good for sound health.	Why it is necessary to be well-educated for an ideal citizen?
Health	To identify the advantages of	*Teacher's Statement* An ideal citizen should have		Fill in the blanks:

(Contd.)

Contents and Items to be Taught	Objective and their Specification	Teacher's Activity	Student's Activity	Teaching Aids	Evaluation
	sound health	sound health because without it he can neither enjoy his life nor perform his duties towards his nation as a citizen.			A healthy man can —— his life and can serve his —— as a citizen.
Equality	Knowledge (Pupils can recognise the fact that we all are children of the same God).	(Pointing towards the Picture) Q. What type of feeling Gandhiji is arousing while sitting amongst harijans?	Pupils will remain unresponded.	A picture of Gandhiji sitting amongst Harijans.	Why we should behave equally with other citizens?
		Explanations: Gandhiji, sitting amongst the harijans, trying to arouse the feeling of equality. According to him, an ideal citizen should behave equally with other citizens because we are the children of the same God.	The pupils will listen carefully.		
		Q. What we call the pupils without eyesight? Q. What is our duty towards blind persons?	1. Persons without eyesights are called blind. 2. We should serve the the blind persons.		

Service	Application (The pupil can serve other citizen)	(Pointing towards the picture) Teacher's Statement: An ideal citizen should have the quality of being social animal and he should have the feeling of social service and serve other citizens accordingly.	The pupils will listen carefully.	A picture of an ideal citizen showing the way to a blind.	Being a social animal, what is the duty of an ideal citizen.
Proper use of Votes.	Knowledge (The pupils can differentiate able and unable citizens)	(Pointing towards the picture) Q. What the citizens are putting into a ballot box? Teacher's Statement: An ideal citizen should use his vote properly keeping himself away from any groupism. Only then, a real government can be formed for the progress of the nation. Blackboard Summary: ——— *Home Work:* What qualities an ideal citizen should possess? Write in detail.	The pupil will listen carefully.	A picture of citizens casting their votes.	Why the citizens should use their voting rights?

16

Technique of Solving Day to Day Teaching-Learning Problems

The process of teaching and learning involves human beings who behave according to their motives, environment, intelligence, socio-cultural and socio-economic conditions, therefore, during actual teaching most effective and efficient teachers as well as most intelligent students at times face various problems which deserve careful consideration and demand just solution. This is only possible through action research.

Modern age is a science age. The man is advancing day by day as a result of progress in science. Remember that the basis of this human progress is the application of the results of the new researches by adopting scientific attitudes in their activities. The field of education is not separate from this. We observe that the teachers do not want to conduct their task of teaching through trial and error only, they also seek the help of researches being conducted in other subjects in order to solve various problems created at the time of teaching.

Hence, in education many researches are being conducted in order to solve various problems.

Meaning of Research and Educational Research

According to P.M. Cook "Research is an honest, exhaustive, intelligent searching for facts and their meanings or implications with reference to a given problem. The product and findings of a given piece of research should be an authentic, verifiable contribution to knowledge in the field studied".

According to Travers "Educational research is that activity which is directed towards the development to a science of behaviour in educational situation which is to provide knowledge that will permit educator to achieve his goals by the most effective methods."

Types of Educational Researches

Educational researches are of following three types:

1. *Historical.* According to John W. Best, "Historical research involves identification and limitation of the problem, formulation of the hypothesis, collection and organization, verification, validation and analysis of data; testing the hypothesis and writing of historical facts."

2. *Descriptive.* In descriptive research a problem concerning education involves. Example of such problem is: "unrest among students and its remedy." According to John W. Best, "It is concerned with conditions or relationships that exist, practices that prevail, belief, point of view or attitudes that are held; processes that are going on, effects that are being felt or trends that are developing."

3. *Experimental.* This method of research is difficult but the results derived are valid and reliable. In the words of John W. Best, "Experimental research is the description and analysis of what will be, or what will occur under controlled conditions."

Meaning and Definition of Action Research

Meaning. Action research means such a scientific search which is concerned with practical aspects of education. In it, a scientific search is conducted for the solution of various problems which come across the day-to-day activities of the pupils, teachers, schools and educational officers. All persons collect evidences relating to their problems, define and delimit the problem, collect all their experiences for action hypothesis method and explore the reasons of the problem. This solves the problem as well as the task too goes on.

Definition. The following definitions explain the meaning of action research more clearly:

1. *Stephen M. Corey:* "The process by which practitioners attempt to study their problems scientifically in order to guide correct and evaluate their decisions and actions in what a number of people have called action research".

2. *McRathote and Others:* "Action research is organized, investigative activity aimed towards the study and constructive change of a given endeavour by individuals or group concerned with such change and improvement".

Action Research and Fundamental Research

In the field of education, two types of researches occur—1. Fundamental, and 2. Applied. Action research is practical. In fundamental research, the basic elements of education are discovered, but in action research, the day-to-day problems of educational process are solved. In the table we are differentiating both types of researches, i.e., fundamental and action research.

Fundamental or Basic Research	*Action Research*
1. Fundamental Research is traditional.	Action research has developed from fundamental research. Hence, in the field of research, it is a new concept.
2. It has a wider area of problem.	It has narrow problematic area.
3. Fundamental research needs special training.	Action research can be conducted by a teacher, manager and educational officer without any special training.
4. In it, standard devices are used.	In it, self-made devices are used.

(Contd.)

Fundamental or Basic Research	Action Research
5. The fundamental researcher needs no relationship with the school.	Action research is conducted by the teacher, managers and administrators.
6. It is based upon the samples.	It is delimited to school only.
7. Its objective is to indoctrinate the principles.	Its objectives is to improve the school working by finding a practical solution to the educational problems and to enhance the knowledge of administrators and to develop curriculum and progress of teachers.
8. Generalization has special importance in fundamental research. The results achieved by this research are general.	The results achieved by action research can be applied to the local situations and directions. Hence, in it, generalization is not necessary.
9. In it, extreme truth is discovered through results which expands the sphere of knowledge.	This imporves the activities and working systems of the school.

Advantages of Action Research

Modern age is democratic. For its success, education is essential. But it is not an easy task to organize education properly. We observe that many day-to-day problems become horrible before the teachers, managers and administrators. In order to solve these problems, action research occupies an important place. In short, action research is useful in many ways. The main advantages are:

1. Action research develops scientific attitude in the teachers.
2. This can raise the achievement level of the pupils.

3. Action research enables the schools to organize proper programmes for the development of the pupils.
4. Teachers can adopt such a teaching method, by studying the interests, needs and abilities of the pupils, so that the teaching may become interesting and an all-round development of the pupils may take place.
5. With the help of action research, curriculum can be developed.
6. This can solve the problem of indiscipline.
7. Action research can preserve the democratic values by eliminating traditional and mechanical environment.
8. Action research can solve the problems of delinquency and backwardness.
9. Action research can remove the discrepancies among pupils and teachers which occur due to social causes.
10. With the help of action research, decisions can be taken regarding the day-to-day problems which occur before the principles, supervisors, administrators and managers. In other words, they can remove them by evaluating their own working systems or working methods.

From the above description, it is very much clear that the action research is much important in the field of education. It inspires all the teachers, managers, and administrators to work together with cooperation. This solves the most difficult educational problems very easily.

Methodology of Action Research

Methodology or steps of action research should proceed in following sequence:

1. *Identification of the Problem.* The first and the most important step of action research is to identify or select a problem. For this, the researcher should select problem from various sources like teaching, training, co-curricular activities, school administration and organization etc. which need solution on priority basis.

But remember that—1. The problem should be related to the school, 2. The need of its solution should be felt, 3. It should come in the score of the researcher, 4. Its scope should neither be so wider nor so narrow, and 5. Its objective type analysis can be conducted.

2. *Defining and Delimiting the Problems.* The second step of action research is the defining and delimiting the problem. Under defining, every aspect of the problem should be made clear. Similarly. in delimiting, the main points of the problem are fixed and the area is delimited. It is done just to make its scientific study more easy.

3. *Analysing the Probable Causes of the Problem.* In the third step of the action research, the probable causes of the problem are analysed. Therefore, the researcher should collect the evidences. Then, on the basis of the evidences, the probable causes should be explored.

In the end, a list of causes is prepared and its scientific analysis is done. For example, there can be many causes of not doing the home task, such as—

(i) lack of intelligence,
(ii) individual differences,
(iii) domestic environment,
(iv) non-understanding of questions given in home task,
(v) to be careless,
(vi) no checking of home work by the teachers,
(vii) no punishment to the defaulters regarding home task.

4. *Formulation of Action Hypothesis.* The fourth and most important step of action research is the formulation of action hypothesis. In this step, after analysing the causes related to the problem, the most important cause is explored which is eliminated and the problem is solved. In this connection, the researcher should write the guessed solution in words with sensitivity, consultation, creative imagination and insight. For example, in order to create a habit of doing home work. This hypothesis is formulated, "If a teacher checks the home work carefully and punishes those who fail to do it, then the pupils will start doing home work timely".

5. *Base Line Data.* In the fifth step of action research, a thought should be given to base line data. In this connection, the researcher should collect all those data which can help in solving the problem.

6. *Tools for Collecting Data.* In this step, the researcher should mention all those tools with the help of which the data are collected to solve the problem.

7. *Formulation of Action Design.* After formulating hypothesis, collecting data regarding that hypothesis and mentioning the tools for collecting the data, such as design should be prepared with which many research points may become clear. These points are—

(i) description of proposed activities,
(ii) the editing method of the activities and the means of doing those activities,
(iii) time taken by the activities.

Then, the real research should be started.

8. *Evaluation of the Results of Action Research:* In this step, the results are derived after analysing the facts on the basis of actions performed according to the design. Then, considering the final evaluation as basis, essential suggestions are derived for the solution of the problem and these are executed. The researcher should use these techniques for evaluating the results. 1. Questionnaire, 2. Interview, 3. Test. 4. Rating, Scale, 5. Check List, 6. Observation, 7. Collection of opinion, and 8. Statistical Methods.

Outline of Action Research

The following is the outline of action research—

1. Name of the teacher:		Mrs. R. K. Sood.
2. Name of the school:		S.D. Inter College, Kanpur.
3. Class:		9th.
4. Area of the problem:		Not doing home work in English
5. Pin-pointed problems:		To create a habit in these pupils, of doing home work in English who shows carelessness and ails to do it in time.
6. Probable Causes:	(i)	Individual differences
	(ii)	Lack in Intelligence
	(iii)	Domestic environment
	(iv)	Lack of furniture in the class-room
	(v)	Weak eye sight
	(vi)	Impaired hearing
	(vii)	Non-understanding of questions given in the home-work
	(viii)	Doing home work carelessly

(ix) No checking of home-work
(x) No marking of home-work
(xi) No punishment to the defaulters

7. Action Hypothesis: If the teacher check the home task in English, carefully, and punishes the defaulters, the pupils will start doing home work carefully and timely.

8. Base Line Data:
(i) History of the pupils
(ii) Knowledge of the family environment
(iii) Knowledge of traits
(iv) Necessary information regarding economical, cultural and physical situation

9. Tools for collecting data:
(i) Observations
(ii) Study
(iii) Questionnaire
(iv) Personal interviews
(v) Exercise books of English

Action Research Design

S. No.	*Month and Week*	*Activities to be started*	*Method*	*Expected Tools*
1.	Ist and 2nd week of September	To know about the interests, attitudes and aptitudes	Self efforts and cooperation of companions.	Personal Interview
2.	3rd and 4th week of September	To know the interests of pupils, their individual attitudes	Self-efforts	Questionnaire
3.	Ist week of October	To decide how many copies of the pupils can be checked.	Self-thinking	Study
4.	2nd week of October	To decide how much home task should be given to the pupils daily.	Conversation with all the teachers who teach the pupils.	Answer-books in English
5.	3rd and 4th week of October	To understand the content regarding home task.	By using a proper method	—

(Contd.)

S. No.	Month and Week	Activities to be started	Method	Expected Tools
6.	Ist and 2nd week of November	To get back the copies from the pupils in definite time.	Self-thinking	Answer copies in English.
7.	Ist and 2nd week of November	To punish those who do the home work carelessly or those who fail to do the home work.	Self-thinking and cooperation of the associates.	Answer-books in English
8.	3rd and 4th week of November.	To know the progress of the pupils.	Self-efforts	Answer-books

Evaluation of the Results of Action Research

By testing the hypothesis on the basis of results received from the activities performed according to the design of the action research, it is revealed that before conducting action research, 48 out of 60 or 80% pupils did not complete the home work. Only 12 or 20% pupils did home work in time. But the research revealed that only 27 or 45% pupils lagged in doing home work, rest 33 or 55% pupils started doing home work carefully. In this way, in three months, the number of pupils who started home work raised upto 35%. Consequently, it can be said that if the pupils are checked carefully daily, their knowledge will definitely enhance. There is possibility of improvement in the education system.

QUESTIONS FOR ANSWER

1. What is research ? Describe its types, while explaining the meaning of educational research.
2. What 'Action Research' means? Differentiate action and fundamental researches.

17

Progress of Educational Technology Programme in India

Though many nations had opted to use and develop educational technology much earlier, yet we in India opted to use and develop educational technology after twenty-five years of our independence, hence we are no match to other developed nations in this field, but in recent years our progress of development in this field is more encouraging and there is a hope that in the near future we would be able to put India at par with the most developed nations in the field of educational technology and thus ensure national progress in all fields at a faster rate which will benefit all sections of our society. In short we can say that our present policy in the field of educational technology will meet our national needs.

Hereunder, we attempt to highlight the process of development of educational technology in India. India's educational technology programme was started in the Central sector in 1972 during the Fourth Plan. It aimed at deploying the resources of educational technology for bringing about a qualitative improvement in education, widening access to education and reducing existing disparities between different regions of the country as well as different sections of the population.

Faced with the problem of high expansion and the need for improvement of the quality of education, the Government of India launched an educational technology project in 1972-73. This project broadly envisages the stimulation and promotion of an integrated use of mass media and instructional technology at all levels of education.

The objective is to bring about qualitative improvement, accelerate the rate of expansion and make instruction more interesting. Implemented with the collaboration of UNDP, the programme involves the setting up of a centre for the development of educational technology under the NCERT and educational technology cells in 21 states. Departments of Education and an Educational Technology unit in the Ministry of Education.

Educational Technology Programme

As per the programme, the centre is expected to plan the way for the introduction of educational technology in the educational processs especially in the area of training and research. Its programme includes development of innovations in education, training of teachers, communicators and administrators, evaluation of materials and programme of building an information bank of educational technology. It will also be concerned with the development of curriculum and preparation of basic scripts for films, radio and television as well as with the production of multi-purpose kits, models and other instructional material including 16 mm films.

Data Bank and Software Bank

A survey of equipment available with educational institutions in the country for the production or use of audio-visual aid materials was sponsored. Nursery rhymes, collected in four languages by the Indian Council for Child Welfare on behalf of the Centre, were set to music and recorded on tapes. The rhymes were translated into Devnagari and English.

Radio

A case study on the utilization of school broadcast programmes in Jaipur was completed. A similar case study is proposed to be conducted in Jalgaon (Maharashtra). Work progressed to locate potential areas where monitoring panels should be set up to monitor children's programmes broadcast from AIR.

Open School

A sub-committee was set up to explore the possibility of starting an open school pilot project in Delhi. The sub-committee has recommended that an open school would be highly suitable and desirable to meet the educational needs of the age-group 14 plus. This plan has already been implemented.

Educational Technology Cells

Initially in 11 states, namely, Maharashtra, Rajasthan, Andhra Pradesh, Orissa, Bihar, Karnataka, Madhya Pradesh, Punjab, Gujarat, Tamil Nadu, and Uttar Pradesh these cells fostered and promoted the development of programme at the state level. The entire expenditure on the setting up and maintenance of the state cells was met by the Government of India up to the end of the Fifth Plan, or for 5 years whichever was earlier.

In the context of the availability of the television facilities of INSAT, the Ministry of Information and Broadcasting suggested that the user ministries should take active part in the production of programmes meant for their specific uses. This would ensure that the programmes are relevant, meaningful and effective. It was, thus, necessary to create production capabilities at a decentralized level. The Ministry of Education decided that the responsibility for the production of educational television programmes would be gradually taken over by the educational authorities from Doordarshan.

Production of Video Programmes in Education

In order to implement this decision, it was necessary to set up programme production centres in the INSAT states in a phased manner. Accordingly, State Institutes of Educational Technology (SIET) are being established in each of the six INSAT states namely, Andhra Pradesh, Orissa, Gujarat, Maharashtra, Uttar Pradesh and Bihar, for promoting production of educational television programmes (ETV) on a decentralised basis.

The non-INSAT states and union territories are being prepared for participation in the INSAT programme through an educational technology scheme under which limited production capabilities were created to enable the states and union territories to experiment in production of programmes and organize training courses.

At the national level, the Central Institute of Educational research and Training by merging the existing Centre for Educational Technology and Department of Teaching Aids was established.

The major priorities identified for educational programmes, particularly in relation to the use of radio and television facilities, for educational purposes are—

(a) universalisation of elementary education, both formal and non-formal;
(b) non-formal education for adults, linking education to economic and social tasks;
(c) development of vocational and professional skills:
(d) training for citizenship;
(e) popularizing science with a view to develop a scientific outlook;
(f) promoting national integration, and
(g) providing information about themes of national importance—population education, energy conservation, preservation of wildlife, environmental sanitation, nutrition and health.

Keeping in view the large requirements for teacher education, the mass media will be used to broaden the horizon of teachers; to provide help in formal school teaching; and to assist in appreciation of the objectives of the educational uses of television and radio to ensure better utilisation.

The state production centres will be responsible for the production of television programmes of acceptable professional quality and educational utility. To begin with, the programmes would be limited to elementary education, non-formal education and teachers' training. Once the production centres become fully operational they will cater to the programme requirement of all levels of education.

Till such time as the state production centres become operational, the CIET is producing programmes which are being telecast in six states. The production of ETV programmes for the INSAT states was hitherto shared between Doordarshan and CIET on 50 : 50 basis.

However, from May 1987, the responsibility has been taken

entirely by CIET. The CIET has also produced capsules for mass orientation of teachers during the summer vacations.

Two programmes are being telecast daily in the regional languages, five days a week, for school children in the age group 5-11 during the normal working hours of the schools. On Saturdays there is a programme for teachers.

In view of the limited production facilities available, CIET is presently producing programmes in Hindi or English and dubbing them into regional languages of the states concerned. Production of programmes (and dubbing of CIET programmes) has been taken up by SIET in Gujarat and Maharashtra, Andhra Pradesh, Bihar and Uttar Pradesh have also started some programme production. The responsibility for radio transmission still rests with AIR.

Multi-media Package

The Centre developed a multi-media package consisting of television programmes, radio programmes, activity guides, enrichment materials and tutorials for in-service training of primary teachers in science teaching. It prepared suitable handbooks for teacher monitors as well as booklets of detailed and non-detailed activities. The package was used to train 47,000 teachers during the Satellite Instructional Television Experiment (SITE).

An evaluation of the in-service teachers training programmes was organized on the impact of SITE. Another study to evaluate the impact of SITE on primary school children was carried out in collaboration with India Space Research Organization (ISRO).

SITE Programme

The Satellite Instructional Television Experiment was launched in the country in August, 1975 for a period of one year. Under this experiment, it was possible to telecast programmes to 2,400 villages in six states, namely Andhra Pradesh, Bihar, Karnataka, Madhya Pradesh, Orissa and Rajasthan. The in-service teachers training programme which was organized in 1975 was repeated in June, 1976 to train 23,000 teachers for teaching science subjects.

Evaluation of Television Programmes

To facilitate understanding of the impact of tèlevision on education, the Ministry of Education undertook evaluation studies of television programmes broadcast to primary schools under the SITE. These studies are a collaborative effort between the several agencies involved in the planning production and utilization of the educational programmes and, therefore, are being carried out by the ET cells in States and the *Upgraha Doordarshan Kendras* in Cuttack, Delhi and Hyderabad.

The studies are programme-oriented and seek to obtain the reactions of select programmes at two levels, of teachers and pupils, both comprising the new television audience.

The Studies are designed to provide valuable insights in to the educational television process which would help to bring about improvement in the quality of television programming and production and in making it relevant to social and educational needs.

The field work of study in Orissa and Karnataka has been completed and analysis of data taken in hand. The preparatory work for studies in Rajasthan and Andhra Pradesh and many more states has also been completed.

Emphasis on Teacher's Role. India's educational technology programme of 1972 emphasised greater role of the teacher in the educational programme of the nation, because in every system of education teachers' role is pivotal and hence, teacher, in the changed circumstances, was asked to own not only educational responsibilities but also socio-cultural and nation-building responsibilities for the greater good of the people, society and the nation and hence, it stressed as follows:

Teachers cannot afford to rest on their oars and allow complacency to set in. They need to constantly improve on their skills. After all any enduring behavioural change that cannot be ascribed to non-volitional activity but has been deliberately caused by systematic well-planned instructional schedule could be labelled "learning" and the very process of effecting such a change upon an individual is termed "teaching".

Unlike a host of behavioural changes that could be attributed to incidental or informal learning, classroom learning is said to be more disciplined, goal-directed and time-bound.

Teacher needs to individualize instruction, make it meaningful to the majority, attend to the need of the mediocre and slow learners, assess them periodically and also prepare them for a terminal public examination—all within the academic year.

Ironically, in our social set up educational institutions are easy targets to express public dissent for real or imaginary inequities and remain closed for weeks at a stretch. Teachers anticipate such eventualities as closure of schools and hence plan, accordingly, so that the least damage is caused to students' interests.

Generally, teachers are meticulous in planning their lessons and strive to deliver them to the best of their capacity. They are sufficiently prepared to clarify doubts and answer the bewildering questions raised by the promising students in the class.

This preparedness and earnestness provide satisfaction to the students and self-fulfilment to the teachers. After all, he is given a limited time to teach an unlimited content, not always under congenial conditions. At least during the initial days of his preparation so as to earn a good name among students and parents.

Every succeeding year he experiences a gradual increase in his mastery of content and pedagogy. One cannot afford to rest on the oars and allow complacency to set in. The initial thrust and drive must be kept upto maintain the momentum all through his career.

Post-graduation and doctoral studies provide a solid content base with the strength of which a lecturer embarks on his teaching career. The thrill and excitement of addressing a gathering of adolescents and the cultivation of fluency provide immense joy to novice at college. He has a syllabus, if not a text-book, to go by and a host of reference materials for gathering information.

He has to be well informed to locate where the requisite information is available. Any attempt on his part to bestow disproportionate attention upon ornamental language at the expense of sound content would not be favoured by serious-minded students.

Teacher-student Interaction

The dynamics of a school classroom with all the question-answer sessions and activity-based teaching seem to be conspicuously missing and substituted by a sort of impersonality, if not non-accountability at the collegiate level.

The higher one ascends in the hierarchy of higher education, the less one gets involved in the business of imparting instruction. Most students are left high and dry after a mesmerising monologue in the lecture-halls. Under the garb of student initiative, many a teacher would avoid undue strain and effort.

However, if this is deliberately planned, fostered and supervised so as to instill such traits like self-reliance, praiseworthy. On the other hand, if it is an offshoot of dereliction and wilful neglect, it is likely to breed unhealthy attitudes among students. The simmering discontent among college students may be partially attributed to the ham-handed treatment meted out to them in the class.

Centrally Sponsored Scheme, 1982

In 1982, with the commissioning of INSAT transmission, it was decided that production of ETV programme will be the responsibility of educational authorities. Accordingly, a scheme was prepared by the Ministry of Education for creating Educational Television (ETV) programme production facilities within the education sector on a decentralised basis by setting up a Central Institute of Educational Technology (CIET) in the NCERT and State Institutes of Educational Technology (SIETs) in six States, i.e., Andhra Pradesh, Bihar, Gujarat, Maharashtra, Uttar Pradesh and Orissa and strengthening of ET Cells in other states.

National Policy of Educational Technology, 1986

The National Policy of Education, 1986 states that, "in order to avoid structural dualism, modern educational technology must reach out to the most distant areas and most deprived sections of beneficiaries simultaneously with the area of comparative affluence and easy availability".

This approach would intrinsically favour the use of broadcast methods with the inherent advantage of greater reach, convenience of management and cost effectiveness. Keeping this in view, the educational technological programme formulated in 1982 was reviewed and a revised scheme formulated by the Department which seeks to consolidate present efforts under the INSAT utilization programme, achieve larger programme production capabilities within the education sector and extend Radio and TV coverage to one lakh and five lakh elementary schools respectively providing receiving sets. The scheme was finalized and started in 1987-88.

Educational Technology Action Plan, 1992

(a) School Education. In school education, the Central Institute of Educational Technology (CIET) and the six State Institutes of Educational Technology (SIET) in Uttar Pradesh, Bihar, Orissa, Gujarat, Maharashtra and Andhra Pradesh continue to define the production facility.

Since April 1988, the responsibility for programme production of ETV transmission is being shouldered by CIET and SIETs. Another important development has been that the Government has decided to make these SIETs autonomous in order to make them more professional. SIETs in UP, Maharashtra, Orissa and Andhra Pradesh have already been conferred autonomous status. The working of the SIETs and their output is still sub-optimal. There is a need to improve the quality of the programmes. Increasing their output has to remain a priority during the 8th Plan.

There would be advantage in defining before-hand the optimum coverage and the objectives to be achieved by transmission of even enrichment programmes and to schedule programme production accordingly. The involvement of non-government organisations (NGOs) has not come about in any substantial manner so far.

An important initiative has been the distribution of radio-cum-cassette players and colour TVs in primary schools under the Educational Technology Scheme. So far 37, 129 schools have been provided with TV sets and 2,56,566 schools have been provided with radio-cum-cassette players.

(b) Adult Education. A beginning has been made for utilizing Education Technology for adult literacy and continuing

education. Short capsules for conveying the message of literacy appear regularly at prime time on the TV. In order to retain the interest of the neo-literates an innovative project called *'Vivek Darpan'* has been jointly launched by the Department of Electronics and Ministry of Human Resource Development.

Under this programme initially 100 villages were provided with a colour TV set and a VCR each (Together called *'Sangha Mitra')*. It is an experimental project and its experience would enable the Government to consider a larger coverage in the subsequent plans.

(c) Primary Education and Teacher Training. Recognizing the need to provide necessary background and orientation to primary and upper primary school teachers, inputs in Educational Technology have been made an integral part of in service as well as pre-service training for teachers in the DIETs. A senior lecturer and lecturer in educational technology are part of the prescribed staffing norm for each DIET.

These faculty members also serve as model points to liaise with the nearest AIR Kendras besides acting as trainers. They help them in producing educational broadcasts. Teachers Training Institutes like DIET, CTE and IASE have been provided with VCRs and colour TVs and efforts are now being made to make available adequate number of software for their optimal utilization.

(d) Higher Education. In higher education, the IGNOU has been provided a half hour slot on the national TV network early in the morning. These country-wide Class-room Programme of UGC is continuing with a two hour transmission daily between 1-2 p.m. and 4.5 p.m.

The UGC has created 15 Educational Media Research Centres (EMRCs) and Audio-Visual Research Centres (AVRCs); through these centres the UGC has been able to achieve a level of 80 per cent for indigenously produced programmes. However, in order to keep abreast with rapid developments in different areas of knowledge, programmes made abroad would have to be used optimally; a level of 15 to 20% seems reasonable.

The UGC has also developed the framework for setting up an Inter-University Consortium for Educational Communication (IUCEC) which will, on the one hand, provide coordination and leadership EMRC-AVRC and on the other, would develop as a forum to bring the Government, Universities, NGOs and other professionals together. IUCEC would also oversee and organize efficient marketing of the educational cassettes.

A notable initiative has been the preparation of a series of cassettes for each subject at undergraduate level, which would make available the benefit of good quality teaching to students all over the country.

(e) Technical Education. In technical education four Technical Teachers' Training Institutes (TTTIs) and some IITs have been provided with reasonable programme production infrastructure. About 300 programmes have been produced and made available to Polytechnics and Engineering Colleges for use through the VCRs and cinematographic equipments. Professional bodies like the Institute of Electronics and Telecommunication Engineers (IETE) have launched their own programmes of distance education and production of video films.

Provision of an educational TV channel by 1991-92 and commissioning of dedicated satellite system for education have made no progress in this period. There is a need for dedicated educational TV channel and a sufficiently larger fixed time segment for radio transmission for educational purposes.

Such stations can cater to the entire school system, non-formal education, adult-education, continuing education, higher education, vocational education and technical education. These requirements can be reasonably serviced only if educational transmission time becomes available for a major part of the day. Radio and TV transmissions have an important role to play in bringing the remote areas within the reach of good quality education. Therefore, a dedicated educational channel is an urgent requirement.

Action Plan Modified

According to Russel, strategy/action plan emphasis would be laid on improving the quality of educational programmes and optimum utilization transmission facility. For this, the following measures should be taken:

1. In SIETs association of professionals on deputation/ contract should be encouraged to professionalise the working environment.

2. Professional talent should be associated through commissioned programmes, to supplement the in-house programme production arrangements. The CIET would seek to have 10 per cent of its programmes transmitted on TV produced by professionals outside CIET.
3. The remaining SIETs should be made autonomous. Production facilities in North East will be set-up. Subject to availability of resources, creation of programme production facilities in other language zones should also be considered.
4. The UGC should set up adequate master's level courses or postgraduate diplomas in various aspects of educational programme production. To optimize returns on the investments such courses should be started where EMRC/AVRC already exist so that the cost on infrastructure does not have to be repeated. To upgrade the skills of existing technical manpower involved in production of educational TV/Radio programmes, the possibility of introducing diploma courses in suitable disciplines in certain polytechnics should be examined.
5. The EMRCs and AVRCs should be converted into autonomous departments of the university concerned and these institutions would associate professional talent from outside on tenure/contract basis to invigorate the EMRC system. One new AVRC should be set up in each of the remaining larger states in the 8th Plan.

Viewing of the educational programmes during the scheduled transmission time by large number of students poses obvious problems both in terms of management and learner outcome. Therefore, individual viewing and viewing in small groups is bound to become more and more important and it is already a fast developing area. To enable more and more students to have access to educational programmes the following measures could be taken:

1. Augmentation of equipments in SIETs/CIET.
2. Provision of receiving sets, radio-cum-cassette player and T.V. sets in larger number of primary school/upper primary schools.

3. Encouragement of educational institutions to raise resources locally to provide electronics hardware, radio, cassette players, T.V. and V.C.R. for group viewing/ listening.
4. Production of programmes for upper primary sector also.
5. Marketing of educational cassettes by the IUCEC. The revenues so earned could be used to improve and expand the programme production and viewing facilities in universities/colleges.
6. Special efforts for production of recorded audio-cassettes by CIET/SIETs to ensure optimal utilization of RCCPs. Special emphasis will be given to production of cassettes dealing with teaching of Hindi and regional languages.
7. Development of IUCEC as the nodal agency for marketing of educational software of all sectors of education.
8. Development by the IGNOU, of a large range of recorded audio of audio-visual cassettes to support its various distance education courses.
9. Setting up of training facilities for technical personnel by CIET and IUCEC on regional basis. The facility may be located either in the universities having EMRCs or in the SIETs.
10. Support by the UGC to the University/department of distance education having enrolment of 5000 or more for supplementing the programme production of the IGNOU. Independent programme production infrastructure would not be created in such departments.

The working of programme production facilities in the TITIs should be professionalised and output from these should be optimized. The IITs and Universities should undertake research for developing innovations in Education Technology and Universities.

In-service training of teachers should receive more importance through both T.V. and radio. The arrangements through CIET, once in a week would be made more effective and similar arrangements should be established under UGC transmission.

The programme of continuing education should be given

more support through *'Vivek Darpan'*, and such other programmes and awareness for literacy should continue to be built up through capsules on the TV/radio.

The IUCEC and the TTTIs/IITs and other professional agencies should make a sizeable beginning for support to professional upgradation programmes for specific professional groups like management, and medicine, etc.

There are at present over 130 universities, besides a number of institutions, which also impart higher learning. These institutions are also deemed to be universities for the purposes of the University Grants Commission Act, 1956. Many of the research laboratories and institutions are recognized by the Association of Indian Universities as centres of higher research.

The Association of Indian Universities, earlier known as Inter-University Board, provides the forum for the discussion of university problems and for the mutual recognition of degrees and diplomas awarded by the universities in India. The functions of the Association are advisory in character.

The University Grants Commission promotes and coordinates university education and determines and maintains standards of teaching, examination and research in the universities. It has the authority of making appropriate grants to different universities and implement development schemes.

Vocational and technical education is provided at school and higher levels. Most of the States have institutions for vocational and technical education at the secondary and higher secondary levels. These provide training in agriculture, commerce, engineering, forestry, medicine, animal husbandry, arts and crafts and primary school teacher training.

The Industrial Training Institutes under the Union Ministry of Labour and State Labour Departments also train persons who have studied upto the 8th or 9th standards. There are also junior technical schools which prepare students especially for the engineering trades.

Five national institutions called Indian Institutes of Technology (IITs) functioning at Mumbai, Kanpur, Kharagpur, Chennai and New Delhi provide facilities for higher level of technical education and research in engineering. These institutions admit about 1500 students annually to undergraduate courses. Besides, these institutions along with the Indian Institute of Science, Bangalore, admit nearly 2500 students every year to the post-graduate and research courses.

In addition, over 135 other engineering colleges and university departments offer facilities for post-graduate courses and research with annual intake of about 5000 students. There are also regional engineering colleges in all the States in the country and number of other technological institutions and polytechnics providing facilities for specialized courses such as mining and metallurgy, industrial engineering, forging and foundry and architecture. A number of centres have been established.

To integrate engineering education with practical training, 150 engineering colleges and polytechnics are now offering 'sandwich' courses in collaboration with the industry. The duration of such courses for degree in engineering is 5½ years and for diploma is 3½ years. India is now in a position to meet the technical manpower requirements of not only of its own industries but also export technical personnel abroad.

In addition to above in last three years, on account of government of India, Ministry of Human Resource and Development has worked very hard to develop and enlarge educational technology in many ways, which had made almost number one in the world in the field of information technology and, thus, we may hope to be so in the field of educational technology too.

QUESTIONS FOR ANSWER

1. Explain progress of Educational Technology in India during 1972-1992.
2. Write a note on the Development of Educational Technology in India during 1992-2002.
3. 'Educational Technology's impact of Teachers' Role in Education is to make teaching and learning more effective'. Justify.
4. Write short notes on:
   A. Evolution of Educational Television Programmes.
   B. Satellite Instructional Television Experiment.
   C. Production of Video Programmes in Education.

18

National Policy on Education and Educational Technology

Since the adoption of the policy on education in 1968, there had been considerable expansion in educational facilities all over the country at all levels. However, the general formulations incorporated in the 1968 policy were not translated into a detailed study of implementation. Problems of access, quality, quantity, utility and financial outlay, accumulated over the years, assumed such massive proportions that they must be talked with the utmost urgency.

Therefore, in January 1985, the Government of India announced that a New Education Policy would be formulated in the country. A Status Paper *Challenge of Education—A Policy Perspective* was issued by the Ministry of Education, Government of India. This document included a comprehensive appraisal of the existing system of education. There was a country-wide debate on educational reforms in the country. Finally, the New National Policy on Education, 1986 was approved by the Parliament in May 1986.

Though, policy formulated in 1968 was not properly implemented, yet between 1968 and 1986 and even prior to it following important educational plans were properly implemented:

Kendriya Vidyalayas

The scheme of Kendriya Vidyalayas was started in 1963-64, primarily for catering to the educational needs of the children of transferable Central Government employees including defence personnel, whose education was disrupted owing to transfer of the parents from one linguistic region to another and the resultant change in courses of study.

In 1965, the autonomous organisation, Kendriya Vidyalaya Sangathan, was established to handle the task of opening and managing Kendriya Vidyalayas. The organisation is wholly financed by the Government of India. Initially, 20 regimental schools, then functioning at places having large concentration of defence personnel, were taken over as Kendriya Vidyalayas during 1963-64. The number of Kendriya Vidyalayas at present is more than 850 in which 10 lakh students are studying.

Kendriya Vidyalayas have also distinguished themselves in co-curricular activities including game and sports, out-door activities, environmental educational programmes and fine and performing arts. Kendriya Vidyalaya students have been wining prizes every year in international and national competitions.

Most of the Kendriya Vidyalayas run nature and adventure clubs which are affiliated to the World Wild Life Fund of India and the National Adventure Foundation of India, respectively. About 10,000 students are trained in rock-climbing and about 550 are sent for trekking to glaciers every year.

Educational Technology Programme

In the previous chapter details of educational technology programme have been given. An educational technology programme was started in the central sector during the Fourth Plan period in 1972 for widening access to and bringing about qualitative improvement in education. Under the scheme a Centre of Educational Technology was set up in the NCERT and cent per cent assistance was provided to 21 States for setting up of Educational Technology (ET) Cells.

In view of the expansion of broadcasting facilities with the advent of INSAT and concomitant demand for educational software, the Ministry of Education decided to take on the responsibility of production of educational television programmes for relay through satellites.

Accordingly, a scheme was prepared by the Ministry of Education for creating Educational Television (ETV) programme production facilities within the education sector on a decentralised basis by setting up Central Institute of Educational Technology (CIET) in the NCERT and State Institutes of Educational Technology (SIETs) in six States viz., Andhra Pradesh, Bihar, Gujarat, Maharashtra, Orissa and Uttar Pradesh and strengthening of ET cells in other States.

To meet the objectives of the National Policy on Education, 1986, the Educational Technology Scheme was revised in 1987 with the broad objectives of strengthening of both ETV and audio programme production capabilities and providing wider access to the same by supplying one lakh colour television (CTV) sets and five lakh radio-cum-cassette players (RCCPs) to primary schools during the Seventh Plan.

Programme production has commenced in CIET and all the six SIETs. In fact from the academic year 1988-89, responsibility for programme production which was hitherto being shared between CIET and Doordarshan on 50 : 50 basis has been taken over by CIET and SIETs.

The satellite based ETV service presently provides educational programmes of 45 minutes duration in each of the five regional languages, viz., Gujarati, Hindi, Marathi, Oriya and Telugu telecast ontime-sharing basis. The programmes for children are telecast from Monday to Friday and for primary level teachers on every Saturday. There are separate programmes for the children in the age group of 5-8 and 9-11 years on each day.

The ETV programmes are relayed by all high and low power transmitters in the six INSAT States. The programmes in Hindi are relayed by the other five Hindi speaking States also, namely Haryana, Himachal Pradesh, Madhya Pradesh, Punjab and Rajasthan and the Union Territory of Chandigarh.

The CIET has produced 715 ETV programmes upto September, 1992 and 914 language versions. It has also produced 540 capsules for the programme of mass orientation of teachers during the summers of 1986, 1987, 1988 and 1989. The NCERT has set up a Committee to evolve modalities for involving outside producers to produce video films for CIET. As many as nine ETV video programmes commissioned to outside producers have been completed and another eight programmes are nearing completion.

Computer Education in Schools

A pilot project on Computer Literacy and Studies in Schools (CLASS) was initiated in 1984-85 in 248 selected secondary/ higher secondary schools jointly by the Department of Electronics and the Department of Education to acquaint students and teachers with the range of computer applications and its potential as a learning medium. Till 1989-90, 2,598 schools were covered under the project. 61 Resource centres were set up to train school teachers and provide logistic support to the participating schools. Installation of hardware and its maintenance continued to be the responsibility of Computer Maintenance Corporation (CMC). NCERT continued as the nodal agency for software development academic support and organisation of teachers-training.

The Steering Committee for the project was jointly headed by the Secretaries of the Department of Electronics and the Department of Education. Upto 1986-87, the schools received a set of two BBC micros, which was increased to five from 1987-88. Since the last financial year, a decision has been taken to provide an additional three BBC micros to 1,249 schools which have so far only two computers each. The evaluation of the project was done in 1986 by the Space Application Centre, Ahmedabad.

In pursuance of the objectives laid down in the NPE, an expanded programme was prepared in 1987-88 to cover 13,000 higher secondary schools all over the country. However, due to paucity of funds this was not finalised. The project is being reviewed for further expansion.

Media and Educational Technology

1. Educational technology will be employed in the spread of useful information, the training and retraining of teachers to improve quality, sharpen awareness or art and culture, inculcate abiding values, etc., both in the formal and non-formal sectors.
2. Radio and T.V. programmes, which clearly militate against proper educational objectives, will be prevented.

3. An active programme will be started to promote the production of children's film of high quality and usefulness.

National Open School

Open School, Delhi, the first of its kind in the country, was started by the Central Board of Secondary Education (CBSE), Delhi in 1979. Based on a Project Report, the Government of India decided to establish the National Open School (NOS) as a registered society and an autonomous body under the administrative control of the Department of Education, Ministry of Human Resource Development in November, 1989 and amalgamated the Open School with it. In October 1990 through a resolution of the Government of India, the NOS was vested with authority to conduct its own bridge, secondary and senior secondary examinations and issue certificates.

The NOS offers an alternative open learning system through distance education made to a heterogeneous clientele comprising the rural people, the urban poor, women, SC/ST, working adults and school drop-outs who are unable to attend the formal school system. It takes education to the doorsteps of the motivated learners and allows them to study at their own pace at places and time convenient to them. The NOS has recently introduced a variety of vocational courses. During 1993-94, 17 vocational curriculum were started.

Currently, the National Open School has a cumulative active enrolment of over two lakh students, literally from every State and UT of India. In the year of 1992-93, 57.14 per cent students were from educationally and socially disadvantaged categories, comprising women (37.29 per cent), scheduled castes and scheduled tribes (18.78 per cent), ex-servicemen (0.39 per cent) and handicapped (0.68 per cent) who are also provided fee concessions. In the NOS scheme of work, accredited institutions (AIs) have a central place and they provide various types of student services including personal contact programmes. Presently, the NOS has 339 AIs (300 for general education and 39 for vocational education) all over the country.

Educational Philosophy of New Policy, 1986

1. *New Acculturating Role of Education.* One of the most

important contributions of New Policy of Education is that it has provided a comprehensive educational philosophy covering the new acculturating role of education by way of refining sensitiveness, building scientific temper and cultivating independence of mind and spirit.

2. *Natural Perspective.* Manpower planning and its educational investment has brought in a national perspective to our development needs. A unifying policy in the development of human resources provides a social dimension to an area of personal perception. The pooling of resources in the area of personnel and research at the national level with the provision for inter-regional mobility with equal access for every Indian of requisite merit is a most welcome and a timely policy statement.

3. *Universalisation.* The universalisation of education upto a given level with access of education of a comparable quality is another positive aspect of the policy.

4. *Equalisation.* The special emphasis laid on the removal of disparities and equalization of opportunity by attending to the specific needs of different groups of distressed people including women, scheduled castes, minorities and the handicapped, should enhance the sense of social responsibility and a fair distribution of justice to all concerned.

5. *Efficiency.* The policy determination to promote efficiency and effectiveness at all levels (though easier said that done) brings in new dimension in the performance of teachers, students, administrators, Government officials and institutions.

6. *Beneficial.* The realisation the education needs to be managed in an atmosphere of utmost intellectual rigour, seriousness of purposes with adequate freedom for innovation and creativity should bear beneficial fruits.

7. *Cultural Perspective.* Another special feature of the policy is the concept of providing a cultural perspective to the formal system of education.

8. *Value Education.* The focus on value education and work experience as an integral part of the learning process will enable us to uphold human values necessary for raising the quality of life for all. The document speaks about combating certain negative values and promoting positive ones from our heritage. It mentions social, ethical and moral values which have to be cultivated.

The Essence and Role of Education

The policy has envisaged the role of education as follows:

1. Education is fundamental to our all- round development, material and spiritual.
2. Education is the highway to derive the maximum benefit from the areas already created by the economic and technical development and a means to ensure that the funds must reach all sections.
3. Education needs to be planned meticulously and developed with great sensitivity so as to make the best use of the human being who is a positive asset and precious national resource.
4. Education must prevent the erosion of long- cherished values.
5. Education should assist in the realisation of goals of secularism, socialism and professional ethics.
6. Education should be an effective instrument of reducing rural-urban disparities.
7. Spread of literacy and education among women is the largest single factor in bringing down the growth of population in India.
8. Education should develop the activity of the coming generation to internalize new ideas constantly and creatively.
9. Education should imbibe the coming generations with a strong commitment of human values and to social justice.
10. Education has an acculturating role. It refines sensitivity and perceptions that contribute to national cohesion, a scientific temper and independence of mind and spirit.
11. Education develops manpower for different levels of the economy.
12. Education is a unique investment in the present and the future.

The National System of Education

The National Policy on Education, 1986 has envisaged the following main features of the National Systems of Education:

1. *Based on Constitutional Principles.* It derives its inspiration

from the ideals and values of democracy, secularism and socialism enshrined in our Constitution.

2. *Access to Education.* It implies that upto a given level all students, irrespective of caste, creed, location, sex, have access to education of a comparable quality. To achieve this, the Government will initiate appropriately funded programmes. Effective measures will be taken in the direction of the Common School System recommended in the 1968 policy.

3. *Common Educational Structure.* It envisages a common educational structure. The 10 + 2 + 3 structure has now been accepted in all parts of the country. Regarding the further break-up of the first 10 years efforts will be made to move towards an elementary system comprising five years of primary education and three years of upper primary, followed by two years of High School.

4. *National Curricular Framework with a Common Core.* It will be based on a national curricular framework which contains a common core along with other components that are flexible. The common core will include the history of India's freedom movement, the constitutional obligations and other contents essentials to nurture national identity.

These elements cut across subject areas and will be designed to promote values such as India's common cultural heritage, egalitarianism, democracy and secularism, equality of the sexes, protection of the environment, removal of social barriers, observance of the small family norms and inculcation of the scientific temper. All educational programmes will be carried on in strict conformity with secular values.

5. *Education for International Understanding.* India has always worked for peace and understanding between nations, treating the whole world as one family. True to this hoary tradition, education has to strengthen this world view and motivate the younger generations for international co-operation and peaceful co-existence. This aspect cannot be neglected.

6. *Equality of Opportunity in Education.* To promote equality it will be necessary to provide for equal opportunity to all not only in access, but also in the conditions for success. Besides, awareness of the inherent equality of all will be created through the core curriculum. The purpose is to remove prejudices and complexes transmitted through the social environment and accident of birth.

7. *Minimum Levels of Learning.* Minimum levels of learning will be laid down for each stage of education. Steps will also be taken to foster among students an understanding of the diverse cultural and social systems of the people living in different parts of the country.

8. *Promotion of Languages.* Besides the promotion of the link language, programmes will also be launched to increase substantially the translation of book from glossaries. The young will be encouraged to undertake the rediscovery of India each in his own image and perception.

9. *Universal Character of Higher Education.* In higher education in general and technical education in particular, steps will be taken to facilitate inter-regional mobility by providing equal access to every Indian of requisite merit, regardless of his origins. The universal character of universities and other institutions of higher education is to be understood.

10. *Priorities in Educational Reform.* The Nation as a whole will assume the responsibility of providing resource support for implementing programmes of educational transformation, reducing disparities, universalisation of elementary education, adult literacy, scientific and technical research, etc.

11. *Open and Distance Learning.* Life-long education is a cherished goal of the education process. This presupposes universal literacy. Opportunities will be provided to the youth, house-wives, agricultural and industrial workers and professionals to continue the education of their choice, and the pace suited to them. The further thrust will be in the direction of open and distance learning.

12. *Strengthening of National Institutions.* National institutions which will be strengthened to play an important role in giving shape to the National System of Education, are the University Grants Commission. The All India Council of Technical Education, the Indian Council of Agricultural Research and the Indian Medical Council.

Integrated Planning will be instituted among all these bodies so as to establish functional linkages and reinforce programmes of research and postgraduate education. These, together with the National Council of Education Research and Training, the National Institute of Educational Planning and Administration and the International Institute of Science and

Technology Education will be involved in implementing the Education Policy.

13. *Meaningful Partnership*. Concurrence signifies a partnership which is at once meaningful and challenging. The Centre and the State shall give effect to it in letter and spirit.

Merits of the New Policy on Education

The 1986 policy laid down under the 12 heads containing 156 paragraphs is a comprehensive statement. It includes all the important ideas and ideals to reform and transform education in India to meet the needs of our fast developing technological society. Sincere efforts of a great magnitude will have to be made by all concerned in the implementation of the educational reforms.

Important merits of the New Policy on Education are as under:

1. *Basic Values*. The New Education Policy is based on the basic and essential values underlying the Preamble of our Constitution.
2. *The Total Man*. The New Educational Policy aims at the education of the whole man, the total man with commitment to higher values.
3. *Synthesis*. The New Education Policy is built on the foundations of ancient spirituality, modern culture and technical sophistication; history being its past experience and modern knowledge its present instrument to achievements in the future.
4. *Framework*. By linking education to development, on the one hand, and to national unity and integration, on the other it has provided a framework which is of current relevance and urgency.
5. *National Pattern*. The New Education Policy continues to be within the existing national pattern of 10 + 2 + 3.
6. *Developmental*. The design of education is truly developmental in character, enabling the students to discover, develop and discipline their talents, abilities and skills.
7. *Core Curriculum*. While emphasizing the need for a national curriculum, it provides for a core curriculum

to give adequate scope for accommodating local and regional needs.

8. *Minimum Standards.* The new system of education provides for a national minimum standard of achievement for the different stages and levels from primary to the university, including professional education.
9. *Targets.* By stressing the need of defining minimal national standards in terms of competence and learning outcomes in all subjects and for the different stages, it has focussed our attention to have clear targets to attain, both for teachers and students.
10. *Performance.* It stresses performance accounting at every level, from the individual school to the highest level.
11. *Decentralisation.* Decentralised education supervision as proposed is likely to provide more impetus to local initiative.
12. *Check on Standards.* It will decrease the present undue stress on getting marks in public examinations, by fair or unfair means and help the supervising institutions to keep a check on standards and performance.
13. *Self-Employment.* The new education policy aims at overhauling the educational systems in such a way that the students are able to practise their own vocations instead of looking for Government jobs.
14. *Anti-Prejudice.* The new education policy intends to remove narrow-mindedness from pupil's mind.
15. *Vocational.* There is the much needed thrust on vocational education under the New Education Policy. Practical and workable suggestions have been made to change the contents of education so as to make youth an instrument of evolving a new developed self-reliant, socialist and democratic India.
16. *Equalisation.* The New Education Policy has suggested important measures for minimising inequalities of opportunity of education on account of status and wealth.
17. *Job Opportunities.* The new system of education has proposed planned linkages with real job opportunities and the world of work.

18. *Delinking of Degrees.* The New Education Policy has rightly accepted that degrees have no longer remained pious documentary proof of one's learning and knowledge. Degree or diploma is not considered a last word of educational achievements.
19. *Reduction in Rush for Degrees.* The recommendations regarding 'delinking of degrees from jobs' that is to refrain employment agencies from prescribing the degrees as essential qualification for a job is likely to reduce the mad rush and craze for higher education. When 'workability' and 'performance' are given preference to degrees, degrees will automatically lose their lustre attractions and false values attached. Jobs like doctors and engineers for which degrees are essentials as a basic qualification will be identified and set aside as exceptions.
20. *Women Development.* The New Education Policy has accepted the need for infusing a spirit of boldness and self-confidence among women.
21. *Population Education.* The New Education Policy has identified the role of population in the development and needs of the society.
22. *Open Universities.* Open Universities for higher education are to be expanded besides formal educational institutions through distance education, self-studies, correspondence courses, evening classes, open university/mobile university, special studies institutes, etc.
23. *Integration with Culture.* It is for the first time that the policy lays down that integration of culture in education will be must.
24. *Primacy of Learner.* The New Education Policy envisages a place of primacy to the learner in the learning process. Self-learning and learning by doing have been recommended. Interactive teaching and relating the process of learning with environment have been emphasised to promote a spirit of discovery and inventiveness.

Eight Bold Steps

1. *National System of Education.* National system of education

to provide access to education of a comparable quality to all students, to have a common educational structure with national curricular framework containing a common core.

2. *Navodaya Schools.* Pace setting Navodaya Schools to be started which will be residential and free of charge.

3. *Vocational Targets.* Vocational courses to cover 10 per cent of higher secondary students by 1990 and 25 per cent by 1995.

4. *Delinking Degree from Jobs.* Beginning to be made in delinking degrees from jobs in selected areas.

5. *Performance and Accountability.* To ensure that all teachers should teach and all students study.

6. *The Management of Education.* Evolving a strategy of decentralization and the creation of a spirit of autonomy for educational institutions.

7. *Indian Education Service.* Constitution of this Service is likely to bring a national perspective in education.

8. *Raising Resources.* Resources to be raised through—

(i) asking beneficiary communities to maintain school buildings,

(ii) raising fees at the higher levels of education and

(iii) levying cess or charge on the user agencies.

Revised Policy Formulations, May, 1992

The National Policy of Education (NPE), 1986 is a landmark in educational development of the country. A review of the NPE, 1986 was conducted during, 1990-92. The Central Advisory Board of Education (CABE) in its 47th meeting held on May 5-6, 1992 considered the report of the CABE Committee on policy set-up to make an in-depth study of the report of the Committee for review of NPE, 1986. While broadly endorsing the policy, it recommended certain modifications in the light of the developments during the last few years and the experience gained in the implementation of the policy. The revised policy formulations containing these modifications recommended by the CABE were tabled in the Parliament on May 7, 1992.

Following the adoption of the revised policy formulations in May 1992, a revised POA was prepared. The POA 1992 was tabled in the Parliament on August 19, 1992.

Universalisation of elementary education, equalisation of educational opportunities, women's education and development, vocationalisation of school education, consolidation of higher education, modernisation of technical education, improvement of quality content and process of education at all levels continue to be the themes of national endeavour in the field of education.

Navodaya Vidyalayas

In order to provide good quality modern education to the talented children predominantly from the rural areas, Government of India launched in 1985-86 a scheme to establish Navodaya Vidyalaya on an average one in each district. 342 Navodaya Vidyalayas covering 24 States and seven Union Territories have been established in the country upto January 31, 1994. Another 17 Vidyalayas have been sanctioned and are likely to be established during 1993-94.

Admission of Navodaya Vidyalaya is at the level of Class VI. In view of the fact that most of the students so admitted would have been taught earlier through the medium of the mother tongue/regional language, instruction is provided through the same medium upto Class VI or VIII, during which time intensive teaching of Hindi/English both as a language subject and co-media is undertaken.

Thereafter, the common medium would be Hindi/English. At this stage, there is a migration of 30 per cent students in Class IX from one Navodaya Vidyalaya to another Navodaya Vidyalaya in a different linguistic region. The migration is mainly between Hindi and non-Hindi speaking districts.

Break-up of the students selected so far in 321 Navodaya Vidyalayas is as follows, as on January 31, 1994:

Boys	*Girls*	*Rural*	*Urban*	*Genl.*	*SC*	*ST*
84,548 70 per cent	35,755 30 per cent	93,058 77 per cent	27,245 33 per cent	81,438 67 per cent	24,772 21 per cent	14,093 12 per cent

Navodaya Vidyalayas are residential, co-educational and

primarily for children from rural areas. Hence, admission of children from urban areas is restricted to a maximum of one-fourth. Efforts are made to ensure that at least one-third of the students in each Navodaya Vidyalaya are girls. Reservation of seats in favour of children belonging to the scheduled castes and scheduled tribes. Upto 1993-94 16,450 vocational sections have been approved by the Central Government creating facilities for diversion of 8.22 lakh students to vocational streams at +2 level. During 1992-93 till February 10, 1993, 1,623 vocational sections have been approved creating additional facilities for diversion of 0.81 lakh students to vocational streams. Job-linked vocational courses have been started in General Insurance, Life Insurance and Railway Commercial. Some health-related vocational courses have also been started. Certain State Governments/UTs have also started some vocational courses.

Improvement of Science Education in Schools

In order to improve the quality of science education and promote a scientific temper as envisaged in NPE, a centrally sponsored scheme of Improvement of Science Education in schools was started during the last quarter of 1987-88. Under this scheme, financial assistance is provided to States/Union Territories for provision of science kits to upper primary schools, upgrade and strengthen science laboratories in secondary and higher secondary schools, upgrade libraries in secondary and higher secondary schools, set up district resource centres for science education, development of instructional materials and training of science and mathematics teachers. It also provides assistance to voluntary organisation active in the field of science education for undertaking innovative projects and resource support activities in science education.

With a view to identifying and nurturing talent in mathematics at the school level, the International Mathematical Olympiad (IMO) is held every year. India has been participating in this Olympiad since 1989. An eight member delegation comprising six student contestants, a team leader and a deputy team leader participated in IMO held in Moscow during July 1992. India ranked 22nd out of 64 participating countries. The Indian team won one silver and four bronze medals.

Environmental Orientation to School Education

In order to promote integration of educational programmes in the schools with environmental conditions, as envisaged in the NPE, a centrally-sponsored scheme of Environmental Orientation to School Education was started in 1988-89. Under the scheme, 100 per cent assistance is provided to the States, Union Territories and voluntary agencies on project basis. The project activities include review of curricular material preparation of textbooks/ instructional material/informative books/ booklets/brochures/ posters/audio-visual materials on environment, organisation of seminars for creating environmental consciousness and orientation of teachers' voluntary organisations are assisted for taking up of various kinds of experimental and innovative programmes in this field.

General Features of National Policy on Education

The above details contain only some of the most important and very special aspects of education. While keeping in view the record of 1000 years of Indian education each of the following general feature may be regarded as a revolutionary in nature and hence hereunder they are being mentioned in briefest form:

1. *The Essence and Role of Education.* Education is the key to our all-round development, material and spiritual.

2. *National System of Education.* The national system of education envisages common educational structure.

3. *A Meaningful Partnership.* There will be a meaningful partnership between the Centre and the States.

4. *Education for Equality.* All possible efforts will be made on the removal of disparities and to equalise educational opportunity by attending to the specific needs of the women, scheduled castes and scheduled tribes, the minorities and the handicapped.

A. Education for Women's Equality

1. *Basic Change.* Education will be used as an agent of basic change in the status of women. It will foster the development of new values through residential curricula, textbooks, the training and orientation of teachers, decision-makers and administrators, and the active involvement of the educational institutions.

2. *Literacy.* The removal of woman's illiteracy will receive overriding priority through provision of special support services.

3. *Participation.* Major emphasis will be laid on women's participation in vocational, technical and professional education at different levels.

B. The Education of the Scheduled Castes

The central focus in the SC's educational development in their equalisation with the non-SC population will be at all stages and levels of education, in all areas and in all the four dimensions—rural male, rural female, urban male and urban female.

C. The Education of Scheduled Tribes

Many urgent measures will be taken to bring the Scheduled Tribes at par with others. These include:

(i) opening of primary schools,
(ii) opening of residential schools including Ashram Schools.
(iii) construction of school buildings,
(iv) promotion of Tribal languages,
(v) promotion of Tribal culture,
(vi) incentive schemes like scholarship,
(vii) special remedial courses and other programmes,
(viii) encouraging educated and promising members of the Scheduled Tribes to take up teaching in tribal areas, and
(ix) opening of Anganwadies, Non-formal Education Centres and Adult Education Centres on priority basis.

D. Education of the Minorities

Greater attention will be paid to the education of minority groups in the interests of equality and social justice.

E. Education of the Handicapped

The objective will be to integrate the physically and mentally handicapped with the general community as equal partners, to prepare them for normal growth and to enable them to face life with courage and confidence.

F. Adult Education

A vast programme of adult and continuing education will be implemented through various ways and channels.

G. Re-organisation of Education at Different Stages

1. *Early Childhood Care and Education.* A full integration of child-care and pre-primary education will be brought about, both as a feeder and a strengthening factor for primary education and to human resource development in general.

2. *Elementary Education. Resolve Regarding Primary Education.* It shall be ensured that all children who attain the age of about 11 years by 1990 will have had five years of schooling or its equivalent through the non formal stream. Likewise, by 1995, all children will be provided free and compulsory education upto 14 years of age.

3. *Secondary Education.*

(i) *Curriculum.* Conscious internationalism of healthy work ethos and of the values of a human and composite culture will be brought about through appropriately formulated curriculum.

(ii) *Pace Setting Schools.* Navodaya Vidyalayas, which will be residential and free of charge, will be established in various parts of the country. These will have scope for innovation and experimentation. These schools are meant for talented children largely rural. They are envisaged to become catalysts of a nation-wide programme of school improvement.

(iii) *Vocationalisation.* The introduction of systematic, well-planned and vigorously implemented programmes of vocational education is crucial in the proposed educational reorganisation. Vocational courses will be provided after the secondary stage. It is proposed that vocational courses cover 10 per cent of higher secondary students by 1990 and 25 per cent by 1995. Steps will be taken to see that a substantial majority of the products of vocational courses are employed or become self-employed.

4. *Higher Education.*

(i) The main emphasis will be on the consolidation of,

and expansion of facilities in the existing institutions.

(ii) Admission will be regulated according to capacity.

(iii) Teacher's performance will be assessed systematically.

(iv) All posts will be filled entirely on the basis of merit.

H. National Testing Service

Concommitant with delinking, an appropriate machinery such as National Testing Service will be established in the appropriate phase.

I. Technical and Management Education

The reorganisation of Technical and Management Education should take into account the anticipated scenario by the turn of the century.

J. Promoting Efficiency and Effectiveness at all Levels

1. The process of maintaining discipline in the system must be strengthened.
2. Modernization will be undertaken to enhance functional efficiency.
3. More effective procedures will be adopted in the recruitment of staff. Institutions will be encouraged to generate resources.
4. Staff development programme will be integrated and made mandatory.
5. Excellence in performance of institutions and individuals will be recognized.
6. Select institutions will be awarded autonomy.
7. Net working systems will have to be established between education and industry.

K. Re-orienting the Content of Education

1. *Cultural Perspective.* Education and its curriculum must bring about the fine synthesis between change-oriented technologies and the country's continuity or cultural traditions. Due attention will be paid to Fine Arts, Musicology, Folklore, etc.

2. *Value Education.* Value education should have a universal appeal and should be oriented towards the unity and integration

of our people. It must be based on our heritage, national and universal goals and perception.

3. *Languages.* Language policy of 1968 must be implemented energetically and purposefully.

4. *Work Experience.* Work experience, an essential component at all stage of education must be provided through well structured and graded programmes.

5. *Environmental Education.* The aspect of environmental consciousness should be integrated in the entire educational process.

6. *Mathematics Teaching.* The teaching of mathematics will be suitably redesigned to bring it in line with modern technological devices like computers.

7. *Science Education.* Science education programmes will be designed to enable the learner to acquire problem-solving and decision-making skills and to discover the relationship of science with health, agriculture, industry and other aspects of daily life.

8. *Sports and Physical Education.* A nation-wide infrastructure for physical education, sports and games will be built into the educational edifice. Appropriate encouragement will be given to those talented in sports and games. Due stress will be laid on indigenous traditional games. Yoga will receive special attention.

L. Re-orientation of the Process of Education

1. Special attention will be paid to the production of quality books for children including textbooks and work books.
2. Provision will be made in all educational institutions for library facilities.

M. The Evaluation Process and Examination Reform

Assessment of performance is an integral part of any process of learning and teaching. As a part of sound educational strategy, examinations should be employed to bring about qualitative improvement in education. The examination system will be recast so as to ensure a method of assessment that is a valid and reliable measure of student development and a powerful instrument for improving teaching and learning. Following measures will be taken in this regard:

1. The elimination of excessive elements of chance and subjectivity.
2. The de-emphasis on memorisation.
3. Continuous and comprehensive evaluation that incorporates both scholastic and non-scholastic aspects of education, spread over the total span of instructional time.
4. Effective use of the evaluation process by teachers, students and parents.
5. Improvement in the conduct of examinations.
6. The introduction of concomitant changes in instructional material and methodology.
7. The use of grades in place of marks.
8. The predominance of external examinations will be reduced.

N. The Teacher

1. *Status of the Teacher.* The status of the teacher reflect the socio-cultural ethos of a society. The pupils cannot rise above the levels of their teachers. The Government and the community should endeavour to create conditions which will help motivate and inspire teachers on constructive and creative lines. Teacher will continue to play a crucial role in the formulation and implementation of educational programmes.

2. *Freedom to Teacher.* Teachers should have the freedom to innovate, to devise appropriate methods of communications and activities relevant to the needs and capabilities of and the concerns of the community.

3. *Pay and Service Conditions.* The pay and service conditions of teachers have to be commensurate with their social and professional responsibilities and with the need to attract talent to the profession.

4. *Teacher Education.* To provide quality education emphasis was laid on teacher education. Details given in the next chapter.

QUESTIONS FOR ANSWER

1. Write a brief note on 'Educational Technology Programme' and its utility in teaching.
2. Discuss Educational Philosophy of the National Policy on Education, 1986.

3. Discuss in brief the 'National System of Education' and its merits as per National Policy on Education, 1986.
4. Write a note on 'General Features of National Policy on Education, 1986' and its Revised Formulation of May, 1992.
5. Write short notes on the following:
   (A) National Open School.
   (B) Essence and Role of Education.
   (C) Eight Bold Steps of NEP 1986.
   (D) Navodaya Vidyalaya.
   (E) Improvement of Science Education in Schools.

19

Teacher Education and National Policy on Education

Teacher's Social Status

Teacher's duty is to devote himself to the work of acquisition, conversation and promotion of knowledge and its transmission to posterity. He learns in order to teach and also teach in order to learn. Thus, since ages teacher enjoys very high social status. Following observations make teachers' social and national status very clear.

Since ages, the teacher has been looked upon by the community as one possessing knowledge superior to that of his students. At the same time, however, he is not expected to be a walking encyclopaedia of knowledge to unfold any thing at any time. It would be a sufficient achievement, if teachers so teach that the young will learn how to discover methods of solving problems that are known or unknown. The young must be taught how to think when a method to be used is not known and the problem to be solved has not been formulated.

In the words of Prof. Humayun Kabir, "Teachers are literally the arbiters of a nation's destiny. It may sound a truism, but it still needs to be stressed that the teacher is the key to any educational, reconstruction." Teacher's influence is everlasting. He shapes the destiny of futures citizens.

The Secondary Education Commission (1952) rightly points

out "we are convinced that the most important factor in the contemplated educational reconstruction, is the teacher—his personal qualities, his educational qualifications, his professional training and the place that he occupies in the school as well as in the community."

The teacher occupies a very important place in society because he brings about the transfer of the intellectual tradition from one generation to the next. He maintains the level of technological skill and keeps the light of civilisation burning bright. "He is expected to help in the silent social revolution that is taking place in the country. His duty does not end in the classroom with his students. He owes a duty to the society and the nation. He should be abreast of the developments in the country and the world. He should be able to constantly adjust his methods and approach to suit the changing times."

The history of teacher education in India is as old as the history of Indian education itself. Education of teachers must have been born in India in 2500 B.C.

Teacher Education in Independent India

Just after independence, the Government of India took up the work of national development on priority basis but it soon realised that qualitative national development depends on qualitative education and for qualitative education good quality of teachers force is pivotal, hence for improving teacher education system in Indian universities a commission was appointed in 1948.

1. *University Education Commission (1948-49).* Appointed in free India in 1948 under the Chairmanship of late Dr. S Radhakrishnan, the then President of India the first Commission in the name of 'University Education Commission' critically scanned the teacher training programme and reported, "Our main criticism of the existing courses (but we repeat that it does not apply to them all) is that too little time is given to school practice, too little weight is given to practice in assessing the student's performance, and conditions of school practice are often unsatisfactory, sometimes, quite grossly unsatisfactory. In some places, a student is required to give only five lessons during the whole of his course."

Prescribing a remedy to this malady, the Commission stated, "We consider that in a year's course not less than twelve weeks should be spent by the students in supervised school practice. This does not mean that the supervisor should be present throughout the twelve weeks. Far from it, the students can only find his feet when he is left, from time to time, to his own unaided efforts."

Recommendations about B.Ed. Course. Regarding the theory part of the B.Ed. curriculum, the Commission suggested that the courses must be flexible and adaptable to local circumstances. In this context, the Commission recommended the following:

(i) School Practice—That the course be remodelled and more time given to school practice and more weight given to practice in assessing the students performance;

(ii) Suitable Schools—That suitable schools be used for practical training;

(iii) Make the Best—That students be encouraged to fall in with the current practices of a school and make the best of it;

(iv) Flexible Courses—That the courses on the theory of education be flexible and adaptable to local circumstances.

2. *Secondary Education Commission (1952-53).* Secondary Education Commission made following observations about teacher training. "During this one year of training the graduate teacher should be trained in methods of teaching at least two subjects... The practical training should not consist only of practice in teaching, observation, demonstration and criticism of lessons, but should include such subjects as construction and administration of scholastic tests, organisation of supervised study and students societies, conducting library periods and maintenance of cumulative records. We feel that the scope of teacher-training, particularly, in its practical aspects, should be broadened to include some of its activities that a student- teacher will be expected to perform when he becomes a full fledged teacher."

3. *Ford Foundation Team (1954).* Government of India in collaboration with Ford Foundation appointed an International team of eight experts in 1954 to study in greater detail the major recommendations of Secondary Education Commission

concerning the recruitment, selection and training of teachers and the structure and content of the curriculum in secondary schools.

The team travelled extensively in India, U.K., U.S.A. and Denmark and made the following recommendations concerning B.Ed. curriculum:

(i) The course of training should be so framed as to prepare the students adequately for the immediate work of teaching.

(ii) The training institutions should be careful not to advocate methods and techniques of teaching that are impracticable and unrealistic.

(iii) For some continuity of practice teaching, there should be the system of block practice with proper arrangements for supervision and guidance.

(iv) The training institutions should be encouraged to organise and conduct demonstration or laboratory schools where, among other things, experiments are made in curriculum construction and progressive methods of teaching are used.

Such Demonstration-schools should not be fettered by rules and regulations externally imposed but should be given freedom in matters of methods and curricula.

(v) The training institutions should expand their programmes of practical training to include other activities, besides actual classroom teaching, which teachers will be called upon to perform, as part of their work.

4. *Pires Committee (1956)*. Prompted by the criticism by the University Education Commission and Secondary Education Commission levelled against the teacher education curriculum, the Ministry of Education, Government of India, appointed a Committee in 1956 with Dr. E.A. Pires as Convener to draft a new syllabus for Secondary Teachers Training.

Draft made by the Committee was later on approved by a Conference of the Principals of Training Colleges in 1957. The Committee recommended that practical work should be given as much weightage as the theory portion. The examination papers reduced to four, as stated below:

(i) Principles of Education and School Organisation.
(ii) Education Psychology and Health Education.
(iii) Methods of Teaching Two School Subjects.
(iv) Current Problems in Indian Education.

5. *Education Commission (1964-66).* Under the Chairmanship of Dr. D.S. Kothari the Education Commission showed keen interest in teacher education, studied its varied aspects and devoted full one chapter, giving their observations and recommendations. The Commission remarked: "A sound programme of professional education of teachers is essential for the qualitative improvement of education....In the absence of other influences, a teacher tries to teach in the way in which he himself was taught by his favourite teachers and thus, tend to perpetuate the traditional methods of teaching."

The Commission observed that the essence of a teacher education curriculum is quality. In its absence, teacher education becomes a financial waste, a source of over-all deterioration of educational standards. The Commission felt that the existing programmes are largely traditional, rigid, and divorced from the realities of schools and devoid of proposed programmes of educational reconstruction. The Commission asked for the reorientation of the subject knowledge of the trainees. It recommended that provision must be made in all the training colleges for a study of the subjects to be taught, in depth as well as in range. It should be a carefully planned content-course including a study of fundamental concepts and their implications for the school syllabus, and of the textbooks and emerging source materials to assist teaching at the school stage.

Proposals About the B.Ed. Curriculum. There is need to eliminate irrelevant matter and to relate the curriculum closely to the teacher's responsibilities and to Indian conditions, problems and studies.... Moreover, student-teachers at this level need to be provided with specific learning experiences in constructing achievement and diagnostic tests in spotting talent, in developing enrichment programmes, in diagnosing difficulties of under-achievers and in planning remedial programmes.

Recommendations

(i) Key Area of Educational Development. The professional preparation of teachers, being crucial for the qualitative

improvements of education, should be treated as a key area in educational development and adequate financial provision should be made for it, both at the State and national levels.

(ii) Brought into Mainstream. In order to make the professional preparation of teachers effective, teacher educaticn must be brought into the mainstream of the academic life of the Universities on the one hand and of school life and educational developments on the other.

(iii) Improvement of Quality. The essence of a programme of teacher education is 'quality' and in it:; absence, teacher education becomes, not only a financial waste but a source of overall deterioration in educational standards. A programme of highest importance, therefore, is to improve the quality of teacher education. This can be done through the following:

(a) *Content Courses*—Organisation of well-planned subject-orientation or content courses, in collaboration with University departments (for postgraduate colleges), leading to insight into basic concepts, objectives and implications of subjects to be taught;
(b) *Integrated Courses*—Introducing integrated courses of general and professional education in universities;
(c) *Professional Studies*—Staticalizing professional studies and basing them on Indian conditions through the development of educational research.
(d) *Improved Methods of Teaching*—Using improved methods of teaching which leave greater score for self study and discussion and improved methods of evaluation which include continuous internal assessment of practical and sessional work as well as practice-teaching.
(e) *Improved Practice Teaching*—Improving practice teaching and making it a comprehensive programme of internship.
(f) *Special Courses*—Developing special courses and programmes; and
(g) *Revision of Curricula*—Revising the curricula and programmes at all levels of teacher-education in the light of fundamental objectives of preparing teachers for their varied responsibilities in an evolving system of education.

6. *First Asian Conference on Teacher Education.* Jointly sponsored by Indian Association of Teacher Education (IATE)

and the International Council on Education for Teaching (ICET) the First Asian Conference on Teacher Education was held from 14 to 19 June 1971, at Bangalore.

The Conference resolved, "The Conference takes note of the socio-economic changes that have taken place in various parts of the world in general and Asian countries in particular and recommends that the programmes of school education and Teacher Education in each country should be modified to meet the new challenges."

7. *'ITEP' Plan of National Council of Educational Research and Training (NCERT).* The Teacher Education Department of National Council of Education Research and Training launched a plan for the comprehensive improvement of teacher training under the name 'Intensive Teacher Education Programme (ITEP)' to work co-operatively with the training colleges involved, to bring about desirable change and improvement in teacher education.

In October, 1969 two conferences of the Principals of Colleges of Education, affiliated to the Punjab University, were held. Outlines of a revised programme were thrashed and following B.Ed. curriculum was agreed upon:

Part I: General Professional Course

1. Principles of Education.
2. Educational Psychology (including elementary statistics).
3. Modern Indian Education and its Problems.
4. School Organisation and Specialization in one area.

5-6. Methodology of Teaching Two School Subjects.

Part II: Student Teaching

(*a*) Preparatory Course.
(*b*) Demonstration.
(*c*) Discussion and Criticism Lessons.
(*d*) Block Practice.

Part III: Work Experience.

Part IV: Sessional Work

(*i*) Preparation and Use of Aids.
(*ii*) Blackboard Work.
(*iii*) Co-curricular Activities.
(*iv*) Psychology Practicals.

(v) Study of School Plant.
(vi) Evaluation and Record Keeping.
(vii) Study of School Records.

8. Efforts of Indian Association of Teacher Educators (IATE). The Indian Association of Teacher Educators, formerly known as All India Association of Training Colleges, the only national organisation of teachers of training institutions, have been organising annual conferences beginning with their first meet at Baroda in 1950.

Baroda Study Group

In collaboration with National Council of Educational Research and Training, IATE constituted a Study Group popularly known as Baroda Study Group to revitalize the B.Ed. Programme which met at Baroda in 1964 and made following broad recommendations regarding B.Ed. courses:

(i) *(a)* The duration of the B.Ed. courses be increased to one complete year of twelve months.
(b) Habit of self-study should be encouraged in B.Ed. trainees.
(c) Provision be made for specialization in a single teaching field rather than in two Special Methods.
(d) A Committee for revising the existing B.Ed. syllabus be appointed. While revising the syllabus, it should have three objectives in view: (*a*) a grounding in the fundamentals of principles of education (*b*) subject matter competency, and (*c*) competence in the art of teaching. The Committee should evolve a suitable system for evaluation.

(ii) There should be a systematic and comprehensive programme of practical work which should include:
(a) Practice teaching.
(b) Observation of pupils and lessons.
(c) Criticism lessons.
(d) Study of different types and grades of schools.
(e) Organisation of and participation in co-curricular activities.
(f) Follow-up assignments given to school children.
(g) Preparation of case studies.

(*h*) Construction and administration of scholastic achievement tests.
(*i*) Black-board work.
(*j*) Socio-metric study of groups in the class-room.
(*k*) Practical work connected with school subjects.
(*l*) Preparation and use of audio-visual aids.
(*m*) Experimental and laboratory work for science students as well as simple workshop practices.

(*iii*) For practical work, the trainee should be placed in a school for 8-12 weeks and associated with the institution as a regular member of the staff.

The B.Ed. Programme

In collaboration with the Education Commission (1964-66), IATE appointed a Working Group with Miss S. Panandikar as convener to design a new B.Ed. programme, which was discussed and approved by their Eighth Conference held at Taradevi (Simla) in 1965. Following recommendations were made:

Part A—Theory

Paper 1—Foundations of Educations (Psychological); Educational Psychology including Evaluation.

Paper 2— Foundations of Education (Philosophical and Sociological).

Paper 3—Education in India.

Paper 4—Teaching of two school subjects (including content courses and teaching methods)

N.B. 1. For those interested, there should be provision for the study of one special field on an optional basis. Subjects offered should be related to school work. These may be:

(*a*) School Library Work.
(*b*) Guidance.
(*c*) Audio-visual Education.
(*d*) A selected art of craft.

2. Under each theory paper, a scheme of organised practical and sessional work should be developed.

Part B—Practice Teaching and Related Practical Work

Practice teaching, extending over 8-10 weeks, should include all aspects of teacher's work. It should be continuous and should be preceded by observation of school programmes in selected schools under the guidance of experienced teachers. The demonstration school of the Training College should also be utilised for this purpose.

Practical work related to Practice Teaching should include the following:

1. Observation of lessons by experienced teachers and staff of the college.

2. Planning units and lessons.

3. Discussion of lesson plans and Unit plans and Lessons given (Criticism Lessons).

4. Organisation of and participation in co-curricular activities.

5. Setting Follow-up assignments.

6. Evaluation in terms of educational objectives; use of teacher-made tests; administration of standardised scholastic achievement tests.

7. Blackboard work.

9. Practical work connected with school subjects.

9. Preparation and use of audio-visual aids related to methods of teaching.

10. Experimental and laboratory work in Science, Home Science, Geography and other subjects needing such work.

11. Study of the organisation of work and activities in the school.

12. Observation and assistance in the Health Education Programme.

13. Observation and assistance in the guidance programme and maintenance of cumulative records.

14. Devising techniques of teaching large classes.

9. *National Commission on Teachers—1 (1983-85)*. Under the Chairmanship of Prof. D.P. Chattopadhyaya, the National Commission on Teachers-I (for school teachers) in their report, wrote one chapter on the training of teachers and made following recommendations:

1. *Four-year Training Course*. A four-year training course after senor secondary, or preferably a 5 year course leading to graduation and training is recommended. Each State may make a beginning during the Seventh Plan Period by starting at least one four-year integrated college of education. The first degree in teaching. B.A./B.Sc., B.Ed., should be considered adequate

to pursue postgraduate courses. Planning of the contents of the four-year integrated course should be done in consultation with university authorities.

2. *Capital Grants.* A four-year integrated college will need a capital grant of Rs. 20 lakhs to enlarge and improve its physical facilities. Its recurring support will imply an expenditure of Rs. 24,000 per annum for every additional member of the faculty during the Seventh Plan Period.

3. *One-year B.Ed. Course.* The duration of one year B.Ed. course should be extended by two summer months ensuring an academic session of 220 days with longer working hours.

4. *Two-year Training Course.* For elementary teachers, it is desirable to have a two-year training course after Class XII. Efforts may be made to have this pattern established as the normal pattern of training for elementary teachers as early as possible. The possibility of developing a four-year integrated programme after Class X with a built-in provision for upward mobility should also be explored.

5. *Criteria for Selection of Trainees.* While selecting a teacher for training, the following factors may be taken into consideration:

(i) Good physique;
(ii) Linguistic ability and communication skills;
(iii) A fair degree of general mental ability;
(iv) General awareness of the world;
(v) A positive outlook on life; and
(vi) Capacity of good human relations.

Selection of trainees should be made through a combination of objective tests, rating scales, group-discussion and personal interviews.

6. *On-the-Job Training.* The approach could also be tried out to recruit an untrained first class graduate/postgraduate and then give him on-the-job training to be followed by full training through correspondence and contact programme.

7. *Elements of Curriculum.* The integrated four-year curriculum for a degree in education should consist of two elements, namely, general education and professional preparation.

A. General Education will include:

(i) Study of a language.

(ii) Three or four discipline from among the subjects taught at school.

(iii) Seminars, Projects and study-visits.

B. The professional preparation part should consist of:

(i) Study of education as a discipline including educational psychology, sociology of education and educational philosophy;

(ii) Practice of teaching and its content-cum-methodology; and

(iii) Learning a variety of skills related to the role of a teacher, including educational technology and preparation of software.

8. *Cadre of Teacher Educators.* A cadre of teacher educators in educational technology may be formed. One such educator may be appointed in each college of education.

9. *Joint Responsibility.* The preparation of a teacher must be considered a joint responsibility of the College of Education and the practice teaching school.

10. *Role Experience.* A part from teaching methods, the pupil teacher should also gain experience of his other roles such as organisation of co-curicular activities and working with the community.

11. *Internship.* The word 'Practice teaching' should be replaced by the word 'Internship' as it suggests a much more comprehensive concept of teacher training. The duration of the Internship should not be less than four weeks in the third year and 3 weeks in the fourth year of study. During this period, stress should be laid on blackboard writing, drawing, skills, making and improving aids to learning, and using technological equipments. Participation in co-curricular activities like games, sports, music, dance, drama should be obligatory.

12. *Tools for Evaluation.* The faculty must evolve the right tools for evaluation of pupil-teacher performance in the class. It must also take into account attitude to work, love for children, scientific outlook etc. Self-assessment and pre-lesson and post-lesson discussion should be encouraged.

13. *Training for One-year B.Ed.* In the case of the one year B.Ed., a period of six weeks, preceded by a general introduction to the life and work at school for one week, should be the minimum.

14. *Review of Teacher Education Curriculum.* The teacher education curriculum prepared by the National Council for Teacher Education, 1978, should be reviewed by Boards of Studies in Education of various universities, and suitably modified.

15. *Preparation of Teacher Educators.* The teacher educators in Colleges of Education should be drawn both from disciplines of various school subjects and educational disciplines like psychology, sociology, philosophy etc. The minimum qualification for a teacher educator should be postgraduate degree in the subject and a B.Ed. preferably an M.Ed. degree. Their continual in-serveice education must also be assured so that Colleges of Education can form part of the mainstream academic life of their respective universities.

16. *Specialised Staff.* As some lecturers in the teachers' training colleges are not qualified to teach the subject entrusted to them, it is desirable that colleges of education should offer only such subjects for specialization for which they have the qualified staff.

17. *Full Strength Staff.* Keeping in view the needs of the trainees, steps should be taken by the universities to ensure full staff strength.

18. *Teacher-Trainers' Proficiency.* The teacher trainers themselves should be proficient in the use of skills they seek to develop among their trainees, particularly, in the service and maintenance of hardware of educational technology and must be knowledgeable about the available sources for software (educational technology).

19. *Trainers' Workshop.* To develop planning and organizational skills in co-curricular activities, colleges should depute their teacher trainers to participate in specially conducted workshops for which help of institutions like Bal Bhavan, National School of Drama and National Film Institute could be taken.

20. *Training Curriculum for Elementary Teachers.* It will consist of general education. Sufficient emphasis needs to be given to the mastering of language and communication skills and to the trainee's value orientation.

21. *Professional Preparation.* Pedagogy, practice teaching, development of skills such as story-telling, recitation, writing

on the black-board, use of new technology etc. are important for professional preparation. A greater emphasis is essential on art, music, craft and dance.

22. *Duration of Practice Teaching.* Not less than six to eight weeks in the first year and twelve weeks in the second year should be allowed to practice teaching. The trainees may start with one or two lessons a day but should gradually be accepted to stay for the whole day and take on full responsibilies of a regular teacher. This alone will develop in them needed professional competence and personal confidence.

23. *The Teacher Education for the Elementary Training Institutes.* There should be drawn primarily from the cadre of practising primary schools. The minimum qualification of the other staff should be a postgraduate degree with B.Ed. training. Their continued in-service education is equally important.

24. *Separate Cadre for Teacher Training.* The practice of transferring least effective district Inspectors of Schools to the Teacher Training Institutes must stop forthwith. A separate cadre for those in teacher training, in-service education and research should be formed, if necessary to ensure qualitative improvement in elementary preparation.

25. *Correspondence-Cum-Contact Courses for B.Ed. Training.* This should be allowed only if, satisfactory arrangements exist for practice and proper supervision.

10. National Policy on Education (NPE) (1986)—

1. *Recommendations.* Teacher education is a continuous process, and its pre-service and in-service components are inseparable. As the first step, the system of teacher education overhauling.

2. *Continuing Education.* The new programmes of teacher education will emphasize continuing education and the need for teacher to meet the thrusts envisaged in this Policy.

3. *District Institutes of Education and Training (DIET).* There will be established with the capability to organize pre-service and in-service courses for elementary school teachers and for the personnel working in non-formal and adult education.

Substandard institutions will be phased out as DIETs get established. Selected Secondary Teacher Training Colleges will be upgraded to complement the work of State Councils of Educational Research and Training.

The National Council of Teacher Education will be provided the necessary resources and capability to accredit institutions of teacher education and provide guidance regarding curricula and methods. Net working arrangements will be created between institutions of teacher education and University Departments of Education.

Programme of Action (1986)

Government of India came out with a concrete, specific and detailed Programme of Action for implementation of Teacher Education as a follow-up measure of National Policy on Education.

1. *Overhaul of Teacher Education.* NPE calls for overhaul of teacher education, as the first step toward educational reorganisation. Selected institutions would be developed as District Institutes of Education and Training (DIET), both for pre-service and in-service courses of elementary school teachers and for continued education of the personnel working in non-formal and adult education programme. Reorganisation of secondary teacher education system is also implied in the policy.

2. *NCTE.* The National Council of Teacher Education will be given the statutory status and necessary resources to play its role.

3. *Reorganisation of Elementary Teacher Education.* Change in the educational system will be brought about by the radical transformation of the present system of Elementary Teacher Education. The functions of an Elementary Teacher Education institution would include:

(i) Pre-service and in-service education of teachers for the formal school system.

(ii) Induction level and continuing education of Non-formal and Adult Education Instructors and Supervisors.

(iii) Training and orientation of heads of institutions in institutional planning and management and micro-level planning.

(iv) Orientation of community leaders, functionaries of voluntary organisations and others influencing school level education.

(v) Academic support to school complex and District Boards of Education.

(vi) Action research and experimentation work.

(vii) Serving as evaluation centre for primary and upper primary schools as well as Non-formal and Adult Education Programme.

(viii) Provision of service of a resource and learning centre for teacher and instructors.

(ix) Consultancy and advice, for example to DBE's.

4. *Task Force.* Keeping in view the various relevant programmes of action each State Government will set up a Task Force for making an assessment of the number of such institutions required in the State. The Task Force will also identify the existing institutions which can be developed as District Institutes of Education and Training. Substandard institutions would be phased out as DIETs get established.

5. *Functions of DIET.* The DIET will perform all the functions mentioned in the preceding paragraph. The head of DIET would be of the status of a Principal of a Degree College/B.Ed. College. Most of the faculty members would be persons with background in elementary education.

Special selection procedure will be established to ensure that ablest persons are selected, given higher scales of pay and are reoriented in co-operation with NCERT, NIEPA, SCERTs, University Departments of Education, some outstanding teachers etc.

The NFE/Adult Education District Resource Units would be an integral part of DIET for which additional faculty will be provided. On this programme, Centrai Government will meet a major share in funding.

6. *Facilities of Latest Technology.* These will be provided at DIETs such as computer-based learning. VCR, TV etc. The teachers receiving training at DIETS would be encouraged to develop their own programmes using the facilities available at DIETs and to use these materials as instructional resources. Capability for making copies of video cassettes, audio cassettes, etc. would also be provided in these institutes. Besides, imaginative use of traditional teaching aids would be emphasized. Teachers would be encouraged to improvise their own instructional materials.

7. *Secondary Teacher Education.* The responsibility for

secondary teacher education would continue to rest with Colleges of Teacher Education, affiliated to universities in co-operation with NCTE the university will exercise responsibility for academic aspects including conduct of examinations, award of degrees, and ensuring quality of secondary teacher education institutions. These institutions would also be responsible for continuing education programme for secondary teachers.

8. *Comprehensive Institution.* Some colleges of Teacher Education will be developed as comprehensive institutions, organising programmes for primary teacher education and possibly also, 4-years' integrated courses after higher secondary stage, in addition to the usual B.Ed., M.Ed courses.

These comprehensive institutions would also be provided facilities and staff for undertaking research and to supplement the efforts of State Councils of Educational Research and Training (SCERT). In order to promote innovations and experimentation, good colleges and departments of education of universities will also be given autonomous status.

9. *In-service Education of Teachers.* The needs for in-service education of teachers arise from several sources, such as, changing national goals, revision of school curricula, additional inputs in teaching-learning system, inadequate background of teachers, etc.

SCERTs would play the major role of planning, sponsoring, monitoring and evaluating the in-service education programme for all levels of teachers, instructors and other educational personnel. The state level agency would take cognizance of all the needs before preparing a programme of in-service education for a given period of times.

10. *Functions of SCERTs.* SCERTs would prepare suitable material for in-service education of teachers, undertake orientation of key persons, monitoring and evaluation of programmes. Similar steps for training of teachers in vocational stream should also be taken be SCERTs.

11. *The District Institutes of Education and Training for the Primary Level.* These would be the major agency to conduct the programme of in-service education for primary teachers. Assistance would be sought from school complexes in the district.

In case of secondary school teachers, the programmes would be extended through teacher training institutions and the Centres for Continuing Education. The district level education officer will help in effective conduct of the programmes.

12. *Distance In-Service Education.* This will be prepared and extended with the help of broadcasting agencies. SCERTs would be equipped with necessary resources for production of learning material other than print. Minimum essential equipment to record audio, video programmes would be provided to each SCERT.

Comprehensive colleges of education as well as DIETs would also be provided production facilities in a phased manner. Production facilities at DIETs and the colleges may not be of professional quality which would produce material which can be used in its own training programmes and can also be shared by other sister-organisations.

Experiences specially those of voluntary organizations should be drawn upon in designing courses, development of material and strategies for in-service education.

13. *Cadre of Teacher Education.* A separate cadre will be created for appointment of staff in SCERTs, secondary teacher education institutions and DIETs. Persons selected to this cadre will receive incentives such as housing and placement in a higher scale of pay.

Special arrangements will be made to ensure their continuing education. An inter-change will be organised between teaching and teacher education. To enable people from this cadre to go as teachers for 1-2 years, every 4-5 years sufficient number of supernumerary/reserve positions will be created in schools.

14. *National Council of Teacher Education (NCTE).* NCTE has been in existence since 1973. To remedy difficulties inherent in its constitution, it will be conferred autonomous and statutory status. It would perform the following functions:

(i) Accreditation/disaccreditation of institutions of teacher education.

(ii) Laying down of standards and norms for institutions of teacher education.

(iii) Development of guidelines for curricula and methods of teacher education.

(iv) Other functions like earning of credit for in-service education, duration of various courses, emphasis to be laid in training programmes for NFE/AE instructors,

place of correspondence education in teacher education etc.

Preparation of learning material, orientation of senior teacher educators etc. may continue to be performed by NCERT, SCERTs, in co-operation with NCTE.

15. *The Curriculum for Teachers' Training*. It needs to be revised in the light of the new policy thrusts. There should be an emphasis on integration of education and culture, work experience, physical education and sports, the study of Indian culture and the problems of the unity and integration of India.

Curriculum should bring out the importance of Planning and Management. Educational technology will influence methodologies contents and design of teaching learning process.

16. *New Learning Material Reflecting Indian Experience.* As there is too much emphasis on textbooks having Western ideas, teachers under training do not get exposed to Indian philosophical and psychological concepts of education.

Therefore, NCERT and UGC should undertake the task of preparing new learning materials, which would include textbooks, reference books, anthologies, slides, films, etc. reflecting the Indian experience in education.

17. *Teacher and Adult Education and Development Programmes.* Adult education is both a process through which effective delivery mechanisms are created for the deprived sections of society, and a forum through which such sections secure information and understanding regarding the processes of development. Hence it is of importance that effective linkage is established between adult education and development programmes. Some of the ways in which this can be done are:

(a) Special literacy primers and other reading material will be developed for the beneficiaries of IRDP and NREP to enable them to understand their rights and responsibilities.

(b) Efficacy of ICDS has suffered due to discontinuance of the competent of functional literacy of adult women. This programme will be restarted in the form of Functional Literacy of Women (FLOW) which would be an integral part of ICDS.

(c) The various programmes for development of SC/ST and other educationally backward sections will include

a component of literacy and adult education wherever possible.

(d) Programmes of labour welfare will give special attention to literacy and adult education. Employers will be required, if necessary by law, to organize literacy and skill development programmes for all their employees. Welfare Funds for various categories of workers, will be used for running literacy and adult education programmes and due attention given in the various schemes for unorganized workers.

(e) Literacy and adult education will also form an important part of the various programmes of women's development.

(f) Starting with 50 Nehru Yuvak Kendras in 1986-87, all NYKs will take up in their district one project of 100 functional literacy centres in one block each.

18. *Teachers for Mass Functional Literacy.* NPE places complete faith in country's youth, teachers, workers and peasants. In conformity with this spirit, it is intended to give a marked slant to NPAE from the present intensive selective activity on a limited scale to a mass programme. Its main features would be as follows:

(a) Literacy work would be taken up by a large number of students as "study service'—viz., specific projects taken up as a part of work experience and social/national service, which would be reflected in students' final result sheets.

(b) Substantial institutional incentive will be provided to universities, colleges, higher secondary/secondary schools for eradication of illiteracy in a well-defined area.

(c) Trade unions, Panchayati Raj agencies and other representative organizations of people will be encouraged to voluntarily take up functional literacy programme for which literacy kits and some organizational expenses would be provided to them.

(d) Encouraging individual to look upon literacy work as a personal commitment and voluntary service, particularly, by women, among women and involvement of voluntary agencies for this purpose.

19. *Teaching for Continuing Education.* Continuing education is an indispensable aspect of the strategy of human resource development and of the goal of creation of a learning society. Continuing education includes post-literacy for neo-literates and school drop-outs for retention of literacy skills, continuation of learning beyond elementary literacy and application of this learning for improving their living conditions.

20. *Teaching of Different Levels.* Detailed planning at the district level for illiteracy eradication would be the responsibility of the District Boards of Education (DBE). Technical assistance would be provided to DBE by the District Resource Units. DBE should undertake:

(a) Spatial allocation of responsibility among the various agencies implementing the programme;
(b) Provide overall guidance to DRUs;
(c) Coordinate the Mass Programme;
(d) Guide and coordinate the adult education programmes undertaken by the employers, etc.

Motivational Plans

With a view to motivate the teachers to be dutiful as well as effective and efficient together with raising the prestige of teachers and teaching profession in the society, following steps have been taken by the government:

1. Teachers Day

On 5th day of September each year, students, their parents, social organizations and even education department of the government gives public recognition to teachers of outstanding merit. No other profession has such a day to observe officially.

2. National Awards to Teachers

The scheme of National Awards to teachers, introduced in 1958 with the object of raising the prestige of teachers and giving public recognition to teachers of outstanding merit, continued in 1989. The number of awards allotted to a state depends upon the number of teachers. However, each State/UT is entitled to at least one award each for the categories of primary and secondary school teachers. The number of awards have been increased in 1986 from 186 to 300. Of these, 272 awards are for primary and secondary school teachers of different States/UTs. Four awards each for teachers of Kendriya Vidyalayas and schools, affiliated to CBSE, 15 awards for teachers of Sanskrit Pathashalas and 5 for Arabic/Persian teachers of Madrassas run on traditional lines due to their limited number. States also give awards to their teachers. Those who receive these award, get extension in service for 2 more years.

3. National Foundation for Teachers' Welfare (NFTW)

The National Foundation for Teachers Welfare (NFTW) was set up in 1962 under th Charitable Endowments Act, 1980.

Financial assistance from the National Foundation for Teachers' Welfare is granted to teachers for the following purposes:

* Construction of Shikshak Sadans.
* Paid holidays to eminent teachers who have rendered meritorious services.
* Support for professional education of children to school teachers.
* Medical reimbursement to teachers suffering from ailments.
* Gratuitous relief to teachers in cases of serious accidents.
* Subsidy for academic activity of teachers.
* Excursion tours of teachers.
* Assistance to teachers and their dependents in indigent circumstances.

QUESTIONS FOR ANSWER

1. Write a note on the efforts made between 1948 and 1983 for improving the teacher education in India.
2. Write a note on Intensive Teacher Education Programme of NCERT.
3. Write a note on the recommendations of National Commission on Education, 1983-85.
4. Discuss the outline of Teacher Education as per National Policy on Education Programme of Action, 1986.
5. Write short notes on the following:
   (a) Kothari Commission's recommendations about Teacher Education.
   (b) Recommendations of Baroda Study Group about B.Ed. Courses.
6. Motivational Plans for the Teachers.

20

Education in the New Millennium: The Task Ahead

India is a developing country but it realises importance of education and hence, since independence it is striving for providing education to its people and developing educational technology to ensure speedy development of the nation but due to financial difficulties, the targets set for the purpose have not been achieved, therefore, much has to be done in the 21st Century. We attempts to discuss the same in this chapter.

All people strive hard to build up their nation in such a way that they could enjoy the fruits of a welfare society. In fact, it is the endeavour of the individual, as well as that of the society, to maximize the benefits through various welfare measures, "Greatest Happiness of the Greatest Number" has been the motto of developing countries. Education has been recognized as the most crucial and significant factor in activising and optimising the welfare of the society through its ramifications in almost all spheres of life.

Economic development, social welfare and cultural progress are the ultimate goals of any nation, but there are innumerable internal and external challenges in attaining these goals in an ever-changing world of science and technology. The New Education Policy, while stressing the vital role of education as vehicle of socio-economic development, raises the clarion call to the nation thus, "Education is the most effective instrument to meet these challenges. Only education can imbue people with knowledge, a sense of purpose and the confidence essential for building a dynamic, vibrant and cohesive nation, capable of providing its people with the wherewithal for creating better, fuller and more purposeful lives."

Knowledge Explosion

It is estimated in an UNESCO study that human knowledge doubled from the beginning of the Christian era to the year 1500, doubled again from 1500 to 1800, from 1800 to 1900, 1900 to 1945, 1945 to 1960, 1960 to 1970. Please note the narrowing down of the period taken for doubling of knowledge. Every decade saw phenomenal progress in this technotronic age.

UNESCO's estimates are presently not applicable to India, therefore, in the 21st century we will have to work hard to achieve the essential features of national educational policy which are as follows:

* Education is fundamentally for an all-round personality development of the individual.
* Education should help to develop the necessary skilled manpower for different levels of the Indian economy.
* Education is no more a mere consumption good but is an investment for the future and hence, greater share of the national economy should be diverted in making the system more effective.
* Education has to be provided to all, at the same time the quality of education has to be maintained, irrespective of the quantitative expansion of study. Modern technological and scientific developments should find an application in improving the efficiency of the education system. To achieve the above goals, we need to take care of the following aspects and develop them accordingly.

Educational Technology

During the last two decades, many significant developments have taken place in the discipline of eduction. Educational technology has become a very major and useful area of knowledge relevant for more efficient and effective functions of teaching-learning system.

There are two subtle aspects of educational technology—Technology in Education and Technology of Education.

Technology in Education covers every possible means by which knowledge or information can be presented interestingly. It is concerned with various equipments such as projectors, overhead projectors, television, computers etc., used for education and training.

Technology of Education is concerned with the better understanding of the learners and learning processes and how best the available resources can be used optimally for producing learning in the minimum time possible.

The new developments in psychology, social and behavioural sciences have shown us many innovative methods, techniques and strategies in maximizing the learning outcomes. There is a practical need to develop all above elements.

Updating Curriculum

It has been found by several research studies that updated education is the core and crux of all developmental activities at all levels, starting from the workers to the top level managers and administrators. We all know that stagnated water becomes polluted; so also knowledge; one should update his knowledge and skills in fast changing world of science and technology otherwise he will be rejected by society.

Curriculum revision and renewal is the only means through which the education system can become a real instrument of social change and development. In the face of all this our efforts sometimes, dissipates because of lack of such updated education among the masses and the expected results cannot be achieved.

The curriculum is to be updated to match the challenges and required curriculum materials are to be designed including application of mass media and educational technology.

The Government of India, which had been inept for eduction reform in spite of its appointment of several commissions, suddenly emphasized the significant role of education in our country's development through the New Education Policy.

Naturally, we witnessed what seemed to be an awakening in the country to modernize the whole of the education system.

Thus, the New Education Policy has been evolved to usher in a golden period in our country's development.

New Inputs

What are to be the new inputs? Instructional processes should be based on the needs, abilities and interest of learners.

* Better organization of space for group learning and independent learning will be applied.
* A teacher should be a facilitator in helping the students to learn rather than a transmitter of knowledge.
* Methods to monitor the progress of student's learning at every stage and to provide guidelines.
* Information technology should find an extensive role in all teaching-learning activities.
* Conventional face to face teaching will be slowly reduced and self-study through various resource materials will be encouraged.
* Open education channels are developing fast.
* Multi-media libraries should be established and promoted in the place of libraries with mere printed material.
* More credit based modular education programmes will be developed and implemented.
* There is great emphasis on the faculty staff development through regular in-service education and training programmes at all levels. The NEP has given us the Academic Staff Colleges in Universities.

Apart from in-service education, continuing, education programmes with credit approach will be promoted.

Curriculum will be designed scientifically and linked with career development of people.

The NEP has also realized that the education system developed by the Britishers is not suitable to attain all the lofty objectives in moulding the modern India. The NEP is attempting to re-link learning with life as it is in India and this is very essential to achieve our aims.

In order to provide education for all including the people in the remote rural areas and to meet the increasing demands of education, there is need to deploy the modern educational technology and mass media. These traditional system of classroom teaching alone would not help us in attaining the universalisation of education through formal and non-formal channels. The launching of satellite will be immensely useful in expanding our educational programmes, which we have done.

National Integration

The New Education Policy rightly emphasises the vital factors in achieving the superb goal of shaping the egalitarian society. In a vast country like India, it is national integration that should receive topmost priority as otherwise all our efforts will be shattered into pieces because of fissiparous tendencies. The strategy adopted to strengthen national integration are many. Out of this the common core curriculum plays a vital role in making the future citizens shed their differences and live as unified people of our nation.

Any effort to jeopardise national integration will damage the entire country's progress. The introduction of common core curriculum with its built-in flexibility to the regional culture, respecting each other's culture will go a long way in strengthening the nation.

In a developing country like ours, if so many are to be employed on skilled jobs, every scrap of potential talent in our national must be utilized. The U.S. found that by providing education for all upto the age of 18, many more skilled workers were produced who were more adaptable and had greater power of concentration.

In our nation, the potentialities of millions of children are yet to be realized despite our efforts.

Literacy Rate

According to the 1991 Census, the national literacy rate for the population aged seven years and above increased from 43.56 per cent in 1981 to 52.21 per cent in 1991 registering an increase by 8.65 percentage points. While male literacy increased by 7.75 per cent, the female literacy rate increased by 9.53 per cent. The number of literates aged seven and above in 1991 at 3,953 lakh compares very well with the number of literates at

2,357 lakh in 1981. The number of illiterates in 1991 was 3,289 lakh which is a marginal increase form the 3,053 lakh in 1981.

The increase in the number of literates in 1991 over 1981 was 1,236 lakh whereas the corresponding increase in the number of illiterate was 236 lakh only. Kerala (89.81 per cent) tops the literacy rates followed by Mizoram (82.27 per cent), Lakshadweep (81.78 per cent), and Chandigarh (77.81 per cent). At the end of the ladder are Bihar (38.48 per cent), Rajasthan (38.55 per cent) and Dadra and Nager Haveli (40.71 per cent). The increase in the literacy rate has been very significant in the States/Union Territories—Sikkim (19·29 per cent), Lakshadweep (17.59 per cent), Nagaland (14.45 per cent), Daman & Diu (12.90 per cent), Haryana (13.57 per cent), Manipur (13 per cent), Andaman and Nicobar Islands (12.63 per cent), Tripura (11.65 per cent) and Kerala (10.47 per cent). The literacy rate is above the all India level of 52.21 per cent in case of 22 States/Union Territories but nine States/Union Territories viz. Bihar, Rajasthan, Arunachal Pradesh, Madhya Pradesh, Uttar Pradesh, Andhra Pradesh, Meghalaya, Orissa and Union Territory of Dadra and Nagar Heveli are still below the threshold level of literacy i.e., 50 per cent. All these States/Union Territories except Meghalaya, are also below the all India level in case of female literacy.

The above figures establish that we are far behind our goal. Almost similar situation is applicable in the following programmes concerning various sections targeted by the NEP:

1. Primary Education,
2. Non-Formal Education,
3. The National Bal Bhavan Project,
4. Lok Jumbish Education for all,
5. Women's education,
6. Mahila Samakhya (Education for Women's Equality),
7. Integrated Education for Disabled Children,
8. Environmental Orientation to School Education,
9. National Talent Search Scheme,
10. Education for S.C. and S.T.,
11. Minorities Education, and
12. Adult Education.

Therefore, greater efforts are to be made to achieve the objectives of National Policy on Education but for that population control is must, otherwise, targets set, will not be achieved. Hence proper planning is needed.

Teacher Education

In the previous chapter, we have mentioned provisons concerning teacher education in India, but we still do not have good number of properly trained teachers in our schools and large number of trained teachers, too, do not have enough knowledge about various basic aspects of educational technology, therefore, in the 21st century National Council for Teacher Education and NCERT both together will have to work hard for creating a qualitative teacher force well trained in educational technology for qualitative, effective and efficient teaching as per socio-politico needs of the nation. This is a major task and if we fail in it, then we will fail in achieving the goals and objectives of NEP, because without qualitative teachers, qualitative education is impossible and the same is applicable to the working of U.G.C. in respect of university education, which too at present is not in good shape. Some facts concerning all these institutions are as follows:

As envisaged in NPE and POA-1986, the centrally sponsored scheme of Restructuring and Reorganisation of Teacher Education was taken up in 1987 to create a viable institutional infrastructure, and academic and technical resources base for orientation/training and continuous upgradation to knowledge, competence and pedagogic skills of elementary education teachers in the country. The scheme envisaged setting up of DIETs in each district to provide academic and resource support to elementary education teachers and NFE/AE instructors.

It also envisaged upgradation of selected Secondary Teacher Education Institutions (STELs) into CTEs and IASEs to organise pre-service and in-service training for secondary teachers and to provide extension and resource-support services to secondary schools.

IASEs were expected to conduct programmes for preparation of elementary teachers educators—to conduct in-service training for elementary and secondary teacher educators and principals of secondary schools; to engage in advanced level fundamental and applied research especially of interdisciplinary nature, and to provide academic guidelines to DIETs and support services to CTEs. Till the end of 1997-98, 444 DIETs have been sanctioned, 76 CTEs and 34 IASEs have been upgraded and 19 SCERTs have been strengthened.

National Council for Teacher Education

The National Council for Teacher Education (NCTE) has been established under the National Council for Teacher Education Act, 1993 as a statutory body with effect from August 17, 1995, with the objectives of achieving planned and co-ordinated development of teacher education system, regulation and proper maintenance of norms and standards of teacher education and for matters connected therewith.

As per provisions of the Act, four Regional Committees for the northern, southern, eastern and western regions have been set up at Jaipur, Bangalore, Bhubaneswar, and Bhopal respectively.

These Committees consider the application of institutions of teacher education for recognition/permission in accordance with the provision of the NCTE Act. The Council has laid down norms and standards for pre-primary, elementary, secondary level teacher education institutions and for B.Ed. through correspondence/distance education mode. During the year 1997-98 the NCTE had held a number of seminars workshops, symposia, awareness meetings etc. The NCTE have also taken up a number of projects and studies for the development of teacher education in the country.

National Council of Educational Research and Training (NCERT)

The National Council of Educational Research and Training (NCERT) was established in September, 1961 in New Delhi as an autonomous body. Qualitative improvement and excellence in school education and teacher education are some of its major objectives. It develops curricula, syllabi and prepares textbooks for Classes I-XII which form the basis for prescription of scheme of studies by Central Board of Secondary Education (CBSE) for the schools affiliated to the Board.

It also develops instructional material for childhood education and training packages for teacher educators and supervisory personnel. It provides technical assistance for national population education programmes designed to introduce population education in the formal education system. NCERT also provides its expertise to States/UTs. It also designs courses and material, generates software systems and sets up resource centres for computer literacy and studies in school projects.

NCERT organises Jawaharlal Nehru Science Exhibition every year in which a large number of school students from all over the country participate. It prepares comprehensive guidelines for curriculum evaluation of teachers on vocationalisation of education. Training courses for the officials involved in the Integrated Education Programme for Disabled Children are also conducted. Major projects entrusted to NCERT include Sixth All India Education Survey, assistance in implementing the District Primary Education Programme (School and Non-Formal Education) etc.

There are four regional institutes under NCERT at Ajmer, Bhopal, Mysore and Bhubaneswar. The North-Eastern Regional Institute at Shillong has also started functioning from the academic session 1996-97.

University Grants Commission

Co-ordination and determination of standards in higher education is a subject of the Union List and hence a special responsibility of the Central Government. This responsibility is discharged mainly through University Grants Commission (UGC) which was established in 1956 under an Act of Parliament to take measures for promotion and co-ordination of university education and determination and maintenance of standards in teaching, examination and research in universities.

To fulfil its objectives, the Commission can enquire among other things into financial needs of the universities; allocate and disburse grants to them, establish and maintain common services and facilities; recommend measures for improvement of university education and give advice on allocation of grants and establishment of new universities.

UGC has approved 119 colleges for autonomous status, 19 in Andhra Pradesh, 44 in Tamil Nadu, 38 in Madhya Pradesh, five each in Orissa and Himachal Pradesh, three in Uttar Pradesh and two each in Maharashtra and Gujarat.

Autonomous Research Organisations

1. *Indian Council of Historical Research, New Delhi.* Set up in 1972, enunciates and implements a national policy on historical research and encourages scientific writing of history, it operates research projects, finances research project by individual scholars, awards fellowships and undertakes publication and translation work.

2. *Indian Council of Philosophical Research.* Starting functioning from 1981 with offices in New Delhi and Lucknow, it reviews the progress, sponsors or assists projects and programmes of research in philosophy, gives financial assistance to institutions and individuals to conduct research in philosophy and allied disciplines.

3. *Indian Institute of Advanced Study, Shimla.* Set up in 1965 it is a residential centre for advanced research on humanities, social sciences and natural sciences. It is a community of scholars engaged in exploring new frontiers of knowledge aimed at conceptual development and offering inter-disciplinary perspectives on questions of contemporary relevance.

4. *Indian Council of Social Science Research, New Delhi.* It is an autonomous body for promoting and co-ordinating social science research. Its main functions are to review the progress of social science research, give advice on research activities in Government or outside sponsor research programmes and give grants to institutions and individuals for research in social sciences.

Priority Areas

Objectives and goals set for the following need to be achieved on priority basis, through special efforts at the earliest in the 21st century:

Elementary Education

The National Policy on Education envisages that free and compulsory education of satisfactory quality should be provided to all children upto the age of 14 years before the commencement of twenty-first century. The target of universalising elementary education has been divided into three broad parameters, i.e., universal access, universal retention and universal achievement during the Eighth Five Year Plan. As a result of the efforts made by the Central Government and State Governments, 94 per cent of country's rural population have been provided primary schools within one km and 84 per cent have upper primary schools within three km. This has resulted in

(i) enrolment of children of 6-14 years of age in primary and upper primary schools has gone up steadily since independence to 87 and 50 per cent respectively;
(ii) significant improvements have taken place in enrolment of girls and SCs/STs.

The Central and State Governments have over a period of time, evolved strategies to check drop-out rates and improve levels of achievements in the school the key elements of which include:

(i) creating parental awareness and community mobilisation.
(ii) involvement of communities and PRIs (73rd and 74th Constitutional Amendments);
(iii) economic incentives,
(iv) improvement in the content and process of schooling (Minimum Levels of Learning);
(v) District Primary Education Programme initiative; and
(vi) National Programme of Nutritional Support to Primary Education (Mid-day Meals Scheme).

The 83rd Constitutional Amendment Bill has been introduced in the Rajya Sabha to make the right to elementary education a fundamental right and a fundamental duty. A Group of experts on educational finance is currently examining the requirement of additional resources to make education compulsory for the 6-14 year-old children.

The National Elementary Education Mission is being set up for facilitating the achievement of (UEE) in a systematic, sustained and integrated manner, involving all segments of civil society in this national endeavour.

An attempt at competency-based learning has been made. The Minimum Levels of Learning (MLL) was introduced in many States over the last six years. This has led to the development of better textbooks-cum-workbooks, supplementary reading materials, Teachers' Handbooks and better systems of pupil evaluation. The Government is now trying to extend the MLL approach to the upper primary stage.

The Central Government plays an important role in funding plan expenditure on elementary education. Ninety-seven per cent of the expenditure incurred by State Governments on education sector goes towards the payment of teachers' salaries. The expansion of the school system and the quality initiatives in elementary education have been possible on account of increased resource availability even during a phase of structural adjustment.

India is one of the few developing countries which have not allowed the expenditure on education to shrink during the reform period. The increase in expenditure on elementary education alone over the last three Five Year Plan period has been more than the increase in expenditure on education as a whole. Forty-eight per cent of the Central Plan was spent on Elementary Education in the Eighth Plan. There are substantial variations between States in terms of per capita expenditure on education.

A media and advocacy plan is being launched for universalisation of elementary education. It will focus on the right of every child to elementary education. Besides radio and television, the media campaign would use traditional and folk forms of communication. The print media would also be fully used to promote education for all.

Women's Education

The National Policy for Education document made a strong commitment to a well conceived edge in favour of women as 'an act of faith and social engineering'. These commitments have been translated into concrete guidelines. They have resulted in a number of interventions which focus on the empowerment of women as the critical pre-condition for their participation in the educational process.

The impact of these programmes is reflected in the decennial growth rate of 9.54 per cent in female literacy (Census 1991) which is significantly higher than the corresponding figure for males (7.76 per cent)

The following special provisions for women have been incorporated in the existing scheme—

(i) Operation Blackboard scheme now provides that at least 50 per cent of the teachers recruited in the future should

be women. Out of the 1.27 lakh posts of the teachers filled under the scheme, 47 per cent are by women;

(ii) An innovative approach taken up in Rajasthan to improve access to education is the Shiksha Karmi Project. It envisaged substitution of the primary school teacher in single teacher schools by a team of two locally resident education workers called Shiksha Karmis, of whom 10 per cent are women;

(iii) Under the scheme of Non-Formal Education, 90 per cent assistance is given for NFE centres exclusively for girls. The scheme has recently been revised so as to provide more facilities for educating girls by increasing the ratio of NFE centres exclusively for girls from 25 per cent to 40 per cent of total;

(iv) Efforts are being made to ensure that at least one-third of the students in each Navodaya Vidyalayas are girls. In Navodaya Vidyalayas and Kendriya Vidyalayas, free education is imparted to girls upto Class XII;

(v) Free education is provided to girls upto Class VIII in Punjab (Government schools), Manipur, Rajasthan (Government schools), U.P., Delhi Meghalaya and Chandigarh and upto secondary stage in Andhra Pradesh, Assam, Bihar (Government schools), Himachal Pradesh (Government schools), Karnataka, Tamil Nadu (Government schools), Mizoram and Lakshdweep and upto senior secondary stage Class XII in the States of Arunachal Pradesh, Goa, J&K, Kerala, Sikkim (Government schools), Tripura, West Bengal, A & N Island, Dadra & Nagar Haveli, Daman and Diu, Pondicherry, Gujarat and Madhya Pradesh.

(vi) Under the Centrally Sponsored Programme, at +2 level vocational programmes with emphasis on entrepreneurship are being designed to cater to the needs of girls when drop out of schools. Efforts are also on to consciously encourage participation of girls in the non-traditional and emergent technologies;

(vii) Women's education at the university and college levels have been diversified and re-oriented in tune with the changing requirement of society, industry and trade. The number of women enrolled institutions of higher

education increased from 40,000 in 1950-51 to about 20,65,000 in 1995-96, an increase of more than 51 times over the 44 year period;

(viii) The enrolment of women students at the beginning of year 1993-94 was 15.90 lakh, as against 15.12 lakh in the previous year. At the postgraduate level the enrolment of women was 34.09 per cent of total enrolment.

(ix) The UGC has been providing assistance to universities for undertaking research projects in women's studies, a number of research projects have been approved for assistance. Also assistance has been provided to 22 universities and 11 colleges for setting up women's studies/cells. The UGC has also created 40 positions of part-time research associateship for women candidates, and

(x) The participation of women in technical and professional streams has also shown a marked increase from a little over 6,000 in 1950-51 to 1.46 lakh in 1986-87, an increase of 23 times. There was also noticeable growth in the number of women students in the engineering and technology streams (in IITs and Polytechnics). As against 40 women students in 1950-51 (0.3 per cent), it rose to 16.67 thousand in 1986-87 (7.7 per cent) and 78.3 thousand in 1993-94 (13.1 per cent).

Vocationalisation of Education

The National Policy on Education (NPE), 1986 accords high priority to vocationalisation of education at the secondary stage. The NPE as revised in 1992 set the target of achieving diversion of 10 per cent of the students at the +2 level to the vocational stream in 1995 and 25 per cent by 2000 A.D.

Accordingly a Centrally Sponsored Scheme of Vocationalisation of Secondary Education was launched in February, 1998. Under the scheme, substantial financial assistance is provided to States/UTs for introduction of vocational courses in Classes XI and XII of the school system.

So far, all States/UTs, except Lakshadweep, have joined the programme. In all 18,719 vocational courses have been sanctioned in 6,486 schools all over the country thereby creating capacity for diversion of about 9.35 lakh students to the vocational stream which is 11 per cent of the enrolment at the +2 stage.

About 150 vocational courses have been introduced in six major areas, i.e., agriculture, business and commerce, engineering and technology, health and paramedical, home science, humanities and others and 94 vocational courses have been notified under the Apprenticeship Act.

Collaborative arrangement has been made with National Institute of Fashion Technology (NIFT) for introducing of courses in Fashion and Garment making in three identified schools at Ludhiana (Punjab), Vizag (AP) and Indore (MP).

Environmental Orientation to School Education

The National Policy on Education, 1986, provides that the protection of environment is a value which along with certain other values, must form an integral part of curricula at all stages of education. Operationalism of this noble objective required that the mind and intellect of the students must be sensitised to the hazards inherent in the utter disregard and over-exploitation of the bounties of nature. This step intends to inculcate awareness and respect among the students for the basic concepts relating to conservation of the environment.

To this end, a Centrally Sponsored Scheme, Environmental Orientation to School Education was initiated in 1997-98 to assist State Government/UT administrations and voluntary agencies. The voluntary agencies are assisted for the conduct of experimental and innovative programmes aimed at the promoting integration of educational programme in schools with local environmental conditions.

Improvement of Science Education in Schools

To improve the quality of science education and promote scientific temper, as envisaged in the National Policy on Education, 1986, a Centrally Sponsored Scheme, "Improvement of Science Education in Schools" was initiated during 1987-88. Under the Scheme, financial assistance is provided to State Governments/Union Territory administrations and voluntary agencies.

While voluntary agencies are provided assistance for conducting experimental and innovative programmes, States/

UTs are assisted for provision of science kits to upper primary schools; upgradation and strengthening of science laboratories in secondary/senior secondary schools, supply of books on science related subjects in secondary and senior secondary schools; and training of science and mathematics teachers.

One of the important components of this scheme is participation of Indian students at school level in the International Mathematical Olympiad (IMO) as well as International Physics Olympiad (IPO). Indian students have been participating in IMO since 1989 and in the IPO from 1998.

QUESTIONS FOR ANSWER

1. 'Education is the most crucial and significant factor in activising and optimising the welfare of the society through its ramifications in almost all spheres of life'. In the light of this statement write a note on the role of the teachers.
2. Write a note on the challenges ahead in education in the 21st century.
3. Write short notes on the following:
   (a) Updating Curriculum.
   (b) Role of Educational Technology.
   (c) Need For New Inputs in Education.
   (d) Women's Education.
   (e) Elementary Education.
   (f) Vocationalisation of Education.

Index